The Wiley Reader
Designs for Writing
(Brief Edition)

Caroline D. Eckhardt
The Pennsylvania State University

David H. Stewart
Texas A&M University

John Wiley & Sons
New York   Chichester   Brisbane   Toronto

Library of Congress Cataloging in Publication Data:

Main entry under title:
The Wiley reader.

   Includes bibliographical references and index.

   1.   College readers.   2.   English language—
Rhetoric.   I.   Eckhardt, Caroline D., 1942–
II.   Stewart, David Hugh, 1926–
PE1417.W48 1979   808′.04275   78-15326
ISBN 0-471-03499-1

Printed in the United States of America

10 9 8 7 6 5 4 3 2

For
Tom

Preface

Like the earlier edition of *The Wiley Reader*, this brief edition is based
on the assumption that you can learn to write well if you practice and
if you follow good models. Good writing does not just "happen." It
is a matter of design, not chance; of craftsmanship, not miracle. The
process of writing is like the process of working clay with your hands:
you need material to work with and a design to give the material
meaning. If all goes well, the finished object will have exactly the
effect you want. In writing, the material you work with comes from
yourself. It may be your memory of a personal experience, or your
interpretation of what you have read or heard. The choice of the design
is yours too. The purpose of *The Wiley Reader* (Brief Edition) is to
offer you designs from which to choose.

The Format of This Book

The introduction, *The Drama of Information*, explains our conviction
that information—knowledge of the world—can be as moving and
powerful as a dramatic fictional story. "Human beings naturally desire
to know," as the Greek philosopher Aristotle said some 2500 years
ago. Have something to say and people naturally will want to listen—
if your way of expressing it helps them to see the dramatic quality of
the information. The sections called *Prewriting, Drafting*, and *Rewriting*
discuss ways to choose and organize your information, write a
first draft, and revise it.

The book is divided into four parts, each beginning with an explanatory
essay. The four parts present four kinds of writing: writing that
aims (1) to inform, (2) to prove, (3) to judge or evaluate, and (4) to
recommend or persuade. Each part shows you several ways of achieving
its objectives—several ways, rather than one, because *in writing
there are many right ways of reaching a goal*. Your personal preferences,
your need to be faithful to your own style, will determine which
are the best choices for you. This freedom to choose among alternatives
permits you to say something about yourself: how you think and
how you go about describing the world. Every time you write, you

fashion a self-portrait that provides additional information for your readers.

The first kind of writing (Part One) is called **Definition**. Here we use this term to include all writing whose primary purpose is to explain what the author means by something, to make readers understand it—the subject, *X*, whatever that may be—the same way the author does. Definitions answer the question, **"What is *X*?"** They may call on a number of techniques, such as clarification by example, comparison and contrast, and narration, as well as upon the type of defining you see in a dictionary.

Part Two, **Substantiation**, presents writing whose primary purpose is to support an opinion that goes beyond what is actually known. Definitions may appear here also. The main goal, however, is to prove that some further claim ("thesis") about *X* is valid—that you can accept this claim as a responsible extension of the known into the unknown. Here the question is, **"What is likely to be true about *X*?"**

Part Three, **Evaluation**, presents writing that establishes the writer's value judgment of *X*: the ways *X* seems good or bad. Having defined the subject (*Definition*), and perhaps also shown what is probably true about it (*Substantiation*), the writer explains how he or she feels about it—doing everything possible to make you feel the same way. Evaluations answer the question, **"Is *X* good or bad?"**

Part Four, **Recommendation**, adds one more step. The writer—having defined the subject, substantiated an interpretation of it, and evaluated it as good or bad—then presents a proposal for change. Recommendations answer the question, **"What should we do about *X*?"**

This fourfold division is simple and practical. It is developmental, because each kind of writing builds on the one preceding it, and it applies to almost all occasions for writing.

The four categories, however, like all categories, are to some extent arbitrary. Each kind shades into the next, just as the colors of a rainbow do. Nevertheless the classification is useful (as the separate names for the colors of a rainbow are). It makes the wide range of nonfiction writing easier to understand, discuss, and practice.

In each section, the readings offered as examples are arranged in two series. In Series One, each selection has an introductory note, a commentary, an outline, and suggestions for writing. In Series Two, each selection has an introductory note only, so that you and your instructor can approach it as best suits the progress of your own course. The sequence within each series ranges from simple to complex and is usually short to long. Toward the end, the selections become more ambitious and shade into the next major category.

The readings include letters, advertisements, and newspaper articles, as well as formal "essays." All demonstrate the variety and vitality of the written language today. Some of the authors represented here are established writers, but others are not. Some are anonymous. Others identify themselves as journalists, factory workers, teachers, business executives, novelists, or government officials. No group or profession has a monopoly on good writing.

Preparing this book gave us a fine excuse to read a tremendous amount of good prose as we looked for selections to include. We enjoyed choosing the best. We hope that you too will enjoy the book, and find in it useful designs for giving shape to your own information. The material to work on is within the reach of your mind. The power to shape it is at the end of your fingers.

A Note of Thanks

The editors are grateful to the following Pennsylvania State University colleagues (at University Park and the Commonwealth campuses) for examining and suggesting revisions of the larger *Wiley Reader*, from which this book repeats certain selections: Evelyn Buckalew, Wilma R. Ebbitt, Evelyn A. Hovanec, David L. Livingstone, Cheryl J. Plumb, and Albert N. Skomra. Portions of the text were class tested in pilot sections of English Composition at The Pennsylvania State University, and we thank the students in those sections and their teachers, Timothy Conley, Michelle Knovic, Laurie Lieb, and Paul Sorrentino. Sue Runk prepared the typescript, and Amy Austin assisted in several ways.

Many others made helpful suggestions for improving the format and content of the text. We are especially grateful to John P. Broderick of Old Dominion University, Greg Cowan of Texas A&M University, C. Jeriel Howard of Bishop College, Russell Meyer of The University of Minnesota, Betty Renshaw of Prince George's Community College, Gary Tate of Texas Christian University, Joseph F. Trimmer of Ball State University, and Jeanne Nelson of the Association of Departments of English, for their helpful comments on the long version of *The Wiley Reader*. We also thank John P. Broderick of Old Dominion University, Linda S. Coleman of The University of Wisconsin-Milwaukee, Pruitt Davis of North Texas State University, David Hoddeson of Hunter College, C. Jeriel Howard of Bishop College, David Livingstone of The Pennsylvania State University, and Robin C. Mitchell of Marquette University for reviewing this revised, brief edition of the reader.

We particularly express our appreciation to Robert B. Eckhardt and Diane S. Stewart and to the many staff members at John Wiley and Sons, who consistently offered a high level of professional support.

Caroline D. Eckhardt
David H. Stewart

Contents

Substantiation, Readings without Commentary

Part three
Evaluation: Introductory Essay   159

Evaluation, Readings with Commentary

Evaluation, Readings without Commentary

A Guide to Rhetorical Forms

This guide lists essays and parts of essays that are useful for studying the traditional rhetorical forms. Within each group, the sequence in which the selections appear in the book has been followed. However, alternative arrangements might be preferable for certain instructional purposes.

The guide offers suggestions; it is not exhaustive. Other examples can be found in the text. Some readings, of course, illustrate more than one of the traditional rhetorical forms, but we have kept multiple listings to a minimum.

One
Formal Definition—introductory material, p. 22

Two
Description—introductory material, p. 8

Ten

Analogy—introductory material, p. 24

Eleven

Persuasion—introductory material, p. 231

Twelve

Irony and Satire—introductory material, p. 297, 163

Introduction

The Drama of Information

Everything written is as good at it is dramatic. . . . Sentences are not different enough to hold the attention unless they are dramatic. . . . That is all that can save poetry from sing-song, all that can save prose from itself. Robert Frost, Preface to **A Way Out***.*

Whenever you read anything—a magazine article, a newspaper, an advertisement, a letter from Aunt Harriet, even the label on a shampoo bottle—you expect it to tell you something. **All good writing begins with information.** As human beings, we have an inborn need for information. From the simple sense-impressions collected by an infant to the complicated statistical data collected by a scientist, information is one of our means of coping with the world.

There are some kinds of information that writing cannot easily convey. If you want to know what Limburger cheese tastes like, a small piece on your tongue will tell you much better than several pages of prose. But the written word too has certain advantages. It can give permanence to what you want to say. An unwritten conversation or an unspoken thought may soon be lost, but a written statement of your viewpoints provides a permanent record. Also, what you write can be shared—with the people you work with or even with everybody on earth—as that bite of Limburger cheese cannot. In addition, the written record of an experience will probably be *more structured, more precise*, and therefore *more truly informative* than the casual conversation or wordless participation that preceded it.

The writer's task, as novelist Joseph Conrad remarked in "The Condition of Art," is to use the power of the written word to make us

hear, to make us feel, to make us *see*. The good writer blocks all irrelevant information out of the picture, concentrates on what we are meant to understand, and presents it so vividly, so dramatically, that we see it as the writer sees it. We respond almost as if we were there ourselves.

The paragraphs below, from Lillian Ross's "Symbol of All We Possess," demonstrate the ability of information-based nonfiction to capture some of the drama inherent in life itself.

There are thirteen million women in the United States between the ages of eighteen and twenty-eight. All of them were eligible to compete for the title of Miss America in the annual contest staged in Atlantic City last month if they were high school graduates, were not and had never been married, and were not Negroes. Ten thousand of them participated in preliminary contests held in all but three of the forty-eight states. Then, one cool September day, a Miss from each of these states, together with a Miss New York City, a Miss Greater Philadelphia, a Miss Chicago, a Miss District of Columbia, a Miss Canada, a Miss Puerto Rico, and a Miss Hawaii, arrived in Atlantic City to display her beauty, poise, grace, physique, personality, and talent. The primary, and most obvious, stake in the contest was a twenty-five-thousand-dollar scholarship fund—a five-thousand-dollar scholarship for the winner and lesser ones for fourteen runners-up—which had been established by the makers of Nash automobiles, Catalina swimsuits, and a cotton fabric known as Everglaze. The winner would also get a new four-door Nash sedan, a dozen Catalina swimsuits, and a wardrobe of sixty Everglaze garments. The contest was called the Miss America Pageant. The fifty-two competitors went into it seeking, beyond the prizes, great decisions. Exactly what was decided, they are still trying to find out.

Miss New York State was a twenty-two-year-old registered nurse named Wanda Nalepa, who lives in the Bronx. She has honey-blond hair, green eyes, and a light complexion, and is five feet three. Some other statistics gathered by Miss American Pageant officials are: weight,108; bust, 34; waist, 23; thighs, 19; hips, 34; calf, 12½; ankle, 7½; shoe size, 5; dress size, 10. She was asked in an official questionnaire why she had entered the Atlantic City contest. She answered that her friends had urged her to.[1]

"Symbol of All We Possess" examines the Miss America Pageant in minute detail. Ross found the pageant crass and dehumanizing. But in 1948, when she wrote her description, the pageant was at the height of its popularity with the American public, and no explosion of indignation would have served to indict it. If the pageant were to be indicted it must indict itself. Therefore Ross simply supplies information: the discriminatory qualifications for contestants, the long list of "Misses" and the qualities they must display, the prizes, the measurements rattled off as though Wanda Nalepa were a side of beef. Ross is not imposing drama on the situation she describes. Instead, she is *making visible the drama inherent in the situation*. She wants her readers

to react negatively to the Miss America Pageant, and she has faith that a precise, factual, and honest description will produce that reaction.

Creative writers of nonfiction strive to make the drama of life visible. They do so by making us *see*. They recreate the real by making the abstract *concrete*, the general *specific*, the vague *clear*. Often the information they deal with is not new. In fact, it may be so old and so well known that we have forgotten its meaning, but **creative writers can make us see old information with new eyes.** For example, Loren Eiseley wanted to dramatize an idea common enough in our time: one's most dangerous enemy is oneself. He put it this way:

As a boy I once rolled dice in an empty house, playing against myself. I suppose I was afraid. It was twilight, and I forget who won. I was too young to have known that the old abandoned house in which I played was the universe. I would play for man more fiercely if the years would take me back.[2]

Eiseley was writing about the progress of the human species: people have conquered the sea, the land, the air; the antagonist we face now is ourselves. This insight takes on a renewed dramatic power when Eiseley expresses it by means of a simple image of childhood. Because we have all been frightened children once, playing our games alone in the twilight, we can respond emotionally to this scene. The idea is nothing new, but it can be made to seem new again and again by a careful choice of information, and information includes metaphors and comparisons. The most effective of these are often the simple shared experiences of life, because we can identify with them at once.

[1] From *Reporting* by Lillian Ross. Copyright © 1964 by Lillian Ross. Reprinted by permission of Simon & Schuster, a Division of Gulf & Western Corporation.

[2] Loren Eiseley, *The Invisible Pyramid* (New York: Scribner's, 1970), pp. 2-3.

The more that writing relies on universal experiences or on simple sensory evidence, the more likely it is to be understood by everybody. But it is hard to write completely in such terms without seeming trite or childish. Therefore most writers draw also upon more complex, less elemental, sources of information. The following paragraph from Harlow Shapley's *View from a Distant Star* requires that we recognize information from the fields of religion, chemistry, natural history, and geology.

> . . . the breath of St. Francis is with us, and of Confucius, and of Mary of Nazareth. That knowledge may give you, I hope, a feeling of brotherhood with the great and holy past, for the nitrogen of the international air crosses the barriers of time as well as space. But each breath of yours, I should hasten to add, contains also nitrogen breathed by ancient sinners; and it probably contains at least six of the nitrogen atoms expelled in each ferocious snort of an ancient dinosaur, as he raised his head from the Mesozoic swamps 100 million years ago and sneered, in his vulgar way, at the primitive little mammals which were just beginning to grow into the most dominant animal form on earth.[3]

This example shows that the writer's decision concerning exactly what information will convey the drama of the subject must be influenced by the *characteristics of the intended audience*. If you have never heard of St. Francis, or Confucius, or nitrogen, or dinosaurs, or the Mesozoic era, your response might be only "What on earth is he talking about?" But Shapely assumed he was writing for an audience with a basic education in many fields. To these people, the paragraph is filled with meaningful information that dramatizes his

[3] Harlow Shapley, *The View from a Distant Star* (New York: Dell, 1963), p. 90.

idea: all of us share kinship with the people who lived before us and with the creatures to whom the earth belonged before there were any people around at all.

Creative nonfiction, then, is writing that recreates some part of the real world by supplying the right information: enough information—but not the surplus that would bore us; information that we will recognize—not obscurities that would merely puzzle us; information carefully arranged—not a hodgepodge. Enough of the right kind in the right order. Such creative nonfiction can achieve a drama equal to that of the finest fiction. It seems to capture reality itself and thus responds to our natural human desire to know always more about the world in which we live, a world partly defined by our presence in it.

Prewriting

How does one write dramatic nonfiction? Lillian Ross, Loren Eisely, Harlow Shapley, and other professional writers show us that it *can* be done—but not *how*.

There isn't any simple answer (or we'd all be Lillian Rosses), but much of the success of a piece of writing depends on the process called preparation for writing, or *prewriting*.

Discovery (Invention)

Prewriting begins with our attitudes and our information; it ends with words on paper. In between occurs the process called **invention** or **discovery**: discovery of the significance, the value, the meaning of whatever information we have at hand. Mere information is both boring and useless. Nobody—except a phone company executive—would want to read the telephone directory cover to cover; although it is densely packed with precise information, the information, taken as a whole, lacks meaning.

Source. Drawn by Arthur Vergara.

Psychologists point out that the human mind naturally records information as *patterns* or *structures* rather than as isolated bits of data. We remember a face as a face—not as a list of facts such as "eyes with speckled irises, a nose with a low bridge, a tongue that sticks out most of the time, a shape of the face shorter than normal top-to-bottom." Information in that form, no matter how accurate and detailed, is meaningless, because each item stands alone. Notice that there is no center or point around which everything else is organized to form a pattern. In prewriting you need to discover that focal point.

There is no set of rules, no magic formula, that can tell you how to find the meaning of your information. Experienced writers say that they "think it through," or that they experience a flash of insight, or that they simply write and rewrite until somehow the act of putting words on paper seems to force the information to take shape. Perhaps you recognized that the speckled eyes, the low-bridged nose, the protruding tongue, and the wide face make a pattern known as Down's syndrome, a type of genetic damage sometimes called mongolism; *that* is the meaning of the information about the face.

The inexperienced writer, however, isn't helped much by being told to think it through, or to wait for a flash of insight, or to write and keep on writing. Here is a procedure that often helps.

Plan from the beginning to present the subject to a *specific audience*. Imagine yourself in the audience's place: you are seeing the information for the first time, and you can see only what the writer tells you. As every new piece of information comes in, you automatically try to relate it to something you've been told before. If you can't do so, you become bored or annoyed. This technique requires that, as a writer, you look at your information

as your reader would—look for the relationship between item 1 and item 2, item 1 or 2 and item 3, and so forth. Whatever does not fit, you set aside to try again later. (If a piece of information never fits, it is set aside for use in some other writing project or else discarded).

Let's assume, for example, that you have been assigned to write a 500-word paper based on personal experience. You want to share what you have just learned from your first formal job interview. You faced a strange city, a new kind of job, a six-page form to fill out, nosey questions to answer. It's all over now, and you want to tell someone else about it. But *what* exactly to say, and *how*?

Try beginning with a different question: *to whom?* **Choose an audience for your paper**—at least identify its age or educational level or occupational interest or personal situation. If this audience is going to care about your paper, there must be some common ground (or you will have to work very hard to create one). Probably your experience would be of interest to other people facing their first job interview. This *shared interest* will be the main characteristic of your audience. For the moment, you won't worry about whether these job seekers are 16 years old or 60, female or male, applying to be waiters or window washers or wildlife managers. What all of them share is that mixture of hope, fear, and anxiety that you felt too. You want them to understand and recognize these emotions. Now you know what you (and your audience) are looking for.

The next step is to **make a first record of your information**: write down whatever you can remember about the job interview. You may fill several pages with rough notes at this point. Then, sort through your information. Keep only what relates to the shared audience interest that you have found.

It's sure hot out; I'm sweaty

Maybe this shirt wasn't the right thing to wear after all

The girl on the magazine cover looks like Sally

I never did like plastic couches

Wonder what Sally's doing now?

Wish I hadn't forgotten my watch... probably on the bathroom sink but if not there, on my desk?

That receptionist sure looks at me in a funny way

HERE I GO....

I'm sweaty
Maybe this shirt wasn't the right thing to wear after all
You stick to plastic couches
This was a fine day to forget my watch! 5 minutes to go, by that clock
That receptionist sure gave me an odd up-and-down look when I first came in. Now she doesn't look at me at all
"You may go in now"--stand up, you idiot; come on knees, work.

Thoughts in the Waiting Room ⟶ Information Sorted for an Audience

Everything now relates to everything else, but you still need to discover the *nature* of the relationship, the *meaning* of the pattern. Put yourself in the audience's place. **Ask the questions your readers would ask.** "Why are you telling me this?" "Are you trying to say that everybody gets nervous? I know that already. What else?" "Do you mean that the problem was in *you*—or do you mean that the whole interview setup was guaranteed to make anybody nervous?" (Perhaps you can find somebody to play the part of the audience at this point; if not, ask the questions yourself.) Each question can help lead you towards a *meaning* for the information. If you ask all the questions that your information permits, you should soon come across the one that makes you answer, "Yes, that's it!" The right question makes the information's meaning (which was really there all the time) stand out.

If none of the questions works, you have probably made a wrong decision along the way. Look at the information you discarded, sort it out, and ask for its meanings too.

By now you should have three things: a collection of focused information; a definition of your audience; and a sense of what the information means.

Choosing a Strategy —
An Organizational Plan

Different kinds of writing have different purposes. In this book, all writing that aims primarily *to clarify what we mean* is called *definition*. Writing that aims *to prove that something is (or is not) true* is called *substantiation*. Writing that evaluates—tries *to show that something is good or bad*—is called *evaluation*. And writing that tries *to persuade people to do something* is called *recommendation*. These categories represent a sequence. Each builds upon the ones that precede it. To make a recommendation, for example, you may need to (1) explain what it is you are concerned with (*definition*); (2) collect evidence to establish that something is true about your subject (*substantiation*); (3) show us what is good or bad about the current situation (*evaluation*); and (4) make us agree that your solution is the best one (*recommendation*).

It's somewhat like building, starting with the ground floor. For some purposes, you put the roof on top of the first story; structures with other purposes need a second, third, or fourth story. In terms of construction, it is a *developmental sequence*: you can't add a fourth story unless you have a third.

All kinds of writing have certain things in common, regardless of their final size or purpose. Whatever the developmental level of your piece of writing, you will need to choose a basic plan to organize your material. These "basics" afford you, as a writer, certain choices. The design alternatives for writing are sometimes called *rhetorical strategies*. Before you write a first draft, you should know something about the design options that are available.

1 **Narration.** Narration—**telling a story**—is one of the most common and dramatic means of conveying information. If someone tells you a story about being mauled by a bear in Glacier Park, you are getting information about bears that no scientific description of them could convey. To be sure, one story is not the *whole* story, about bears or anything else. But it may tell you just what you need to know should a bear happen to step on your sleeping bag.

Narrative is the basic structure of fiction. In nonfiction writing, a story is told not only for its own sake, but also to do something else—to fulfill one of the major purposes mentioned above. Stories can be told to *clarify* what it is like when you meet a bear head-on, or to *substantiate* a thesis about why couples choose not to have children, or to *evaluate* your high school, or to *recommend* that we un-sex the English language. Many people find narration the easiest way to structure their writing because it almost "writes itself." The narrative design automatically supplies you with a time sequence, characters, setting, action, and personal involvement. Concrete details—the information that makes writing effective—are readily available. However, in nonfiction writing, narration needs something more: a strong unifying purpose, a clear sense of *why* you are telling this story.

2 **Description.** While narration reports events, description records **the evidence of your senses**—how something looks (or feels or smells or tastes or sounds). A good description requires care. Where do you start? If you are describing a fish, the head-to-tail pattern may be natural and effective, but if you are describing a car, do you start with its body style or engine design? Usually, you should choose one pattern—left to right, outside to inside, near to far, center to edges, and so forth—and follow it consistently throughout.

It is important to record those sense-impressions precisely, not vaguely. *Diction* (your exact choice of words) will make the difference between a description that provokes the response "So what?" and one that is rewarded with "Yes, I see!" Should you write *run* (or *sprint, trot, gallop, canter, race*) when you describe a bridegroom arriving late to his wedding? If you are describing a restaurant, do you want to say that the lighting made it look *dim* (or *dark, dingy, gloomy, cozy*)? Do you want to call our attention to the lighting at all? And use descriptive terms that are not likely to be misunderstood.

3 **Process Analysis.** This form of writing combines *narration* with *description*. You explain **how to do something** (or **how something happens** on its own) using chronological order, as in narration, and you present each step in the process with careful attention to descriptive detail. Process analysis is often used in giving directions. You may have looked at an owner's manual to find out how to make your car start on cold mornings, or you may have tried to follow instructions for assembling a build-it-yourself bookcase. One key element of a successful process analysis is *clarity of detail* (not "apply glue" but "apply a thin thread of casein glue along the side and back

MR. SMITH! THE RENAISSANCE MAN YOU ADVERTISED FOR IS HERE!

Source. Reprinted by permission of Chuck Vadun.

edges of the shelf"). Another key element is inclusion of every step in the process—in its correct order. You might practice process analysis by telling someone how to perform a familiar action—how to change gears in a manual-transmission car or make a paper airplane (if you begin by saying "Fold a piece of paper," you are likely to be asked "Which way?").

4 **Division and Classification.** When a subject is large or complicated, it often becomes clearer if you **divide the subject into parts and then arrange the parts according to a principle**, such as simple-to-complex or small-to-large. A familiar illustration of this process asks you to imagine that you are the owner of a grocery store; on the morning after a slight earthquake, you must sort out the merchandise lying around in random heaps. "Groceries" being too large a category, you divide it into major classes: frozen foods, refrigerated

foods, canned goods, baked products, and so forth. Then you subdivide the frozen-food pile into TV dinners, juices, ice cream. . . . Eventually you have restored order to your merchandise and made it manageable again.

We follow such a procedure quite often. College students are classified by majors, grade-levels, living quarters (those who live in the dorms, in fraternities or sororities, in apartments, at home). Biologists classify animals and plants according to an elaborate system of groups, families, species, subtypes. People can be classified according to their occupations, marital status, educational level, nationality, religion. When you're on the receiving end of a blood transfusion, it can be a matter of life and death to have someone know "This one's a B-negative!"

In addition, division and classification can be especially useful for dealing with unfamiliar things, since it permits you to take a new idea one part at a time. John D. Stewart divides "vulture country" into three main parts:

> There are three essential qualities for vulture country: a rich supply of unburied corpses, high mountains, a strong sun. Spain has the first of these, for in this sparsely populated and stony land it is not customary, or necessary, to bury dead animals. Where there are vultures in action such burials would be a self-evident waste of labor, with inferior sanitary results. Spain has mountains, too, in no part far to seek; and the summer sun is hot throughout the country. But it is hottest in Andalusia, and that is the decisive factor.

An overuse of this technique can produce writing that sounds anything but dramatic—a mere listing of parts: "there are two main types . . . there are four factors . . . there may be three reasons," and so on. But division and classification need not be deadening if you use it as a basic means of *organizing*

information rather than simply as an announcement.

5 **Comparison and Contrast.** If *description* in some ways resembles a photographic record, comparison and contrast suggests a double exposure, since **you are dealing with two (or more) subjects at the same time.** Sometimes what you want to write about is important mostly because of its relationship to other things. If so, it is probably best presented by showing how it resembles them and differs from them. In a description of the latest change in clothing fashions, for instance, you would need to compare this year's styles with last year's or those of 10 years ago—or else we wouldn't understand exactly what "change" you wanted us to see.

In using comparison and contrast, you have a choice between two varieties of this structure. You can describe *one of your subjects fully* first, and *then the other*, adding a summarizing conclusion if that seems necessary. Or, you can provide *one kind of information* about *both* of your subjects, then a *second kind* of information about *both* of them, and so forth, again summarizing at the end if you need to.

Comparison and contrast reminds us that there can also be two emphases. **Comparison emphasizes the resemblance, contrast the difference.** However, the two are mutually reinforcing, since seeing the overlap between X and Y helps us focus on the areas in which they don't overlap. A Manx cat is almost completely like any other cat—except at the end.

6 **Cause and Effect.** Sometimes the most important aspect of a subject is its cause. Someone has a car wreck. A witness says, "reckless driving!" Examining the car, however, you notice that a front shock absorber has collapsed: perhaps this mechanical failure is what caused the car to go out of control. And sometimes it is the effect that matters most.

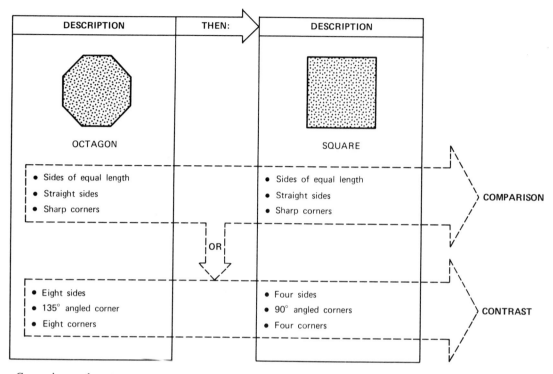

Comparison and contrast

You may be explaining a proposed change in your college's graduation requirements. The most important thing to know about the change may well be "How will it affect me?" You need to be very careful in identifying causes and effects. Are you sure that your school's basketball team lost the game mainly because of prejudiced referees? What do you think of the beaver's sense of cause and effect? (See cartoon p. 11)

Cause and effect, as a rhetorical strategy, specifies what kind of information you will be looking for rather than how you will organize it. An organizing strategy such as *division and classification, process analysis,* or *comparison and contrast* may be helpful.

The six writing strategies discussed above don't exhaust the possibilities. You will meet others. However, these six are enough to suggest that the process of prewriting involves choosing among a number of patterns of organization. To go back to the collection of information about a job interview on page 6, you could use:

1 **Narration** to tell us the story of the interview.

2 **Description** to make us understand what the waiting room (or the secretary or the personnel manager) was like.

3 **Process analysis** to describe the sequence of steps that you went through.

4 **Division and classification** to separate your complex emotional state into parts—resentment at the scornful secretary, satisfaction at having gotten this

Cause and effect   *Source.* © King Features Syndicate Inc.

far, doubt as to whether you've worn the right clothing, and so forth.

5 **Comparison and contrast** to make it clear that this way of getting a job is quite different from the casual drop-in method you had used before.

6 **Cause and effect** to identify the characteristics that eventually produced the manager's "Report Monday morning!"

You could write six different drafts, in fact. To write even one of them, however, you need to have a clear idea of which rhetorical strategy you will use. Perhaps you have been told which one to use. If it's up to you to decide, consider (1) **your own preferences**—what comes most easily to you; (2) **the nature of your audience**—what will have most appeal to your readers; and (3) **the nature of your information and the main point you have discovered**—which pattern of organization will make your material's meaning most evident.

Drafting—Writing a First Draft

At the end of the prewriting process, you have a collection of focused information, a definition of your audience, a sense of what the information means to that audience, and an organizational plan. If you are writing in re-

sponse to an assignment, you also know about how long your paper is supposed to be, and you may have been given other specifications too.

The actual process of putting words on paper is hard for many writers. Two suggestions will help. One is to remember that *a first draft is just that—a first attempt.* Its purpose is simply to get you started, to give you something you can later improve. Second, if you find it difficult to begin at the beginning, you can begin in the middle of your organizational plan and come back to the beginning later. And if you find it hard to begin with a blank piece of paper challenging you, then begin with a piece of paper on which you've already written some notes. In fact, many writers find that their notes naturally grow into a first draft. Others find that an easy way to get started is to make an outline and then let the outline gradually become fuller, changing from key words into sentences.

In writing a first draft, the important task is combining your information and your rhetorical strategy (organizational plan). Assemble your notes into several piles according to the parts of your paper's organization. For example, if you are using a **comparison and contrast** plan, put all of your information about Chevys into one pile, about Fords into an-

Source. © 1972 United Feature Syndicate, Inc.

other. (Cut up your pages of notes into strips if necessary.) Then pick up the Chevy pile, put its items into some order, and write them out in sentence form. Sort the Ford items into the same order and write *them* out in sentence form. You still need to add an introductory paragraph to explain what you are doing and a conclusion to summarize the results of the comparison, but the central part of your first draft has been written.

```
I'm sweaty
Maybe this shirt wasn't
the right thing to wear
after all
You stick to plastic
couches
This was a fine day to
forget my watch! 5 min-
utes to go, by that
clock
That receptionist sure
gave me an odd up-and-
down look when I first
came in.  Now she doesn't
look at me at all
"You may go in now"--
  stand up, you idiot;
come on knees, work.
```

```
I've forgotten my watch,
but the clock on the
office wall says 2:25 ...
five minutes to wait
before my interview (if
the manager's on time).
What if this orange shirt
is too wild? This morning
I thought it would make
me seem cheerful and
lively--just the sort of
person they'd want to
have working in an
advertising agency.  But
the receptionist's up-
and-down glance when I
came in was hardly
appreciative.
"You may go in now," she
is saying, still with-
out looking up. Come on,
knees, work!
```

Information Sorted for an Audience ⟶ First Written Version
(Prewriting)   *(Drafting)*

If your rhetorical strategy is **narration**, arrange your information into chronological order and write it out in sentence form. Later, you might decide to vary that order—to use a flashback, for instance—but you can follow a straightforward "first things first" principle in the draft. If your rhetorical strategy is **description**, arrange your information in far-to-near order (or in whatever order you have chosen) and write it out in sentence form.

In fact, whatever your rhetorical strategy, the process is the same: **(1) arrange the information according to the strategy,** and **(2) put sentences on paper.** Keep going. Don't worry about whether each sentence is grammatically correct, or even about whether it should be there at all—you'll come back to such questions later. Begin wherever in the plan you feel most comfortable. *Write forward to the end. Then go back and fill in any missing parts.*

Rewriting

Almost nobody can write a good paper on the first attempt. Even professionals write and rewrite and rewrite, polishing off a rough edge here, sharpening a point there. That first draft (looking at it objectively) is probably a collection of sentences and paragraphs, not a finished composition. Some parts may be very dramatic, others repetitive or floundering or dull. As you rewrite it, you will need to do four things:

1 Edit the language. This aspect of rewriting involves making all aspects of style—grammar, spelling, punctuation, word choice, paragraphing, and so forth—correspond to standard American usage. Use a good dictionary or a handbook, if you're uncertain about correctness (is it "*wierd*" or "*weird*"?). No simple error of language should be permitted to confuse the reader.

Editing the language involves more than correctness, however. It also involves attention to *style*. Style is the *personality* of language—those qualities that go beyond the bare necessities of communication. Both a brand-new Ferrari and a 1955 Chevrolet will get you to town: the difference is style. Your writing style is an extension of your whole personal style. Just as you adjust your personal approach for different situations, *you adjust your writing style to the subject matter of your paper and to the characteristics of your audience.* Your writing style supplies an additional kind of information to your readers: it tells them what kind of (writing) person you are, at least on this occasion. In general, it is usually good to be fairly direct and straightforward, avoiding false chumminess on the one hand, and false stiffness or strained "literary effects" on the other.

Source. © 1974 United Feature Syndicate, Inc.

I've forgotten my watch, but the clock on the office wall says 2:25... five minutes to wait before my interview (if the manager's on time). What if this orange shirt is too wild? This morning I thought it would make me seem cheerful and lively--just the sort of person they'd want to have working in an advertising agency. But the receptionist's up-and-down glance when I came in was hardly appreciative.

"You may go in now, "she is saying, still without looking up. Come on, knees, <u>work</u>!

Blaze orange? For a job interview? Sure. It will make me seem creative and lively--just the sort of person they'd want to have working in an advertising agency.

That's what I thought this morning, but the receptionist's up-and-down glance when I came in was hardly appreciative. 2:25 by the wall clock (what a day to have forgotten my watch)... 5 minutes to go. I could still get up and say, "Oh, I forgot something," and walk out of here and not have to face whoever's behind that blank door.

But if I run away again it will only be worse afterwards.

"You may go in now," she is saying, still not looking at me. Is it <u>that</u> bad? Come on, knees: <u>work</u>!

First Draft ⟶ Revised Draft

2 Improve the organization. Does the paper *go* somewhere? It should have a recognizable sequence or order, consistently followed—for example, chronological order, a simple-to-complex sequence, a good-to-bad contrast, a near-to-far spatial development. A paper without a clear sense of organization will seem incomplete or confusing, like an abstract painting without a label: which way is up?

3 Emphasize the major idea. The major idea, usually called the **thesis**, expresses what you have discovered to be the meaning of your information. This is the idea or impression that you most want your readers to remember. Short compositions usually concentrate on one thesis rather than trying to present several. *Even if your thesis consists of a group of related ideas, the overall impact* *will be greater if you make one idea the center of attention.* The thesis is often presented as a **thesis sentence**, which appears near the beginning or near the end of the paper. However, the information you provide should make the thesis clear whether you decide to state it as a thesis sentence or not.

4 Sort the information once again. With the main idea clear in your mind (if not yet clear in the paper), look hard at every piece of in-

---

INAUGURAL ADDRESS OF JOHN F. KENNEDY[4]
(EDITORIAL CHANGES)

First Draft	Next-to-Last Draft	Last Draft
We celebrate today not a victory of party but the sacrament of democracy.	We celebrate today not a victory of party but a convention of freedom.	We observe today not a victory of party but a celebration of freedom.
Each of us, whether we hold office or not, shares the responsibility for guiding this most difficult of all societies along the path of self-discipline and government.	In your hands, my fellow citizens, more than in mine, will be determined the success or failure of our course.	In your hands, my fellow citizens, more than mine, will rest the final success or failure of our course.
Nor can two great and powerful nations forever continue on this reckless course, both overburdened by the staggering cost of modern weapons.	. . . neither can two great and powerful nations long endure their present reckless course, both overburdened by the staggering cost of modern weapons.	. . . neither can two great and powerful groups of nations take comfort from our present course—both sides overburdened by the cost of modern weapons . . .

TWO SENTENCES FROM EARLIER SPEECHES WHICH GAVE SUGGESTIONS FOR THE *INAUGURAL ADDRESS*[5]

. . . It is time, in short, for a new generation of Americans.

. . . the torch has been passed to a new generation of Americans.

We do not campaign stressing what our country is going to do for us as a people. We stress what we can do for the country, for all of us.

And so, my fellow Americans, ask not what your country can do for you; ask what you can do for your country.

---

[4] Theodore C. Sorensen, *Kennedy* (New York: Harper and Row, 1965), pp. 241–42.
[5] *Ibid.*

formation in your draft. *Which details deserve to be kept? Which can be omitted? What is missing from the information? Is every paragraph adequately developed?* Wherever possible, increase the drama of the information by using a *concrete word* rather than a vague one, a *new phrase* rather than a cliché. Let "late afternoon" become "four-thirty."

Notice the editorial changes that Kennedy made. Is every change an improvement?

Any change you make affects the entire piece of writing in some way. Therefore, you will need to make a final revision to adjust one change to another. If somewhere along the way you have slightly revised your main idea, for instance, you will need to discard some information that is no longer relevant. You may also need to add new information to fill the new blank spaces.

Most writers find that they need help along the way—in prewriting, drafting, and rewriting. Perhaps part of your first draft can be discussed in class, so that you can ask for help from other students who are struggling with the same writing problems. Some things will come more easily to you, some more easily to them, and so you should be able to help each other. Ask your instructor, who has been through the writing process many times. And, indirectly, ask the writers whose works appear in this book.

Creative Reading

So far we have been concerned with the process of writing, but this book is called a *reader*. What does reading have to do with writing? You may have heard arguments about whether good writing comes from firsthand experience or from reading and imitating other writers. The answer is both. Without experience, you would have nothing to say. But anyone's experience is a limited thing. Read-

ing is a way of expanding your experiences by sharing other people's. As you learn how to write, reading not only adds information to your stockpile. It also provides models. It's not enough for someone to describe *narration* or *process analysis* to you. You need to see the real thing, not just hear about it. And once the real thing arrives at the end of a leash, or neatly wrapped in brown paper, or between the pages of a book, you still need to know how to deal with it. (Do you give that thing on the leash fish or cracked corn?)

Source. Illustration courtesy of Fidelity Municipal Bond Fund.

This book offers more than fifty examples of good writing. Exactly what do you do with them as you read—how do you make the transition between "That's a good job" and your own efforts to put words on paper? You must know how to *read creatively* if your reading is to help you write creatively.

1 **Read once for content and overall impression.** Read (this first time) as you might listen to someone talking: let the writer tell you, without interruption, whatever he or she wants to say. Afterward, make a brief note of your response, just as you

might respond if the writer were in the room with you: "Yes, I see what you mean" or "Well, I never knew that!" or "Let's think this thing over—there's got to be a better way."

2 **Analyze the piece of writing.** You are now going to study its parts to see *how* it produced that response in you. Exactly what you will see depends, of course, on the particular piece of writing, and on what it was trying to do. However, most pieces of writing will show you how they work if you examine the following characteristics.

a **Structure** (organization). Often the best way to see the structure of a piece of writing is to make an outline or brief notes. "First it's all about sheep, then it's all about goats" will help you see that a *comparison and contrast* structure is being used.

b **Development.** How is the basic structure developed? What kinds of information are used? How does the writer make transitions between one section and another? For example, how does the writer help you move from the introduction—often based on an attention-getting bit of information—to the next part of the structure? How is the piece of writing tied together at the end?

c **Style.** Now you are looking at the particular words chosen and the way those words are made into sentences. Has the writer tried to seem close to you by choosing informal, everyday words and short, easy sentence structures? Or has the writer tried to seem authoritative by using some formal or technical words and more compli-

cated sentence structures? (There are of course many other possibilities.) What you need to do, at this point, is examine all relevant aspects of the writer's "personality-on-paper."

3 **Reread the piece of writing.** After having seen its parts, you need to put it together again. See whether your initial response has been modified. It will at least have been *clarified*—you will know why your response is what it is.

4 **Relate the piece of writing to yourself as a writer.** Now you are considering which aspects of the piece of writing can be useful to you. Nobody would suggest that you try to reproduce everything. If you did, your paper wouldn't be your own. You'd be guilty of *plagiarism*—literary theft. However, you might decide that the overall structure can be used, or that the subject is one you can write on too (because you have further information), or that certain qualities of the style—perhaps the writer's ability to describe an action in two or three vivid adjectives—would be good for you to practice. Be honest with yourself. You may have to say "I don't know anything about railway travel in 1890, so I can't write about that," or "If I use long words and complicated sentences I'll only sound stuffy—that's not *me*." Even if the piece of writing serves mostly as a *negative example* (an example of characteristics that fit another writer's style and information and purpose, but not yours), it can help you understand your own realistic choices.

The aim of creative reading is not to copy—that's pointless—but to *see what the possibilities are*. When you are planning to decorate a room, you can get a lot of good ideas by seeing what colors other people have painted their walls and how they have used lighting to create atmosphere. But you should choose whatever suits your own abilities and purposes and needs.

This book can show you ways to design your own writing. But the sense of direction must come from *you* and *your particular writing task*.

> "Would you tell me, please, which way I ought to go from here?" [Alice in Wonderland asks the Cheshire Cat].
> "That depends a good deal on where you want to get to," said the Cat.
> "I don't much care where—" said Alice.
> "Then it doesn't matter which way you go," said the Cat.

No amount of advice or collection of examples can be of much use to you if you don't know where you want to go—what you want to say, and to whom. Even then, as reading this book

will show you, you can't please all of the people all of the time. Readers help determine what succeeds in being dramatic by their willingness to receive the subject matter. A superb article on guns or quasars might receive the comment "Dull—I can't stand guns," or "Astronomy is a bore." And a second-rate article on the clothing of thirteenth-century European aristocrats might be read with avid interest by a reader who likes that sort of thing.

You are not trying, then, to conquer the world (although once in a while that happens). You are trying to reach a limited audience and to present your subject to that audience in the most effective way. Whether your subject is animal, mineral, or vegetable, reality or fantasy, dream or nightmare, tomorrow or yesterday—somebody will listen. Somebody has listened to the essays in this book, which discuss everything from automobiles to zoology, with birth and death and love and the Lone Ranger in between. Somebody out there is ready to listen, and the rest is up to you.

Summary

1 All good writing begins with information—presented vividly so that we see what is meant.
2 *Prewriting* (preparing for writing) involves (1) gathering information; (2) choosing an audience; (3) discovering the meaning, or central focus, of what you want to say; and (4) choosing a rhetorical strategy—such as *narration, description, process analysis, division and classification, comparison and contrast, cause and effect*.
3 *Drafting* (writing a first draft) involves preparing a first version that arranges your information into sentences and par-

agraphs, according to your structure.
4 *Rewriting* (revising your draft) involves (1) editing the language for both correctness and style; (2) improving the organization; (3) emphasizing the major idea; (4) sorting the information again to check that the right details are there, presented as vividly as possible; and (5) adjusting one change to another so that you produce a unified piece of writing.
5 *Creative reading* involves (1) reading once for a first response; (2) analyzing such aspects as structure, development, and style; (3) rereading; and (4) choosing the qualities that are useful to you.

Part One
Definition: Introductory Essay

Definition—the explanation of what we mean by the words we use—is the basis of any kind of writing. Many discussions are pointless because people do not first establish what exactly they mean by *X*, the subject they are considering. You may remember, in Lewis Carroll's *Through the Looking Glass*, Alice's puzzlement when she couldn't make sense of the strange ways in which other characters were using language.

> "I don't know what you mean by 'glory,'" Alice said.
>
> Humpty Dumpty smiled contemptuously. "Of course you don't—till I tell you. I meant 'there's a nice knock-down argument for you!'"
>
> "But 'glory' doesn't mean 'a nice knock-down argument,'" Alice objected.
>
> "When *I* use a word," Humpty Dumpty said in a rather scornful tone, "it means just what I choose it to mean—neither more nor less." . . .
>
> Alice was much too puzzled to say anything. . . .

Unless our aim is to produce an astonished silence, we must make sure that the words we use are understood. Most words we do not stop to define, since we use them in their conventional meanings. But the central thing a writer wants to discuss often needs to be clarified.

Short definitions may be expressed as single words (synonyms) or brief sentences. Diction-ary definitions of *mitosis* or *metaphor* or *metropolis* aim only at specifying the normal meaning of a word. Longer (extended) definitions may require several hundred pages. Book-length presentations of the theory of relativity or the history of English literature aim at explaining their subjects in full breadth and detail.

Whether short or long, simple or complex, definitions always respond to the question: "What is *X*?"

X might be some aspect of an event, a process, a structure, a living organism, a theory, and so forth. It might be an episode in the writer's own experience, the form of a Shakespearean sonnet, the average size of the dinosaur *Tyrannosaurus rex*, the voting patterns of college students in the last presidential election, the provisions for birth control in medieval Europe, or the ways to maximize the yield of wheat per acre. Regardless of its subject, definition intends primarily to present *X* so that readers will understand it the way the writer does. It does not primarily intend to argue for or against it. (That is the province of *substantiation, evaluation,* and *recommendation,* types of writing discussed later in this book.)

In many books about writing, the term "definition" is used for only one pattern, the "*X* = class term + distinguishing terms" pattern (see *formal definition* below, p. 22). The more extended forms (see pp. 22-25) are called *description, explanation,* or *exposition*. In this book, we include them all in the category *definition* because all have the same intention, the same purpose: to provide the information necessary to a shared understanding of the subject.

Planning a Definition

When you write a definition, you face certain decisions. First, you usually know more about your subject than you can say. You may be limited by space, by the characteristics of your audience (their prior information about the subject and their interest in it), or by some special requirement of an assignment. **The first decisions, therefore, are matters of selection.** Of everything I know about hiking, what shall I say? Of everything I have learned about the practical applications of lasers, what will I include?

Second, because you are so familiar with your subject, you can see it from a number of viewpoints simultaneously. You can begin almost anywhere without becoming confused. Your readers, however, probably know much less than you—which is why *you* are the one doing the explaining. They must be guided carefully through the field of information, or they will get lost. **The second set of decisions, therefore, concerns matters of organization:** What should be said first? Later? Why should the material in the second paragraph be there and not in the first or third? Is this *X* clearest if seen first as a whole thing and then taken apart, or should you show it one part at a time and put it together afterwards?

Finally, you must adjust your style to your readers so that the information you want to convey, once selected and organized into a logical sequence, will be fully comprehensi-

ble. **The third set of decisions, therefore, has to do with style:** vocabulary, syntax, sentence structure, and tone of voice. Such questions as whether your *X* needs a diagram to clarify it, or whether references to the sources of your information should be included, can also be considered matters of style. And a good writing style must be free of surplus words. You don't want to insult your readers' intelligence by including the obvious, as in "The bird's wings are bright yellow in color" (what else could they be bright yellow in?).

A well-written definition, whether brief or extended, resembles a well-designed automobile. Efficiently and comfortably, with all its parts cooperating, it functions to take someone from here (relative ignorance of *X*) to there (relative familiarity with *X*). Normally, like the automobile, it is not an end in itself, but the means by which some further purpose can be accomplished. Often a definition forms part of a larger piece of writing that has other purposes. The primary task of definition itself, however, is simply to present *X* so that your readers will understand it the way you do. In addition, the act of examining *X* in order to make it clear to somebody else often makes it clearer to you as well.

Objective and Subjective Definition

The general question, "What is *X*?" may be interpreted in an **objective** or **subjective** way. The difference between these two types of definition is important, for neither can do the job of the other. **Objective definition explains the normal or typical characteristics of *X*,** characteristics that are public, apparent to anyone who looks at the evidence, based on assumptions that our entire society shares. Dictionary definitions—which record the conventional meanings assigned to words—belong to this type, as do scientific explanations of the natural world, descriptions of historical events, and so forth. The purpose of objective definition is to present X as it is potentially accessible to everybody.

Subjective definition, on the other hand, explains characteristics of X that are private, dependent on the experience of an individual, based on one person's assumptions. The purpose of subjective definition is to express what X means to *you*, whether it means the same thing to anyone else or not.

Subjective definition is not in opposition to objective. It would be pointless to call one true and the other false. They simply have different intentions. If we ever knew any X completely, we would discover that its total meaning consists of what it has meant to *everybody*, here and now as well as in every other time and place—*the sum of all public and private experiences of it*. In practice, our understanding of X is limited to the accepted public interpretations, plus whatever private interpretations we can add. Both types enlarge our understanding of the world.

Occasionally the two types of definition coincide. When your private experience happens

Source. "The Average Voter" by Bob Englehart, *Dayton Journal Herald*. Used by permission.

This cartoon depicts three *subjective definitions* of "the average voter." How might you *objectively* define that term?

to resemble someone else's, the objective and subjective presentations, which normally run like separate and parallel lines, merge. Daniel Inouye, in explaining what homecoming meant to him (p. 52), records his personal experience but touches on the universal qualities of home as well.

Techniques of Definition

How do you define something? We don't usually divide each definition into a series of techniques, and perhaps it wouldn't even be good to try. (Such an operation would wrongly imply that good writing is a patchwork quilt—here a formal dictionary definition, there two examples, next an analogy, all neatly stitched together.) However, it does help to be aware of certain techniques that many writers have found useful so that you can see where, and how, and how well they work. No traditional technique of definition is in itself good or bad. Its value is always determined by whether it helps you do what you want to at a particular time.

Formal Definition

A *formal* or *lexical* or *dictionary* definition consists of three parts: (1) the word to be defined; (2) the *genus* or *class term*; and (3) the *differentia* or *distinguishing terms*. The class (category) term relates X to other things by naming a larger category in which X belongs. It tells us what kind of thing X is. The distinguishing terms separate it from other members of that class.

For example, in a discussion of how a thermostat works, you might need to define *bimetallic strip*, one of the thermostat's basic parts. You might say that a bimetallic strip is *a short metal strip* (class term—now we know what sort of thing this is) *consisting of two different metals, bonded back to back* (distin-

guishing terms—now we know what makes this metal strip different from others). That example illustrates a useful formula:

$$X \text{ (subject)} = class\ term\ +\ distinguishing\ terms$$

Forster (p. 31) defines *plot* as *a narrative of events* (class term), *the emphasis falling on causality* (distinguishing term). Karp (p. 57) defines an *omnibuilding* as *a kind of building* (class term) *in which the street becomes an integral part of the structure, and a house a "unit" slotted into the system the way a cabinet is fitted into one's kitchen* (distinguishing terms).

Formal definitions are useful especially in two situations: when X is totally unfamiliar, or when X is a familiar word being used in a new or special way. In the first case, we need the precision of a formal definition to give us an initial understanding of what X is. In the second case, we also need it to give us a clear understanding of what X is not. Consider these examples:

1 A *bear* is someone who sells stocks and bonds in hopes of buying them back more cheaply later when their market price will have fallen.
2 A *argali* is a wild Asiatic sheep with unusually large horns.

In (2), most of us have no idea what the word *argali* means until the writer defines it. In (1), we *do* have a prior idea what the word *bear* means—but that idea is irrelevant here. The formal definition prevents us from imagining Smokey the Bear wandering around the New York Stock Exchange.

Illustration, or Definition by Example

Often the liveliest way to clarify something is to give examples. Donald (p. 64) relies on a series of examples to explain the funny misuse of language called a *Spoonerism*. In *The Wild Flag*, E. B. White attempts to define democracy by a list of particular details:

July 3, 1943

We received a letter from the Writers' War Board the other day asking for a statement on "The Meaning of Democracy." It presumably is our duty to comply with such a request, and it is certainly our pleasure.

Surely the Board knows what democracy is. It is the line that forms on the right. It is the don't in Don't Shove. It is the hole in the stuffed shirt through which the sawdust slowly trickles; it is the dent in the high hat. Democracy is the recurrent suspicion that more than half of the people are right more than half of the time. It is the feeling of privacy in the voting booths, the feeling of communion in the libraries, the feeling of vitality everywhere. Democracy is the score at the beginning of the ninth. It is an idea that hasn't been disproved yet, a song the words of which have not gone bad. It's the mustard on the hot dog and the cream in the rationed coffee. Democracy is a request from a War Board, in the middle of a morning in the middle of a war, wanting to know what democracy is.

White cites 13 examples to explain what democracy means to him (this is clearly a subjective definition). It would be easy enough to supply generalizations instead. "The line that forms on the right," for instance, suggests orderliness and cooperation—waiting your turn—as well as a system of priority based on when you get there, rather than on who you are. "The don't in Don't Shove" suggests restricting each person's freedom so that other people will not suffer. But White's use of illustration is much more vivid—therefore more dramatic—than a list of generalizations would be.

A word of caution: when definition relies heavily on illustrations, it is sometimes advisable to make very clear just what the common principle is that unifies the illustrations. It might be said of White's "Democracy" statement, for instance, that the 13 separate items do not add up to a coherent whole. We know, to some extent, what it may be like to live in a democracy, but not what democracy *is*. For that, we still need a dictionary.

When in doubt, you can combine a formal definition with one or more examples and have the best of both worlds—the clarity of the formal definition and the liveliness of the example. Here is Charlie Chaplin defining laughter (as Max Eastman recalls it):

"It seems to me," he said, "that there are two different kinds of laughter. Superficial laughter is an escape. The waiter comes in and the duck isn't cooked properly, and you pick it up and throw it at him—yes, and by God, he throws it back! That's an escape. It's a break in the monotony of normal conduct. That's superficial humor, slapstick. Subtle humor shows you that what you think is normal, isn't. This little tramp *wants* to get into jail. The audience thinks at first that he's ridiculous. But he isn't. He's right. The conditions are ridiculous. If I make them laugh that way, it's what I call subtle laughter."

That paragraph contains enough information for a formal definition *and* a definition by example—in fact, two of each. For instance, we could rephrase the second half of the paragraph into a formal definition: *subtle humor* or *subtle laughter* (X, to be defined) is *a form of comedy consisting of a funny incident* (class term) *that shows you that what you think is normal, isn't* (distinguishing term). We could then supply the example, the story of a little tramp told in such a way that the audience gradually realizes that the tramp's enthusiasm for jail is the right attitude. Charlie Chaplin's version, of course, is more dramatic because it eliminates the obvious.

Analogy

When something is totally unfamiliar to us, or else so overfamiliar that it is indistinct, it can often be clarified by analogy. **Analogy is a type of comparison in which the two things compared are really quite different, but they share some similarity that it is useful to point out.** Above, a written definition was compared to an automobile. Although different in almost every way, both exist in order to perform a task efficiently and conveniently, and their task is to take us from here to there. Hayakawa (p. 77) uses an analogy between a map and language; what they have in common is that both guide us through experience.

The analogy below uses the familiar concept of a 24-hour day to help us understand an unfamiliar concept—the immense span of time during which life on earth has existed and, in comparison, the brevity of our 5000 years of human history.

> If the period from the origin of life (suggested to be about 2 billion years ago) up to the present time is seen in terms of a twenty-four hour day, then fossils do not become abundant until about 4:30 in the afternoon. Plants begin to grow upon the land shortly before 7 p.m., insects and amphibians invade the land just before 8 p.m., and the Age of Reptiles stretches from about 9:30 until 11 p.m. At that point the Age of Mammals begins. At about 2 seconds before midnight the mammal called *homo sapiens* appears—and all of recorded human history takes place during the last one-fourth of a second before midnight. (Adapted from George Gaylord Simpson and William S. Beck, *Life: An Introduction to Biology*, 2nd ed., Harcourt, Brace, & World, Inc., 1957, 1965, p. 753.)

The following analogy is intended to make us see a familiar thing—a football team—more vividly.

> The offensive line . . . was much maligned during the pre-season as being a question mark on a team of exclamation points. (Eric Yoder, "Top Performance," *The* [Pennsylvania State University] *Daily Collegian*, Sept. 19, 1977, p. 11.)

If it is going to help, an analogy must use something we are already acquainted with or can easily imagine. But it must not be something we are weary of, or we will not pay attention. To present the world as if it were a ball is probably useful only to young children, for whom that analogy may be new. *The dangers in using analogy, then, are obscurity and triteness.*

Functional Definition

Sometimes the most important way to clarify the nature of X is to explain its function: what it does, or what it is used for. "Meet the Cow" (p. 29) emphasizes the functions of a cow's component parts. Look at this statement about Stonehenge:

> These days, Stonehenge serves as a memorial to a proud ancient past—and as a source of income to the surrounding towns, whose shopkeepers and innkeepers are glad to welcome the thousands of tourists who come each year. In its own time, however, in those long prehistoric centuries that we are only now coming to understand and to respect, Stonehenge served as a place of worship, as a burial ground, and as an astronomical observatory.

This passage assumes that we already have some idea of what Stonehenge is (we know that it is not a local housing development, for example). Therefore, we do not need a simple formal definition such as *Stonehenge is a prehistoric circular assemblage of upright stones in England*. The writer wants us to concentrate on the *functions* of this monument—in fact, *five functions* are named. You may notice that this functional definition uses a comparison-and-contrast principle of organization (after the two modern functions are named, the word *however* signals a change or contrast in idea).

Here is Percy Marks' definition of punctuation:

> Punctuation properly used is an analysis of thought. In effect, the writer says to the reader, "These commas indicate that this matter is parenthetical; this semicolon indicates that the thought in my first clause balances the thought in my second clause; this colon indicates that the clauses preceding it are equal in my mind to whatever may succeed it," and so forth. Only with punctuation can the writer make clear to the reader what one part of his sentence means to another part. . . .[1]

Marks could also have defined punctuation by using division and classification: punctuation consists of commas, semicolons, colons, periods, and so forth. However, that would be telling us the obvious. The new information he has to tell us, the information that justifies one more definition of punctuation, concerns what he sees as punctuation's function: a signal from writer to reader about the logical relationships of parts of ideas.

A negative functional definition specifies what *X* does *not* do. "Far be it from God, that he should do wickedness," says the Bible (Job 34:10). Almost by definition, it is the function of God to do good.

Identification of Essential (Distinguishing) Characteristics.

Sometimes *X* is very similar to other things, and you need to direct your readers' attention

[1] Percy Marks, *The Craft of Writing* (New York: Harcourt Brace, 1932), p. 75.

to the one or two crucial characteristics that you think make it different: "The pizza that Tom made was always spiced with cloves." And sometimes *X* is very large (*cities, families, Montana*); unless you point out the precise features that matter to you, your readers may have a different idea of what you're talking about than you intend. In this case, you need to *limit* their interpretation of *X*: "The thing to remember about the atmosphere is its size," writes Hughes (p. 41). There are many kinds of information that can clarify the nature of the atmosphere, but for Hughes's purpose—which is to explain how "a parcel of air" becomes a hurricane—*size* is the essential quality for us to have in mind.

Other Techniques of Definition.

All of the rhetorical patterns discussed in "The Drama of Information" can be used to clarify *X*. *Narration, description, process analysis, division and classification, comparison and contrast,* or *cause and effect*—with or without one of the special defining techniques presented here—might be helpful in making your readers see *X* as you do. If you want someone to understand the meaning of an event, for example, narration would be a natural way to organize your information. If you want someone to understand the working parts of a device, division and classification, perhaps cooperating with process analysis, might be best.

Two final suggestions. First, when you define something, keep the subject within bounds. (An old joke runs: "Define the universe and give two examples.") Second, don't be surprised if your effort to define seems to produce changes in the thing itself. When you begin, you will be starting with what you *think*

Source. © 1961 The New Yorker Magazine, Inc.

Identifying essential characteristics. *Shape* is a major characteristic of a great many things—so many, in fact, that it doesn't clearly distinguish one thing from another. If your definition relies upon identifying a few major characteristics, you'll need to make sure that they are clear and specific enough to depict your *X* alone, not a dozen other things too.

you mean. But as you look closely you may discover that your first ideas about *X* no longer seem accurate. Writing is a gradual process of coming closer to the essence of things. Most of the best writers keep revising and revising, which means reseeing. If each time you resee, you see more clearly, then change will be progress. You may discover, as Alice did (to come back to Lewis Carroll), that what you first thought was a most dis-

agreeable baby is really a perfectly agreeable piglet. "It would have made a dreadfully ugly child," Alice remarks, "but it makes rather a handsome pig."

In the following readings you will find blind people who can suddenly see, buildings big enough to be whole towns, spinning hurricanes and whirling dervishes, even a well-boiled icicle. None of these pieces was written, by the way, solely as an example of definition. All were written because their authors had something to say, information they wanted to share, or—as Julian Huxley puts it—because "it is one of the duties and privileges of man to testify to his experience, to bear witness to the wonder and variety of the world in which he finds himself."[2]

Summary

1 **Definition**—clarifying the meanings of words—is basic to any successful writing. You can clarify not only single words, but also general concepts, experiences, and so forth. Here, definition includes all writing that aims primarily to inform your readers about what X (your subject) means, so that they will see it the way you do.

2 **Objective definition** explains the normal or typical characteristics of X—what X is likely to mean to anybody. **Subjective def-**inition explains characteristics that are personal—what X means to you.

3 **Techniques of definition** include *formal definition, illustration* (definition by example), *analogy, functional definition,* and *identification of essential characteristics.* In addition, the rhetorical strategies of *narration, description, process analysis, division and classification, comparison and contrast,* or *cause and effect* may be useful in explaining what X means.

[2] Julian Huxley, *From An Antique Land* (London: Max Parrish, 1954), p. 303.

Definition, Series One
Readings with Commentary

Meet the Cow
Nova Scotia Farm News

This brief **functional definition** (see p. 24), obviously intended partly in fun, forms part of an advertisement for a store selling ice cream and other dairy products. It succeeds in looking at a familiar item in a new way. However, to do so it uses a number of traditional techniques of definition, including a **lexical definition** (see p. 22), which here forms the first sentence.

MEET THE COW

The cow is a mobile, animated machine housed in unprocessed leather. On one end it is equipped with a power mower, grinder, and other standard equipment including bumpers, headlights, wing flaps and foghorn. At the other end there is a milk dispenser, a fertilizer spreader, and an insect repeller. Centrally located is a conversion plant consisting of a combination storage and fermentation vat, three converters in series, and an intricate arrangement of conveyor tubes. Special equipment includes a device for self-reproduction at yearly intervals and a central pumping system. The machine is mysterious and secret, but unpatented, and is available in various colors, sizes, and qualities, ranging from one to twenty tons of milk production yearly, at prices ranging from fifty dollars up.

—Nova Scotia
Farm News

Meyer Dairy Store and Ice Cream Parlor

South Atherton Street
between State College and Harris Acres
Open 10-10 daily

Source. "Meet the Cow" from *Nova Scotia Farm News*. Reprinted by permission.

Commentary

Some definitions attempt to introduce us to a new X. Others give us additional information about an X that we have known only partly or incorrectly. "Meet the Cow," however, offers a whole new way of seeing a familiar X. The writer avoids repeating information we already know *in its usual form*. Thus we are not told that the cow eats grass. Instead we are told that it "is equipped with a power mower." The usual information is still there, but the manner of presentation, which involves **analogy** (see p. 24), makes it new and interesting again.

Suggestion for Writing

Write a short, one-paragraph definition that presents one of the following items in a new way: the telephone, the frying pan, the traffic light, the snail. For example, present the telephone as a device for keeping people from working, the frying pan as a device for decreasing the nutritional content of vegetables, the traffic light as a means of concentrating accidents in one place, the snail as a way of keeping the water in a bowl from becoming stagnant. Consider the following example:

> A Boy is an inexpensive device for pulling legs off chairs, leaving fingerprints on paint, abandoning bicycles in the livingroom, falling into ponds, and correcting pomposity in his elders. Although seldom seen at rest, Boys may be recognized by their darting flight, their mud-colored plumage, and their characteristic cry resembling a kazoo heard through a public address system. Good places to look for Boys are sand lots, marshes, the bottoms of quarries, and the rafters of buildings under construction.
>
> . . . To protect itself from the crushing vigor of Boys, adult society sentences them to spend several hours a day in restraining institutions called schools. A school is a place where a Boy has no difficulty in spelling "superjet" but finds it impossible to learn to spell "cat." Some new schools have tried to disguise themselves by using glass walls instead of brick, but they cannot conceal their true penal character from Boys. Any Boy who is seen at about 8:30 in the morning dragging himself along as if he were very sick is going to school. Any Boy who is seen running with the speed of light in the opposite direction has decided that he is too sick to go to school that day.[1]

[1] From "Concerning Boys," *The Welcomer* [newsletter of the Welcome House Adoption Agency, Doylestown, Pa.], May, 1977, p. 4.

Plot
E. M. Forster

This one-paragraph definition combines the **comparison and contrast** structure (see p. 9) with **formal definition** (see p. 22) and **definition by illustration** (see p. 22). Forster defines *plot* by distinguishing it from *story* and illustrates both concepts by a series of mini-tales, each only one sentence long. Finally, he relates plot to the kind of people who prefer it to mere story.

Let us define a plot. We have defined a story as a narrative of events arranged in their time-sequence. A plot is also a narrative of events, the emphasis falling on causality. "The king died and then the queen died," is a story. "The king died, and then the queen died of grief " is a plot. The time-sequence is preserved, but the sense of causality overshadows it. Or again: "The queen died no one knew why, until it was discovered that it was through grief at the death of the king." This is a plot with a mystery in it, a form capable of high development. It suspends the time-sequence, it moves as far away from the story as its limitations will allow. Consider the death of the queen. If it is in a story we say "and then?" If it is in a plot we ask "why?" That is the fundamental difference between these two aspects of the novel. A plot cannot be told to a gaping audience of cave men or to a tyrannical sultan or to their modern descendant the movie-public. They can only be kept awake by "and then—and then—" They can only supply curiosity. But a plot demands intelligence and memory also.

Commentary

Forster has only a very brief space in which to clarify the essential difference between two types of storytelling. He must find the one **distinguishing characteristic** (see p. 25) that is most important. Since this characteristic—*causality*—is a rather abstract idea whose meaning may not be immediately clear, **he illustrates it**. In choosing an illustration, why does he use a king and a queen (rather than, for example, a dog and a cat, or a ship and a lifeboat)?

Forster also suggests a contrast between audiences, but, because this is not really his main subject, does not take the time to work it out as fully. Do you see what he means by the implied contrast between "the movie-public" and people who can appreciate a good novel? Albert Einstein once claimed that cu-

Source. From *Aspects of the Novel* by E. M. Forster, copyright, 1927, by Harcourt Brace Jovanovich, Inc.; renewed, 1955 by E. M. Forster. Reprinted by permission of Harcourt Brace Jovanovich, Inc. and Edward Arnold (Publishers) Ltd.

riosity and inquisitiveness were the greatest human virtues—the driving forces behind all discovery and progress. But Forster has a low opinion of curiosity. What does the word mean to him?

Outline

I Introduction: statement of purpose (sentence 1)

II Lexical (formal) definitions (sentences 2 and 3)

III Examples (illustrations) of the contrast (sentences 4–12)

IV Contrasting kinds of audience (sentences 13–16)

Suggestions for Writing

1 Briefly distinguish between two related subjects—pump and semiautomatic shotguns, German shepherds and Old English sheepdogs (both "working dogs"), Texas-style barbecue and Georgia-style barbecue.

2 Using your own experience to help clarify, distinguish between the two kinds of audience Forster mentions—people who like to go to the movies and people who like to read. There will be a substantial area of overlap (in fact, some people belong in both classes). What characteristics distinguish the two audiences?

The Merry-Go-Round
Stephen Crane

The merry-go-round seems to be vanishing from American amusement parks and carnivals. Fifty years ago, it was a leading attraction. Crane's **description** (see p. 8) tries to capture the merry-go-round's spirit in a single paragraph. As you read, try to imagine your own favorite carnival ride or sports activity described in equally dramatic language.

Within the Merry-Go-Round there was a whirling circle of ornamental lions, giraffes, camels, ponies, goats, glittering with varnish and metal that caught swift reflections from windows high above them. With stiff wooden legs, they swept on in a never-ending race, while a great orchestrion clamored in wild speed. The summer sunlight sprinkled its

Source. From "The Pace of Youth" in *Men, Women, and Boats* by Stephen Crane. New York: Alfred A. Knopf, 1921.

gold upon the garnet canopies carried by the tireless racers and upon all the devices of decoration that made Stimson's machine magnificent and famous. A host of laughing children bestrode the animals, bending forward like charging cavalrymen, and shaking reins and whooping in glee. At intervals they leaned out perilously to clutch at iron rings that were tendered to them by a long wooden arm. At the intense moment before the swift grab for the rings one could see their little nervous bodies quiver with eagerness; the laughter rang shrill and excited. Down in the long rows of benches, crowds of people sat watching the game, while occasionally a father might arise and go near to shout encouragement, cautionary commands, or applause at his flying offspring. Frequently mothers called out: "Be careful, Georgie!" The orchestrion bellowed and thundered on its platform, filling the ears with its long monotonous song. Over in a corner, a man in a white apron and behind a counter roared above the tumult: "Popcorn! Popcorn!"

Commentary

One of the best ways to see what Crane has accomplished is to compare his description with a dictionary definition of the word "merry-go-round." Here is a definition from *Webster's Third International Dictionary*:

> a contrivance commonly found at amusement parks and carnivals that consists of a circular platform having seats often in the form of horses or other animals and rotating around a fixed center usually to calliope music—called also *carousel*.

Crane's description shares hardly a single word with this definition. The words *contrivance, platform, rotate*, and *music* never appear. Instead, **everything is concrete and specific**. We see giraffes and garnet canopies, we hear whooping cavalrymen and a bellowing orchestrion. And the entire paragraph seems to sweep "in a never-ending race"—at least in our imaginations. To write this way, **you must avoid lazy words that generalize and use vivid words that appeal to the senses**. Crane concentrates on two of the senses—*sight* and *hearing*—but also suggests *taste* and *smell* ("Popcorn!") and perhaps even *touch* to those of us who recall clutching at an iron ring.

And note: Crane's vividness conveys not only the sights and sounds of the merry-go-round but also the excitement and enthusiasm that he felt.

Suggestions for Writing

1 Today most merry-go-rounds are not as elaborate as the one that Crane describes. Describe a merry-go-round that you have seen—or a ferris wheel or other "contrivance" in an amusement park.

2 Choose some common object or place (kitchen, automobile, gymnasium, restaurant, disco) and describe it in ways that will appeal to the senses—record its sights, sounds, smells, and so forth. Convey your attitude toward it by selecting details carefully.

33

The Costume of Women in Mostar
Rebecca West

Sometimes we need to describe, and understand, strange objects that we see around us.

Traveling through Yugoslavia, Rebecca West noticed that in the town of Mostar the women wore an extraordinary garment. West offers first a **description** of what the Mostar women wore and then her ideas about the attitudes that might have **caused** the adoption of this odd costume.

1   The traditional Mostar costume for women consists of a man's coat, made in black or blue cloth, immensely too large for the woman who is going to wear it. It is cut with a stiff military collar, very high, perhaps as much as eight or ten inches, which is embroidered inside, not outside, with gold thread. It is never worn as a coat. The woman slips it over her, drawing the shoulders above her head, so that the stiff collar falls forward and projects in front of her like a visor, and she can hide her face if she clutches the edges together, so that she need not wear a veil. The sleeves are allowed to hang loose or are stitched together at the back, but nothing can be done with the skirts, which drag on the ground.

2   We asked the people in the hotel and several tradesmen in Mostar, and a number of Moslems in other places, whether there was any local legend which accounted for this extraordinary garment, for it seemed it must commemorate some occasion when a woman had disguised herself in her husband's coat in order to perform an act of valour. But if there was ever such a legend it has been forgotten. The costume may have some value as a badge of class, for it could be worn with comfort and cleanliness only by a woman of the leisured classes, who need not go out save when she chooses. It would be most inconvenient in wet weather or on rough ground, and a woman could not carry or lead a child while she was wearing it. But perhaps it survives chiefly by its poetic value, by its symbolic references to the sex it clothes.

3   It has the power of a dream or a work of art that has several interpretations, that explains several aspects of reality at one and the same time. First and most obviously the little woman in the tall man's

Source. "The Costume of Women in Mostar" from *Black Lamb and Grey Falcon* by Rebecca West. Copyright 1940, 1941 by Rebecca West. Reprinted by permission of The Viking Press.

coat presents the contrast between man and woman at its most simple and playful, as the contrast between heaviness and lightness, between coarseness and fragility, between that which breaks and that which might be broken but is instead preserved and cherished, for the sake of tenderness and joy. It makes man and woman seem as father and daughter. The little girl is wearing her father's coat and laughs at him from the depths of it, she pretends that it is a magic garment and that she is invisible and can hide from him. Its dimensions favour this fantasy. The Herzegovinian[1] is tall, but not such a giant as this coat was made to fit. I am barely five-foot-four and my husband is close on six-foot-two, but when I tried on his overcoat in this fashion the hem was well above my ankles; yet the Mostar garment trails about its wearer's feet.

4   But it presents the female also in a more sinister light: as the male sees her when he fears her. The dark visor gives her the beak of a bird of prey, and the flash of gold thread within the collar suggests private and ensnaring delights. A torch is put to those fires of the imagination which need for fuel dreams of pain, annihilation, and pleasure. The austere yet lubricious beauty of the coat gives a special and terrifying emphasis to the meaning inherent in all these Eastern styles of costume which hide women's faces. That meaning does not relate directly to sexual matters; it springs from a state of mind more impersonal, even metaphysical, though primitive enough to be sickening. The veil perpetuates and renews a moment when man, being in league with death, like all creatures that must die, hated his kind for living and transmitting life, and hated woman more than himself, because she is the instrument of birth, and put his hand to the floor to find filth and plastered it on her face, to affront the breath of life in her nostrils. There is about all veiled women a sense of melancholy quite incommensurate with the inconveniences they themselves may be suffering. Even when, like the women of Mostar, they seem to be hastening towards secret and luxurious and humorous love-making, they hint of a general surrender to mortality, a futile attempt of the living to renounce life.

Commentary

West begins with an objective **description** of the Mostar women's garment (paragraph 1). She then moves (paragraphs 2 to 4) to her subjective explanation of the "poetic value," the "symbolic references" that she decides must be responsible, if not for the costume's origin, at least for its survival. These symbolic references are of two kinds: suggestions of playfulness, fragility, and tenderness associated with women (paragraph 3) and "more sinister" suggestions of fear, pain, and hatred of women (paragraph 4). The garment that

[1] [Herzegovina is a region in Yugoslavia; Mostar is a town in that region—Eds.]

35

women wear in the male-dominated society of Mostar thus reflects, according to West, the contradictory attitudes of men—both the male appreciation of woman as a pretty little plaything and the male resentment of woman as "the instrument of birth."

Outline

I Description of the garment—paragraph 1

II Absence of a rational explanation—paragraph 2

III The symbolic function of the garment

A Appreciation of woman as child—paragraph 3

B Resentment of woman as mother—paragraph 4

Suggestions for Writing

1 Using West's pattern (beginning with **objective description** and moving into **subjective interpretation**), consider some current American costume and its meaning. For example:

> In America, a common garment for young women, especially those who are college students, is the type of trousers called 'blue jeans.' These trousers fit almost skintight from the hips to the knees. Then they may be cut straight or else flare slightly to the ankles. They are made of dark blue denim, which is a heavy, twill-woven, rather stiff fabric otherwise used mostly for working-men's garments such as the overalls of farmers, and for similar 'blue jeans' worn by young men.

2 Examine the costumes worn at an earlier period, perhaps when your parents or grandparents were your age. You might look at family photographs, back issues of newspapers or magazines in the library, old Sears catalogues, old paintings, a book about the history of costume, and so forth. For example, during the Victorian period (the latter half of the nineteenth century and the first few years of the twentieth), "respectable" women usually wore garments that concealed their natural shapes and covered virtually all skin except that on the hands and face. What docs such a style imply? Describe an earlier style and interpret its meaning.

3 Apply West's pattern of description to some aspect of our lives other than clothing (household furnishings, cars, recreation equipment, "labor-saving" devices, whiskey-bottle shapes, etc.). Move from a brief **objective description** into **subjective interpretation**. "Most middle-class homes in America have at least one television, an electronic device that provides instant audio-visual entertainment" (etc.).

The Santa Ana
Joan Didion

"We had nothing to talk about but the weather," you may have heard someone say, as if the weather were always insignificant. Didion describes a peculiar kind of weather—the wind called a *Santa Ana*—and its effects on the people of the Los Angeles area.

Although a **formal definition** (see p. 22) is supplied in paragraph 3, Didion's approach is mainly **subjective** (see p. 21). She wants us to understand this wind not as a meteorologist might analyze it, but *as people respond to it*: it makes them unhappy. The wind comes to symbolize the impermanence and unreliability of life in Los Angeles (paragraph 6).

How much information does this definition supply about the Santa Ana wind? How much information does it supply about the people of Los Angeles? And how much about writer Didion herself?

1   There is something uneasy in the Los Angeles air this afternoon, some unnatural stillness, some tension. What it means is that tonight a Santa Ana will begin to blow, a hot wind from the northeast whining down through the Cajon and San Gorgonio Passes, blowing up sandstorms out along Route 66, drying the hills and the nerves to the flash point. For a few days now we will see smoke back in the canyons and hear sirens in the night. I have neither heard nor read that a Santa Ana is due, but I know it, and almost everyone I have seen today knows it too. We know it because we feel it. The baby frets. The maid sulks. I rekindle a waning argument with the telephone company, then cut my losses and lie down, given over to whatever it is in the air. To live with the Santa Ana is to accept, consciously or unconsciously, a deeply mechanistic view of human behavior.

2   I recall being told, when I first moved to Los Angeles and was living on an isolated beach, that the Indians would throw themselves into the sea when the bad wind blew. I could see why. The Pacific turned ominously glossy during a Santa Ana period, and one woke in the night troubled not only by the peacocks screaming in the olive trees but by the eerie absence of surf. The heat was surreal. The sky had

37

a yellow cast, the kind of light sometimes called "earthquake weather." My only neighbor would not come out of her house for days, and there were no lights at night, and her husband roamed the place with a machete. One day he would tell me that he had heard a trespasser, the next a rattlesnake.

3   "On nights like that," Raymond Chandler once wrote about the Santa Ana, "every booze party ends in a fight. Meek little wives feel the edge of the carving knife and study their husbands' necks. Anything can happen." That was the kind of wind it was. I did not know then that there was any basis for the effect it had on all of us, but it turns out to be another of those cases in which science bears out folk wisdom. The Santa Ana, which is named for one of the canyons it rushes through, is a *foehn* wind, like the *foehn* of Austria and Switzerland and the *hamsin* of Israel. There are a number of persistent malevolent winds, perhaps the best known of which are the mistral of France and the Mediterranean sirocco, but a *foehn* wind has distinct characteristics: it occurs on the leeward slope of a mountain range and, although the air begins as a cold mass, it is warmed as it comes down the mountain and appears finally as a hot dry wind. Whenever and wherever a *foehn* blows, doctors hear about headaches and nausea and allergies, about "nervousness," about "depression." In Los Angeles some teachers do not attempt to conduct formal classes during a Santa Ana, because the children become unmanageable. In Switzerland the suicide rate goes up during the *foehn*, and in the courts of some Swiss cantons the wind is considered a mitigating circumstance for crime. Surgeons are said to watch the wind, because blood does not clot normally during a *foehn*. A few years ago an Israeli physicist discovered that not only during such winds, but for the ten or twelve hours which precede them, the air carries an unusually high ratio of positive to negative ions. No one seems to know exactly why that should be; some talk about friction and others suggest solar disturbances. In any case the positive ions are there, and what an excess of positive ions does, in the simplest terms, is make people unhappy. One cannot get much more mechanistic than that.

4   Easterners commonly complain that there is no "weather" at all in Southern California, that the days and the seasons slip by relentlessly, numbingly bland. That is quite misleading. In fact the climate is characterized by infrequent but violent extremes: two periods of torrential subtropical rains which continue for weeks and wash out the hills and send subdivisions sliding toward the sea; about twenty scattered days a year of the Santa Ana, which, with its incendiary dryness, invariably means fire. At the first prediction of a Santa Ana, the Forest Service flies men and equipment from northern California into the southern forests, and the Los Angeles Fire Department cancels its ordinary non-firefighting routines. The Santa Ana caused Malibu to burn the

way it did in 1956, and Bel Air in 1961, and Santa Barbara in 1964. In the winter of 1966–67 eleven men were killed fighting a Santa Ana fire that spread through the San Gabriel Mountains.

5   Just to watch the front-page news out of Los Angeles during a Santa Ana is to get very close to what it is about the place. The longest single Santa Ana period in recent years was in 1957, and it lasted not the usual three or four days but fourteen days, from November 21 until December 4. On the first day 25,000 acres of the San Gabriel Mountains were burning, with gusts reaching 100 miles an hour. In town, the wind reached Force 12, or hurricane force, on the Beaufort Scale; oil derricks were toppled and people ordered off the downtown streets to avoid injury from flying objects. On November 22 the fire in the San Gabriels was out of control. On November 24 six people were killed in automobile accidents, and by the end of the week the Los Angeles *Times* was keeping a box score of traffic deaths. On November 26 a prominent Pasadena attorney, depressed about money, shot and killed his wife, their two sons, and himself. On November 27 a South Gate divorcée, twenty-two, was murdered and thrown from a moving car. On November 30 the San Gabriel fire was still out of control, and the wind in town was blowing eighty miles an hour. On the first day of December four people died violently, and on the third the wind began to break.

6   It is hard for people who have not lived in Los Angeles to realize how radically the Santa Ana figures in the local imagination. The city burning is Los Angeles's deepest image of itself: Nathanael West perceived that, in *The Day of the Locust*; and at the time of the 1965 Watts riots what struck the imagination most indelibly were the fires. For days one could drive the Harbor Freeway and see the city on fire, just as we had always known it would be in the end. Los Angeles weather is the weather of catastrophe, of apocalypse, and, just as the reliably long and bitter winters of New England determine the way life is lived there, so the violence and the unpredictability of the Santa Ana affect the entire quality of life in Los Angeles, accentuate its impermanence, its unreliability. The wind shows us how close to the edge we are.

Commentary
Below is a definition of the Santa Ana from a meteorology handbook.

Santa Ana—A hot, dry, foehn-like desert wind, generally from the northeast or east, especially in the pass and river valley of Santa Ana, California, where it is further modified as a mountain-gap wind. It blows, sometimes with great force, from the deserts to the east of the Sierra Nevada Mountains and may carry a large amount of dust. It is most frequent in winter; when it comes in spring, however, it does great damage to fruit trees.[1]

You can see immediately that Didion's intention is quite different from that of the handbook writer. Both of them define the Santa Ana. **Didion, however, is centrally interested in the effects of the wind on people, not in the wind itself.** Thus she begins with her personal experience (paragraphs 1–2), and then gives us mystery writer Raymond Chandler's comment—which is also in terms of *people*, not the wind (paragraph 3). Didion is writing what

[1] Ralph E. Husche, ed., *Glossary of Meteorology* (American Meteorological Society, Boston, Mass., 1959), p. 491.

we call a *personal essay*, an essay in which the writer wants to express a *personal response* to some aspect of human experience and to keep in close *personal touch with the audience*. However, Didion wants us to see that her personal response to the Santa Ana is shared by many other people and is even borne out by scientific evidence. **She is trying to bridge the gap between the personal essay and more objective writing.**

Didion's essay ends on a very subjective note: "The wind shows us how close to the edge we are." A part of the natural environment is being seen as a *symbol* of the frustrations of human life in a tense, urban society. This vision is very close to the use of symbols in poetry.

Outline

I Introduction: the Santa Ana is expected (paragraph 1)

II An earlier experience with the Santa Ana (paragraph 2)

III Expansion beyond Didion's personal experience (paragraphs 3–5)

    A Chandler's comment on the wind

    B Science supports Didion's impression

    C The Southern California climate

    D The Santa Ana brings fire

    E The Santa Ana of November-December 1957

IV Conclusion: what the wind means to "the local imagination" (paragraph 6)

Suggestions for Writing

1 Describe some part of the natural environment of your home: the coldness of winter in upper Michigan; the fog in a Pennsylvania mountain valley; the relentless flatness of the land in northern Texas; the rainy season in Seattle. Provide objective information. In addition, clarify the *effect* on the people who live there.

2 Describe some object that human technology has added to the natural environment: the courthouse in your city, a local highway edged with barbed-wire fences, the cable cars of San Francisco, the mailboxes along a country road. Be specific; you are trying to make your audience see a *particular* pizza parlor, not pizza parlors in general. As you present X, suggest what aspect of modern American life it seems to stand for.

Definition, Series Two
Readings without Commentary

The Hurricane
Richard Hughes

In this short **process analysis** (see p. 8), Hughes explains how a hurricane develops. He points out the natural conditions involved (warm air rising, the earth turning, and so forth) so that we will be able to understand why the hurricane develops as it does. To help us visualize it, he brings in an **analogy** (see p. 24) to a more familiar object—an engine.

1   The thing to remember about the atmosphere is its size. A little air is so thin, so fluid; in small amounts it can slip about so rapidly, that the conditions which give rise to a hurricane cannot be reproduced on a small scale. In trying to explain a hurricane, therefore, one must describe the large thing itself, not a model of it. For it is only when one thinks of the hugeness of a parcel of air on the world, the big distance it may have to shift to equalize some atmospheric difference, that one can realize how slow and immobile, regarded on a *large* scale, the air is.

2   It happens like this. The air above a warm patch of sea, somewhere near the Canaries, is warmed: so it will tend to be pushed up and replaced by the colder, weightier air around. In a warm room it would rise in a continuous gentle stream, and be replaced by a gentle draught under the door—no excitement. But on a large scale it cannot: that is what is different. It rises in a single lump, as if it were encased in a

Source. ''The Hurricane'' by Richard Hughes is from *In Hazard* by Richard Hughes. Published by Chatto & Windus and reprinted by permission of David Higham Associates Limited.

gigantic balloon—being actually encased in its own comparative sluggishness. Cold air rushes in underneath not as a gentle draught but as a great wind, owing to the bodily lifting of so great a bulk of air.

3   Air moving in from all round towards a central point: and in the middle, air rising: that is the beginning. Then two things happen. The turning of the earth starts the system turning: not fast at first, but in a gentle spiral. And the warm air which has risen, saturated with moisture from the surface of the sea, cools. Cooling, high up there, its moisture spouts out of it in rain. Now, when the water in air condenses, it releases the energy that held it there, just as truly as the explosion of petrol releases energy. Millions of horse-power up there loose. As in a petrol-motor, that energy is translated into motion: up rises the boundless balloon still higher, faster spins the vortex.

4   Thus the spin of the Earth is only the turn of the crank-handle which starts it: the hurricane itself is a vast motor, revolved by the energy generated by the condensation of water from the rising air.

5   And then consider this. Anything spinning fast enough tends to fly away from the centre—or at any rate, like a planet round the sun, reaches a state of balance where it cannot fly inwards. The wind soon spins round the centre of a hurricane so fast it can no longer fly into that centre, however vacuous it is. Mere motion has formed a hollow pipe, as impervious as if it were made of something solid.

6   That is why it is often calm at the centre of a hurricane: the wind actually cannot get in.

7   So this extraordinary engine, fifty miles or more wide, built of speed-hardened air, its vast power generated by the sun and by the shedding of rain, spins westward across the floor of the Atlantic, often for weeks together, its power mounting as it goes. It is only when its bottom at last touches dry land (or very cold air) that the throttle is closed; no more moist air can be sucked in, and in a few days, or weeks at most, it spreads and dies.

The Dance of the Dervishes
Julian Huxley

Most of us have heard the phrase *a whirling dervish*. This short description of an activity shows what dervishes really do when they whirl and what this whirling—certainly a peculiar way to behave, in the opinion of Westerners—means to the people who do it.

Huxley writes from the viewpoint of an objective observer, a "casual visitor" as he puts it, and therefore *the information he gives us is limited to what he was able to see.*

1   There are very few dancing dervisheries left in the region. The one at Tripoli stands among olive groves just outside the city, on the banks of the Kadesha river. The Sheikh of the community, a dignified little man with a greying beard, led us through the various domed dwellings to the separate building set aside for the ceremonial dancings, or turnings as they might better be called. This was a square hall, open on the valley side, with balconies round the other three, supported on wide white arches. We took our places to the left of the Sheikh, with the musicians on his right. The rest of the seats were soon filled up with privileged spectators. After a time the dozen or so dervishes walked in slowly with folded hands, and sat down cross-legged on carpets. They were wearing tall khaki fezzes protruding from small turbans, and brown abbas—sleeved robes like heavy dressing-gowns, but without a belt, and made of camel's hair. The musicians began chanting chants full of semi-tones, and prayers were intoned. The dancers rose and began to walk slowly round and round in a heavy ritualized step, with a solemn pause at each forward pace, and a turn and a bow each time they passed one corner of the hall. A flute and drums struck up, and after some twenty minutes the dervishes took off their abbas, disclosing full white skirts with weighted hems, reaching from waist to feet. Then, each in his appointed spot, they began their turning.

2   Turning consists essentially in pivoting on the left foot, with two or

Source. "The Dance of the Dervishes" by Julian Huxley is from *From an Antique Land* by Julian Huxley. Published by Chatto & Windus Ltd. and reprinted by permission of A. D. Peters & Co. Ltd.

43

three steps of the right foot to each full turn. As the speed of turning increases, the white skirt flares out into a great rotating cone. One handsome young dervish elaborated the movement by making a graceful dip during each turn, and by varying the position of head and arms. His most beautiful pose was one with arms and hands fully extended in line, one diagonally upwards, the other downward, with head inclined against the upward arm, and a serene, absorbed, prayer-like expression on his face. Then there was a stoutish middle-aged little turner, who spun round with head thrown back. He lacked the effortless grace of the young man, but achieved the same look of rapt serenity. He was a policeman by profession.

3   The turning went on for an hour or more, its monotony remaining strangely beautiful and fascinating instead of becoming boring. Most of the dancers stopped at intervals for a short rest, but the policeman and the graceful young dervish never broke their turning. The Sheikh later told us that the policeman had a weak heart, and that his deepest desire was that he might die while dancing.

4   At the private ceremonies of the community, turning may go on for many hours, until the dancers fall immobile on the floor in a state of exalted and complete exhaustion. The Sheikh covers them with their abbas, and there they lie until they recover.

5   I had got it into my head that the dances we were to see would be orgies of violent and frenzied motion, but I had been confusing the dancing dervishes with a quite different confraternity, the howling dervishes. The turning ritual seems designed to give a sense of liberation and ecstasy, but a serene and orderly one. It was clear that the turners could, through their controlled and long-continued rotation, spin themselves into a state in which the world of everyday was transcended. We are apt to look down on such simple physical methods of achieving a sense of ecstasy or transcendence as barbarous or childish. I can only say that, to the casual visitor like myself, it looked like a satisfying form of ritual and, for some of the participants at least, seemed to provide a quality of real fulfilment.

The Death of the Moth
Virginia Woolf

In this subjective presentation of an event, Virginia Woolf uses a quite common occurrence of our everyday lives to represent some of the most serious aspects of existence. In the course of this short **narrative** , an ordinary moth is associated with the vigor, energy, light, and activity which (to Woolf) are the essence of life itself, and then it dies: a miniature enactment of humanity's own life-into-death drama.

What does Woolf want us to understand about living—and dying?

1 Moths that fly by day are not properly to be called moths; they do not excite that pleasant sense of dark autumn nights and ivy-blossom which the commonest yellow-underwing asleep in the shadow of the curtain never fails to rouse in us. They are hybrid creatures, neither gay like butterflies nor sombre like their own species. Nevertheless the present specimen, with his narrow hay-coloured wings, fringed with a tassel of the same colour, seemed to be content with life. It was a pleasant morning, mid-September, mild, benignant, yet with a keener breath than that of the summer months. The plough was already scoring the field opposite the window, and where the share had been, the earth was pressed flat and gleamed with moisture. Such vigour came rolling in from the fields and the down beyond that it was difficult to keep the eyes strictly turned upon the book. The rooks too were keeping one of their annual festivities; soaring round the tree tops until it looked as if a vast net with thousands of black knots in it had been cast up into the air; which, after a few moments, sank slowly down upon the trees until every twig seemed to have a knot at the end of it. Then, suddenly, the net would be thrown into the air again in a wider circle this time, with the utmost clamour and vociferation, as though to be thrown into the air and settle slowly down upon the tree tops were a tremendously exciting experience.

2 The same energy which inspired the rooks, the ploughmen, the

45

horses, and even, it seemed, the lean bare-backed downs, sent the moth fluttering from side to side of his square of the window-pane. One could not help watching him. One was, indeed, conscious of a queer feeling of pity for him. The possibilities of pleasure seemed that morning so enormous and so various that to have only a moth's part in life, and a day moth's at that, appeared a hard fate, and his zest in enjoying his meagre opportunities to the full, pathetic. He flew vigorously to one corner of his compartment, and, after waiting there a second, flew across to the other. What remained for him but to fly to a third corner and then to a fourth? That was all he could do, in spite of the size of the downs, the width of the sky, the far-off smoke of houses, and the romantic voice, now and then, of a steamer out at sea. What he could do he did. Watching him, it seemed as if a fibre, very thin but pure, of the enormous energy of the world had been thrust into his frail and diminutive body. As often as he crossed the pane, I could fancy that a thread of vital light became visible. He was little or nothing but life.

3   Yet, because he was so small, and so simple a form of the energy that was rolling in at the open window and driving its way through so many narrow and intricate corridors in my own brain and in those of other human beings, there was something marvellous as well as pathetic about him. It was as if someone had taken a tiny bead of pure life and decking it as lightly as possible with down and feathers, had set it dancing and zig-zagging to show us the true nature of life. Thus displayed one could not get over the strangeness of it. One is apt to forget all about life, seeing it humped and bossed and garnished and cumbered so that it has to move with the greatest circumspection and dignity. Again, the thought of all that life might have been had he been born in any other shape caused one to view his simple activities with a kind of pity.

4   After a time, tired by his dancing apparently, he settled on the window ledge in the sun, and, the queer spectacle being at an end, I forgot about him. Then, looking up, my eye was caught by him. He was trying to resume his dancing, but seemed either so stiff or so awkward that he could only flutter to the bottom of the window-pane; and when he tried to fly across it he failed. Being intent on other matters I watched these futile attempts for a time without thinking, unconsciously waiting for him to resume his flight, as one waits for a machine, that has stopped momentarily, to start again without considering the reason of its failure. After perhaps a seventh attempt he slipped from the wooden ledge and fell, fluttering his wings, on to his back on the window sill. The helplessness of his attitude roused me. It flashed upon me that he was in difficulties; he could no longer raise himself; his legs struggled vainly. But, as I stretched out a pencil, meaning to help him to right himself, it came over me that the failure

and awkwardness were the approach of death. I laid the pencil down again.

5   The legs agitated themselves once more. I looked as if for the enemy against which he struggled. I looked out of doors. What had happened there? Presumably it was midday, and work in the fields had stopped. Stillness and quiet had replaced the previous animation. The birds had taken themselves off to feed in the brooks. The horses stood still. Yet the power was there all the same, massed outside indifferent, impersonal, not attending to anything in particular. Somehow it was opposed to the little hay-coloured moth. It was useless to try to do anything. One could only watch the extraordinary efforts made by those tiny legs against an oncoming doom which could, had it chosen, have submerged an entire city, not merely a city, but masses of human beings; nothing, I knew had any chance against death. Nevertheless after a pause of exhaustion the legs fluttered again. It was superb this last protest, and so frantic that he succeeded at last in righting himself. One's sympathies, of course, were all on the side of life. Also, when there was nobody to care or to know, this gigantic effort on the part of an insignificant little moth, against a power of such magnitude, to retain what no one else valued or desired to keep, moved one strangely. Again, somehow, one saw life, a pure bead. I lifted the pencil again, useless though I knew it to be. But even as I did so, the unmistakable tokens of death showed themselves. The body relaxed, and instantly grew stiff. The struggle was over. The insignificant little creature now knew death. As I looked at the dead moth, this minute wayside triumph of so great a force over so mean an antagonist filled me with wonder. Just as life had been strange a few minutes before, so death was now as strange. The moth having righted himself now lay most decently and uncomplainingly composed. O yes, he seemed to say, death is stronger than I am.

Why the Sky Looks Blue
Sir James Jeans

Jeans wants to clarify why the sky looks blue—to define the
process by which the blue waves of light become the ones that
we see everywhere, although the sun itself (which looks yellow)
sends out light that is composed of many colors. Jeans depends
upon **analogy** (see p. 24) as a technique of clarification. What
characteristics make his analogy a good choice? How does he
make the transition between the X used as an analogy and the
X that is his main subject?

Notice that Jeans is not trying to *prove* this theory that the
sky looks blue because blue light waves are easily scattered.
*His purpose here is simply to make us understand the process
of scattering.*

1   Imagine that we stand on an ordinary seaside pier, and watch the
waves rolling in and striking against the iron columns of the pier.
Large waves pay very little attention to the columns   they divide right
and left and reunite after passing each column, much as a regiment of
soldiers would if a tree stood in their road; it is almost as though the
columns had not been there. But the short waves and ripples find the
columns of the pier a much more formidable obstacle. When the short
waves impinge on the columns, they are reflected back and spread as
new ripples in all directions. To use the technical term, they are
"scattered." The obstacle provided by the iron columns hardly affects
the long waves at all, but scatters the short ripples.

2   We have been watching a sort of working model of the way in which
sunlight struggles through the earth's atmosphere. Between us on earth
and outer space, the atmosphere interposes innumerable obstacles in
the form of molecules of air, tiny droplets of water, and small particles
of dust. These are represented by the columns of the pier.

3   The waves of the sea represent the sunlight. We know that sunlight
is a blend of many colors—as we can prove for ourselves by passing
it through a prism, or even through a jug of water, or as nature
demonstrates to us when she passes it through the raindrops of a
summer shower and produces a rainbow. We also know that light

Source. "Why the Sky Looks Blue" by Sir James Jeans is from *The Stars in Their
Courses* by Sir James Jeans. Published by Cambridge University Press, 1931 and reprinted with their permission.

consists of waves, and that the different colors of light are produced by waves of different lengths, red light by long waves and blue light by short waves. The mixture of waves which constitutes sunlight has to struggle past the columns of the pier. And these obstacles treat the light waves much as the columns of the pier treat the sea-waves. The long waves which constitute red light are hardly affected but the short waves which constitute blue light are scattered in all directions.

4   Thus the different constituents of sunlight are treated in different ways as they struggle through the earth's atmosphere. A wave of blue light may be scattered by a dust particle, and turned out of its course. After a time a second dust particle again turns it out of its course, and so on, until finally it enters our eyes by a path as zigzag as that of a flash of lightning. Consequently the blue waves of the sunlight enter our eyes from all directions. And that is why the sky looks blue.

With Legs Like These . . . Who Needs Wings?
George E. Hollister

Hollister's subject is the roadrunner. A technical description of this bird (taken from a field guide) is as follows:

Roadrunner *Geococcyx Californianus*
Field marks: A cuckoo that runs on the ground (tracks show 2 toes forward, 2 backward). Slender, heavily streaked; long, maneuverable, white-tipped tail, shaggy crest, strong legs. In flight the short rounded wings display a white crescent.
Voice: Song, 6–8 dovelike *coo*'s descending in pitch (last note about pitch of Mourning Dove). The bird makes a clattering noise by rolling mandibles together.

Where found: Sw. U.S. (east to e. Oklahoma, nw. Louisiana); south to c. Mexico. **West:** *Resident* from n. California (n.

Source. "With Legs Like These . . . Who Needs Wings?" by George Hollister. Copyright 1973 by the National Wildlife Federation. Reprinted from the August-September issue of *National Wildlife* magazine.

Sacramento Valley), s. Nevada, s. Utah, c. Colorado, sw. Kansas south. **Habitat:** Open country with scattered cover, stony deserts, dry brush, open piñon-juniper. **Nest:** A shallow saucer in bush, cactus, low tree. Eggs (3–8; 12) white.[1]

This technical account differs from Hollister's informal description in a number of ways. One is length. The technical account is kept very brief. Another is intention. Readers consult a field guide in order to be able to *identify* a bird. The technical description lists *distinguishing characteristics* of the bird's appearance and way of life, so that we will know what to look for and in what likely places.

Hollister's informal description (from a popular journal), though somewhat fuller, is also brief, with short sentences and paragraphs that create a "staccato" rhythm. How much more do we learn about roadrunners here than in the technical field guide? What is the purpose of Hollister's account?

1   He's half tail and half feet. The rest of him is head and beak. When he runs, he moves on blurring wheels. He can turn on a dime and leave change. He doesn't need to fly because he can run faster. He kicks dirt in a snake's face, and then eats the snake. He chases lizards, and watches hawks with one eye.

2   He's "Meep-meep" and a cartoon favorite of three generations. He's an odd bird, but a real one—the roadrunner.

3   Early southwestern settlers were surprised to see a wildly colored bird dart onto a trail, race ahead of a lone horse and rider, slide to a dusty halt and then bob and bow in salute. Scientists later labeled him *Geococcyx californianus*, a member of the cuckoo family, but settlers aptly named him "roadrunner."

4   Because of his foot structure, Indians of the Southwest believed he had special power. His toes form an X, with two pointed forward and two backward. This arrangement held special meaning to the Indians, who scratched duplicate X figures near new graves and, for extra protection from evil spirits, decorated infant cradleboards with roadrunner feathers.

5   The footprint X's are unique in a more concrete way—they show the roadrunner may take 22-inch strides in high gear. He's been clocked at fifteen miles per hour (the rate of a four-minute miler). This means his thin muscular legs are taking 12 steps every second.

6   The combination of fast feet and a flat, wide tail serving as rudder

[1] "The Cuckoo Family, The Roadrunner Species" is from *A Field Guide to Western Birds* by Roger Tory Peterson. Copyright © 1969 renewed by Roger Tory Peterson. Reprinted by permission of Houghton Mifflin Company.

gives the roadrunner a double advantage over lizards and low-flying insects. He simply darts and twists after his prey, screeching into ninety-degree turns, careening around sagebrush and spurting into a straightaway as he catches his meals on the run.

7   In the roadrunner's hot, dry desert environment, all this hyperactivity would seem likely to dehydrate the bird. (He also frequents many plains, prairies, and oak-hickory forests.) But he has adapted remarkably well to temperatures over one hundred degrees and dry winds. His biggest problem—water—is solved by careful budgeting. He rests in the shade during the hottest part of the day, and replenishes body water through his diet; he eats things like lizards, whose bodies have a high water content, and then manufactures liquid by oxidation of the food into carbon dioxide.

8   The remainder of his diet is no problem, mainly because he eats most anything he can catch that's smaller than he is. He prefers insects (high water content), plants, lizards, snakes, and mammals like mice and rats.

9   His manner of catching a snake is especially noteworthy. He dashes in circles around a coiled snake, stops within striking distance, shuffles his feet, swishes his tail in the dirt, and stirs up a blinding cloud of dust.

10   Then begins Act II. Roadrunner ruffles his feathers to reduce penetration from a direct strike, and leaps back into a dizzying series of circles around the bewildered snake. He often reverses directions in mid-stride, catches the snake going the other way, and clouts him with his long, sharp beak. Finally, the tired, wounded snake catches several pecks to the brain and succumbs.

11   Eating the snake requires almost as much talent as catching it; the bird is dealing with a dinner frequently longer than itself. Roadrunner swallows his prey headfirst, forcing the snake as far down his gullet as possible. If there is excess snake, the bird simply waits for his superactive digestive juices to do their part, and in a matter of hours the snake is completely eaten.

12   Compared to snakes, insects are easy pickings. Most are simply snapped off mesquite and cacti, or flushed from under rocks with a tail flick. To catch cicadas, so erratic in flight that man can hardly catch them, Roadrunner simply dogs their odd flight pattern.

13   Roadrunner's eyesight is spectacular. He can spot a lizard skittering out of reach and watch an enemy hawk overhead at the same time. When he really wants to concentrate, he can focus all attention through one eye. Roadrunners have been observed standing entranced, with head tilted sideways, one eye focused on the ground and the other scanning the sky for airborne enemies.

14   In the spring, Roadrunner gets restless, grows a few sporty new feathers in his head crest, and begins stepping out. When he finds a

likely prospect for his affections, he starts acting like a normal road-runner—odd. His call to establish territory is normal: his series of six or eight calls descends in pitch until the last one resembles a mourning dove's plaintive coo.

15   He'll offer some food, flutter his tail, shuffle his feet in another dust-stirring dance, then end the performance with a graceful bow and more coos. If the hen thinks he's acceptable, she takes the food, they dance and bow, and then begin to look for a suitable place to build a nest.

16   Nest building, roadrunner style, usually results in a disorganized pile of sticks, feathers, old snakeskins, and rubble. The hen tramples a slight hollow in the center of this debris and lays three to eight white eggs at infrequent intervals. This haphazardly planned parenthood usually results in the first hatched young stumbling over a freshly laid egg or two.

17   It remained for Warner Brothers to enshrine the incredible roadrun-ner. From cartoons, the screwball bird and "meep-meep" branched out to emblems, decals, and patches. And not only for the toddler set—unofficial military insignia also bear his picture.

18   And he's not done yet. Next time you see a whirling cloud of dust, watch for some fast soft-shoe, a little artful bobbing and weaving. In the center of that cloud will be a roadrunner, the king of the cuckoos, doing his bit to enliven your hours on the road.

Homecoming
Daniel K. Inouye

In about a thousand words, this selection recreates the age-old experience of a soldier's homecoming. Inouye was not only a war hero (he lost his arm in the Italian campaign of World War II) but also a man who overcame racial prejudice to become the first American of Japanese ancestry elected to the U.S. Senate. The selection printed here, from his book *Journey to Washington*, tells the story of his return home after the war. The narrative begins in San Francisco with his attempt to get a seat on a Hawaii-bound plane.

Source. "Homecoming" by Daniel K. Inouye from the book *Journey to Washington* by Daniel K. Inouye with Lawrence Elliott. © 1967 by Prentice-Hall, Inc. Published by Prentice Hall, Inc., Englewood Cliffs, New Jersey and reprinted with their permission.

In this example of defining by personal **narrative** (see p. 7), Inouye captures the complexity of homecoming: he is a changed person now, inevitably affected by his wartime experiences, and yet home is still home.

1   In the end, of course, I did get to the coast, but still had to wangle a flight on that last, long trans-Pacific leg. I managed to hitch a jeep ride from San Francisco to the Air Corps base at Hamilton Field, and promptly ran into fresh trouble. As I checked through the guard post at the entrance, a captain—I suppose he was officer of the day—noticed that I returned the M.P. sentry's salute with a nod of my head, and he came storming through the door.

2   "Where'd you learn your military courtesy, Lieutenant?" he bellowed at me. "That guard is entitled to a salute. It's officers like you that make it so tough to maintain any sense of discipline in this man's army . . ."

3   He ranted on and on while, in the narrow confines of the jeep seat, I tried to get my overcoat open. Then he noticed what I was doing:

4   "Listen, don't show me your ribbons. They don't excuse . . ."

5   "Captain," I finally broke in, "you haven't given me a chance to say anything so I was trying to show you, not my ribbons"—here I finally got my coat open and pulled my hook out—"but the fact that I don't have an arm to salute with. I don't think you'd want me doing it with a hook, would you?"

6   I thought the poor man was going to burst into tears. He started to apologize, couldn't make it, leaned close and just touched my shoulder. "I didn't know," he whispered at last. "I . . . didn't know."

7   "Forget it, sir. No harm done."

8   "No, listen, where are you bound? Is there anything I can do for you?"

9   Well, that's how I got my ride home. I told that captain my problem and he just about broke his back to get me a seat on a troop carrier flight bound for Hickam Field that very day. That's what I call really atoning for an error.

10   And sometimes when your luck changes, it really changes. I had to wait to board the plane, since it was done by rank and I was very nearly the most junior passenger. And somewhere in the lounge, the most senior officer, a brigadier general, noticed me. Anyway, once we were aboard, he sent his aide back to my seat to ask if I'd like to join him up forward. And so he was my seatmate on the trip, and given his rank, the service was as good as the company. We chatted about Hawaii—this was to be his first visit—and I told him a little about the ins and outs of Honolulu. He asked if this was my first trip back and

53

I said yes. He asked if I had a ride home and I said no, and thought no more about it until we bumped down at Hickam, just past midnight. No sooner had the props stopped spinning than a staff car with a gleaming single star on the front bumper came tearing up under the wing.

11   "There's your ride, Lieutenant," the general said with a smile. "Just tell the sergeant where to take you."

12   "But . . . but that's your car, sir," I stammered. "How will you . . ."

13   "Oh, I imagine I'll get a lift somehow. But I want you to take my car tonight." And he didn't look at my hook when he said, "It's little enough for what you've given."

14   And so Dan Inouye, who'd barely made it into the army and had gone off to war with a uniform that didn't fit and high hopes of making corporal, came home in a general's car, a staff sergeant carrying his bag. I had called from the terminal—"Hello, Papa, I'm sorry to wake you up, but I'm at Hickam Field and I'll be there in twenty minutes"— and now as I stood outside the house in the still, deserted street I suddenly couldn't believe it. Was I really home? Had all those incredible things happened to me in the more than two and a half years that had passed since I last saw this place? Then the door opened and light poured into the dark street and my mother was saying, "Ken?"

15   I had my arm around her and felt her tears. I had my arm around all of them, my father, my sister May who had been a child when I left and was now grown and beautiful, my brothers John and Robert flushing with embarrassment and the pride plain in their faces. It was a sublimely happy moment, that homecoming, those few first minutes when we dispelled the long years with our joy and gratitude.

16   John took my bag from the sergeant, who saluted smartly as he left. Robert took my coat and May brought me a chair. "Shall I bring you something?" my mother whispered. "Tea? You're hungry! I'll make . . ."

17   "No, no, Mama. I'm fine."

18   I was. I looked around the house, my home, suddenly grown smaller and yet just the same. There was the picture of President Roosevelt on the wall, with one of me next to it. A blue star hung in the window. When I turned back, they were all looking at me, at my uniform and the ribbons on my chest, and, of course, at the hook. Now there had come that moment of awkward silence, the fumbling for a thought after the first heedless and loving greeting.

19   I lit a cigarette—tense, stomach tight—and had taken a deep-down drag before I realized what I was doing. May's eyes widened. My father, who must have had a pretty clear idea about my little vices— he'd once sent me a cigarette lighter, cautioning me never to mention it to my mother—tried to pretend he was in another city. And Mother came to her feet as though pinched.

20 ''Daniel Ken Inouye!'' she said in exactly the old way.

21 I looked sheepishly at the cigarette, then at her, then at the rest of them. And then we all began to laugh, my mother, too, and I knew that I was home.

Omnibuildings
Walter Karp

Karp uses a variety of techniques to define *omnibuildings*—for example, **lexical definition** (see p. 22) in paragraph 2, **comparison and contrast** (see p. 9) in paragraphs 3–6, **definition by example** (see p. 22) in paragraph 8. He also uses pictures. As you read the essay, try to identify what information you acquire from the words and what from the photographs of model omnibuildings. How do you decide whether your *X* needs a picture or diagram to clarify its meaning?

Notice that Karp avoids discussing whether he would like to live in one of these designer's dreams. His purpose is to inform, not to judge. He gives us the basic information and lets us form our own impressions. You might imitate his objectivity in explaining the nature of a college dormitory, a high-rise apartment complex, a country house in disrepair, a suburban home with all the ''extras'' such as deck, patio, two-car garage, lawn full of conquering crabgrass.

1 The curious structure shown on page 56 looks like a prefabricated coliseum waiting to be assembled. In fact it is a scale model of a Mediterranean town soon to be built on a man-made spit of land extending out from the shores of Monaco. The curved sections are towering artificial hills into which townhouses, shops, offices, and cafés will be inserted when the ''hills'' are completed in a few years' time. The cross section shows what the entire structure will look like from the sea. Monaco's satellite town is a prime example of perhaps the most striking endeavor in contemporary architecture: the designing

Source. ''Omnibuildings'' by Walter Karp. © 1970 by American Heritage Publishing Co., Inc. Reprinted by permission from *Horizon* (Winter 1970).

Source. Manfredi Nicoletti—Project for the Satellite Town of the Principality of Monaco. Reprinted by permission of Manfredi Nicoletti.

of "omnibuildings," a kind of structure that defies our sense of what a "building" is.

2   A building, we suppose, is an individual container, housing an office, a factory, a school, or a residence. When several of these containers— each with its own independent arrangements—spring up in one place, we have a town, an aggregate of "buildings" separated by open spaces called "streets." Suppose, however, that the factory, office, residence, and school are components of a single continuous structure, with each part "plugged" into a centrally organized system of transportation, plumbing, heating, and so forth. Then, in a word coined by *Progressive Architecture*, you have an "omnibuilding," a kind of building in which the street becomes an internal part of the structure, and a house a "unit" slotted into the system the way a cabinet is fitted into one's kitchen.

3   The omnibuilding is not entirely without historic antecedents. A luxury liner, with its unified system of residences (cabins), public commons (decks), work places, offices, dining quarters, vertical and horizontal interior streets, is an omnibuilding of sorts. On land an even closer approximation was the multipurpose castle, such as the Louvre, below, of Charles V. Like other castles, the Louvre combined in one structure a royal residence, court, fortress, military garrison, village,

Early Omnibuilding, The Louvre c. 1380

Sunset Mountain Park, California (see p. 60).

Source. Reprinted by permission of Daniel, Mann, Johnson & Mendenhall, Los Angeles, California.

and governmental offices. Like the contemporary omnibuildings, too, many castles had streets that were integral parts of the structure, namely the footpaths atop walls and parapets.

4   Both the luxury liner and the castle lack essential features of the ideal omnibuilding, however. One of these is what some architects call "open-endedness"—the capacity for change. In the ideal omnibuilding new units can be integrated into the system—sometimes called the "armature" or "infrastructure"—as the need for them arises. An omnibuilding, in other words, combines the planned organization of a rigid, conventional building with a town's flexible capacity for growth.

5   In addition, no ancestor of the modern omnibuilding can approach it in sheer complexity. The luxury liner, after all, performs the limited function of transportation, whereas Monaco's omnibuilding-by-the-sea

Sea City, to sit 15 miles out at sea (see p. 61).
Source. Used by permission of Pilkington Brothers Limited.

is a real town in which people will live permanently and whose needs, propensities, and convenience are, in consequence, many times more complicated and pressing. The Louvre combined a great many functions, but it did not have to include, for example, the integration of central heating, plumbing, automobile traffic, and storage into its design.

6   There is one other key feature of the omnibuilding, the one, perhaps, that is most difficult to grasp. That is its quality of being a three-dimensional system. Taken as a group, a cluster of ordinary buildings functions in two dimensions. People using one building reach another by moving horizontally across non-building space called a street. In the concentrated world of an omnibuilding people might just as easily pass between units by aerial footbridge or rooftop walkway; they may be able to drive their cars "upstairs." The omnibuilding designer, therefore, must conceive his entire design with all these varieties of spatial interconnection in mind and arrange them in the most efficient,

Buckminster Fuller's Floating City (see p. 61).
Source. Courtesy Buckminster Fuller Archives.

harmonious, and sociable way, a task that stands to ordinary building design as three dimensional chess stands to the flat variety.

7   Indeed there are critics who suggest that the chief charm of omni-buildings is precisely the awesome challenge they provide for their designers. As one architect has said, present omnibuilding designs "are more indicative of technological feats than of emerging spatial institutions." However that may be, the designers of the structures shown on these pages have risen to the challenge and wrought spectacularly.

Single-Structure Cities

8   Omnibuildings as cities in themselves include the model, page 58, for Sunset Mountain Park, a town proposed for a site overlooking Santa

Monica, California. At the mountain's crest sits the center of town (or omnibuilding). The terraced extensions reaching downhill are neighborhoods of townhouses. Residents would commute within the structure by means of inclined elevators. On page 59 is a rendering of the British-designed Sea City, a more visionary amphitheatre-like structure intended to sit on concrete stilts fifteen miles out in the North Sea. Its thirty thousand inhabitants would live chiefly on the tiered inner face of the edifice. Within the artificial lagoon would be numerous floating islets for private homes and boat moorings, linked by footbridges to the "mainland." Sea City's natural-gas heating plant would raise the surface temperature of the lagoon several degrees, creating a bubble of relatively balmy weather. The final model is Buckminster Fuller's "floating city," designed to serve as an offshore colony of a crowded coastal city. Created under the sponsorship of the Federal Department of Housing and Urban Development, Fuller's floating city is composed of several prefabricated "town" units, each capable of being built in a shipyard. They would be fitted together to form the full city.

Elizabeth Eckford, the Guards, and the Mob
Daisy Bates

The event defined here belongs to the painful story of school desegregation in America. In 1957, a court granted nine black students the right to enter Central High School in Little Rock, Arkansas. When they tried to go to school, they found their way blocked by white townspeople and by Arkansas National Guardsmen. One of the nine students, 15-year-old Elizabeth Eckford, later described that experience to writer Daisy Bates.

Elizabeth's **narrative** is remarkable for three qualities: first, its *realism* (such details as "I was pressing my black and white dress—I had made it to wear on the first day of school"—make her an individual rather than a name in a newspaper); second, its *balance* (she remembers to mention the white people who helped her as well as the ones who were cruel); third, its *control* (she never gives way to childish emotionalism such as name calling). These qualities of maturity in the telling of the story imply maturity in her own character and offer a dramatic contrast to the behavior of the mob. The *style* of the narrative is therefore as important as its substance. We learn about the event. We also learn about the kinds of people who made it.

1   She remained quiet for a long time. Then she began to speak.

2   "You remember the day before we were to go in, we met Superintendent Blossom at the school board office. He told us what the mob might say and do but he never told us we wouldn't have any protection. He told our parents not to come because he wouldn't be able to protect the children if they did.

3   "That night I was so excited I couldn't sleep. The next morning I was about the first one up. While I was pressing my black and white dress—I had made it to wear on the first day of school—my little brother turned on the TV set. They started telling about a large crowd gathered at the school. The man on TV said he wondered if we were going to show up that morning. Mother called from the kitchen, where she was fixing breakfast, 'Turn that TV off!' She was so upset and worried. I wanted to comfort her, so I said, 'Mother, don't worry.'

4   "Dad was walking back and forth, from room to room, with a sad expression. He was chewing on his pipe and he had a cigar in his hand, but he didn't light either one. It would have been funny, only he was so nervous.

5   "Before I left home Mother called us into the living-room. She said we should have a word of prayer. Then I caught the bus and got off a block from the school. I saw a large crowd of people standing across the street from the soldiers guarding Central. As I walked on, the crowd suddenly got very quiet. Superintendent Blossom had told us to enter by the front door. I look at all the people and thought, 'Maybe I will be safer if I walk down the block to the front entrance behind the guards.'

6   "At the corner I tried to pass through the long line of guards around the school so as to enter the grounds behind them. One of the guards pointed across the street. So I pointed in the same direction and asked whether he meant for me to cross the street and walk down. He nodded 'yes.' So, I walked across the street conscious of the crowd that stood there, but they moved away from me.

7   "For a moment all I could hear was the shuffling of their feet. Then someone shouted, 'Here she comes, get ready!' I moved away from

the crowd on the sidewalk and into the street. If the mob came at me I could then cross back over so the guards could protect me.

8   "The crowd moved in closer and then began to follow me, calling me names. I still wasn't afraid. Just a little bit nervous. Then my knees started to shake all of a sudden and I wondered whether I could make it to the center entrance a block away. It was the longest block I ever walked in my whole life.

9   "Even so, I still wasn't too scared because all the time I kept thinking that the guards would protect me.

10   "When I got right in front of the school, I went up to a guard again. But this time he just looked straight ahead and didn't move to let me pass him. I didn't know what to do. Then I looked and saw that the path leading to the front entrance was a little further ahead. So I walked until I was right in front of the path to the front door.

11   "I stood looking at the school—it looked so big! Just then the guards let some white students go through.

12   "The crowd was quiet. I guess they were waiting to see what was going to happen. When I was able to steady my knees, I walked up to the guard who had let the white students in. He too didn't move. When I tried to squeeze past him, he raised his bayonet and then the other guards closed in and they raised their bayonets.

13   "They glared at me with a mean look and I was very frightened and didn't know what to do. I turned around and the crowd came toward me.

14   "They moved closer and closer. Somebody started yelling, 'Lynch her! Lynch her!'

15   "I tried to see a friendly face somewhere in the mob—someone who maybe would help. I looked into the face of an old woman and it seemed a kind face, but when I looked at her again, she spat on me.

16   "They came closer, shouting, 'No nigger bitch is going to get in our school. Get out of here!'

17   "I turned back to the guards but their faces told me I wouldn't get help from them. Then I looked down the block and saw a bench at the bus stop. I thought, 'If I can only get there I will be safe.' I don't know why the bench seemed a safe place to me, but I started walking toward it. I tried to close my mind to what they were shouting, and kept saying to myself, 'If I can only make it to the bench I will be safe.'

18   "When I finally got there, I don't think I could have gone another step. I sat down and the mob crowded up and began shouting all over again. Someone hollered, 'Drag her over to this tree! Let's take care of the nigger.' Just then a white man sat down beside me, put his arm around me and patted my shoulder. He raised my chin and said, 'Don't let them see you cry.'

19   "Then, a white lady—she was very nice—she came over to me on the bench. She spoke to me but I don't remember now what she said. She put me on the bus and sat next to me. She asked me my name and tried to talk to me but I don't think I answered. I can't remember much about the bus ride, but the next thing I remember I was standing in front of the School for the Blind, where Mother works.

20   "I thought, 'Maybe she isn't here. But she has to be here!' So I ran upstairs, and think some teachers tried to talk to me, but I kept running until I reached Mother's classroom.

21   "Mother was standing at the window with her head bowed, but she must have sensed I was there because she turned around. She looked as if she had been crying, and I wanted to tell her I was all right. But I couldn't speak. She put her arms around me and I cried."

Will Someone Please Hiccup My Pat?
William Spooner Donald

Donald has two purposes. One is to define the term *Spoonerism*. The other is to present the personality of the man whose comic misuse of language gave rise to that term. In this brief account of Spooner's life, conventional biographical data (date of birth, etc.) are kept to a minimum, while the incidents during which Spooner made his silly remarks such as "Will someone please hiccup my pat?" are emphasized. The collection of Spoonerisms, worked chronologically into the narrative, functions as a **definition by example**. The narrative itself serves to connect and explain the separate Spoonerisms and to help us see the man behind the mistakes. The resultant combination is neither standard biography nor standard definition of a term, but a delightful hybrid of the two.

Source. "Will Someone Please Hiccup My Pat?" by William Spooner Donald. Reprinted by permission of the author.

1 One afternoon nearly a hundred years ago the October wind gusted merrily down Oxford's High Street. Hatless and helpless, a white-haired clergyman with pink cherubic features uttered his plaintive cry for aid. As an athletic youngster chased the spinning topper, other bystanders smiled delightedly—they had just heard at first hand the latest "Spoonerism."

2 My revered relative William Archibald Spooner was born in 1844, the son of a Staffordshire county court judge. As a young man, he was handicapped by a poor physique, a stammer, and weak eyesight; at first, his only possible claim to future fame lay in the fact that he was an albino, with very pale blue eyes and white hair tinged slightly yellow.

3 But nature compensated the weakling by blessing him with a brilliant intellect. By 1868 he had been appointed a lecturer at New College, Oxford. Just then he would have been a caricaturist's dream with his freakish looks, nervous manner, and peculiar mental kink that caused him—in his own words—to "make occasional felicities in verbal diction."

4 Victorian Oxford was a little world of its own where life drifted gently by; a world where splendid intellectuals lived in their ivory towers of Latin, Euclid, and Philosophy; a world where it was always a sunny summer afternoon in a countryside, where Spooner admitted he loved to "pedal gently round on a well-boiled icicle."

5 As the years passed, Spooner grew, probably without himself being aware of the fact, into a "character." A hard worker himself, he detested idleness and is on record as having rent some lazybones with the gem, "You have hissed all my mystery lessons, and completely tasted two whole worms."

6 With his kindly outlook on life, it was almost natural for him to take holy orders; he was ordained a deacon in 1872 and a priest in 1875. His unique idiosyncrasy never caused any serious trouble and merely made him more popular. On one occasion, in New College chapel in 1879, he announced smilingly that the next hymn would be "Number One seven five—Kinkering Kongs their Titles Take." Other congregations were treated to such jewels as ". . . Our Lord, we know, is a shoving Leopard . . ." and ". . . All of us have in our hearts a half-warmed fish to lead a better life. . . ."

7 Spooner often preached in the little village churches around Oxford and once delivered an eloquent address on the subject of Aristotle. No doubt the sermon contained some surprising information for his rustic congregation. For after Spooner had left the pulpit, an idea seemed to occur to him, and he hopped back up the steps again.

8 "Excuse me, dear brethren," he announced brightly, "I just want to say that in my sermon whenever I mentioned Aristotle, I should have said Saint Paul."

65

9   By 1885 the word ''Spoonerism'' was in colloquial use in Oxford circles, and a few years later, in general use all over England. If the dividing line between truth and myth is often only a hairsbreadth, does it really matter? One story that has been told concerns an optician's shop in London. Spooner is reputed to have entered and asked to see a ''signifying glass.'' The optician registered polite bewilderment.

10   ''Just an ordinary signifying glass,'' repeated Spooner, perhaps surprised at the man's obtuseness.

11   ''I'm afraid we haven't one in stock, but I'll make inquiries right away, sir,'' said the shopkeeper, playing for time.

12   ''Oh, don't bother, it doesn't magnify, it doesn't magnify,'' said Spooner airily, and walked out.

13   Fortunately for Spooner, he made the right choice when he met his wife-to-be. He was thirty-four years old when he married Frances Goodwin in 1878. The marriage was a happy one, and they had one son and four daughters. Mrs. Spooner was tall, good-looking girl, and on one occasion the family went on a short holiday in Switzerland. The ''genial Dean,'' as he was then called, took a keen interest in geology, and in no time at all he had mastered much information and many technical definitions on the subject of glaciers.

14   One day at lunchtime the younger folk were worried because their parents had not returned from a long walk. When Spooner finally appeared with his wife, his explanation was: ''We strolled up a long valley, and when we turned a corner we found ourselves completely surrounded by erotic blacks.''

15   He was, of course, referring to ''erratic blocks,'' or large boulders left around after the passage of a glacier.

16   In 1903 Spooner was appointed Warden of New College, the highest possible post for a Fellow. One day walking across the quadrangle, he met a certain Mr. Casson, who had just been elected a Fellow of New College.

17   ''Do come to dinner tonight,'' said Spooner, ''we are welcoming our new Fellow, Mr. Casson.''

18   ''But, my dear Warden, I *am* Casson,'' was the surprised reply.

19   ''Never mind, never mind, come along all the same,'' said Spooner tactfully.

20   On another occasion in later years when his eyesight was really very bad, Spooner found himself seated next to a most elegant lady at dinner. In a casual moment the latter put her lily-white hand onto the polished table, and Spooner, in an even more casual manner, pronged her hand with his fork, remarking genially, ''My bread, I think.''

21   In 1924 Spooner retired as Warden. He had established an astonishing record of continuous residence at New College for sixty-two years first as undergraduate, then as Fellow, then Dean, and finally as Warden. His death in 1930, at the age of eighty-six, was a blushing

crow to collectors of those odd linguistic transpositions known by then throughout the English-speaking world as Spoonerisms.

Seeing
Annie Dillard

Most of us take the ability to see for granted. However, to a blind person who suddenly acquires sight, seeing is a remarkable experience—''pure sensation'' (paragraph 2). Dillard uses examples from the book *Space and Sight* to illustrate the effects of newly acquired vision. *Notice how these brief examples rely on a few vivid details.* Then Dillard goes one step further: she explains the effects of this book's information on her own way of seeing. This analysis of **cause and effect** (see p. 9) thus defines two related concepts: (1) what seeing means to the newly sighted, and (2) what her own enlarged concept of seeing is.

1   I chanced on a wonderful book by Marius von Senden, called *Space and Sight*. When Western surgeons discovered how to perform safe cataract operations, they ranged across Europe and America operating on dozens of men and women of all ages who had been blinded by cataracts since birth. Von Senden collected accounts of such cases; the histories are fascinating. Many doctors had tested their patients' sense perceptions and ideas of space both before and after the operations. The vast majority of patients, of both sexes and all ages, had, in von Senden's opinion, no idea of space whatsoever. Form, distance, and size were so many meaningless syllables. A patient ''had no idea of depth, confusing it with roundness.'' Before the operation a doctor would give a blind patient a cube and a sphere; the patient would tongue it or feel it with his hands, and name it correctly. After the operation the doctor would show the same objects to the patient without letting him touch them; now he had no clue whatsoever what

he was seeing. One patient called lemonade "square" because it pricked on his tongue as a square shape pricked on the touch of his hands. Of another postoperative patient, the doctor writes, "I have found in her no notion of size, for example, not even within the narrow limits which she might have encompassed with the aid of touch. Thus when I asked her to show me how big her mother was, she did not stretch out her hands, but set her two index-fingers a few inches apart." Other doctors reported their patients' own statements to similar effect. "The room he was in . . . he knew to be but part of the house, yet he could not conceive that the whole house could look bigger"; "Those who are blind from birth . . . have no real conception of height or distance. A house that is a mile away is thought of as nearby, but requiring the taking of a lot of steps. . . . The elevator that whizzes him up and down gives no more sense of vertical distance than does the train of horizontal."

2   For the newly sighted, vision is pure sensation unencumbered by meaning: "The girl went through the experience that we all go through and forget, the moment we are born. She saw, but it did not mean anything but a lot of different kinds of brightness." Again, "I asked the patient what he could see; he answered that he saw an extensive field of light, in which everything appeared dull, confused, and in motion. He could not distinguish objects." Another patient saw "nothing but a confusion of forms and colours." When a newly sighted girl saw photographs and paintings, she asked, " 'Why do they put those dark marks all over them?' 'Those aren't dark marks,' her mother explained, 'those are shadows. That is one of the ways the eye knows that things have shape. If it were not for shadows many things would look flat.' 'Well, that's how things do look,' Joan answered. 'Everything looks flat with dark patches.' "

3   But it is the patients' concepts of space that are most revealing. One patient, according to his doctor, "practices his vision in a strange fashion; thus he takes off one of his boots, throws it some way off in front of him, and then attempts to gauge the distance at which it lies; he takes a few steps towards the boot and tries to grasp it; on failing to reach it, he moves on a step or two and gropes for the boot until he finally gets hold of it." "But even at this stage, after three weeks' experience of seeing," von Senden goes on, " 'space,' as he conceives it, ends with visual space, i.e., with colour-patches that happen to bound his view. He does not yet have the notion that a larger object (a chair) can mask a smaller one (a dog), or that the latter can still be present even though it is not directly seen."

4   In general the newly sighted see the world as a dazzle of color-patches. They are pleased by the sensation of color, and learn quickly to name the colors, but the rest of seeing is tormentingly difficult. Soon after his operation a patient "generally bumps into one of these

colour-patches and observes them to be substantial, since they resist him as tactual objects do. In walking about it also strikes him—or can if he pays attention—that he is continually passing in between the colours he sees, that he can go past a visual object, that a part of it then steadily disappears from view; and that in spite of this, however he twists and turns—whether entering the room from the door, for example, or returning back to it—he always has a visual space in front of him. Thus he gradually comes to realize that there is also a space behind him, which he does not see.''

5   The mental effort involved in these reasonings proves overwhelming for many patients. It oppresses them to realize, if they ever do at all, the tremendous size of the world, which they had previously conceived of as something touchingly manageable. It oppresses them to realize that they have been visible to people all along, perhaps unattractively so, without their knowledge or consent. A disheartening number of them refuse to use their new vision, continuing to go over objects with their tongues, and lapsing into apathy and despair. ''The child can see, but will not make use of his sight. Only when pressed can he with difficulty be brought to look at objects in his neighbourhood; but more than a foot away it is impossible to bestir him to the necessary effort.'' Of a twenty-one-year-old girl, the doctor relates, ''Her unfortunate father, who had hoped for so much from this operation, wrote that his daughter carefully shuts her eyes whenever she wishes to go about the house, especially when she comes to a staircase, and that she is never happier or more at ease than when, by closing her eyelids, she relapses into her former state of total blindness.'' A fifteen-year-old boy, who was also in love with a girl at the asylum for the blind, finally blurted out, ''No, really, I can't stand it any more; I want to be sent back to the asylum again. If things aren't altered, I'll tear my eyes out.''

6   Some do learn to see, especially the young ones. But it changes their lives. One doctor comments on ''the rapid and complete loss of that striking and wonderful serenity which is characteristic only of those who have never yet seen.'' A blind man who learns to see is ashamed of his old habits. He dresses up, grooms himself, and tries to make a good impression. While he was blind he was indifferent to objects unless they were edible; now, ''a sifting of values sets in . . . his thoughts and wishes are mightily stirred and some few of the patients are thereby led into dissimulation, envy, theft and fraud.''

7   On the other hand, many newly sighted people speak well of the world, and teach us how dull is our own vision. To one patient, a human hand, unrecognized, is ''something bright and then holes.'' Shown a bunch of grapes, a boy calls out, ''It is dark, blue and shiny. . . . It isn't smooth, it has bumps and hollows.'' A little girl visits a garden. ''She is greatly astonished, and can scarcely be per-suaded to answer, stands speechless in front of the tree, which she

only names on taking hold of it, and then as 'the tree with the lights in it.' '' Some delight in their sight and give themselves over to the visual world. Of a patient just after her bandages were removed, her doctor writes, ''The first things to attract her attention were her own hands; she looked at them very closely, moved them repeatedly to and fro, bent and stretched the fingers, and seemed greatly astonished at the sight.'' One girl was eager to tell her blind friend that ''men do not really look like trees at all,'' and astounded to discover that her every visitor had an utterly different face. Finally, a twenty-two-year-old girl was dazzled by the world's brightness and kept her eyes shut for two weeks. When at the end of that time she opened her eyes again, she did not recognize any objects, but, ''the more she now directed her gaze upon everything about her, the more it could be seen how an expression of gratification and astonishment overspread her features; she repeatedly exclaimed: 'Oh God! How beautiful!' ''

8   I saw color-patches for weeks after I read this wonderful book. It was summer; the peaches were ripe in the valley orchards. When I woke in the morning, color-patches wrapped round my eyes, intricately, leaving not one unfilled spot. All day long I walked among shifting color-patches that parted before me like the Red Sea and closed again in silence, transfigured, wherever I looked back. Some patches swelled and loomed, while others vanished utterly, and dark marks flitted at random over the whole dazzling sweep. But I couldn't sustain the illusion of flatness. I've been around for too long. Form is condemned to an eternal danse macabre with meaning: I couldn't unpeach the peaches. Nor can I remember ever having seen without understanding; the color-patches of infancy are lost. My brain then must have been smooth as any balloon. I'm told I reached for the moon; many babies do. But the color-patches of infancy swelled as meaning filled them; they arrayed themselves in solemn ranks down distances which unrolled and stretched before me like a plain. The moon rocketed away. I live now in a world of shadows that shape and distance color, a world where space makes a kind of terrible sense. What gnosticism is this, and what physics? The fluttering patch I saw in my nursery window—silver and green and shape-shifting blue—is gone; a row of Lombardy poplars takes its place, mute, across the distant lawn. That humming oblong creature pale as light that stole along the walls of my room at night, stretching exhilaratingly around the corners, is gone, too, gone the night I ate of the bittersweet fruit, put two and two together and puckered forever my brain. Martin Buber tells this tale: ''Rabbi Mendel once boasted to his teacher Rabbi Elimelekh that evenings he saw the angel who rolls away the light before the darkness, and mornings the angel who rolls away the dark-

ness before the light. 'Yes,' said Rabbi Elimelekh, 'in my youth I saw that too. Later on you don't see these things any more.' "

Why didn't someone hand those newly sighted people paints and brushes from the start, when they still didn't know what anything was? Then maybe we all could see color-patches too, the world unraveled from reason, Eden before Adam gave names. The scales would drop from my eyes; I'd see trees like men walking; I'd run down the road against all orders, hallooing and leaping.

My Search for Roots:
A Black American's Story
Alex Haley

One of the most exciting kinds of information is information about yourself. In such cases, the question "What is *X*?" becomes "What am *I*?" Sometimes the search for self focuses on the past. Haley, deprived of part of his past, set out to recover it.

This article (the introduction to a book on the African roots of black Americans) describes the process of search that led Haley to reunion with his African relatives. *The article is dramatic because of its subject matter*—the story of a person in search of himself is always appealing, since all of us need to "find ourselves" in some way. *It is dramatic also because Haley makes us share his emotional involvement.*

1   My earliest memory is of Grandma, Cousin Georgia, Aunt Plus, Aunt Liz and Aunt Till talking on our front porch in Henning, Tennessee. At dusk, these wrinkled, graying old ladies would sit in rocking chairs and talk, about slaves and massas and plantations—pieces and patches of family history, passed down across the generations by word of mouth. "Old-timey stuff," Mamma would exclaim. She wanted no part of it.

2   The furthest-back person Grandma and the others ever mentioned was "the African." They would tell how he was brought here on a

ship to a place called "Naplis" and sold as a slave in Virginia. There he mated with another slave, and had a little girl named Kizzy.

3   When Kizzy became four or five, the old ladies said, her father would point out to her various objects and name them in his native tongue. For example, he would point to a guitar and make a single-syllable sound, *ko*. Pointing to a river that ran near the plantation, he'd say "Kamby Bolongo." And when other slaves addressed him as Toby—the name given him by his massa—the African would strenuously reject it, insisting that his name was "Kin-tay."

4   Kin-tay often told Kizzy stories about himself. He said that he had been near his village in Africa, chopping wood to make a drum, when he had been set upon by four men, overwhelmed, and kidnaped into slavery. When Kizzy grew up and became a mother, she told her son these stories, and he in turn would tell *his* children. His granddaughter became my grandmother, and she pumped that saga into me as if it were plasma, until I knew by rote the story of the African, and the subsequent generational wending of our family through cotton and tobacco plantations into the Civil War and then freedom.

5   At 17, during World War II, I enlisted in the Coast Guard, and found myself a messboy on a ship in the Southwest Pacific. To fight boredom, I began to teach myself to become a writer. I stayed on in the service after the war, writing every single night, seven nights a week, for eight years before I sold a story to a magazine. My first story in the Digest was published in June 1954: "The Harlem Nobody Knows." At age 37, I retired from military service, determined to be a full-time writer. Working with the famous Black Muslim spokesman, I did the actual writing for the book *The Autobiography of Malcom X*.

6   I remembered still the vivid highlights of my family's story. Could this account possibly be documented for a book? During 1962, between other assignments, I began following the story's trail. In plantation records, wills, census records, I documented bits here, shreds there. By now, Grandma was dead; repeatedly I visited other close sources, most notably our encyclopedic matriarch, "Cousin Georgia" Anderson in Kansas City, Kansas. I went as often as I could to the National Archives in Washington, and the Library of Congress, and the Daughters of the American Revolution Library.

7   By 1967, I felt I had the seven generations of the U.S. side documented. But the unknown quotient in the riddle of the past continued to be those strange, sharp, angular sounds spoken by the African himself. Since I lived in New York City, I began going to the United Nations lobby, stopping Africans and asking if they recognized the sounds. Every one of them listened to me, then quickly took off. I can well understand: me with a Tennessee accent, trying to imitate African sounds!

8   Finally, I sought out a linguistics expert who specialized in African

languages. To him I repeated the phrases. The sound "Kin-tay," he said, was a Mandinka tribe surname. And "Kamby Bolongo" was probably the Gambia River in Mandinka dialect. Three days later, I was in Africa.

9   In Banjul, the capital of Gambia, I met with a group of Gambians. They told me how for centuries the history of Africa has been preserved. In the older villages of the back country there are old men, called *griots*, who are in effect living archives. Such men know and, on special occasions, tell the cumulative histories of clans, or families, or villages, as those histories have long been told. Since my forefather had said his name was Kin-tay (properly spelled Kinte), and since the Kinte clan was known in Gambia, they would see what they could do to help me.

0   I was back in New York when a registered letter came from Gambia. Word had been passed in the back country, and a *griot* of the Kinte clan had, indeed, been found. His name, the letter said, was Kebba Kanga Fofana. I returned to Gambia and organized a safari to locate him.

11   There is an expression called "the peak experience," a moment which, emotionally, can never again be equaled in your life. I had mine, that first day in the village of Juffure, in the back country in black West Africa.

12   When our 14-man safari arrived within sight of the village, the people came flocking out of their circular mud huts. From a distance I could see a small, old man with a pillbox hat, an off-white robe and an aura of "somebodiness" about him. The people quickly gathered around me in a kind of horseshoe pattern. The old man looked piercingly into my eyes, and he spoke in Mandinka. Translation came from the interpreters I had brought with me.

13   "Yes, we have been told by the forefathers that there are many of us from this place who are in exile in that place called America."

14   Then the old man, who was 73 rains of age—the Gambian way of saying 73 years old, based upon the one rainy season per year—began to tell me the lengthy ancestral history of the Kinte clan. It was clearly a formal occasion for the villagers. They had grown mouse-quiet, and stood rigidly.

15   Out of the *griot's* head came spilling lineage details incredible to hear. He recited who married whom, two or even three centuries back. I was struck not only by the profusion of details, but also by the Biblical pattern of the way he was speaking. It was something like, "—and so-and-so took as a wife so-and-so, and begat so-and-so. . . ."

16   The *griot* had talked for some hours, and had got to about 1750 in our calendar. Now he said, through an interpreter, "About the time the king's soldiers came, the eldest of Omoro's four sons, Kunta, went away from this village to chop wood—and he was never seen again. . . ."

73

17   Goose pimples came out on me the size of marbles. He just had no way in the world of knowing that what he told me meshed with what I'd heard from the old ladies on the front porch in Henning, Tennessee. I got out my notebook, which had in it what Grandma had said about the African. One of the interpreters showed it to the others, and they went to the *griot*, and they all got agitated. Then the *griot* went to the people, and *they* all got agitated.

18   I don't remember anyone giving an order, but those 70-odd people formed a ring around me, moving counterclockwise, chanting, their bodies close together. I can't begin to describe how I felt. A woman broke from the circle, a scowl on her jet-black face, and came charging toward me. She took her baby and almost roughly thrust it out at me. The gesture meant "Take it!" and I did, clasping the baby to me. Whereupon the woman all but snatched the baby away. Another woman did the same with her baby, then another, and another.

19   A year later, a famous professor at Harvard would tell me: "You were participating in one of the oldest ceremonies of humankind, called 'the laying on of hands.' In their way, these tribespeople were saying to you, 'Through this flesh, which is us, we are you and you are us.' "

20   Later, as we drove out over the back-country road, I heard the staccato sound of drums. When we approached the next village, people were packed alongside the dusty road, waving, and the din from them welled louder as we came closer. As I stood up in the Land Rover, I finally realized what it was they were all shouting: "Meester Kinte! Meester Kinte!" In their eyes I was the symbol of all black people in the United States whose forefathers had been torn out of Africa while theirs remained.

21   Hands before my face, I began crying—crying as I have never cried in my life. Right at that time, crying was all I could do.

22   I went then to London. I searched and searched, and finally in the British Parliamentary records I found that the "king's soldiers" mentioned by the *griot* referred to a group called "Colonel O'Hare's forces," which had been sent up the Gambia River in 1767 to guard the then British-operated James Fort, a slave fort.

23   I next went to Lloyds of London, where doors were opened for me to research among all kinds of old maritime records. I pored through the records of slave ships that had sailed from Africa. Volumes upon volumes of these records exist. One afternoon about 2:30, during the seventh week of searching, I was going through my 1023rd set of ship records. I picked up a sheet that had on it the reported movements of 30 slave ships, my eyes stopped at No. 18, and my glance swept across the column entries. This vessel had sailed directly from the Gambia River to America in 1767; her name was the *Lord Ligonier;* and she had arrived at Annapolis (Naplis) the morning of September 29, 1767.

4   Exactly 200 years later, on September 29, 1967, there was nowhere in the world for me to be except standing on a pier at Annapolis, staring sea-ward across those waters over which my great-great-great-great-grandfather had been brought. And there in Annapolis I inspected the microfilmed records of the *Maryland Gazette*. In the issue of October 1, 1767, on page 3, I found an advertisement informing readers that the *Lord Ligonier* had just arrived from the River Gambia, with "a cargo of choice, healthy SLAVES" to be sold at auction the following Wednesday.

5   In the years since, I have done extensive research in 50 or so libraries, archives and repositories on three continents. I spent a year combing through countless documents to learn about the culture of Gambia's villages in the 18th and 19th centuries. Desiring to sail over the same waters navigated by the *Lord Ligonier*, I flew to Africa and boarded the freighter *African Star*. I forced myself to spend the ten nights of the crossing in the cold, dark cargo hold, stripped to my underwear, lying on my back on a rough, bare plank. But this was sheer luxury compared to the inhuman ordeal suffered by those millions who, chained and shackled, lay in terror and in their own filth in the stinking darkness through voyages averaging 60 to 70 days.

Reports, Inferences, Judgments
S. I. Hayakawa

Hayakawa defines the kinds of statement we make. He begins by classifying statements into three types: *reports*, *inferences*, and *judgments*. To explain each type, he uses **formal definition**, a great many specific **examples**, and a recurrent **analogy** that compares (1) life to a territory through which we move and (2) language to the map we make of that territory.

Hayakawa's governing idea is that we can make an accurate map of experience only if we describe it impartially or, in his terms, only if we offer *reports* of what we see, hear, feel, and so forth, rather than *inferences* and *judgments*. He asks us to

Source. "Reports, Inferences, Judgments" by S. I. Hayakawa is from *Language in Thought and Action*, Second Edition, by S. I. Hayakawa, copyright © 1964 by Harcourt Brace Jovanovich, Inc. and reprinted with their permission.

write *objectively,* to let others see *X* as *X* is and to avoid writing *subjectively,* to avoid asking others to see *X* ''our way.'' To what extent is such neutrality possible? When might it not be desirable?

To put it briefly, in human speech, different sounds have different meanings. To study this co-ordination of certain sounds with certain meanings is to study language. This co-ordination makes it possible for man to interact with great precision. When we tell someone, for instance, the address of a house he has never seen, we are doing something which no animal can do.

LEONARD BLOOMFIELD

Vague and insignificant forms of speech, and abuse of language, have so long passed for mysteries of science; and hard or misapplied words with little or no meaning have, by prescription, such a right to be mistaken for deep learning and height of speculation, that it will not be easy to persuade either those who speak or those who hear them, that they are but the covers of ignorance and hindrance of true knowledge.

JOHN LOCKE

1   For the purposes of interchange of information, the basic symbolic act is the *report* of what we have seen, heard, or felt: ''There is a ditch on each side of the road.'' ''You can get those at Smith's hardware store for $2.75.'' ''There aren't any fish on that side of the lake, but there are on this side.'' Then there are reports of reports: ''The longest waterfall in the world is Victoria Falls in Rhodesia.'' ''The Battle of Hastings took place in 1066.'' ''The papers say that there was a smash-up on Highway 41 near Evansville.'' Reports adhere to the following rules: first, they are *capable of verification;* second, they *exclude,* as far as possible, *inferences* and *judgments.* (These terms will be defined later.)

2   Reports are verifiable. We may not always be able to verify them ourselves, since we cannot track down the evidence for every piece of history we know, nor can we all go to Evansville to see the remains of the smash-up before they are cleared away. But if we are roughly agreed on the names of things, on what constitutes a ''foot,'' ''yard,'' ''bushel,'' and so on, and on how to measure time, there is relatively little danger of our misunderstanding each other. Even in a world such as we have today, in which everybody seems to be quarreling with everybody else, *we still to a surprising degree trust each other's reports.* We ask directions of total strangers when we are traveling. We follow directions on road signs without being suspicious of the people who put them up. We read books of information about science,

mathematics, automotive engineering, travel, geography, the history of costume, and other such factual matters, and we usually assume that the author is doing his best to tell us as truly as he can what he knows. And we are safe in so assuming most of the time. With the interest given today to the discussion of biased newspapers, propagandists, and the general untrustworthiness of many of the communications we receive, we are likely to forget that we still have an enormous amount of reliable information available and that deliberate misinformation, except in warfare, is still more the exception than the rule. The desire for self-preservation that compelled men to evolve means for the exchange of information also compels them to regard the giving of false information as profoundly reprehensible.

At its highest development, the language of reports is the language of science. By "highest development" we mean greatest general usefulness. Presbyterian and Catholic, workingman and capitalist, East German and West German, *agree* on the meanings of such symbols as $2 \times 2 = 4$, $100°C.$, HNO_3, $3:35$ A.M., *1940* A.D., *1000 kilowatts, Quercus agrifolia,* and so on. But how, it may be asked, can there be agreement about even this much among people who disagree about political philosophies, ethical ideas, religious beliefs, and the survival of my business *versus* the survival of yours? The answer is that circumstances *compel men to agree,* whether they wish to or not. If, for example, there were a dozen different religious sects in the United States, each insisting on its own way of naming the time of the day and the days of the year, the mere necessity of having a dozen different calendars, a dozen different kinds of watches, and a dozen sets of schedules for business hours, trains, and television programs to say nothing of the effort that would be required for translating terms from one nomenclature to another, would make life as we know it impossible.[1]

The language of reports, then, including the more accurate reports of science, is "map" language, and because it gives us reasonably

[1] According to information supplied by the Association of American Railroads, "Before 1883 there were nearly 100 different time zones in the United States. It wasn't until November 18 of that year that . . . a system of standard time was adopted here and in Canada. Before then there was nothing but local or 'solar' time. . . . The Pennsylvania Railroad in the East used Philadelphia time, which was five minutes slower than New York time and five minutes faster than Baltimore time. The Baltimore & Ohio used Baltimore time for trains running out of Baltimore, Columbus time for Ohio, Vincennes (Indiana) time for those going out of Cincinnati. . . . When it was noon in Chicago, it was 12:31 in Pittsburgh; 12:24 in Cleveland; 12:17 in Toledo; 12:13 in Cincinnati; 12:09 in Louisville; 12:07 in Indianapolis; 11:50 in St. Louis; 11:48 in Dubuque; 11:39 in St. Paul; and 11:27 in Omaha. There were 27 local time zones in Michigan alone. . . . A person traveling from Eastport, Maine, to San Francisco, if he wanted always to have the right railroad time and get off at the right place, had to twist the hands of his watch 20 times en route." Chicago *Daily News* (September 29, 1948).

accurate representations of the "territory," it enables us to get work done. Such language may often be dull or uninteresting reading: one does not usually read logarithmic tables or telephone directories for entertainment. But we could not get along without it. There are numberless occasions in the talking and writing we do in everyday life that *require that we state things in such a way that everybody will be able to understand and agree with our formulation.*

Inferences

5   The reader will find that practice in writing reports is a quick means of increasing his linguistic awareness. It is an exercise which will constantly provide him with his own examples of the principles of language and interpretation under discussion. The reports should be about first-hand experience—scenes the reader has witnessed himself, meetings and social events he has taken part in, people he knows well. They should be of such a nature that they can be verified and agreed upon. For the purpose of this exercise, inferences will be excluded.

6   Not that inferences are not important—we rely in everyday life and in science as much on *inferences* as on reports—in some areas of thought, for example, geology, paleontology, and nuclear physics, reports are the foundations, but inferences (and inferences upon inferences) are the main body of the science. An inference, as we shall use the term, is *a statement about the unknown made on the basis of the known.* We may *infer* from the material and cut of a woman's clothes her wealth or social position; we may *infer* from the character of the ruins the origin of the fire that destroyed the building; we may *infer* from a man's calloused hands the nature of his occupation; we may *infer* from a senator's vote on an armaments bill his attitude toward Russia; we may *infer* from the structure of the land the path of a prehistoric glacier; we may *infer* from a halo on an unexposed photographic plate that it has been in the vicinity of radioactive materials; we may *infer* from the sound of an engine the condition of its connecting rods. Inferences may be carelessly or carefully made. They may be made on the basis of a broad background of previous experience with the subject matter, or no experience at all. For example, the inferences a good mechanic can make about the internal condition of a motor by listening to it are often startlingly accurate, while the inferences made by an amateur (if he tries to make any) may be entirely wrong. But the common characteristic of inferences is that they are statements about matters which are not directly known, statements made on the basis of what has been observed.

7   The avoidance of inferences in our suggested practice in report-writing requires that we make no guesses as to what is going on in other people's minds. When we say, "He was angry," we are not

reporting; we are making an inference from such observable facts as the following: "He pounded his fist on the table; he swore; he threw the telephone directory at his stenographer." In this particular example, the inference appears to be fairly safe; nevertheless, it is important to remember, especially for the purposes of training oneself, that it is an inference. Such expressions as "He thought a lot of himself," "He was scared of girls," "He has an inferiority complex," made on the basis of casual social observation, and "What Russia really wants to do is to establish a world communist dictatorship," made on the basis of casual newspaper reading, are highly inferential. We should keep in mind their inferential character and, in our suggested exercises, should substitute for them such statements as "He rarely spoke to subordinates in the plant," "I saw him at a party, and he never danced except when one of the girls asked him to," "He wouldn't apply for the scholarship although I believe he could have won it easily," and "The Russian delegation to the United Nations has asked for A, B, and C. Last year they voted against M and N, and voted for X and Y. On the basis of facts such as these, the newspaper I read makes the inference that what Russia really wants is to establish a world communist dictatorship. I agree."

8   In spite of the exercise of every caution in avoiding inferences and reporting only what is seen and experienced, we all remain prone to error, since the making of inferences is a quick, almost automatic process. We may watch a car weaving as it goes down the road and say, "Look at that *drunken driver*," although what we *see* is only *the irregular motion of the car*. The writer once saw a man leave a one-dollar tip at a lunch counter and hurry out. Just as the writer was wondering why anyone should leave so generous a tip in so modest an establishment, the waitress came, picked up the dollar, put it in the cash register as she punched up ninety cents, and put a dime in her pocket. In other words, the writer's description to himself of the event, "a one-dollar tip," turned out to be not a report but an inference.

9   All this is not to say that we should never make inferences. The inability to make inferences is itself a sign of mental disorder. For example, the speech therapist Laura L. Lee writes, "The aphasic [brain-damaged] adult with whom I worked had great difficulty in making inferences about a picture I showed her. She could tell me what was happening at the moment in the picture, but could not tell me what might have happened just before the picture or just afterward."[2] Hence the question is not whether or not we make inferences; the question is whether or not we are aware of the inferences we make.

[2] "Brain Damage and the Process of Abstracting: A Problem in Language Learning," *ETC.: A Review of General Semantics*, XVI (1959), 154-62.

Judgments

10 In our suggested writing exercise, judgments are also to be excluded. By judgments, we shall mean *all expressions of the writer's approval or disapproval of the occurrences, persons, or objects he is describing.* For example, a report cannot say, "It was a wonderful car," but must say something like this: "It has been driven 50,000 miles and has never required any repairs." Again statements such as "Jack lied to us" must be suppressed in favor of the more verifiable statement, "Jack told us he didn't have the keys to his car with him. However, when he pulled a handkerchief out of his pocket a few minutes later, a bunch of car keys fell out." Also a report may not say, "The senator was stubborn, defiant, and uncooperative," or "The senator courageously stood by his principles"; it must say instead, "The senator's vote was the only one against the bill."

11 Many people regard statements such as the following as statements of "fact": "Jack *lied* to us," "Jerry is a *thief*," "Tommy is *clever*." As ordinarily employed, however, the word "lied" involves first an inference (that Jack knew otherwise and deliberately misstated the facts) and second a judgment (that the speaker disapproves of what he has inferred that Jack did). In the other two instances, we may substitute such expressions as, "Jerry was convicted of theft and served two years at Waupun," and "Tommy plays the violin, leads his class in school, and is captain of the debating team." After all, to say of a man that he is a "thief" is to say in effect, "He has stolen *and will steal again*"—which is more of a prediction than a report. Even to say, "He has stolen," is to make an inference (and simultaneously to pass a judgment) on an act about which there may be difference of opinion among those who have examined the evidence upon which the conviction was obtained. But to say that he was "convicted of theft" is to make a statement capable of being agreed upon through verification in court and prison records.

12 Scientific verifiability rests upon the external observation of facts, not upon the heaping up of judgments. If one person says, "Peter is a deadbeat," and another says, "I think so too," the statement has not been verified. In court cases, considerable trouble is sometimes caused by witnesses who cannot distinguish their judgments from the facts upon which those judgments are based. Cross-examinations under these circumstances go something like this:

WITNESS: That dirty double-crosser Jacobs ratted on me.
DEFENSE ATTORNEY: Your honor, I object.
JUDGE: Objection sustained. (Witness's remark is stricken from the record.) Now, try to tell the court exactly what happened.
WITNESS: He double-crossed me, the dirty, lying rat!
DEFENSE ATTORNEY: Your honor, I object!

JUDGE: Objection sustained. (Witness's remark is again stricken from the record.) Will the witness try to stick to the facts.

WITNESS: But I'm telling you the facts, your honor. He did double-cross me.

This can continue indefinitely unless the cross-examiner exercises some ingenuity in order to get at the facts behind the judgment. To the witness it is a "fact" that he was "double-crossed." Often patient questioning is required before the factual bases of the judgment are revealed.

3   Many words, of course, simultaneously convey a report and a judgment on the fact reported, as will be discussed more fully in a later chapter. For the purposes of a report as here defined, these should be avoided. Instead of "sneaked in," one might say "entered quietly"; instead of "politicians," "congressmen" or "aldermen" or "candidates for office"; instead of "bureaucrat," "public official"; instead of "tramp," "homeless unemployed"; instead of "dictatorial set-up," "centralized authority"; instead of "crackpots," "holders of nonconformist views." A newspaper reporter, for example, is not permitted to write, "A crowd of suckers came to listen to Senator Smith last evening in that rickety firetrap and ex-dive that disfigures the south edge of town." Instead he says, "Between seventy-five and a hundred people heard an address last evening by Senator Smith at the Evergreen Gardens near the South Side city limits."

Snarl-Words and Purr-Words

14   Throughout this book, it is important to remember that we are not considering language as an isolated phenomenon. Our concern, instead, is with language in action—language in the full context of the nonlinguistic events which are its setting. The making of noises with the vocal organs is a muscular activity and, like other muscular activities, often involuntary. Our responses to powerful stimuli, such as to things that make us very angry, are a complex of muscular and physiological events: the contracting of fighting muscles, the increase of blood pressure, a change in body chemistry, clutching of our hair, *and* the making of noises, such as growls and snarls. We are a little too dignified, perhaps, to growl like dogs, but we do the next best thing and substitute series of words, such as "You dirty double-crosser!" "The filthy scum!" Similarly, if we are pleasurably agitated, we may, instead of purring or wagging the tail, say things like "She's the sweetest girl in all the world!"

15   Speeches such as these are, as direct expressions of approval or disapproval, judgments in their simplest form. They may be said to be human equivalents of snarling and purring. "She's the sweetest girl in

all the world'' is not a statement about the girl; it is a purr. This seems to be a fairly obvious fact; nevertheless, it is surprising how often, when such a statement is made, both the speaker and the hearer feel that something has been said about the girl. This error is especially common in the interpretation of utterances of orators and editorialists in some of their more excited denunciations of "Reds," "greedy monopolists," "Wall Street," "radicals," "foreign ideologies," and in their more fulsome dithyrambs about "our way of life." Constantly, because of the impressive sound of the words, the elaborate structure of the sentences, and the appearance of intellectual progression, we get the feeling that something is being said about something. On closer examination, however, we discover that these utterances merely say, "What I hate ('Reds,' 'Wall Street,' or whatever) I hate very, very much," and "What I like ('our way of life') I like very, very much." We may call such utterances "snarl-words" and "purr-words." They are not reports describing conditions in the extensional world in any way.

16   To call these judgments "snarl-words" and "purr-words" does not mean that we should simply shrug them off. It means that we should be careful to *allocate the meaning correctly*—placing such a statement as "She's the sweetest girl in the world" as a revelation of the speaker's state of mind, and not as a revelation of facts about the girl. If the "snarl-words" about "Reds" or "greedy monopolists" are accompanied by verifiable reports (which would also mean that we have previously agreed as to who, specifically, is meant by the terms "Reds" or "greedy monopolists"), we might find reason to be just as disturbed as the speaker. If the "purr-words" about the sweetest girl in the world are accompanied by verifiable reports about her appearance, manners, character, and so on, we might find reason to admire her too. But "snarl-words" and "purr-words" as such, unaccompanied by reports, offer nothing further to discuss, except possibly the question, "Why do you feel as you do?"

17   It is usually fruitless to debate such questions as "Is President Kennedy a great statesman or merely a skillful politician?" "Is the music of Wagner the greatest music of all time, or is it merely hysterical screeching?" "Which is the finer sport, tennis or baseball?" "Could Joe Louis in his prime have licked Bob Fitzsimmons in his prime?" To take sides on such issues of conflicting judgments is to reduce oneself to the same level of stubborn imbecility as one's opponents. But to ask questions of the form, "Why do you like (or dislike) Kennedy (or Wagner, or tennis, or Joe Louis)?" is to learn something about one's friends and neighbors. After listening to their opinions and their reasons for them, we may leave the discussion slightly wiser, slightly better informed, and perhaps slightly less one-sided than we were before the discussion began.

8   A judgment ("He is a fine boy," "It was a beautiful service," "Baseball is a healthful sport," "She is an awful bore") is a conclusion, summing up a large number of previously observed facts. The reader is probably familiar with the fact that students almost always have difficulty in writing themes of the required length because their ideas give out after a paragraph or two. The reason for this is that those early paragraphs contain so many judgments that there is little left to be said. When the conclusions are carefully excluded, however, and observed facts are given instead, there is never any trouble about the length of papers; in fact, they tend to become too long, since inexperienced writers, when told to give facts, often give far more than are necessary, because they lack discrimination between the important and the trivial.

9   Still another consequence of judgments early in the course of a written exercise—and this applies also to hasty judgments in everyday thought—is the temporary blindness they induce. When, for example, a description starts with the words, "He was a real Madison Avenue executive," or "She was a typical sorority girl," if we continue writing at all, we must make all our later statements consistent with those judgments. The result is that all the individual characteristics of this particular "executive" or this particular "sorority girl" are lost sight of; and the rest of the account is likely to deal not with observed facts but with the writer's private notion (based on previously read stories, movies, pictures, and so forth) of what "Madison Avenue executives" or "typical sorority girls" are like. The premature judgment, that is, often prevents us from seeing what is directly in front of us, so that clichés take the place of fresh description. Therefore, even if the writer feels sure at the beginning of a written account that the man he is describing is a "real leatherneck" or that the scene he is describing is a "beautiful residential suburb," he will conscientiously keep such notions out of his head, lest his vision be obstructed. He is specifically warned against describing *anybody* as a "beatnik"—a term (originally applied to literary and artistic Bohemians) which was blown up by sensational journalism and movies into an almost completely fictional and misleading stereotype. If a writer applies the term to any actual living human being, he will have to spend so much energy thereafter explaining what he does *not* mean by it that he will save himself trouble by not bringing it up at all.

20   In the course of writing reports of personal experiences, it will be found that in spite of all endeavors to keep judgments out, some will creep in. An account of a man, for example, may go like this: "He had apparently not shaved for several days, and his face and hands were covered with grime. His shoes were torn, and his coat, which was several sizes too small for him, was spotted with dried clay." Now, in spite of the fact that no judgment has been stated, a very

obvious one is implied. Let us contrast this with another description of the same man. "Although his face was bearded and neglected, his eyes were clear, and he looked straight ahead as he walked rapidly down the road. He seemed very tall; perhaps the fact that his coat was too small for him emphasized that impression. He was carrying a book under his left arm, and a small terrier ran at his heels." In this example, the impression about the same man is considerably changed, simply by the inclusion of new details and the subordination of unfavorable ones. Even if explicit judgments are kept out of one's writing, implied judgments will get in.

21   How, then, can we ever give an impartial report? The answer is, of course, that we cannot attain complete impartiality while we use the language of everyday life. Even with the very impersonal language of science, the task is sometimes difficult. Nevertheless, we can, by being aware of the favorable or unfavorable feelings that certain words and facts can arouse, attain enough impartiality for practical purposes. Such awareness enables us to balance the implied favorable and unfavorable judgments against each other. To learn to do this, it is a good idea to write two accounts of the same subject, both strict reports, to be read side by side: the first to contain facts and details likely to prejudice the reader in favor of the subject, the second to contain those likely to prejudice the reader against it. For example:

FOR	AGAINST
He had white teeth.	His teeth were uneven.
His eyes were blue, his hair blond and abundant.	He rarely looked people straight in the eye.
He had on a clean white shirt.	His shirt was frayed at the cuffs.
His speech was courteous.	He had a high-pitched voice.
His employer spoke highly of him.	His landlord said he was slow in paying his rent.
He liked dogs.	He disliked children.

22   This process of selecting details favorable or unfavorable to the subject being described may be termed *slanting*. Slanting gives no explicit judgments, but it differs from reporting in that it deliberately makes certain judgments inescapable. Let us assume for a moment the truth of the statement "When Clyde was in New York last November he was seen having dinner with a show girl. . . ." The inferences that can be drawn from this statement are changed considerably when the following words are added: ". . . and her husband and their two children." Yet, if Clyde is a married man, his enemies could conceivably do him a great deal of harm by talking about his "dinner-date with a New York show girl." One-sided or biased slanting of this kind, not

uncommon in private gossip and backbiting, and all too common in the "interpretative reporting" of newspapers and news magazines, can be described as a technique of lying without actually telling any lies.

Discovering One's Bias

23   Here, however, a caution is necessary. When, for example, a newspaper tells a story in a way that we dislike, leaving out facts we think important and playing up important facts in ways that we think unfair, we are tempted to say, "Look how unfairly they've slanted the story!" In making such a statement we are, of course, making an inference about the newspaper's editors. We are assuming that what seems important or unimportant to us seems equally important or unimportant to them, and on the basis of that assumption we infer that the editors "deliberately" gave the story a misleading emphasis. Is this necessarily the case? Can the reader, as an outsider, say whether a story assumes a given form because the editors "deliberately slanted it that way" or because that was the way the events appeared to them?

24   The point is that, by the process of selection and abstraction imposed on us by our own interests and background, experience comes to all of us (including newspaper editors) already "slanted." If you happen to be pro-labor, pro-Catholic, and a stock-car racing fan, your ideas of what is important or unimportant will of necessity be different from those of a man who happens to be indifferent to all three of your favorite interests. If, then, some newspapers often seem to side with the big businessman on public issues, the reason is less a matter of "deliberate" slanting than the fact that publishers are often, in enterprises as large as modern urban newspapers, big businessmen themselves, accustomed both in work and in social life to associating with other big businessmen. Nevertheless, the best newspapers, whether owned by "big businessmen" or not, do try to tell us as accurately as possible what is going on in the world, because they are run by newspapermen who conceive it to be part of their professional responsibility to present fairly the conflicting points of view in controversial issues. Such newspapermen are *reporters* indeed.

25   The writer who is neither an advocate nor an opponent avoids slanting, except when he is seeking special literary effects. The avoidance of slanting is not only a matter of being fair and impartial; it is even more importantly a matter of making good maps of the territory of experience. The profoundly biased individual cannot make good maps because he can see an enemy *only* as an enemy and a friend *only* as a friend. The individual with genuine skill in writing—one who has imagination and insight—can look at the same subject from many points of view. The following examples may illustrate the fullness and

solidity of descriptions thus written:

> Adam turned to look at him. It was, in a way, as though this were the first time he had laid eyes on him. He saw the strong, black shoulders under the red-check calico, the long arms lying loose, forward over the knees, the strong hands, seamed and calloused, holding the reins. He looked at the face. The thrust of the jawbone was strong, but the lips were heavy and low, with a piece of chewed straw hanging out one side of the mouth. The eyelids were pendulous, slightly swollen-looking, and the eyes bloodshot. Those eyes, Adam knew, could sharpen to a quick, penetrating, assessing glance. But now, looking at that slack, somnolent face, he could scarcely believe that.

ROBERT PENN WARREN, *Wilderness*

> Soon after the little princess, there walked in a massively built, stout young man in spectacles, with a cropped head, light breeches in the mode of the day, with a high lace ruffle and a ginger-coloured coat. This stout young man [Pierre] was the illegitimate son of a celebrated dandy of the days of Catherine, Court Bezuhov, who was now dying in Moscow. He had not yet entered any branch of the service; he had only just returned from abroad, where he had been educated, and this was his first appearance in society. Anna Pavlovna greeted him with a nod reserved for persons of the very lowest hierarchy in her drawing-room. . . .
>
> Pierre was clumsy, stout and uncommonly tall, with huge, red hands; he did not, as they say, know how to come into a drawing-room and still less how to get out of one, that is, how to say something particularly agreeable on going away. Moreover, he was dreamy. He stood up, and picking up a three-cornered hat with the plume of a general in it instead of his own, he kept hold of it, pulling the feathers until the general asked him to restore it. But all his dreaminess and his inability to enter a drawing-room or talk properly in it were atoned for by his expression of good-nature, simplicity and modesty.

COUNT LEO TOLSTOY, *War and Peace*
(Translated by Constance Garnett)

Part Two
Substantiation: Introductory Essay

In one of G. K. Chesterton's mystery stories, detective Father Brown is called to investigate the disappearance of the Earl of Glengyle. At the earl's castle, Father Brown finds a puzzling collection of items: a pile of jewels without settings; little heaps of snuff; piles of small metal springs, tiny wheels, and so forth; and 25 candles, without a single candlestick. A police inspector declares that no theory could account for this assortment of oddities. Rising to the challenge, Father Brown provides three separate theories to account for the evidence:

1 The earl was a burglar. He carried candles in a portable lantern, threw snuff into the faces of his pursuers, and used the diamonds and small steel pieces to cut out panes of glass.

2 The earl was a madman who tried to reenact the lives of the French royal family just before the French Revolution. He kept snuff because it was a luxury, candles because they were the method of lighting then, bits of metal because King Louis XVI had played at being a locksmith, jewels because Queen Marie Antoinette had had a famous diamond necklace.

3 The earl was the victim of con men, who had planted the loose jewels to persuade him that there was buried treasure on his estate. The pieces of steel were to be used

for cutting the jewels, the snuff for bribing local shepherds to secrecy, the candles for light as the earl explored caves and other likely hiding places.

The problem, as Father Brown points out, is not a shortage of theories. "Ten false philosophies will fit the universe. Ten false theories will fit Glengyle Castle. But we want the *real* explanation of the castle and the universe."

Finding real explanations is the province of substantiation. **When we want to know something about *X*, substantiation is the process of determining which among any number of theories is the one most likely to be true.**

Essays of substantiation respond to the question "What is likely to be true about *X*?" They differ from essays of definition in that the main purpose is no longer to clarify what something *is* (or how it looks to us). *The purpose is to demonstrate that some further assertion about X—some claim about its relationship to other things in the world—is justified.*

Types of Assertions
Most assertions belong to one of the following three classes.

1 Causal explanations—claims that *X* was caused by something else. (Father Brown

is looking for the right one of this class: the correct cause of the collection of objects he sees.)

2 **Predictions—claims that** X **will happen at some time in the future.** ("Do you think it will stop?" inquired a friend of Mark Twain, looking out at a pouring rainstorm. "Why yes—it always *has*," Twain is said to have answered.)

3 **Attributions—claims that some action or characteristic can be assigned to** X **, either now or at some time in the past.** This class is sometimes divided into **generalizations**, in which X is a whole category ("Most American colleges offer physical education courses"); and **specifications**, in which X is an individual ("Roger Bannister ran the first four-minute mile").

Each of these classes includes both positive and negative assertions. A *causal explanation* may assert that X was or was *not* caused by something; a *prediction* may claim that X will or will *not* occur; an *attribution* may state that George did or did *not* do it.

Occasionally, an assertion may belong to more than one category. Consider "College students are less physically fit than highschool students, because they get less sleep." The first part of that assertion is an *attribution* (more specifically, a *generalization*); the second part is a *causal explanation*.

Steps in the Process of Substantiation

Every assertion is the answer to some question. "Nero fiddled while Rome burned" answers the question "What was Nero doing while Rome burned?" In theory, the question always comes before the answer, and the logical process of substantiation consists of the following four steps.

1 **Statement of the question in a well-defined form.**

2 **Collection of information.**

3 **Formation of a tentative assertion** (a hypothesis or thesis) **in answer to the question.**

4 **Verification of the hypothesis:** a check to make sure that it accounts for all the evidence, that it does so better than any competing hypotheses do, and that it does not conflict with any other facts or concepts accepted as true.

In practice, however, these logical steps often get out of sequence. Father Brown begins with a question (step 1): "What happened to the Earl of Glengyle?" He is then shown the evidence (step 2), and the police inspector revises the question (back to step 1) to "What could account for this stuff?" Immediately Father Brown constructs three hypotheses (step 3). But he takes none of them on to verification (step 4), since he simply made them up to prove that he could, and he feels they are silly. Then more evidence is presented (step 2): a walking-stick from which the top knob is missing and some old Bibles with the haloes cut out of the pictures. While Father Brown is devising new hypotheses (step 3 again), further evidence is discovered (step 2): the body of the earl, with no head.

Sometimes you may begin not with a question but with an *answer*. You might hear someone assert "labor unions are responsible for inflation" (**causal explanation**), or "we will never see a lasting peace in the Middle East" (**prediction**), or "UFOs are nonsense" (**general attribution**), or "the last horserace at Belmont yesterday was fixed" (**specific attribution**). If you wanted to substantiate one of these assertions—or substantiate your disagreement with it—you might well begin by putting it into question form.

Who (or what) is responsible for inflation?

Will we ever see a lasting peace in the Middle East?

What are UFOs?

Was the last horserace at Belmont fixed?

Shifting the *assertion* (which is really the logical *end point* of an inquiry) into the form of a *question* (the logical *beginning* of an inquiry) usually makes it easier to organize the investigation. You can now follow, more or less, the four-step process outlined above. That process, by the way, is a simplified version of what is called the *Scientific Method*. It might better be called the *Rational Method*, since it describes a method for problem solving not only in scientific research but also in every inquiry where we want the most rational solution.

Different Degrees of Certainty

The process of substantiation tries to clarify the relationship between a *body of evidence* and an *assertion* (thesis). Usually, you want to know whether the assertion is *true*—an accurate representation of *reality*. But the best we can ordinarily do is determine whether the assertion is *valid*—the most accurate representation of *the evidence as we have it.*

We can rarely arrive at absolute certainty. Our basic question recognizes this limitation by asking not "What is true about *X*?" but instead, "What is *likely* to be true?" Our legal system also recognizes it by requiring not absolute proof, but only proof "beyond a reasonable doubt."

It usually helps to distinguish degrees of our less-than-absolute certainty. Questions to which we can be (reasonably) certain of having the right answer are called **matters of fact**. These tend to be issues involving reports of our actual experiences. Questions to which we must regard any answer as only probably right are called **matters of opinion** or **matters**

of inference. These tend to be issues involving the *interpretation* (not just the report) of our experiences (see Hayakawa, p. 78).

Techniques of Substantiation: Deduction and Induction

Given a question of the type "What is likely to be true about *X*?" and a certain amount of information and a number of theories, how do you determine which theory best fits the data and deserves to be presented as your thesis?

The two traditional types of reasoning used to bring information and theses together are called **deduction** and **induction**. Chances are that you will use both of them, because they do rather different things.

Deduction

Deduction is the process of bringing together (1) a general statement or principle—the "major premise," and (2) a more limited statement or principle—the "minor premise," and drawing from these two (3) a new statement— the "conclusion"—that joins parts of the two premises. The complete pattern is called a syllogism. The classic example is the following argument:

1 All men are mortal (*major premise*).
2 Socrates is a man (*minor premise*).
3 Therefore, Socrates is mortal (*conclusion*).

Deductive reasoning is a way of clarifying what, given certain statements, must follow from them. It does not add new information. Instead, it rearranges existing information so that all of the relationships come out in the open.

The validity of deductive arguments depends on two factors: (1) whether the premises are correct, and (2) whether the conclusion joins the premises properly. As for the

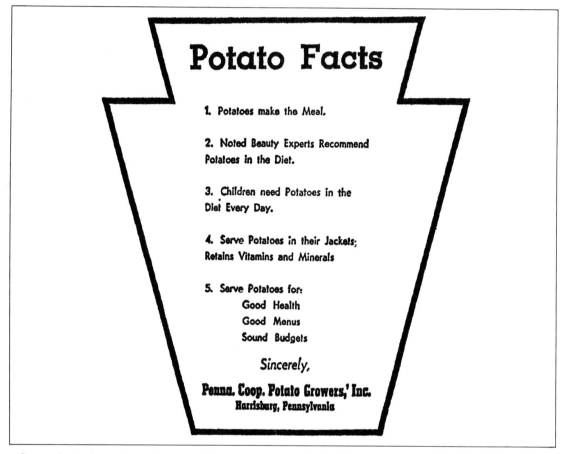

Potato Facts

1. Potatoes make the Meal.

2. Noted Beauty Experts Recommend Potatoes in the Diet.

3. Children need Potatoes in the Diet Every Day.

4. Serve Potatoes in their Jackets; Retains Vitamins and Minerals

5. Serve Potatoes for:
   Good Health
   Good Menus
   Sound Budgets

Sincerely,

Penna. Coop. Potato Growers,' Inc.
Harrisburg, Pennsylvania

Source. Pennsylvania Potato Growers' Ad: Reprinted by permission of Pennsylvania Co-operative Potato Growers, Inc.

The notice above appeared on a package of potatoes. Which of its five statements really concern *matters of fact*? Try changing them into question form. Item 1 becomes "Do potatoes make the meal?" Can we be certain of having the right answer to that question? No, because people will define "make the meal" in different ways. We would have to change the question to something like "Do most people expect to have potatoes at each meal?" before we could say that the answer would be a statement of fact.

Remember that there is such a thing as a *false statement of fact.* If you say "New York City is the capital of New York State," your statement is *false*. Nevertheless, it belongs to the category *statement of fact,* since we can all look at the evidence and come to a *definite and objective conclusion* about the underlying question ("Is New York City the capital of New York State?").

correctness of the premises, the deductive pattern does *not* establish that. It simply takes it for granted. Consider the following paragraph.

> The main characteristic of the modern American is his perpetual restlessness. This may take the form of an endless moving-on to some new part of the country, a search for those greener pastures which always seem just beyond wherever we are now; or the American restlessness may manifest itself in a continuing search for a new philosophy which will explain our perplexing world better than the last one did. Each of us must come to terms with this problem as best we can. If the impulse seizes us physically we must move on, uprooted again and again; if it seizes us mentally we must move our minds on, uprooting our ideas again and again. In either case, there can be no final peace, no ultimate complacency, for you—or for me.

The flow of the prose here somewhat conceals the deductive pattern. In syllogistic form, it would look like this:

1 The main characteristic of the modern American is his perpetual restlessness.
2 You are a modern American. (This second premise is not stated but is implied by the pronouns: "we," "each of us," "us," etc. The argument takes it for granted that the readers are Americans.)
3 You will never be at peace for very long.

A matter of opinion at best—not fact—because to be "at peace," and other key terms, are only vaguely defined. In addition, it is probably not a true conclusion because the *major premise* may well be untrue. We "modern Americans" are repeatedly told that this, that, or the other thing is our distinguishing characteristic ("We are the world's most violence-prone people"; "Americans are mad for

power"; "You can tell an American by the bulges in his wallet, his belly, and his ego").

The deductive argument we have just looked at is weak because it includes an inaccurate (or suspicious) *premise*. A deductive argument can also be flawed because the premises, accurate in themselves, are improperly connected in the *conclusion*. Let's look at a single example. Lewis Carroll's Alice, having eaten a bit too much of the Wonderland mushroom that made people grow, became taller than the treetops and found herself addressed as "Serpent!" by a very grumpy pigeon. When she protested that she was a little girl, not a serpent, the pigeon replied:

> "I've seen a good many little girls in my time, but never *one* with such a neck as that! No, no! You're a serpent; and there's no use denying it. I suppose you'll be telling me next that you never tasted an egg!"
>
> "I *have* tasted eggs, certainly," said Alice, who was a very truthful child; "but little girls eat eggs quite as much as serpents do, you know."
>
> "I don't believe it," said the Pigeon; "but if they do, then they're a kind of serpent: that's all I can say."

Alice's egg-eating confession settles her identity for this birdbrain because it has constructed this syllogism:

1 Serpents eat eggs.
2 Alice and other little girls eat eggs.
3 Alice and other little girls are serpents.

There is nothing inaccurate about the *premises* here. Unfortunately for birds, both snakes and children *do* eat eggs. Where the syllogism goes astray is in the *conclusion*. Here is why:

To go anywhere at all—even astray—a set of premises must include a *common term*—in other words, some phrase or idea that appears in both of them. If there is no common term to hitch the premises together, nothing at all follows from them. A remark such as "Professor Lefkowitz is a hard grader—I hate eight o'clock classes" has two premises not joined to each other by any common term or idea. It is only a grumble, not an argument.

But the pigeon's syllogism about Alice *has* a common term ("eat eggs"). The problem is that the tendency to eat eggs, which the pigeon takes as decisive—as proof of what a thing's nature is—is not really decisive. Too many creatures eat eggs for that characteristic to be useful in deciding what any given creature is.

In dealing with deductive arguments, (1) try to make them into a **syllogism** (a set of *premises* containing a *common term* and a *conclusion*); (2) try to check whether the premises are accurate; (3) check whether the connection being made in the conclusion is a reasonable one.

If the deductive argument passes all these checkpoints, you can accept its conclusion with as much confidence as you can give to anything in this world. If the premises are accurate and the connection between them valid, the conclusion *must* be right.

Induction

Induction is the process of bringing together a set of observations and seeing what they mean. The basic pattern of deduction is recombination—the rearrangement of parts of the premises.

The basic pattern of induction is simple addition—observation 1 plus observation 2 plus observation 3 (any number can play) add up to what? A dozen up-and-down unemployment statistics add up to what trend or principle?

The complete inductive pattern consists of a body of evidence and a conclusion that *in-*

terprets the evidence: identifies its meaning, explains it, states what it adds up to. In this case, the whole is always greater than the sum of the parts because *the conclusion, by interpreting, goes beyond the evidence itself.* The "jump" from evidence to conclusion is called the **inductive leap.**

The validity of inductive reasoning depends on two factors: (1) the quality of the evidence (its *accuracy* and its *sufficiency*—we will come back to these terms), and (2) the size of the inductive leap. **High-quality evidence and a small inductive leap yield reliable inductions. Accuracy.** Usually, you have no way of checking the accuracy of the evidence someone else presents. If you read in the newspaper that the statewide unemployment rate rose 0.6 percent last month, you assume that the figures have not been falsified. You make such assumptions unless the "evidence" seems absurd, or unless you suspect the honesty of the people from whom it comes.

As for checking the accuracy of your own evidence, that is easier. If you have measured, measure again; if you are remembering, verify your recollection; if you are running an experiment, run it once or twice more.

If you still have reservations about the accuracy of your data, just level with your readers about the possible errors (notice that du Bois, p. 121, explains she is relying on a letter from a stranger). Then go forward with the inductive process.

Sufficiency. The criterion of *sufficiency* can be met in one of two ways. The evidence will certainly be sufficient if you get *all* of it. If someone asks, "How many of the students in your class are women?" you can count them all. If you want to know where your congressperson stands on aid to higher education, you can get the *Congressional Record* and see how he or she voted on every higher education bill.

But if the evidence cannot be sufficient in

How Women Are Faring at West Point and Annapolis

The Air Force Academy, the United States Military Academy at West Point, and the United States Naval Academy at Annapolis admitted women last year for the first time. While the dropout rate at the Army and Navy service schools was higher than the Air Force's, the female students who remained performed admirably.

At West Point, the most traditional of the three, the dropout rate for females in the class of 1980 was 31 percent; at Annapolis, 22 percent. In each case, that was about 10 percent higher than the dropout rate for men. A Naval Academy spokesman attributed higher female attrition simply to "small numbers" of women entering. A West Point spokesman suggested that "it reflects the type of service the different academies represent. Ground-combat soldiers are the farthest in polarity from traditional women's roles." In contrast, Air Force Academy spokesmen feel their school has made a far greater effort to welcome women into its ranks.

In its new class of 1981, West Point began with 104 women, down from 119 in the first sex-integrated class. At Annapolis, the new class began with 90 women, compared with 81 in the class a year earlier.

At all three academies, women and men performed equally well in academic studies. At the end of the first semester, a man and a woman were tied for first place in general academic excellence. The woman, Liz Belzer, was also selected as a regimental commander.

Women at the academies showed off their physical fitness to best advantage in freshmen sports. The Annapolis women's basketball and volleyball teams last year won their state divisional titles. The women's basketball team at West Point, nicknamed the Sugar Smacks ("smack" is traditional slang for plebe, or freshman), did so well they achieved varsity status in just one year. This season, they will play leading Eastern and Middle Western schools. The one game everyone would like to see — Army vs. Navy — has not materialized yet. "We would love to see *that* rivalry pick up," said the West Point spokesman.

Nevertheless, very few concessions to the presence of women have been made at West Point and Annapolis, where the same "no fraternization" rule exists between plebes and upperclassmen. There is one change in the Maryland dorms. Previously, an upperclassman could barge uninvited into any plebe room any time he wanted to. Now, he has to knock and wait an appropriate few seconds. —G.L.

Source. "How Women Are Faring At West Point and Annapolis." *The New York Times Magazine*, September 11, 1977. © 1977 by The New York Times Company. Reprinted by permission.

Consider this short newspaper article as an example of substantiation. The subject, the performance of women in the service academies, is identified in paragraph 1. The thesis (also in paragraph 1) is an answer to the underlying question "How well are women doing in the service academies?" Paragraph 2 discusses the dropout rate (West Point, Annapolis, the Air Force Academy). The next paragraphs discuss the new entering class and the performance of the women who have remained.

Look carefully at the evidence presented about women in the three schools. What parts of the evidence are missing? What extra material—material that does not help support paragraph 1's thesis—is put in?

this sense of completeness, it may be instead a **representative sample** of the whole. Evidence based on a *sample*, rather than on the *whole* of what you are concerned with, is sufficient only if the sample is a miniature replica of the whole—that is, *only if it represents, in proper proportion, all elements of the whole.*

Occasionally, the only evidence available is one case history—perhaps your own experience. Such a small sample is not likely to be sufficient. People are so different from each other that nobody's experience is representative of everybody's. That does not mean, however, that arguments based on individual experience are worthless. Each person is contributing one piece of evidence to a gradually growing amount. Just be sure that, in basing an argument on limited experience, you don't present it as more than it is. Rather than talking in general terms of "the child who grows up in a small rural town," talk in terms of yourself, if your own childhood in Hicksville, Ohio is your evidence. Your logic will be stronger as a result, and your style will probably be more dramatic too.

Connecting the Evidence. Once your evidence is in good shape (*accurate* and *sufficient*), what next? How do you decide what it adds up to? This is the hard part, the part over which experts disagree.

Traditionally, it has been thought that when there are several hypotheses that account for the evidence, you should choose the one with the following characteristics: (1) it is the *simplest* hypothesis that accounts for all the evidence; (2) it not only fits this body of evidence but is also congruous with (or at least does not contradict) everything else we know; and (3) it goes beyond merely explaining its own body of evidence to throw light on other matters as well. If you have doubts about this list of characteristics, you are in good company. The principle of simplicity, for one, may not

really apply to logical inquiries involving human (=complex) beings.

The one sure guide in dealing with an inductive argument is the principle that **the smaller the inductive leap is, the more reliable the whole argument will be.** Let us assume that you are investigating whether Shakespeare's plays have as many lines for female characters as for male. You can get a standard edition of Shakespeare's plays, count all the lines for male and female characters (the evidence will be *sufficient* because complete), recheck your count (the evidence should be *accurate*, unless you keep falling asleep at the task), and total things up with the aid of an adding machine. Once the two totals have been rung up, you can give a one-word answer to the question. The inductive leap here is extremely small; the conclusion is little more than a statistical *summary* of the evidence.

But if your question is whether Shakespeare was antifeminist, and if you are trying to answer *that* on the basis of your line-count evidence, your induction will require a kangaroo's leap.

You can avoid the need for a kangaroo by *increasing the range of evidence.* You can collect evidence on other kinds of male-female comparisons, for instance, from Shakespeare's plays. You can also *decrease the scope of the question* and decide to consider not whether "Shakespeare was antifeminist" but only whether "Shakespeare's *plays* are antifeminist." Both of these techniques will narrow the gap between the evidence and the conclusion and increase the chances that your readers will be willing and able to follow your logical gymnastics.

In dealing with inductive arguments, then, **check to see whether the evidence is accurate**, if you can. Next, **check whether it is sufficient** (whether all of it is there, or a representative sample is there); and then **check whether the**

Unfortunately, there have been too many bad
translations. Ralph Manheim's well-known assertion
that "most of the great prose literature of the nineteenth century was translated with an ax" supports this
argument.[1]

_____

[1]Ralph Manheim, "The Trials of Translation: The Translator
Speaks," Publishers Weekly (N.Y.), September 24, 1973, p. 118.

Notice the use of *authority* to support a generalization: the writer cites the opinion of a well-known expert. This technique of substantiation resembles a shortened inductive argument—we are given the conclusion although we do not see the evidence.

The technique is useful if we agree that the expert knows what he or she is talking about, and probably we *will* agree, unless we know of evidence to the contrary. The technique of *appeal to authority* is not usually strong enough by itself, though, to support a writer's main point or an assertion that is controversial.

[This example is from Robert Lima's paper "The Translator as Editor and Anthologist," *Translators and Translating . . .*, ed. P. Ellen Crandell (Binghamton, N.Y.: SUNY Binghamton Dept. of Comparative Literature, 1974), p. 25.]

inductive leap is small. You may also want to apply the traditional tests given above (i.e., whether the proposed thesis is the *simplest* one that accounts for the evidence, whether it corresponds to what else is known, and whether it serves to illuminate further data as well as those with which you began).

The Logical Importance of Inspiration

You may think, by now, that defending your concept of what is likely to be true—proving your thesis—is a wholly objective process. But solving a problem sometimes requires a dash of the intellectual magic that we call *inspiration* or *intuition* or *creative insight*.

Father Brown got nowhere with his problem of the Earl of Glengyle until he suddenly realized, in a flash of inspiration, that each piece of evidence he had seen was *half* a piece of evidence. Each item he had been shown was missing a container or trimming made of gold. After this realization, everything else was easy. The earl had died a natural death, as it turned out—no mystery there. But he had once promised "all the gold of Glengyle" to a simple-minded village boy. When the earl died, the boy took him up on that promise. He took everything made of gold, but nothing else. After extracting the gold from the teeth, he replaced the earl's head in its coffin. This last act confirmed Father Brown's hunch that what explained Glengyle Castle was merely a simple person 'taking, bit by bit, precisely what had been given to him.

Like Father Brown's hunch, your personal contribution to the process of substantiation is important. You see the evidence through your own eyes. You interpret it in terms of your own experience. Is a German shepherd dog big? Yes, if it's sharing an armchair with you; no, if you are used to taking care of elephants. In writing essays of substantiation, you need to be careful that the extent of your own involvement is clear. Your main purpose is to clarify the relationship between X and some other aspect of the world. You can't do that at all unless you involve yourself. But you can't do that responsibly if you *overinvolve* yourself; you have to be willing to ac-

cept the evidence—once you see it—for whatever it is.

In the readings that follow, you will find *causal explanations*—explaining, for example, why a growing number of married couples do not want any children. And *predictions*—for example, that boys and girls will behave differently no matter how similar their upbringing is. And *generalizations*—that the comics have gone relevant; that we can't tell in advance what the consequences of our actions will be. And *specifications*—that the "Loch Ness Monster" could have evolved from a sea-water creature; that the meaning of Tonto's phrase *kemo sabe* can't be pinned down.

You may be thoroughly convinced by some of these essays of substantiation. You may have reservations about others. If you come away feeling that the writers have made good cases for their claims, though, then the job of substantiation will have been done.

Summary

1 Substantiation is the process of arriving at—and defending—*assertions*. There are three main kinds of assertions:
   a *Causal explanations*, claims that X causes (or is caused by) something.
   b *Predictions*, claims that something will happen.
   c *Attributions*, claims that a general or a specific X has certain characteristics.
2 The *scientific or rational method* of substantiation includes four steps:
   a Statement of the question or problem.
   b Collection of information.
   c Formulation of a hypothesis to answer the question.
   d Verification of the hypothesis.
3 Achieving a *high degree of certainty* in substantiation may require:
   a *Deduction* (inferring conclusions from general principles).
   b *Induction* (reaching general conclusions from accumulated evidence).
   c *Inspiration or intuition* (seeing that the evidence has certain shape or implication).

Substantiation, Series One
Readings with Commentary

Things: The Throw-Away Society
Alvin Toffler

Toffler's thesis (paragraph 3) is that our "relationships with *things* are increasingly temporary." His evidence is the Barbie doll. His thesis goes far beyond his evidence, which is intended to function as a **representative sample** (see p. 94) rather than as a summary of all of the evidence that might be available. Would other forms of evidence be more appropriate?

1   "Barbie," a twelve-inch plastic teen-ager, is the best-known and best-selling doll in history. Since its introduction in 1959, the Barbie doll population of the world has grown to 12,000,000—more than the human population of Los Angeles or London or Paris. Little girls adore Barbie because she is highly realistic and eminently dress-up-able. Mattel, Inc., maker of Barbie, also sells a complete wardrobe for her, including clothes for ordinary daytime wear, clothes for formal party wear, clothes for swimming and skiing.

2   Recently Mattel announced a new improved Barbie doll. The new version has a slimmer figure, "real" eyelashes, and a twist-and-turn waist that makes her more humanoid than ever. Moreover, Mattel announced that, for the first time, any young lady wishing to purchase a new Barbie would receive a trade-in allowance for her old one.

3   What Mattel did not announce was that by trading in her old doll

Source. "Things: The Throw-Away Society" by Alvin Toffler is from *Future Shock*, by Alvin Toffler. Copyright © 1970 by Alvin Toffler. Reprinted by permission of Random House, Inc.

for a technologically improved model, the little girl of today, citizen of tomorrow's super-industrial world, would learn a fundamental lesson about the new society: that man's relationships with *things* are increasingly temporary.

4   The ocean of man-made physical objects that surrounds us is set within a larger ocean of natural objects. But, increasingly, it is the technologically produced environment that matters for the individual. The texture of plastic or concrete, the irridescent glisten of an automobile under a streetlight, the staggering vision of a city-scape seen from the window of a jet—these are the intimate realities of his existence. Man-made things enter into and color his consciousness. Their number is expanding with explosive force, both absolutely and relative to the natural environment. This will be even more true in super-industrial society than it is today.

5   Anti-materialists tend to deride the importance of "things." Yet things are highly significant, not merely because of their functional utility, but also because of their psychological impact. We develop relationships with things. Things affect our sense of continuity or discontinuity. They play a role in the structure of situations, and the foreshortening of our relationships with things accelerates the pace of life.

6   Moreover, our attitudes toward things reflect basic value judgments. Nothing could be more dramatic than the difference between the new breed of little girls who cheerfully turn in their Barbies for the new improved model and those who, like their mothers and grandmothers before them, clutch lingeringly and lovingly to the same doll until it disintegrates from sheer age. In this difference lies the contrast between past and future, between societies based on permanence and the new, fast-forming society based on transience.

Commentary

Toffler's subject is not new. Even in 1970, when he wrote the book from which this selection is taken, many other people were pointing out how much Americans use "disposables." Paper napkins, styrofoam cups, nonreturnable bottles, automobiles with built-in obsolescence—from small items to major machines, all are manufactured with the understanding that they will be used temporarily and then thrown out.

Toffler wants us to see this familiar situation in a new way, to see how disposables affect our outlook on life: "things are highly significant, not merely because of their functional utility, but also because of their psychological impact" (paragraph 5). Therefore he ignores all of the evidence about environmental problems, economic factors, the consumer's desire for convenience, and other aspects of the large subject of the "throwaway society." **For his purpose here, only information that suggests the psychological impact of disposables is relevant.** Even this limited body of evidence is too broad to be discussed in a short space: *he must find the single piece of evidence that can stand for all the rest.*

What characteristics of the Barbie doll make it a good choice? Would the tin can (which is really made of steel, with a thin tin coating) have done as well?

Outline

I The evidence: the Barbie doll—paragraphs 1-2

II Thesis statement—paragraph 3

III Discussion of the thesis—paragraphs 4-6 (return to the Barbie doll, for *comparison and contrast*, in paragraph 6)

Suggestions for Writing

1 Using one central (representative) piece of evidence, substantiate your own version of Toffler's thesis about our relationships with things. Perhaps he is not completely correct, or perhaps he has not identified the whole meaning of the situation. Consider the plastic Christmas tree, for example. Since it can be stored in a cardboard box from one Christmas to the next, it lasts *longer* than a natural Christmas tree.

2 Substantiate a version of the thesis "our relationships with *places* are increasingly temporary." Look for evidence about how frequently American families move now, as compared to a generation ago. Or look for evidence about how rapidly the places themselves are changing.

3 Look at Toffler's pattern of development. He begins with a brief review of the evidence, then states the thesis, then discusses the implications of the thesis, then returns to the evidence with which he began. Apply that pattern to a subject of your own choosing.

Growing Up Rich
Anonymous

In this selection, the writer uses personal experience to substantiate her claim that being rich can make you hate yourself—and everyone else—just as being poor can. Growing up rich meant, to this person, knowing that she was ugly and bad. Even now she feels rejected by people who blame her for the wealth of her family.

Notice that this substantiation essay (originally a letter to the editor of *Ms.* magazine) relies on *definition*. Paragraph 1 sketches the **essential characteristics** (see p. 25) of being rich so that you will understand what follows.

Source. "Growing Up Rich" is reprinted from *Ms.* magazine, September, 1974.

1   Much is said about the pain of growing up in poverty, but not much about the pain of growing up rich. My wealthy family never had to worry about a lack of material possessions. Growing up in this environment, especially as a woman, was a deadening experience. Because she had money, Mom hired other people to live for her: to take care of her children, to wash the clothes, to clean the house. She hated herself. There was nothing for her to be except a social ornament for Dad to introduce to his business friends. She never had a job—didn't know how to go about getting a job, didn't even consider that she was capable of working or of supporting herself.

2   Dad was the provider. I have a gut hatred for ruthlessness and competitiveness because both killed my father. He didn't die of starvation, in jail, or in a fight; he died from alcoholism.

3   When Dad died, Mom almost died. All of her repressed anger tore her up inside when her main identity as a wife was taken away. After Mom got home from a mental hospital, her upper-class "proper" facade was totally destroyed. She went crazy. For 10 years she was crazy angry. She became an alcoholic. No one could be near her.

4   When I was a little girl, I was, in many ways, like Mom was when she was crazy. I was angry all the time. I didn't have any friends. I didn't know how to be a friend. All I could hope for was to be recognized by people, and the only way I knew to be recognized was to be angry. If I hit you, you knew I was there. And your anger at me for hitting you reinforced my feeling of not being able to have any friends. Mom knew deep inside that she was ugly and bad; and I knew I was, too.

5   In the last five years I have really been struggling to tear down the walls of my isolation—not only to be seen, but also to be heard.

6   Most of my friends these days didn't grow up in a wealthy environment. One aspect of my relationship with these friends throws me back into the painful isolation I am trying to overcome. I feel a subtle rejection from some of them because I grew up in a family with money. I belong to the class of the oppressors. I will "never really know what the pain of poverty is like." And I want to say to these friends, "Do you know what the pain of wealth is like? Do you know how it crippled my mother, and, through her, me? Don't push me away. Money didn't keep me from suffering. Your pain and my pain may be different, but the pain I feel is as intense as the pain you feel."

7   Dad made his money by being able to ignore the pain of others, and this ignorance (the same ignorance which causes racism and war) eventually killed him.

8   My father's insensitivity isn't restricted to wealthy people. I've seen the same insensitivity and desire to exploit others in the actions of people without money. Take the money away from all the wealthy

people and give it to all the poor; unless there is a corresponding change in attitudes, the violence and exploitation will still remain. Wealthy or poor, until we can share our pain together, the world will remain a cold and brutal place.

(name withheld)

Commentary

This letter to the editor shows how *personal experience* can be used—how information about yourself can be selected, controlled, and presented in effective order—as evidence to substantiate a thesis that goes well beyond that experience. The writer has available some 20 or 25 years' worth of memories, a collection of data far too large and varied for her to be able to use all of it. Some of it must be discarded because it is irrelevant to the subject at hand, or not quite clear in itself (many of our memories are shadowy), or repetitive of other material to be kept, or perhaps too painful to be stated in words to be read by strangers. **What appears here is a small portion of the original body of evidence, focused around two people only (the writer herself and her mother, with subordinate attention given to her father) and organized into two chronological blocks.** The writer's childhood is presented as one period of indefinite duration because it would be irrelevant to keep introducing details of months and years. The writer's present situation is called simply "these days." (The verb tenses move from past to present to indicate the chronological development.)

A very strict process of elimination has resulted in the exclusion of every piece of information that is not evidence for the point to be made. In the section about "these days," for example, we find out nothing about the writer's life beyond what the thesis requires: she is still suffering the pain of growing up rich. We don't even know whether she is still wealthy or whether, as she suggests in the last paragraph, she has tried to end her pain by giving her money away.

Would you be more convinced of the writer's point, more willing to agree that growing up rich causes tremendous emotional distress, if you knew more about her? Or has she told you enough?

Is her personal experience adequate to support her generalization?

Outline

I Introduction: statement of the subject, brief definition of the life of the rich (emphasis on the woman)—paragraph 1

II Evidence: narrative about the writer's life
  A Childhood—paragraphs 1–4
  B Transition toward the present—paragraph 5

  C The present ("these days")—paragraph 6

III Development of thesis: summary of the damage that wealth did to her father, extension of the problem beyond wealth itself to the attitudes behind it—insensitivity, desire to exploit—which appear among the poor also—paragraphs 7–8

Suggestions for Writing

1 In about 500 words (approximately the same length as the letter above), state and substantiate some thesis relating to your personal experience in growing up. Keep the introduction very brief and move rapidly into the presentation of the evidence. The difficult part will be compressing all of your memories into 500 words or, more accurately, choosing the particular memories you can present in 500 words.

　If your thesis is as wide ranging as the one in the letter—which discusses such large concepts as poverty and wealth—you may find that no selection of your evidence leaves you satisfied. If so, try a more limited thesis, for instance ''living in a trailer makes a close-knit family,'' or ''being the football coach's kid isn't all fun and games.''

2 Examine magazine ads for evidence to support the following thesis: ''Ads still imply that money can buy happiness.''

3 If you have read F. Scott Fitzgerald's novel *The Great Gatsby* (or seen the film), summarize the evidence in it to show how that story makes a point about the effects of wealth. Use a different novel or film if you prefer.

Good-bye To All T--t!
Wallace Stegner

This is an essay about calling spades *spades*. Stegner dislikes both the prudish suppression of profanity and the constant use of it in print. As a teacher of creative writing and a successful novelist, he is concerned about effective language. His thesis is that too much obscenity defeats its own purpose. It loses its flavor. His crucial evidence is the little story (paragraph 9) where language turns a somersault from obscenity back to the meekest gentility in order to recover its force.

　Stegner's title indicates that he may intend to tease as well as be serious—a reminder that good titles are important.

1　Not everyone who laments what contemporary novelists have done to the sex act objects to the act itself, or to its mention. Some want it valued higher than fiction seems to value it; they want the word

Source. ''Goodbye to All T--t!'' by Wallace Stegner. Copyright © 1965 by Wallace Stegner. Reprinted by permission of Brandt & Brandt.

"climax" to retain some of its literary meaning. Likewise, not everyone who has come to doubt the contemporary freedom of language objects to strong language in itself. Some of us object precisely because we value it.

2 I acknowledge that I have used four-letter words familiarly all my life, and have put them into books with some sense that I was insisting on the proper freedom of the artist. I have applauded the extinction of those d----d emasculations of the Genteel Tradition and the intrusion into serious fiction of honest words with honest meanings and emphasis. I have wished, with D. H. Lawrence, for the courage to say shit before a lady, and have sometimes had my wish.

3 Words are not obscene: naming things is a legitimate verbal act. And "frank" does not mean "vulgar," any more than "improper" means "dirty." What vulgar does mean is "common"; what improper means is "unsuitable." Under the right circumstances, any word is proper. But when any sort of word, especially a word hitherto taboo and therefore noticeable, is scattered across a page like chocolate chips through a tollhouse cookie, a real impropriety occurs. The sin is not the use of an "obscene" word; it is the use of a loaded word in the wrong place or in the wrong quantity. It is the sin of false emphasis, which is not a moral but a literary lapse, related to sentimentality. It is the sin of advertisers who so plaster a highway with neon signs that you can't find the bar or liquor store you're looking for. Like any excess, it quickly becomes comic.

4 If I habitually say shit before a lady, what do I say before a flat tire at the rush hour in Times Square or on the San Francisco Bay Bridge? What do I say before a revelation of the inequity of the universe? And what if the lady takes the bit in her teeth and says shit before *me*?

5 I have been a teacher of writing for many years and have watched this problem since it was no bigger than a man's hand. It used to be that with some Howellsian notion of the young-girl audience one tried to protect tender female members of a mixed class from the coarse language of males trying to show off. Some years ago Frank O'Connor and I agreed on a system. Since we had no intention whatever of restricting students' choice of subject or language, and no desire to expurgate or bowdlerize while reading their stuff aloud for discussion, but at the same time had to deal with these young girls of an age our daughters might have been, we announced that any stuff so strong that it would embarrass us to read it aloud could be read by its own author.

6 It was no deterrent at all, but an invitation, and not only to coarse males. For clinical sexual observation, for full acceptance of the natural functions, for discrimination in the selection of graffiti, for boldness in the use of words that it should take courage to say before a lady, give me a sophomore girl every time. Her strength is as the strength of ten, for she assumes that if one shocker out of her pretty

mouth is piquant, fifty will be literature. And so do a lot of her literary idols.

7   Some acts, like some words, were never meant to be casual. That is why houses contain bedrooms and bathrooms. Profanity and so-called obscenities are literary resources, verbal ways of rendering strong emotion. They are not meant to occur every ten seconds, any more than—Norman Mailer to the contrary notwithstanding—orgasms are.

8   So I am not going to say shit before any more ladies. I am going to hunt words that have not lost their sting, and it may be I shall have to go back to gentility to find them. Pleasant though it is to know that finally a writer can make use of any word that fits his occasion, I am going to investigate the possibilities latent in restraint.

9   I remember my uncle, a farmer who had used four-letter words ten to the sentence ever since he learned to talk. One day he came too near the circular saw and cut half his fingers off. While we stared in horror, he stood watching the bright arterial blood pump from his ruined hand. Then he spoke, and he did not speak loud. "Aw, the dickens," he said.

10   I think he understood, better than some sophomore girls and better than some novelists, the nature of emphasis.

Commentary

The main point of this essay is that too much of anything loses its impact. Stegner's thesis statement appears in paragraph 3: "When any sort of word . . . is scattered across a page like chocolate chips through a tollhouse cookie, a real impropriety occurs." He attempts repeatedly to show us what happens when language is abused, either by evasion or by overuse. His "genteel dashes" (d----d) in paragraph 2 and in the title are evidence for the point that an excess of prudery is silly.

His anecdotes about his classroom experience and his uncle are evidence for the point that an excess of four-letter words renders them meaningless: language is power, but any word or device of language will lose its strength if it is overworked.

Are Stegner's examples sufficient evidence to convince you? If he provided more, would he himself be overworking *that* device of writing?

Outline

I   Introduction: the subject identified and the author's attitude stated—paragraphs 1–2

II   Thesis: propriety of language determined by circumstances—paragraph 3

III Evidence: hypothetical examples ("If I say . . ."); classroom experience— paragraphs 4–6

IV   Thesis restated and affirmed—paragraphs 7–8

V   Evidence: the uncle who cut his hand— paragraph 9

VI   Summary: referring to paragraphs 5–6 and paragraph 1—paragraph 10

Suggestions for Writing

1 Extend Stegner's analysis to a recent film you have seen. Examine the effect of excessive profanity, sex, or violence.

2 Use personal experience to show that the overuse of something makes it wear out its welcome. One piece of candy is wonderful, 2 better yet, 5 more than enough, 15 nauseating.

3 Does Stegner himself rely excessively on some characteristic of style? Use his essay, especially paragraphs 4–8, as evidence to substantiate the thesis that he overworks the female stereotype.

Of Beowulf, Boxing, and the Ali Myth
Edmund Fuller

Fuller's *thesis*, in this newspaper article, is that "The myths do not die . . . they are acted out around us all the time" (paragraph 1). His *evidence* is the fight between world heavyweight boxing champion Muhammad Ali and challenger Leon Spinks. In February 1978, Ali lost his championship to Spinks. This event, according to Fuller, illustrates two of the most profound and recurring human experiences ("myths"): (1) the myth of the falling hero, the old King who must die to make way for the new; and (2) the myth of the "nobody, the unknown challenger," who is free to take every risk because he has nothing to lose.

Obviously, one example cannot prove Fuller's general thesis (in fact, you may feel that the Ali-Spinks fight supports some quite different thesis). However, you can test Fuller's thesis against life as you see it. Does his claim that *the old myths still live* fit the evidence of your experience? Does David still aim his slingshot at Goliath—and win? Do parents and children still struggle against each other (see Fuller's paragraph 13)?

[Note: In a rematch in September, 1978, after Fuller's article was written, Ali defeated Spinks and regained his crown. How does this fact affect Fuller's thesis?]

1 The myths do not die, my friends; they are acted out around us all the time.

Source. "Beowulf, Boxing, and the Ali Myth" by Edmund Fuller. From *The Wall Street Journal*, February 28, 1978. Reprinted by permission of *The Wall Street Journal*, © Dow Jones & Company, Inc. 1978. All Rights Reserved.

2   I almost didn't watch the fight but some prudential intuition guided me unbeknownst to myself and I saw it from brawling start to brawling finish. What fight? There was only one, of course: Ali-Spinks. If there is a rematch, it will be Spinks-Ali, but I agree with one of the chattering men on TV, Ali's doctor I think, in hoping that "the greatest" will hang up the gloves.

3   Sports are not my true bag, yet I have followed the fights ever since, as a boy, I always rooted against Dempsey. That was not due to a consistent pro-underdog bias in my temperament, for later I always rooted for Joe Louis and Sugar Ray Robinson and Archie Moore. Indeed, I always rooted for Floyd Patterson, which was paradoxically like rooting for the champion as underdog, for Mr. Patterson was the most Dostoyevskian, self-psyched-out fighter ever to enter the squared circle.

4   But I digress. The Ali-Spinks fight inspired me to devote an entire English class session the next morning to a discussion of it as an event not unrelated to a curriculum pursuing "Beowulf," "King Lear," "Hamlet," "Oedipus Rex," and "Paradise Lost." For just as primal myths bounce and rebound through all those works, so the fight unexpectedly flashed forth as the embodiment of a myth—a dual myth. "Myth" in this sense does not mean something unreal or false but means the expression, in universal metaphor, of a profound and recurring human experience.

5   In Muhammad Ali we saw reenacted the myth of the falling hero, for he has been one of the dancing legends of the ring—"The Fancy," as they used to call prizefighting when William Hazlitt wrote his great 18th-century essay "The Fight." Ali was the idol of millions, especially but not exclusively of blacks. Here I must confess that I have always, in the loose language of fan or antifan, "hated" him, always rooted for anyone against him. That was because I detested his persona, his strutting and chest beating, his doggerel predictions of knockout rounds, his ring clowning and "rope-a-dope" tricks, his braying, "I'm the Greatest!"

6   Mind you, it was not the man but the persona I hated, knowing full well that it was deliberately put on just to inflame such feelings in some of us because the wish to see somebody get beaten is at least as big a box-office draw—or bigger—than the wish to see someone win. But I felt no guilt; if it was his right to adopt that mask it was my right to loathe it, knowing his skills, aware that he was a great ring figure— though I shall go to my grave certain that Louis in his prime would have knocked out Ali in his.

7   Yet watching him that night against Leon Spinks, I experienced a sudden deep ambivalence as it began to appear that he was really losing. This was the first time I had ever liked or admired him. Nothing in his championship so became him as his leaving it. There had been

a premonitory note in the live interview a few moments before he entered the ring. He was quiet, even somber, declined to make predictions, said, not meaning it so literally, "I'm at the end of my career."

8   Afterwards, there were no recriminations or excuses. Asked if different tactics in the early rounds might have won, he said starkly, "I did the best I could." He added, "It was God's will." (It was a good night for God; Spinks averred that He gave him the strength.) So always the myth must be reenacted; the King must die. Age and the young Lochinvar carried him away.

9   After the dreary, cautious shuffle of the last preliminary bout it was galvanizing to see Leon Spinks race forward before the bell was silent, throwing punches with all ten of his arms—so it seemed in that blizzard of aggression. Here was the myth of the hungry nobody, the unknown challenger, guarding nothing, contemptuous of peril, risking all to gain all. It was the thing we feel never happens while knowing that ultimately it always happens. The difference is that it seldom happens quite so unexpectedly or in such purity of form as here.

10   Pity the men discussing the action. Spinks couldn't keep up that pace. They knew it. Ali knew it. Spinks didn't know it, and he did keep it up. When Ali began to dance and jab and toy and show apparent control, everybody but Spinks knew the decisive turn had come. When the 24-year-old challenger passed the mystical barrier of 10 rounds into the realm he had never entered before, but where the 35-year-old champion dwelt, all said, "Now he's in Ali's territory." Now Ali would calmly carve him up.

11   The mini-epic 15th round, a jaded crowd on its feet and screaming, brushed close to another kind of myth, the never-never movie land of "Rocky." The unflagging fury of those three minutes, the all-out mutual risk, was as close as one gets to the choreographed constant action of movie prizefights, short of course of the bloody, mangled faces and gallant struggles to rise from the floor. It was a remarkably bloodless fight, except for Ali's cut lip, and there were no knockdowns. Yet it was a gripper. The single-purposed drive of Spinks, looking extraordinarily little in the ring with Ali, kept any round from being dull.

12   J. V. Langmead-Casserley, a theologian no less, once said that the ending of the tragedy of Hamlet is the beginning of the tragedy of young Fortinbras. The spotlight passed to young Spinks, and with it the glory, the purse, even if only for one title defense, but also all the temptations to hubris and the certainty that, in time, he must fall.

13   At the last one is tempted by the remotest possibility of a future super-myth. Michael Spinks, Leon's brother, a light heavyweight, also won in a preliminary bout. This poses the riddle of the Spinks: Might we see a title fight someday of Spinks vs. Spinks? That would match

the myth of the mortal father-son battle of Sohrab and Rustum. After all, Leon Spinks said about cutting down his own one-time idol that in the ring you do what you have to do, and that is to get the top man.

14   No, the myths don't die. But the King does.

Commentary

Fuller's thesis is a very broad *generalization*: the old myths of literature are still acted out around us. He could have chosen to assemble many *pieces of evidence* to support this claim. He could have pointed out, for example, that Grace Kelly—born in Philadelphia—became a princess, enacting the Cinderella tale; that a peanut farmer became President, enacting the country-lad-makes-good pattern; that people have finally landed on the moon, enacting the age-old dream of conquering the skies; and so forth. (Naturally, each instance fits the pattern only approximately; as Fuller points out in paragraph 9, a pure example is rare.)

Instead, Fuller chose to concentrate on one example, the Ali-Spinks fight. What details make this a good choice? You might note, for example, that Ali had openly cast himself in the role of the traditional champion by proclaiming, "I'm the Greatest." Ali had always aroused strong responses—positive or negative—so that people would feel the same sense of involvement that they do in reading great literature. The boxing ring provides a very intense and obvious instance of the struggle for power. At the time, the event was fresh in the minds of millions of Americans. What other characteristics make this fight a good choice?

Fuller's tone shows his self-involvement.

He tells us his opinion of Ali (paragraphs 5-6), which changed once Ali seemed to be losing (paragraph 7). He lets his personal and professional interests show through: he is a teacher of literature, and the literary references (paragraph 4) come naturally to him. Beowulf, the hero of an Old English epic, conquered monsters in his youth but died fighting a monster in his old age. King Lear, hero of Shakespeare's play, abandoned his throne and was attacked by two of his daughters and their husbands in his old age. Hamlet, hero of another Shakespeare play, died in his struggle to understand and avenge his father's murder (the next ruler would be Fortinbras, paragraph 12). The play *Oedipus Rex*, by Sophocles, tells of the downfall of an old king who discovered that he had killed his father and married his mother. *Paradise Lost*, Milton's epic poem, recounts the fall of Adam and Eve. All of these literary works illustrate the "myth of the falling hero." Finally, Lochinvar (paragraph 8) enacts the myth of the young man bearing off the prize—in his case the bride, as told in a ballad in Walter Scott's novel *Marmion*; and Sohrab and Rustum (paragraph 13) represent the battle of the son against the father, as told in Matthew Arnold's poem "Sohrab and Rustum."

Outline

108

Suggestions for Writing

1 Using Fuller's thesis statement as your own first paragraph, write an essay that uses some other incident as evidence.

2 Use Fuller's pattern of offering a broad generalization and supporting it by means of one well-chosen example. For example, develop an example to support the thesis "Romantic love is not dead," or

"People learn from making their own mistakes," or "Television newscasts present a very fragmented view of reality."

3 Write an essay that, like Fuller's, investigates the relationship between literature and life. With your instructor's help, limit your subject so that you can handle it.

The Body in the Bog
Geoffrey Bibby

This is an essay in logical inference from an extremely limited amount of data: a naked body, male, its throat slit, found in a peat bog in Denmark. There would be no point in looking for witnesses, since whatever happened took place 1500 years ago.

Bibby describes the process of investigation that establishes what can be known with certainty about *X* and what, in addition, can be logically inferred. The investigation involves assembling medical, botanical, and chemical evidence, and comparing this body with others recovered from the peat bogs in northern Europe. The range of information brought to bear upon this murder mystery then widens to include facts about the burial customs of prehistoric peoples, artifacts found in the bogs, early histories of Germanic tribes, surviving remnants of pagan religious practices, and finally—returning to the bodies themselves—the contents of their stomachs (the food the victims ate at their last meals). On the basis of this accumulated evidence, Bibby offers an explanation of the murder.

The business of the archaeologist is the digging up of the past, the reconstruction of remote history. He does his best to find out what our remote ancestors did and thought and felt from the material remains they left in the ground. A distinguished archaeologist has un-

Source. "The Body in the Bog" by Geoffrey Bibby. © 1968 by American Heritage Publishing Co., Inc. Reprinted by permission from *Horizon* (Winter 1968).

flatteringly described himself and his colleagues as surgeons probing into the workings of the human brain with picks, shovels, and builders' trowels. "Fortunately," he adds, "our patients are already dead."

2   This comparison must not be taken too literally. When Sir Mortimer Wheeler describes the archaeologist as investigating people who are dead, he means, I am afraid, that we are trying to find out about these dead-and-gone people by studying the things they left behind them, their implements and weapons and coins and pots and pans. The nearest we normally get to the people themselves is their skeletons, and there is a limit to what can be deduced from dry bones.

3   I wish to tell an archaeological detective story that is different—a detective story that begins with a body and no artifacts.

4   My part in the story began on Monday, April 28, 1952, when I arrived at the Prehistoric Museum of Aarhus, in mid-Denmark, to find a dead body on the floor of my office. On an iron sheet stood a large block of peat, and at one end of it the head and right arm of a man protruded, while one leg and foot stuck out from the other end. His skin was dark brown, almost chocolate colored, and his hair was a brownish red.

5   He had been found on Saturday afternoon by workers cutting peat in a little bog near Grauballe, about twenty miles away. He lay a yard below the surface, but peat had been dug for generations there so that the "surface" had lain much higher, even within living memory. The finders had informed the local doctor of their discovery, not so much because he was a doctor but because he was known to be an antiquary of repute. And he had informed Professor Peter Glob, who was the director of our museum.

6   This was not Professor Glob's first "bog body"; he knew what to expect and made preparations accordingly. The next day he drove out to the bog, cut a section through the peat exposing the lie of the body, drew and photographed that section, took samples of the peat surrounding the body, and then cut out the whole block in which the body lay and brought it in to the museum in a truck.

7   That Monday we carefully dug away the peat covering the body, taking samples every two inches. The body lay face down, with one leg drawn up and the arms twisted somewhat behind it. It was completely naked. When we removed the peat from below the body (after turning it over in a plaster cast to preserve its original position), we still found nothing, no trace of clothing, no artifacts—nothing except the naked body.

8   At this point we turned for help to the professor of forensic medicine at Aarhus University, who carried out a thorough autopsy and presented us with a lengthy and detailed report:

9   "This most unusually well-preserved body has, as a result of the particular composition of the earth in which it has lain, undergone a

process of conservation which appears to resemble most closely a tanning. This has made the skin firm and resistant, and has to a high degree counteracted the various processes of decay which normally commence soon after death. . . . The subject is an adult male, and the condition of the teeth suggests that he was of somewhat advanced age. . . . On the front of the throat was found a large wound stretching from ear to ear. . . . This wound may with certainty be interpreted as an incised lesion, probably caused by several cuts inflicted by a second person. The direction of the wound and its general appearance make it unlikely that it could be self-inflicted or accidentally inflicted after death. . . . The investigation of the hair suggests that the subject was dark-haired. The reddish coloration is presumably accounted for by the body having lain in peat."

10   So the man from Grauballe had had his throat cut, and we had a murder mystery on our hands.

11   The investigation went on. The police expert reported: "There is nothing unusual about the fingerprints obtained. I myself possess the same type of pattern on the right thumb and middle finger—without therefore claiming any direct descent from Grauballe Man. Among the present-day Danish population the two patterns occur with a frequency of, respectively, 11.2 and 68.3 per cent."

12   More important were the results we got from the peat samples and from a portion of the liver region that we had excised and sent to the radioactive-carbon laboratory.

13   It happens that the botanists of Scandinavia have worked out in great detail the changing composition of the vegetation of the region since the last ice age ended more than ten thousand years ago. They do this by means of the thousands of infinitesimal grains of pollen to be found in any cubic centimeter of peat. The time within this sequence when any particular specimen of peat was formed is shown by the proportion of certain types of pollen grains, particularly of tree pollen. And the pollen analysts could tell us that the peat immediately below Grauballe Man had been formed early in the period the Danes call the Roman Iron Age, a period extending from the beginning of the Christian Era to about A.D. 300.

14   But they could tell us more. The peat *above* the body was of *earlier* date than that directly below and around the body, and the peat at a little distance to either side of the body was earlier still. The body had clearly been buried in a hole cut in the peat—but not in a hole cut to receive it. The only explanation to fit the facts was that a hole had been cut, probably to obtain peat for fuel, had stood open for some years (long enough for new peat to form in the water at the bottom of the hole), and then Grauballe Man had been thrown into this new peat and the hole had been filled in with peat from the surface layers.

5   The radio-carbon laboratory—which determines the age of organic

substances by measuring the residual carbon-14 in the specimen—could tell us that this had occurred and that Grauballe Man had died in A.D. 310, with a possible error of a hundred years in either direction. This did not surprise us; for, though local newspapers and gossip had made much of a certain "Red Christian," a drunkard farmhand who was said to have disappeared one night some sixty years before, not far from the Grauballe peat bog, we should have been very surprised indeed if the pollen laboratory and the radio-carbon laboratory had *not* given us a date in the region of 100 B.C.—A.D. 300.

16   For Grauballe Man was far from being an isolated example. Bodies have always been turning up in the peat bogs of Denmark—and not only in Denmark. They are frequently found in northwest Germany and even as far south as Holland. In that area there are records of something like two hundred bog bodies. Since the earlier records are not very detailed, sometimes merely an entry in a parish registry of the "body of a poor man drowned in such and such a bog," the statistics are far from exact. The earliest doubtful record of this nature is from 1450, at Bonstorf in Germany. And the first detailed report is from 1773, when a completely preserved body of a man was found three feet deep in the peat at Ravnholt on the Danish island of Fünen. The body lay on its back with its arms crossed behind it—"as though they had been bound," says the parish clerk. Apart from a sheepskin around the head, it was naked. When the sheepskin was removed, it could be seen that the man had had his throat cut.

17   In 1797, in southwest Jutland, another well-preserved male body was found, naked save for one oxhide moccasin but covered with two calfskin cloaks. The cause of death is not recorded, and the body was hurriedly buried in a nearby churchyard when it began to dry out and decompose.

18   And so it went. Every few years a body would be found, would be a nine-day wonder in its immediate locality because of its surprising state of preservation, and would be buried again when it began to smell.

19   A few of the bodies achieved more than local fame. In 1853, about fifty miles south of Copenhagen a body was found, probably that of a woman, though there was little left besides the skeleton and the long, fair hair. The body was noteworthy because it was accompanied by a bronze brooch and seven glass beads, which even then could be dated to the Iron Age and which we can now date to about A.D. 300.

20   Eight years earlier a much more complete female body had been found at Haraldskaer, in south Jutland, not far from the burial mounds of Gorm, the last heathen king of Denmark, and his queen, nor from the site of the first Christian church in Denmark, built about A.D. 950 by Gorm's son, Harald Bluetooth. The body lay in the peat with its hands and feet held down by forked sticks, and it achieved

some notoriety in Denmark because some learned antiquaries claimed that it was Queen Gunhild of Norway, who, according to legend, had been enticed to Denmark by Harald Bluetooth and drowned by him in a morass. Even at the time of discovery, though, the evidence for this identification was regarded as too slender.

1   The first photograph of a peat-bog body dates from 1873 and is of a body found near Kiel. It was a man's body with a triangular hole in the forehead. He was naked except for a piece of leather bound around the left shin, but his head was covered with a large square woolen blanket and a sewn skin cape. An attempt was made to preserve him for exhibition by smoking, and several photographs were taken, some extravagantly posed. The first photograph of a body *in situ* was taken in 1892. The body was found not many miles away from where Grauballe Man was discovered sixty years later, and very close indeed to another recent find, the Tollund Man.

2   The list could be continued almost indefinitely. But it is only within recent years that pollen analysis has been developed to a stage where the bodies can be accurately dated. And all the bodies found since have proved to date to the same restricted period of Danish prehistory, the first three centuries of the Christian Era. This fact makes it possible—indeed essential—to regard them as a single "case."

3   Apart from Grauballe Man, four bodies have been found in the peat bogs of Denmark since World War II, and all have been subjected to the same thorough analysis that we have Grauballe Man. Three came from the same bog, the large peat area of Borremose in north Jutland. The first was a man, naked like so many of the others but with two cloaks of skin beside him. Around his neck was a rope noose, which may have been the cause of death, although the body was too badly preserved to be certain. There were odd features about the noose; it had been knotted at the neck, and both of the fairly short ends had been bent over and lashed with leather thongs to prevent them from unraveling, surely an unduly elaborate treatment for an ordinary hangman's noose.

4   The second body was that of a woman, again poorly preserved. The upper part of the body appeared to have been naked, while the lower part was covered with a blanket, a shawl, and other bits of clothing. There was a leather cord around the neck, but the cause of death was apparently a crushing blow on the skull.

5   The third body was also a woman's, a rather stout lady who lay face downward in the peat with only a blanket wrapped around her middle and held in place by a leather strap. She was no sight for squeamish archaeologists—she had been scalped and her face battered to pieces, though perhaps after death.

6   It is with quite unjustified relief that one turns from the rather macabre Borremose bodies to the well-known Tollund Man, whose

portrait has been in the press of the world and who has had the honor of appearing on British television. Tollund Man was discovered in 1950, two years before Grauballe Man and under the same circumstances, by farmers cutting peat. The discovery was reported to the police, and they called in Professor Glob, who described what he saw:

27   "In the peat cut, nearly seven feet down, lay a human figure in a crouched position, still half-buried. A foot and a shoulder protruded, perfectly preserved but dark-brown in color like the surrounding peat, which had dyed the skin. Carefully we removed more peat, and a bowed head came into view.

28   "As dusk fell, we saw in the fading light a man take shape before us. He was curled up, with legs drawn under him and arms bent, resting on his side as if asleep. His eyes were peacefully shut; his brows were furrowed, and his mouth showed a slightly irritated quirk as if he were not overpleased by this unexpected disturbance. . . ."

29   Tollund Man was found to be naked except for a leather belt around his waist and a leather cap upon his head, a cap made of eight triangular gussets of leather sewn together. There was one other item. Around his neck was the elaborately braided leather rope with which they had hanged him.

30   It is clear, I think, that we have a case of mass murder. There are too many points of similarity between the killings for it to be possible to consider each independently of the others. I should point out, though, that their generally fantastic state of preservation is not one of these points of similarity. It is merely our good fortune. The preservation is due to the fact that the peat bogs contain sufficient humic acid and tannic acid to halt the processes of decay and start a tanning process that can preserve the body. (This process, incidentally, we have carried to its logical conclusion with Grauballe Man. Eighteen months in an oak vat in a concentrated solution based on oak shavings has completed the tanning process that nature commenced some eighteen hundred years ago. Grauballe Man, on exhibition at the Prehistoric Museum in Aarhus, needs only a little linseed oil now and then in order to last indefinitely.)

31   There is one condition for preservation, however, for otherwise the peat bogs would be full of the bodies of every animal that falls into them. The body must be *buried* in the peat, deep enough down to be below the oxygen-containing surface levels. And this—the fact that all these bodies were disposed of in old cuttings in the peat—*is* one of the common factors that cause us to regard all the killings as a single phenomenon.

32   Another is the fact that all the bodies are naked. Though it is the rule rather than the exception for articles of clothing to be found with the bodies, and sometimes wrapped around the bodies, they are never

regularly clothed in the garments. But the most obvious similarity is that all have died violent deaths and that all are found in bogs.

33   And that leads to the next step in the inquiry: the question of motive. Why are these bodies there at all?

34   These are not ordinary burials. Archaeologists are very well acquainted with the burials of this period of Danish prehistory. They were elaborate, clearly showing evidence of belief in an afterlife in which the dead would have need of material things. The graves are large and edged with stones. The body lies carefully arranged on its side, together with a whole set of pottery vessels, or in the case of the wealthy, with glass and silver ware imported from the Roman Empire. The vessels must have held provisions for the journey to the afterworld, for there is often a leg of pork or of mutton with the rest of the provisions, and even a knife to carve the joint.

35   It is clear that whatever it was that resulted in the deaths of the bodies in the bogs also deprived them of regular, ritual burial.

36   We must dismiss the most obvious explanation—that the bodies were victims of robbery with violence. All are dated to the comparatively short period of three hundred years at the beginning of our era. It may have been a lawless time—though farther south it is the period of the Pax Romana—but certainly it was no more lawless than many other periods: the period before, of the great Celtic and Germanic wanderings; or the period after, when the Roman Empire was breaking up and all the vultures flocked to the kill; or the Viking period; or much of the Middle Ages. We should expect a much greater spread in date if the bodies are to be explained as the victims of robber bands.

37   We must widen our scope and look not so much at the bodies as at the bogs. What do we find there?

38   Any Danish archaeologist can answer that question at length. And he can illustrate his answer at the Danish National Museum in Copenhagen, where room after room is full of things found in bogs. More than half of the best treasures of Danish prehistory have been found in bogs, and the archaeologist will tell you that these treasures were offerings to the gods.

39   Now, archaeologists have often been accused of calling in hypothetical gods and cult practices whenever they find anything they cannot explain by obvious mundane means. A theory of offerings in the peat bogs must not be accepted uncritically. But how else is one to explain why a Stone Age farmer, some four thousand years ago, very carefully laid seven large, new, unused stone axes side by side in a row in a peat bog? How is one to explain why several pairs of the big bronze trumpets known as lurs, the finest known products of the Danish Bronze Age, have been found in the bogs in good working order?

40   It begins to look as though anything of prehistoric date found in the bogs of Denmark is a priori likely to be an offering to the gods. If we move forward to the actual period of the bog bodies, we find the offerings in the bogs getting more numerous and more varied and richer. In the early 1950's I spent three years a few miles south of our museum, helping to dig out an immense offering of weapons—several thousand iron swords and spearheads and arrowheads and shield bosses—all of them burned, bent, hacked to pieces, and then deposited in a lake in the middle of a peat bog. They had been deposited at various times—it was a regular place of offering—but all during the period A.D. 150—300. Among the weapons lay the skeletons of two horses—and here perhaps we approach quite close in spirit to the bog bodies, for the horses had been beheaded before they were offered, and marks on the bones showed quite clearly where spears had been stuck into the carcasses, before or after death.

41   We are entering a dark region. Our probings into the minds of our distant ancestors are lifting a corner of a veil that seems to cover an area of deep superstition, a time when the peat bogs were the abodes of gods and spirits, who demanded sacrifice. When we look now at the bodies in the bogs it seems by no means impossible that they, too, were offerings; that the sacrifices to the gods also included human sacrifices.

42   We must ask ourselves what we know about the gods and goddesses of this period.

43   At the northern end of that very bog at Borremose in which three of the bodies were found, there was discovered in 1897 a large caldron of solid silver. In itself the Gundestrup caldron is far and away the most intrinsically valuable of all the bog offerings. But it is more than that; it is a picture book of European religion around the beginning of the Christian Era. Its sides are decorated, inside and out, with a series of panels bearing pictures, in relief, of gods and goddesses, of mythical animals, and of ritual scenes. Admittedly the caldron is believed to have been manufactured in southeast Europe and to have been brought to Denmark as booty, but the deities portrayed are like the native Danish gods of the period.

44   It is particularly noteworthy that each one of these deities, although otherwise naked, bears a torque, or broad necklet, at the throat, which appears to have been a symbol of kingship and of divinity. It has even been suggested—perhaps not entirely fancifully—that the oddly elaborate nooses around the necks of Tollund and Borremose Man in some way set them apart as consecrated to the gods. We know from the sagas, not many hundreds of years later, that in Viking times hanged men were sacred to Odin, the chief god of the Viking pantheon.

45   One of the interior caldron panels shows clearly that the idea of human sacrifice was not alien to the religion of the time. It is admit-

tedly a different ceremony of sacrifice, with the victim dropped head-first into, or perhaps slaughtered above, a caldron, perhaps the Gundestrup caldron itself. The cutting of the throats of animal victims and the draining of their blood into a caldron was not unknown even among the civilized Greeks and Romans—and Grauballe Man, like many of the victims in the Danish bogs, had had his throat cut.

6   Speculation concerning details of ritual, though fascinating, can hardly be justified by the slender evidence at our disposal. But the general picture cannot be questioned: the Danes of the early Christian centuries worshiped torque-bearing gods and goddesses; they were not averse to human sacrifice; and the holy places of the divinities were the peat bogs.

7   There is one source of information that we have not yet tapped. The historians and geographers of the Roman Empire wrote books, some of which describe the manners and customs of peoples beyond the imperial frontiers. The books must be used with caution; few of the authors had visited the regions they describe, and their accounts may well be as full of misunderstandings and fanciful explanations as any-thing the modern archaeologist can invent to explain what he finds.

8   But there is a passage in Tacitus's *Germania*, an account of the peoples beyond the Rhine written in A.D. 98, that bears on our study of the Danish bog bodies. Tacitus names seven tribes to the north of Germany, including the Angles, who are known to have lived in south Jutland before they invaded England in the fifth century together with the Saxons and Jutes. And he says: "these people . . . are distin-guished by a common worship of Nerthus, or Mother Earth. They believe that she interests herself in human affairs and rides through their peoples. In an island of Ocean stands a sacred grove, and in the grove stands a car draped with a cloth which none but the priest may touch. The priest can feel the presence of the goddess in this holy of holies, and attends her, in deepest reverence, as her car is drawn by oxen. Then follow days of rejoicing and merrymaking in every place that she honors with her advent and stay. No-one goes to war, no-one takes up arms; every object of iron is locked away; then, and only then, are peace and quiet known and prized, until the goddess is again restored to her temple by the priest, when she has had her fill of the society of men. After that, the car, the cloth and, believe it if you will, the goddess herself are washed clean in a secluded lake. This service is performed by slaves who are immediately afterwards drowned in the lake. Thus mystery begets terror and a pious reluctance to ask what that sight can be which is allowed only to dying eyes."

9   Here we may be getting close to an answer. Nerthus—Mother Earth—is clearly a goddess of fertility; she may be the "goddess with the torque." And the time of peace and rejoicing when the goddess is driven around the countryside in her draped carriage will be the time

of sowing, the vernal equinox. Pagan survivals of this spring festival still exist in many parts of Europe, in mummers' plays and Maypole dancing and Queens of the May. And in the National Museum in Copenhagen may be seen one of the ox-drawn carriages that almost certainly was used to carry the image of the fertility goddess around the fields. It was found—inevitably—in a peat bog, at Dejbjerg in east Jutland, in the 1880's. Richly carved and decorated with ornaments of bronze, it is far too fine a wagon to have been used for mundane purposes. Upon it stands a palanquin, a carrying chair with a canopy, within which the image of the goddess must have rested.

50   A final point brings the evidence full circle to the bodies in the bogs. Microscopic examination of the stomach contents of the men from Borremose, Tollund, and Grauballe shows that their food for several days before death had been vegetarian. It seems to have consisted of some sort of porridge or mash composed of various kinds of corn, of sorrel and heart's-ease (both cultivated during the Iron Age), and of the seeds of such weeds as were accidentally harvested along with the corn. It has been suggested that this was a ritual diet, part of the ceremony needed to make the corn grow. Be that as it may, it is significant that there was no trace of any of the edible plants or fruits of summer in the stomach contents. So whatever our uncertainty about the precise year of death, we can say with confidence that the season of the year was winter or early spring.

51   Further we cannot go. We have been probing, with our picks and shovels and builders' trowels, not merely into the brains but perhaps also into the souls of men, and we must be content if our diagnosis is imprecise and inconclusive. But it does take us a little way beyond the conventional archaeological picture of the material lives of the simple peasants of barbarian Europe. Behind the material life, inter-leaved with it and perhaps dominating it, was the world of taboos and magic and superstition, the spirits of the earth and of the heavens, who had to be bribed or placated or bought off. One of the occupa-tional risks of Iron Age Europe, right up to the end of the Viking period scarcely a thousand years ago, was that of being chosen as victim, as the price to be paid for prosperity in the next harvest or victory in the next war. It was only with the coming of Christianity that human sacrifice ceased in Europe; looking on the bodies from the Danish bogs we should do well to realize that there, but for the grace of God, lie we.

Commentary

After a brief introduction about the work of archaeologists, who "dig up the past" and attempt to understand it, Bibby describes the case he is interested in—a body of a murdered man, found preserved in a Danish peat bog. After summarizing the information that can be gathered from this body (radiocarbon analysis, for example, shows that the victim was killed in approximately the fourth century A.D.), Bibby expands the mystery by reviewing several other cases of murder victims found in bogs. He then states the problem: why were these people killed and buried in peat bogs?

The question can be answered only by gathering other kinds of data. One of the crucial aspects of any logical investigation is the decision about what kinds of information are to be considered. Bibby's inquiry has reached the point where no further progress can be made by examining the bodies themselves, and he therefore turns to other sources of data about the society in which the victims lived. He is on less certain ground here, since someone might object that these other sources are inappropriate, misleading, or irrelevant, and his dependence on them means that his conclusion about the bodies can be only tentative. However, when an inquiry reaches an impasse, the investigator has no choice except to involve new kinds of information or leave the problem unresolved.

Bibby's information about primitive European peoples, gathered from various sources—

some, as he acknowledges, less reliable than others—permits him to reach the tentative conclusion that the murder victims were human sacrifices in pagan religious ceremonies. This interpretation allows him to make sense of one final observation about the bodies themselves, the contents of their stomachs, which indicate that the victims were killed in the winter or early spring. They were probably sacrificed, then, to a fertility goddess, perhaps to a god of battle, "as the price to be paid for prosperity in the next harvest or victory in the next war."

The mystery has been only partially solved. We still do not know exactly when or by whom the man with whose body we began was murdered; we do not even know who he was. Bibby realizes the incompleteness of his answer, remarking, "we must be content if our diagnosis is imprecise and inconclusive."

The essay illustrates both the process by which one can go from information to a conclusion and the need to refrain from making that conclusion seem more definite than it really is. A less responsible writer might have concealed the incompleteness of his data and presented an answer with a fraudulent aura of certainty.

Outline

I Introduction: the archaeologist's business—paragraphs 1–3

II The body in the bog and what can be learned directly from it—paragraphs 4–15

III Other bog bodies—paragraphs 16–29

IV Common elements in all the cases—paragraphs 30–36

V Other kinds of information about primitive European society—paragraphs 37–49

VI A final fact about the bodies—paragraph 50

VII Conclusion: summary of the interpretation and of its limits—paragraph 51

Suggestions for Writing

1 The discovery of new evidence often requires reinterpretation of the whole body of material. Suppose that you were to discover several more bog bodies. Their stomach contents include foods available at various times of the year (not only winter or early spring). The people have been killed by a number of methods, but each

body has tied onto it some valuable object—a piece of jewelry, a gold cup, a decorated bronze bowl. What reinterpretation of the whole bog-body problem would this new evidence suggest? Write Bibby a letter describing the new discoveries and presenting your revised resolution of the mystery.

2 Apply Bibby's investigative process—what is known about X, what must be added from related areas of knowledge, conclusion—to some problem in your experience. For example, you might attempt to predict what would happen if students were to organize into unions (as faculty members have at some institutions). You have some information about students and about their behavior in groups. However, no data on students organized into unions is available, and your inquiry can go no further unless you turn to related kinds of material: the behavior of faculty members organized into unions or the behavior of students united into less formal or less inclusive interest groups (action movements, foreign students' associations, etc.). You will need to do some library research unless you have had personal experience to use as evidence. Avoid, as Bibby does, suggesting any unwarranted certainty for your conclusion.

Substantiation, Series Two
Readings without Commentary

A House Named Hamerika
Cora du Bois

This brief and terrible story uses personal experience to sub-stantiate the thesis that everything we do involves other people in ways we cannot predict. Cora du Bois, an American scholar, went to the Indonesian island of Alor before World War II to study the people who lived there. They received her most kindly. In the village of Atimelang, they named a house "Ham-erika" after the country from which their visitor said she came. A man named Malelaka and other islanders became her friends.

The selection below, which deals with the consequences of du Bois' visit, appeared as a 1960 appendix to the original preface of her book (first published in 1944).

1   In the fifteen years that have elapsed since this first preface was written I have not returned to Alor. In that interim World War II swept over the area. In July, 1942, four months after the Dutch forces capitulated in Java, the Japanese garrisoned the island. The Dutch, having foreseen several years in advance the possibility of a Japanese invasion, are rumored to have had standing orders for the evacuation of their personnel from the outer islands of Indonesia. In any event, the Japanese took possession of Alor without opposition. . . .

2   After the war I received a letter from a young controleur who was sent to Alor during the Dutch interregnum before Indonesia achieved

Source. "A House Named Hamerika" by Cora du Bois; Reprinted by permission of the author and publishers from *The People of Alor*, Vol. I, by Cora du Bois, Cambridge, Mass.: Harvard University Press, Copyright 1944 by the University of Minnesota; © 1960, 1972 by Cora du Bois.

independence. It was a jovial, almost a flippant, letter. I don't remember his name, but he offered me every hospitality if I wished to return and asked me for a copy of this book. He told quite casually the story of Atimelang and the house called Hamerika. The Japanese had used it as a patrol station, for the Japanese, like the Dutch, sent small groups of troops to crisscross the island at irregular intervals to maintain order and prevent uprisings. Word reached the Japanese command in Kalabahi that the village leaders of Atimelang were claiming that Hamerika would win the war. This could have been nothing but the most innocent fantasy to my friends in Atimelang since they had never even heard of the United States prior to my arrival. But to the Japanese, suffering from all the nervous apprehensions of any occupying power in a strange and therefore threatening environment, such talk could mean only rebellion. As the Dutch, years before, had sent a punitive expedition to the area after the murder of the radjah, as they had later imprisoned Malelaka because he had visions of the arrival of "good beings" (nala kang), so the Japanese sent troops to arrest five of my friends in Atimelang. I am not sure who all of them were from the young controleur's letter, but apparently Thomas, Malelaka, and the Chief of Dikimpe were among them. In Kalabahi they were publicly decapitated as a warning to the populace.

3   There is no end to the intricate chain of responsibility and guilt that the pursuit of even the most arcane social research involves. "No man is an island."

Women Drivers in the Trucking Industry
Abigail Lambert

The writer of this letter to the editor of *Ms.* magazine uses her personal experience to substantiate the thesis that the trucking industry discriminates against women drivers—women who want to be truck drivers, that is. The trucking companies' objections to women truck drivers show that the companies are reasoning in circles rather than in acceptable logical patterns.

Source. "Women Drivers in the Trucking Industry" by Abigail Lambert. From *Ms.* magazine, June, 1974.

Do you think that Lambert makes her case adequately? Or is she seeing only part of the picture?

1   Although I am in perfect health, certified by a truck-driving training school, and in possession of a valid Class-One California driving license, I am running into problems getting employment in the trucking industry because I am female.

2   You may have heard that in recent years, more and more women have been entering the trucking profession. But here's the catch: in most cases, women are able to enter the trucking profession only as part of a husband-wife driving team. As for putting a single woman on with a male co-driver for long-distance hauling (where the best money in trucking is to be made), the companies that I've been to refuse, on the grounds that they could get into trouble for condoning fornication and adultery.

3   Even though two drivers sharing long-distance hauling are expected to alternate driving and sleeping shifts to keep running 20 or 22 hours a day, employers have told me they feel that inevitably I and a male co-driver would wind up spending all our time in the sleeper berth! In short, it's assumed that because I'm a woman, I'm incapable of behaving responsibly on the road, of enforcing any responsible attitude in my co-driver—who, of course, would be incapable of regarding me as anything other than a sex object, placed conveniently at his disposal by the firm while he's on the road. I've also been told that I could be hired by the company in question if only they had another woman driver to put me on with; but the company doesn't hire women anyway, so there's no woman driver to put me on with, so. . . .

4   There you have a nice circular argument trucking firms use to protect themselves against uppity women who dare to stay single, operate 35 tons of tractor-trailer assembly, and try to gross $14,000 to $50,000 income yearly, God forbid!

Abigail Lambert
San Jose, Calif.

123

Loch Ness:
The Logic is There
John Noble Wilford

Is there life on Mars? Is there an abominable snowman somewhere in the Himalaya Mountains? Is ESP real?

People who want to answer such questions usually first try
to substantiate a preliminary thesis: there *could* be life on Mars
(and so forth). Once we see that *X* is possible, we may be
willing to spend the time and money—sometimes involving
personal risks—to conduct a systematic search.

Wilford's question is whether there could be giant creatures
living in Loch Ness. In this portion of a newspaper article, he
is not trying to prove that a ''Loch Ness monster'' definitely
exists, but only that it *could* exist. After a **description** of Loch
Ness itself and the **process** by which it was formed (paragraphs
1-4), he concentrates on whether a salt-water creature could
have adapted to life in the fresh-water loch. His conclusion is
stated in his title: logically, at least, it seems possible. Now it's
up to someone else to see whether the monster—as well as the
logic—is there.

1 Eons ago, a crack opened in the surface of the restless earth, causing
a side-ways slippage of crust between the north and south of the
Scottish highlands. The result is a northeast-southwest trending fault,
visible as the beautiful 100-mile-long Great Glen. Through this rift
valley, between steep green hills, stretches a navigable link between
the North Sea and the Atlantic Ocean, a system of rivers, canals and
lakes, called the Caledonian Canal, running from Moray Firth in the
northeast to the Firth of Lorne in the southwest.

2 During the most recent ice age, a mass of ice perhaps a mile thick
covered this region. When the ice melted, about 10,000 years ago, the
sea rose, but so did Scotland, now that it was relieved of its great
frozen burden. For a long time, Loch Ness, probably the entire Glen,
was a salt-water strait. But as the land continued to rise, Loch Ness
was reduced to being an estuary of Moray Firth. Finally, with the land
reaching some 50 feet above sea level, as it has been for several
thousand years now, the loch became effectively cut off from the sea.

Source. ''Loch Ness: The Logic is There'' by John Noble Wilford. *The New York
Times*, June 6, 1976. © 1976 by The New York Times Company. Reprinted by permission.

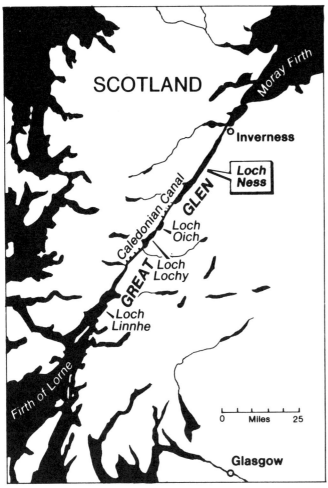

Source. *The New York Times*, June 6, 1976. © 1976 by The New York Times Company. Reprinted by permission.

3   There is a shallow river, running a short distance from the loch to Moray Firth, at the city of Inverness. But this was not sufficient to prevent the loch from changing gradually from salt water to fresh. The runoff from the many rivers and burns, emptying into the loch, made the change complete.

4   The result is the largest fresh water body by volume in the British Isles—23 miles long, as much as a mile and a half wide, up to 975 feet deep in places but generally 700 feet deep along the fault line. It teems with trout, pike, sticklebacks, Arctic char, eels and salmon. But could there also be giant creatures inhabiting the loch?

5   Legends abound, and hundreds of reported sightings in the last 43 years. If there is a Loch Ness monster of some sort, a common assumption is that it belongs to a family of creatures that got trapped when the loch was cut off from the sea and somehow managed to adapt to fresh water. Some 150 to 250 of their descendents could be there now, according to estimates based on what would be necessary to support a viable breeding population these many years.

6   Such adaptation is not impossible, according to Dr. Christopher McGowan, a zoologist of the Royal Ontario Museum in Toronto. Many animals that live in estuaries, he said, can tolerate the wide fluctuations in salinity that come with the ebb and flow of the tides. How well an animal could make a permanent transition to fresh water would in many cases depend on its skin and kidneys.

7   The problem is that many sea creatures coming into fresh water become bloated, some more than others, through a higher absorption of water through the semi-permeable membrane of their skin. This is a breakdown in the process known as osmosis. They have evolved systems in which the water pressure inside their bodies was accustomed to the pressures of sea water outside, not fresh water.

8   But if there was time for evolutionary processes to operate, Dr. McGowan explained, it might be possible for creatures to adapt fairly impermeable skins to reduce the inflow and larger kidneys to flush their systems. He noted that in Lake Ontario the alewife, migrating from the sea through the St. Lawrence, have adapted to fresh water. The lampreys now infesting the Great Lakes have successfully accomplished the same adaptation, and certain species of North American salmon, entirely landlocked in fresh water, are indistinguishable from their relatives who live in the sea, ascending rivers only to spawn. Dr. Roy P. Mackal, a University of Chicago biochemist, points to a species of sea cows, a type of mammal sometimes associated with the monster, that has adapted to the Amazon and Orinoco Rivers in South America. This, he said, "proves that sirenas (sea cows) can exist exclusively in fresh water, if necessary, and provides a parallel with Loch Ness and its phenomena." A similar parallel may exist in the fresh-water seals of Lake Baikal in Siberia.

Speak Up, Chicano
Armando M. Rodriguez

Rodriguez's thesis is that *Chicanos* (Mexican-Americans) ''are
beginning to stand up and make their voices heard'' (paragraph
13). To convince us that this is indeed the case, Rodriguez
begins with a scene in San Antonio, a scene that uses conversation to let us hear those voices directly. He then moves to a
larger perspective—a summary of other such meetings, general
information about Spanish-speaking Americans, a glimpse
backwards into his own personal past—to further support his
thesis.

Notice that Rodriguez organizes his material so that, as we
read, we follow the **inductive process** (see p. 92). We first meet
the evidence—as if we were investigating the situation ourselves. The conclusion (thesis) is not stated until afterward.

I sat quietly and listened as 15 Mexican-American citizens who had
gathered in a crumbling adobe community center in San Antonio's
oldest slum talked about their schools. As director of the U.S. Office
of Education's Mexican-American Affairs Unit, I was there to learn
what the local citizens and school people felt were their most pressing
educational needs.

''We ought to be consulted more about what goes on in our
schools,'' the president of the Mexican-American Community Club
said heatedly. ''Our high school needs a Mexican-American on the
counseling staff. But the school people say they can't find a qualified
one to hire. Over 60 percent of the kids are Mexican-Americans and
most of them have trouble speaking English. Yet we have only five
Spanish-speaking teachers, and not a single person in the school office
speaks Spanish. Is it any wonder the kids drop out like flies? The hell
with the requirements. Let's take care of these kids' needs, and one
of the first is to get somebody who can talk to them.''

''Now wait just a minute,'' interrupted the school district's assistant
superintendent. We have to follow state regulations, you know. You
can't put just anybody in the counseling office. You tell us where to
find a qualified Mexican-American teacher or counselor and we'll be
delighted to hire him.''

''At least you could have Mexican-Americans in the school as aides,

Source. ''Speak Up, Chicano'' by Armando M. Rodriguez. From *American Education*, May, 1968. Reprinted by permission of *American Education*.

couldn't you?'' asked a neighborhood representative on the community action program board. "But you folks downtown made the requirements so high that none of our people could get a job. Why?"

5   "We have to have qualified people to work with the youngsters," answered the director of instruction.

6   "Qualified?" the president broke in. "What could be better qualifications than speaking the language and understanding the kids?"

7   "Well, we haven't seen much show of interest from the parents," countered a schoolman. "We can't get them out to PTA meetings, can't even get many of them to come to parent's night. We hired a Mexican-American school-community coordinator for some of our schools, but she's finding it an uphill battle getting the parents to take an interest in school matters."

8   And so it went at meeting after meeting that I attended with Lupe Anguiano and Dean Bistline, my coworkers in the Mexican-American Affairs Unit. We visited 17 communities on our three-week tour of Arizona, California, Colorado, New Mexico, and Texas. Both Mexican-American community leaders and school people—some 1,700 altogether—poured out their frustrations, and we learned a great deal about what the people want and need and in what priority.

9   In those five states alone, there are more than 5.5 million people of Spanish surname. Eight out of 10 live in California or Texas. Their numbers are constantly reinforced by a stream of immigrants from Mexico. Add the 1.5 million other Spanish-speaking people—Cuban, Puerto Rican, Central and South American, and Spanish—who live in Florida and the Northeast and Midwestern industrial cities, and it becomes apparent that the United States has a substantial second minority group. They are a minority whose historical, cultural, and linguistic characteristics set them apart from the Anglo community as dramatically as the Negro's skin sets him apart. Few people outside the Southwest realize the degree of discrimination this difference has brought about.

10   For me the introduction to discrimination began 37 years ago when my father brought the family to California from Durango, Mexico. I was nine years old when we settled in San Diego in an extremely poor but well-integrated community of Mexican-Americans, Negroes, and poor Anglos. The trouble was in school. I knew only a dozen words of English, so I just sat around the first few weeks, not understanding a thing. I was not allowed to speak Spanish in class. But after school each day I played with neighborhood kids, so I soon picked up enough English to hold my own on the playground. Then I made this smattering of English do in class.

11   It didn't occur to me or my family to protest. In those days people didn't talk much about ethnic differences or civil rights. The *chicanos* (our favorite nickname for fellow Mexican-Americans) pretty much

stayed "in their place," working as domestics and laborers in the cities or as wetback stoop laborers in the fields and orchards. Only a few became professionals or businessmen.

I remember being advised by my high school counselor to forget my dreams of going to college and becoming a teacher. "They don't hire Mexican-Americans," he said. Then World War II came along, and when I got out of the Army in 1944 the G.I. Bill of Rights saw me through San Diego College. I got a teaching job and eventually became a junior high school principal in San Diego. But my experience was a rare one for the times.

Since then, conditions have changed a good deal. There is spirit in the Mexican-American community now. On my recent trip I saw a pride in the young people that was not so evident when I was growing up. The *chicano* today is proud of his role as an American. Many parents, even those who are illiterate, as were mine, are determined that their children will not be like them. And they see education as the means. But along with their determination has come a new impatience. Gone is the meek, long-suffering separateness of the *chicanos*. They are beginning to stand up and make their voices heard.

Hands Across the Sea
Alexander Woollcott

Woollcott uses personal experience, presented in narrative form, to substantiate two theses. One thesis (paragraph 1) is that it is "the small, unimportant days" we remember, not the events that might find their way into history books. To demonstrate this point, Woollcott, writing about World War I, tells a story not about a major battle but about an incident that has "no part in history at all," an incident depicting everyday characteristics of human nature: boredom, resentment at being ordered around, the tendency to take advantage of others.

Woollcott's second thesis is implied by the narrative itself, not openly stated. The sequence of events demonstrates that an apparently pointless everyday incident can contain a very dramatic meaning. You have to wait until later, until the whole story unfolds, to see what the meaning of apparently meaningless experiences will be.

The night of the strange, swift inspection, held under a fitful light at all of the camps which American troops had pitched in the mud of Brittany.

1   In the World War, when chance made me a spellbound witness of some great occasions, some part of me—the incorrigible journalist, I suppose—kept saying: "This will be something to remember. This will be something to remember." Well, it seems I was wrong about that. I find I do not often think of the war at all, and when I do, it is the small, unimportant days that come drifting back, the ones that have no part in history at all. For example, of late my thoughts have taken unaccountably to jogging back along the road to Savenay, an ancient Breton village of steep, cobbled streets, and windmills that still, I suppose, turn sleepily against the sunset sky. And here I am, bent to the task of telling you about the evening of the strange inspection there.

2   It was at Savenay, in August of '17, that the base hospital recruited at the Post-Graduate in New York was established, with an enlisted personnel consisting, to an impressive extent, of bouncing undergraduates from Princeton and Rutgers who had enlisted early in May in order to escape the June exams. This frustrated group was part of a shipment of two thousand soldiers who sailed stealthily from Hoboken on a hot morning in July aboard the *Saratoga*, which aged transport got as far as Staten Island before being rammed and sunk. A week later, the same outfit tried again with another boat and got as far as Savenay. Then followed an interminable and corrupting wait through that bleak autumn of '17 when the war seemed to stretch ahead of us as a sterile condition of life of which we, at least, would never see the end. A time when only the real stalwarts were strong enough to keep from becoming silly or servile or both. A time of inaction and suspense and only the most sporadic and belated news from home. A time when no rumor could be too monstrous to be believed.

3   I emphasize this matter of rumors riding on every wind which came up the valley of the Loire only so that you may remember what tinder we all were for wild surmise, and what an outbreak of fantastic speculation there must have been one frosty December afternoon when, just after sundown, the bugles began blowing a summons which none of us, as we came tumbling out of quarters, could account for. "Line up, everybody! Line up! Line up!" This from the sergeants, all con-

scientiously gruff and authoritative, exhorting us and pushing us in any order into hastily formed queues which at once began shuffling docilely along in the quick-gathering darkness. Within sight, there were several such lines, each apparently working its way up to an appointed table, where there seemed to be muster-rolls spread out. We caught the gleam from officers' caps, bent in candle-lit conference. At the table, the line would pause for a moment, then move on and be swallowed up in the darkness. During this pause a light would flash on and off, on and off, like a winking beacon. What was up? It seemed to be some new kind of inspection. A curious hour for any kind. It was like a nightmare pay-day. But we had just *been* paid the week before. Perhaps the fool quartermaster wanted his francs back. Too late. Too late. There was smothered laughter, and a few foul but constructive suggestions as to what the quartermaster could do if he felt so inclined. A distant line had started up a song, and in a moment you could hear nothing else in the courtyard. It was that fine old pessimistic refrain to the tune of "Glory Hallelujah":

> *Every day we sign the pay-roll,*
> *Every day we sign the pay-roll,*
> *Every day we sign the pay-roll,*
> > *But we never get a*
> > *God-damned cent.*

4   By this time my place in line was so far advanced that I could see something of what was going on. As each soldier reached the table, his name would be checked on the roll. Then he would be told to spread his hands on the table, palms down. An electric flash would spotlight them. The officers all bent low to examine them. Then palms up. Again the light. Again the close inspection. And that was all. No more than that. Well, for Christ's sake, was it leprosy they thought we had *this* time? The soldier would move on, bewildered. The next man would take his place. A moment later my own hands were spread out. By now the entire outfit was humming with surmise. It was a kind of off-stage hubbub with only the recurrent word "hands" distinguishable. Hands. Hands. Hands. Why did they want to see our hands? From the gossipy orderly in the adjutant's office we learned there had been a telephone call from the base and within half an hour, every hand in that outfit was being checked. Patients', orderlies', doctors', cooks', mechanics', everybody's. Except the nurses'.

5   We drifted out through the gate onto the road to Nantes. It lay hard as flint in the frost, white as snow in the light of the new-risen moon. Across the fields was a camp of the Seventeenth Engineers. There, too, the same puzzled line was forming, writhing. The same candle-lit table, the same winking flashlight. They were looking at all the American hands in Savenay. We later learned that, at that same moment,

in Nantes, some thirty kilometers away, and in all the camps pitched in the frozen mud outside St. Nazaire, the same swift inspection was going on. Also, still later, we learned why. In a barn near the port that afternoon, a fourteen-year-old girl in a torn black smock had been found unconscious. She had been raped. They could learn from her only that she had been dragged there by a soldier in a brown uniform, and that, while she was struggling with him, she had caught his hand and bitten it. Bitten it until she tasted blood.

6   Well, that is the story. Not, as you see, an important one. It was unrelated to the major forces launched to make the world safe for democracy. But, every now and again, some sight of a line shuffling in the torch-lit darkness—a not altogether unfamiliar sight in *this* rescued democracy—some Proustian invocation of a bygone moment brings it all back to me.

7   And the end of the story? You want to know, perhaps, whether they found a man with a bitten hand. Yes, they did.

The Comics
on the Couch
Gerald Clarke

Clarke's thesis is that even the comics have gone "relevant." They have left behind their traditional plots and characterizations and are concerning themselves with the real problems of modern life. They are now talking about poverty, race relations, politics, countercultures. Their heroes are becoming more like the rest of us. Superman, who isn't so super any more, has identity hang-ups and is tempted to seek the comfort of a psychiatrist's couch.

Clarke's evidence is exactly what you would expect—illustrations from the comics themselves—and the nature of this evidence influences his tone. He keeps his sense of humor and avoids drawing heavy conclusions. His purpose is limited to demonstrating that an important change has occurred in American comic-book culture.

Source. "The Comics on the Couch" by Gerald Clarke. From *Time*, December 13, 1971. Reprinted by permission from TIME, The Weekly Newsmagazine; Copyright Time Inc. 1971.

1 He was someone you could always count on, the savior of the helpless and oppressed, society's sword against the forces of evil and injustice. He could, among other things, "hurdle skyscrapers, leap an eighth of a mile, run faster than a streamline train—and nothing less than a bursting shell could penetrate his skin." He was, in short, a good buy for a dime. Even by today's hyped-up standards, Superman was quite a guy.

2 Yes, was. The man of steel that many Americans grew up with is not what he used to be. For one thing, his alter ego, Clark Kent, has given up the *Daily Planet* to become a newscaster for the Galaxy Broadcasting System, getting in and out of blue tights and red cape during commercial breaks. ("Personally, I still prefer Walter Cronkite," a mini-skirted Lois tells him. She, at least, is unchanged—as obnoxious as ever.) For another, Superman has succumbed to urban jitters; he obviously needs to spend some time on the couch. Just listen to some of his recent complaints: "I'm finished being anybody's Superman! . . . For years I've been dreaming of working and living as a plain man—without the responsibilities, the loneliness of Superman . . . I've a right to bitterness. No man has a better right. I've denied myself the comforts of home and family to continue helping these ingrates. I thought they admired me—for myself! I've lived in a fool's paradise!"

3 Superhang-ups for a superhero, but Superman is not the only hero hanging his cape outside Dr. Feelgood's door. Today almost all comic-book characters have problems. As in many fields, the word is relevance. The trend may have begun a decade ago, but in the socially

Source. "Superman" © 1971 DC Comics Inc.

aware '70s it has reached full blossom. The comics' caped crusaders have become as outraged about racial injustice as the congressional Black Caucas and as worried about pollution as the Sierra Club. Archfiends with memorable names like the Hulk and Dr. Doom are still around, but they are often pushed off the page by such new villains as air pollution and social injustice. Sometimes, indeed, the comics read like a *New York Times Illustrated*.

4   Recently the comics have discovered yet another field—a mixture of science fiction and the occult that lies somewhere beyond Consciousness III. In a comic book called *The New Gods*, for example, the forces of the good, the beautiful, under-30s, battle the forces of evil, the ugly militarists of Apokolips, in weird sequences that look and read like nightmares. Whatever they are doing, American comics, both the books and the strips, are full of life. In their 75th year, they are bursting—WUMP, BOMP, OOF! and ZAP!—from the page in a dozen new directions.

5   Along with responsibility has come respectability. One of the newest things about the new comics is that more than ever before they are being taken seriously as an art form by critics and as an authentic cultural expression by sociologists. Half a dozen or so learned histories have been written about them, and art galleries give them serious exhibitions. The comics have been included in courses at Brown University, and the creators of the new styles, particularly Marvel Comics' Stan Lee, who invented the idiom, are mobbed like rock stars on the campuses. So popular is Lee, in fact, that he will give a kind of sound and light show at Carnegie Hall next month.

6   Not all of the comics are trying to be with it, of course. *Blondie,* a strip that is syndicated in 1,164 newspapers and is one of the most widely read series in the world, still exists in a timeless never-never land of middleclass clichés where only Daisy the dog seems to have a spark of intelligence. Despite wrist TVs and spaceships, Dick Tracy continues to chase odd-looking crooks like Retsen Nester, a bald-domed, bespectacled type who hides heroin in volumes of Mother Goose. In the same old way, Little Orphan Annie and Sandy still fight the Red Menace and bleeding-heart liberals, and will probably continue to do so well into the 21st century. In a recent episode Annie was trying to find a poor but honest person who needed only Daddy Warbucks' "survival kit," $11,000, to make good. Daddy, a billionaire, is convinced that the "good old-fashioned pioneer spirit that made this country great is not dead" but "just kinda takin' a nap."

7   Many of the other oldtimers, however, have changed just about everything but their costumes. Evil, they are discovering, was much easier to spot when it had a funny name and wore an ugly mask. In a recent comic-book adventure, the Green Lantern collars a kid who has been beating up a fat man. But after being bombarded with garbage

by the kid's ghetto neighbors, the Emerald Crusader learns that the man he has saved is a corrupt slumlord who is about to tear down the block for a parking lot. "I been readin' about you," says an old black who is soon to be evicted. "How you work for the blue skins and how on a planet someplace you helped out the orange skins, and you done considerable for the purple skins. Only there's skins you never bothered with—the black skins! I want to know: How come? Answer me that, Mr. Green Lantern!"

8   Now it's no good just to zap a few uglies either, as of yore. The Green Lantern and his superhero colleagues are constantly being reminded these days that the funny fiends are just front men for some very unfunny social ills. The Green Lantern and his chum, the Green Arrow, are lectured by a youthful victim: "Drugs are a symptom, and you, like the rest of society, attack the symptom, not the disease." Another big change has been the introduction of black characters, who now appear in such strips as *Peanuts, Archie, Li'l Abner* and *Beetle Bailey; Friday Foster*, a swinging soul sister from Harlem, has a strip all her own. Until a few years ago, the color barrier blocked all but a few Negro caricatures from the comics.

9   When it comes to politics, *Li'l Abner* and *Pogo*, which have satirized it for years, are at least as up to date as the men in Washington. Two characters that bear a remarkable resemblance to Senators Hubert Humphrey and Hugh Scott were recently dispatched to Li'l Abner's Dogpatch to learn why it is the one pollution-free spot in the U.S. Reason: the Gobbleglops, which look like pigs with bunny tails, gobble up, in the words of Mammy Yokum, "all glop, irregardless . . . They's natcheral-born incinerators. Thass why glop goes in 'em an' none comes out!!" *Pogo* has been invaded in recent months by an odd beast, half Great Dane and half hyena, that looks and alliterates like Spiro T. Agnew, by a bulldog that might be taken for J. Edgar Hoover, and by a pipe-smoking, improbable baby eagle that might fool even Martha Mitchell into thinking she had seen John. This trio of animal crackers spends most of its time trying to decipher messages from an unseen chief who chooses to communicate by means of undecipherable paper dolls. "Dashing deep digging thought dominates his delectable display," asserts the Spiroesque Great Dane-hyena, who wears the uniform—or half the uniform—of a Greek colonel.

0   While the political spectrum of the regular comic strips ranges from the moderately liberal (*Pogo*) to the arch-conservative (*Little Orphan Annie*), a relatively new phenomenon, underground comics, is pursuing radical political and sexual themes that their aboveground brothers would never dare to touch. Begun in the mid-'60s, the undergrounds, or head comic books, such as *Zap* and *Despair* and strips in papers like the Berkeley *Barb* and Manhattan's *East Village Other,* speak for the counterculture in a zany, raunchy and often obscene idiom. In one

135

Source. Copyright © 1971 Walt Kelly. Courtesy Field Newspaper Syndicate. Permission of Selby Kelly, Executrix.

issue of the *East Village Other,* a strip depicts an Army company in Viet Nam. The sergeant's command "Present arms!" literally brings out the arms of the men in his company, heroin addicts all. Later, when all of the men are dead of overdoses—including the sergeant, whose name is, of course, Smack—it turns out that the CIA is the ultimate pusher. "Put it this way," says the agency's spook in charge, "we consider this something of an investment." . . .

Source. © R. Crumb.

11   With a few exceptions—*Wonder Woman* was into Women's Lib 20 years before Betty Friedan—the comics have always appealed to men more than women, to little boys more than little girls. One reason is the inevitable boy companion that the ten-year-old could identify with—*Batman's* Boy Wonder Robin, the Sandman's Sandy, the Shield's Rusty, to name only a few. Even when the ten-year-old identified too closely with that clever brat on paper as a rival, it was good for sales. Cartoonist Jules Feiffer, who has lately turned to writing for the theater and the movies (*Carnal Knowledge*), was both repelled and drawn to the Boy Wonder. "One need only look at him," Feiffer writes, "to see he could fight better, swing from a rope better, play ball better, eat better, and live better. For while I lived in the East Bronx, Robin lived in a mansion, and while I was trying somehow to please my mother—and getting it all wrong—Robin was rescuing Batman and getting the gold medals. You can imagine how pleased I was when, years later, I heard he was a fag."

12   Feiffer's was a love-hate relationship that the comic books lost for a while in the '50s and early '60s, when sales dropped and the industry appeared headed for extinction. In a world where almost anything was possible and usually visible on a 21-in. screen, outracing a locomotive or buzzing around like an ugly bug in drag seemed somehow tame and tedious. Young readers today, the comic men soon discovered, are more interested in their own problems and the problems they see around them. It is possible, indeed, to see the comics as an art of the people, offering clues to the national unconscious. Superman's enormous popularity might be looked upon as signaling the beginning of the end for the Horatio Alger myth of the self-made man. In the modern world, he seems to say, only the man with superpowers can survive and prosper. Still, though comics are indeed a popular art form, it is going a bit far to compare, as Critic Maurice Horn does, *Gasoline Alley* to Goethe's *Wilhelm Meister* and *Little Orphan Annie* to the works of Charles Dickens and Victor Hugo. As Mammy Yokum might say: "Some folks don't know when to stop."

13   Walt Kelly, still one of the best cartoonists, is a more solid expert on the genre. "A comic strip is like a dream," Turtle tells Bear in *Pogo*. "A tissue of paper reveries. It gloms an' glimmers its way thru unreality, fancy an' fantasy." To which Bear naturally responds: "Sho' 'nuff?" Sho' 'nuff.

The No-Child Family: Going Against 100,000 Years of Biology
Rita Kramer

This article looks for a *causal explanation* of an aspect of human behavior. It raises the question of whether married couples who decide not to have children do so because they are "immature, self-centered egotists," or because they are "responsible adults considering the consequences of their decisions" (paragraph 18). Two kinds of evidence are presented: (1) the statements of the childless wives and husbands themselves, given in their own words so that we can judge whether they sound like immature egotists or responsible adults; and (2) the opinions of experts on human behavior—psychiatrists, psychoanalysts, psychologists—presented in their own words so that we can judge them also. Kramer herself avoids giving any answer to a question about which the experts disagree. Her conclusion is only that the increasing frankness about such issues ought to help people make the decisions that will be best for their individual lives.

Does the evidence she presents warrant any stronger conclusion? What do you think the motives of the "childfree" couples are?

1 Cathy and Wayne N. are in their late 20's, have been married five years, and are childless. The last time a member of Cathy's family asked, "When are you going to start a family?" her answer was, "*We're* a family!"

2 Cathy and Wayne belong to a growing number of young married couples who are deciding not to have children. A recent survey showed that in the last five years the percentage of wives aged 25 to 29 who did not want children had almost doubled and among those 18 to 24 it had almost tripled. What lies behind this decision which seems to fly in the face of biology and society?

3 Perhaps the most publicly outspoken childless (or "childfree" as they like to put it) couple are Ellen Peck, author of *The Baby Trap*,

and her husband William, an advertising executive who is president of the National Organization for Non-Parents, which the Pecks founded last year to defend the social and economic interests of what they feel is a discriminated-against minority group: couples without children. The Pecks insist neither they nor the organization are against parenthood, just against the social pressures that push people into parenthood whether it is what they really want and need or not.

4   "It's a life-style choice," Ellen says. "We chose freedom and spontaneity, privacy and leisure. It's also a question of where you want to give your efforts—within your own family or in the larger community. This generation faces serious questions about the continuity of life on earth as well as its quality. Our grandchildren may have to buy tickets to see the last redwoods or line up to get their oxygen ration. There are men who complain about being caught in a traffic jam for hours on their way home to their five kids but can't make the association between the children and the traffic jam. In a world seriously threatened by the consequences of overpopulation we're concerned with making life without children acceptable and respectable. Too many children are born as a result of cultural coercion. And the results show up in the statistics on divorce and child-abuse."

5   Her husband adds, "Every friend, relative and business associate is pressuring you to have kids 'and find out what you're missing.' Too many people discover too late that what they were missing was something they were totally unsuited for."

6   And Ellen again: "From the first doll to soap operas to cocktail parties, the pressure is always there to be parents. But let's take a look at the rate of parental failure. Perhaps parenthood should be regarded as a specialized occupation like being a doctor. Some people are good at it and they should have children; others aren't, and they should feel they have other alternatives."

7   Less evangelical than the Pecks, who appear regularly in the media extolling the virtues of nonparenthood, but equally convinced that having children is not for them, a number of young husbands and wives who were asked about their decision not to have children made these comments:

8   *The main reason we enjoy our lives together is because we are together. I am not in the kitchen washing baby bottles while he thinks of an excuse to get out of the house because the baby is screaming.*

9   *The thing I find amusing is there are people our age with two or three children, struggling along, and they tell us we are missing something. Meanwhile we ride in a new car, own our own lakefront home, spend our summers on our boat, go away every weekend, and spend every Christmas holiday skiing in Europe. And they tell us we are missing something.*

10   *I'm sure there are some very happy families with children, but the*

unhappy ones far outnumber the happy ones. I don't want to take that chance.

11   *Most married people I know had no choice. They were programed to have three children and be Cub Scout leaders. Then there are those of us who stop to think about the big fantastic world out there waiting to be explored. I feel that most people are so busy washing diapers and trying to balance the budget that they merely exist and look around them, but never see. They're too busy wiping runny noses.*

12   *After five years, both sets of parents are putting on the pressure for us to have kids. They have taken to calling our cat and two dogs their "grandchildren."*

13   *A man's life isn't anywhere near as greatly altered as a woman's once the baby arrives. He may need to increase his earnings, but there is still the job, a productive life outside. The woman will have to sacrifice many things. I would feel trapped in that role.*

14   *It's depressing how crucial my sister and I are to my mother—she more or less lives for us. I will never let that happen to me.*

15   *I want to live my life while I'm young. My parents were always telling me that after my younger brother and I were out of school they would do all the things they wanted to do. My father will be 60 by the time my brother's out of college.*

16   *I don't think it's selfish to stay childless. Who are your hurting? It would be worse to become pregnant and not really want the baby. It might start out as a great ego trip, but all you'd wind up with would be problems.*

17   *When we say we don't want kids, people ask us, "What if everyone felt the way you do?" What a silly question.*

18   Are these the voices of immature, self-centered egotists or of responsible adults considering the consequences of their decisions?

19   Professional observers agree that many people have children for the wrong reasons, sometimes for no reason at all. Men often drift into fatherhood without ever making a deliberate choice. For many women pregnancy can be a way to escape from unresolved conflicts, to achieve instant identity or strengthen a poor self image, to gratify a need for the attention and affection they feel they never had as children.

20   I talked with a number of specialists in the field of human behavior about what these couples had said. Their reactions varied widely. A family therapist described the decision not to have children as "a basic instinctual response to the world situation today," implying that something like the herd instinct in animals was operating as a response to the dangers of overpopulation, crowding, pollution and nuclear war, causing women to feel a reluctance to reproduce and leading them to seek new ways of realizing themselves outside of family life.

21   More than one psychiatrist suggested that those who want to remain

childless are narcissistic—making a virtue out of necessity by rationalizing their inner conflicts about giving care *vs.* being taken care of. "These are people who can't tolerate the idea of caring for children, who have no margin of love to spare them," said one, adding, "You're going against something with 100,000 years of biology behind it." A colleague of his chimed in, "Well, we all rationalize our deficits, and these people probably *shouldn't* have children whatever their real motives are, for the same reason there ought to be liberal abortion laws. There should only be enthusiastic parents in this world."

22 Some observers suggest that perhaps what we are seeing is not a real change at all, that, like the sexual revolution, it is not really a revolution in behavior but in expression. "It may be," says one Connecticut psychoanalyst, "that an identifiable group that has existed all along is simply coming out of the closet, like homosexuals or swingers. The spirit of the time is to do your own thing and not hide it, and these people may reflect an increased frankness and openness rather than any real change."

23 Dr. Helen Kaplan, associate professor of psychiatry at The New York Hospital—Cornell Medical Center and head of its Sexual Disorder Program, thinks there has been a kind of sexual revolution and that what it amounts to is the separation of morality and sexuality. "Sex used to be permissible only for purposes of procreation in marriage. We no longer think it is immoral to have sex without having children and that leaves couples with a choice about whether they want to have them or not. They no longer have to feel guilty about not wanting it."

24 Dr. Kaplan believes there is a strong maternal urge in many women from early childhood on—"and it's not just culturally determined, either"—but that women vary tremendously in their degree of maternal need. And while women who experience deep maternal drives can't give up having children without feeling a real sense of deprivation, not all women feel this way.

25 Psychologist Donald M. Kaplan (no relation to Helen) believes that while some people have always opted not to have children, the increased frequency we are seeing is in those children of the nineteen-forties and fifties who were raised by parents whose character style had shifted from what sociologist David Riesman called "inner-directed" to "other-directed," and that these other-directed parents had two relevant effects on their children. One was to give them a greater feeling of "narcissistic entitlement"—what one expects from life. The other was the loss of a sense of certainty. They are more open to self-doubt, he says, more preoccupied with their bodies, their life-styles, less able to maintain stable attachments to others. The decision to have a baby, he thinks, is the kind of decision such people might be most likely to postpone. It can't be modified, can't be undone.

26   "Many of these young adults are ambivalent about relinquishing the role of the one who is cared for and taking on that of the one who does the caring," says Dr. Kaplan.

27   Dr. E. James Anthony is professor of child psychiatry at Washington University School of Medicine and co-author of "Parenthood, Its Psychology and Psychopathology." In a recent conversation Dr. Anthony said, "Many people I've talked to are very concerned about their own future and the future of children in this rather troubled world. In the past there was always a feeling implicit in the culture that parenthood was something very significant, attractive, enriching, creative. Now it seems to be going by the board. There seem to be so many other opportunities for women to express themselves creatively and family life requires them to give up so many things that the emphasis on family life as a good and creative thing, a way to contribute to the future of the world, doesn't really ring a bell with many young people.

28   "I think that part of what's happening is that the ambivalence of parents today is being passed on unconsciously to their children. Children are a great deal of trouble, and perhaps more so today than ever before. They can be a pain in the neck. Their precocious development, adolescent acting-out, drug-taking, all loom as problems. The young people feel, 'If they don't really want us, why should *we* want to have children?' Then they rationalize this feeling in terms of the external questions like what the world has to offer. They ask questions like, 'Why add to the population explosion? Why create people who will have to face all the problems that are approaching in the next century?'

29   "Just how deeply ingrained are mothering and fathering? Does such a thing as fatherliness really activate men? Can they do without it easily? Some suggest it's just a question of having a fling and then nine months later having to think about the responsibilities of a family. Many young men say they don't feel the need to immortalize themselves in children.

30   "With women, there's the question of what has been called 'the disappointed womb'—whether there is a real need in women to experience something in what Erikson calls that 'inner space.' Many women I talk with are conscious of this kind of enrichment, they talk about being fulfilled in pregnancy, of feeling complete and better than they have ever felt in their lives—but, later, many find handling children is a bit of a nuisance. Still, having a child has been experienced as marvelous, miraculous. What happens if a woman abrogates this experience? It's a much more serious decision for her than for a man. There is something powerful about this basic biological means of creation. To deny oneself may be a little like Beethoven having this powerful talent and being told you must never use it.

31   "Despite their stated motives for not having children, the question arises whether young people really in fact lead richer lives today. I find that many college students today feel strangely empty. They live in a world full of stimuli of all sorts but lack a sense of inner satisfaction that may relate to these basic biologic things."

32   Whatever else they disagree on, the experts all seem to be saying that it's not whether you have children or don't that really matters, what matters is that you are comfortable about what you do. If you don't have children and you have much inner conflict about it, you'll be miserable in your childlessness; if you have children and regret it, you'll be miserable and your children will be miserable too. The point seems to be to know yourself, to accept your deeper feelings and not make such an important life decision because it's the thing to do or to satisfy unrealistic fantasies, or to give your parents what they want or to escape from other responsibilities.

33   Some people are afraid to admit their own feelings of the kind many of the childless couples interviewed could accept about themselves— what they called being "selfish." They are ashamed to admit they would rather travel than bring up children. But what if that *is* what would make them happiest? Deeply held feelings are not easily changed and if you do not recognize what yours really are, you will not make the choices that are right for you.

34   For many, if not most people, the joys of parenthood as well as its problems are what life is all about. To see one's children grow and develop into individuals, and to see oneself continue on in them, can be the richest experience between one's own birth and death. But there are also people for whom living a full life and realizing themselves take other routes. And we live in a time in which attitudes seem to be freeing up in a way which enables increasing numbers of men and women to question the way "everybody" lives if that is not the way that is right for them. The more people continue to ask themselves such questions as whether or not they really want to raise a family before they begin to do so, the fewer unhappy parents and troubled children there will be.

The Macbeth Murder Mystery
James Thurber

Thurber's thesis (unstated) is that different people, looking at precisely the same body of evidence, will come up with different conclusions. His evidence is a personal-experience narrative about a murder-mystery fan who thinks that everyone has missed the clues in Shakespeare's play *Macbeth*.

What assumptions does the "murder specialist" bring to bear in forming the theory that it wasn't Macbeth who killed the old king?

1 "It was a stupid mistake to make," said the American woman I had met at my hotel in the English lake country, "but it was on the counter with the other Penguin books—the little sixpenny ones, you know, with the paper covers—and I supposed of course it was a detective story. All the others were detective stories. I'd read all the others, so I bought this one without really looking at it carefully. You can imagine how mad I was when I found it was Shakespeare." I murmured something sympathetically. "I don't see why the Penguin-books people had to get out Shakespeare plays in the same size and everything as the detective stories," went on my companion. "I think they have different-colored jackets," I said. "Well, I didn't notice that," she said. "Anyway, I got real comfy in bed that night and all ready to read a good mystery story and here I had 'The Tragedy of Macbeth'—a book for high-school students. Like 'Ivanhoe.' " "Or 'Lorna Doone,' " I said. "Exactly," said the American lady. "And I was just crazy for a good Agatha Christie, or something. Hercule Poirot is my favorite detective." "Is he the rabbity one?" I asked. "Oh, no," said my crime-fiction expert. "He's the Belgian one. You're thinking of Mr. Pinkerton, the one that helps Inspector Bull. He's good, too."

2 Over her second cup of tea my companion began to tell the plot of a detective story that had fooled her completely—it seems it was the old family doctor all the time. But I cut in on her. "Tell me," I said. "Did you read 'Macbeth'?" "I *had* to read it," she said. "There wasn't a scrap of anything else to read in the whole room." "Did you

Source. The Macbeth Murder Mystery by James Thurber. Copyright © 1942 James Thurber. Copyright © 1970 Helen W. Thurber and Rosemary Thurber Sauers. From *My World and Welcome To It*, published by Harcourt Brace Jovanovich. Originally printed in *The New Yorker*. Reprinted by permission of Mrs. James Thurber.

like it?" I asked. "No, I did not," she said, decisively. "In the first place, I don't think for a moment that Macbeth did it." I looked at her blankly. "Did what?" I asked. "I don't think for a moment that he killed the King," she said. "I don't think the Macbeth woman was mixed up in it, either. You suspect them the most, of course, but those are the ones that are never guilty—or shouldn't be anyway." "I'm afraid," I began, "that I—" "But don't you see?" said the American lady. "It would spoil everything if you could figure out right away who did it. Shakespeare was too smart for that. I've read that people never *have* figured out 'Hamlet,' so it isn't likely Shakespeare would have made 'Macbeth' as simple as it seems." I thought this over while I filled my pipe. "Who do you suspect?" I asked, suddenly. "Macduff," she said, promptly. "Good God!" I whispered, softly.

3   "Oh Macduff did it, all right," said the murder specialist. "Hercule Poirot would have got him easily." "How did you figure it out?" I demanded. "Well," she said, "I didn't right away. At first I suspected Banquo. And then, of course, he was the second person killed. That was good right in there, that part. The person you suspect of the first murder should always be the second victim." "Is that so?" I murmured. "Oh, yes," said my informant. "They have to keep surprising you. Well, after the second murder I didn't know *who* the killer was for a while." "How about Malcolm and Donalbain, the King's sons?" I asked. "As I remember it, they fled right after the first murder. That looks suspicious." "Too suspicious," said the American lady. "Much too suspicious. When they flee, they're never guilty. You can count on that." "I believe," I said, "I'll have a brandy," and I summoned the waiter. My companion leaned toward me, her eyes bright, her teacup quivering. "Do you know who discovered Duncan's body?" she demanded. I said I was sorry, but I had forgotten. "Macduff discovers it," she said, slipping into the historical present. "Then he comes running downstairs and shouts, 'Confusion has broke open the Lord's anointed temple' and 'Sacrilegious murder has made his masterpiece' and on and on like that." The good lady tapped me on the knee. "All that stuff was rehearsed," she said. "You wouldn't say a lot of stuff like that, offhand, would you—if you had found a body?" She fixed me with a glittering eye. "I—" I began. "You're right!" she said. "You wouldn't! Unless you had practiced it in advance. 'My God, there's a body in here!' is what an innocent man would say." She sat back with a confident glare.

4   I thought for a while. "But what do you make of the Third Murderer?" I asked, "You know, the Third Murderer has puzzled 'Macbeth' scholars for three hundred years." "That's because they never thought of Macduff," said the American lady. "It was Macduff, I'm certain. You couldn't have one of the victims murdered by two ordinary thugs—the murderer always has to be somebody important."

"But what about the banquet scene?" I asked, after a moment. "How do you account for Macbeth's guilty actions there, when Banquo's ghost came in and sat in his chair?" The lady leaned forward and tapped me on the knee again. "There wasn't any ghost," she said. "A big, strong man like that doesn't go around seeing ghosts—especially in a brightly lighted banquet hall with dozens of people around. Macbeth was *shielding somebody*!" "Who was he shielding?" I asked. "Mrs. Macbeth, of course," she said. "He thought she did it and he was going to take the rap himself. The husband always does that when the wife is suspected." "But what," I demanded, "about the sleep-walking scene, then?" "The same thing, only the other way around," said my companion. "That time *she* was shielding *him*. She wasn't asleep at all. Do you remember where it says, 'Enter Lady Macbeth with a taper'?" "Yes," I said. "Well, people who walk in their sleep *never carry lights*!" said my fellow-traveler. "They have a second sight. Did you ever hear of a sleepwalker carrying a light?" "No," I said, "I never did." "Well, then, she wasn't asleep. She was acting guilty to shield Macbeth." "I think," I said, "I'll have another brandy," and I called the waiter. When he brought it, I drank it rapidly and rose to go. "I believe," I said, "that you have got hold of something. Would you lend me that 'Macbeth'? I'd like to look it over tonight. I don't feel, somehow, as if I'd ever really read it." "I'll get it for you," she said. "But you'll find that I am right."

5   I read the play over carefully that night, and the next morning, after breakfast, I sought out the American woman. She was on the putting green, and I came up behind her silently and took her arm. She gave an exclamation. "Could I see you alone?" I asked, in a low voice. She nodded cautiously and followed me to a secluded spot. "You've found out something?" she breathed. "I've found out," I said, triumphantly, "the name of the murderer!" "You mean it wasn't Macduff?" she said, "Macduff is as innocent of those murders," I said, "as Macbeth and the Macbeth woman." I opened the copy of the play, which I had with me, and turned to Act II, Scene 2. "Here," I said, "you will see where Lady Macbeth says, 'I laid their daggers ready. He could not miss 'em. Had he not resembled my father as he slept, I had done it.' Do you see?" "No," said the American woman, bluntly, "I don't." "But it's simple!" I exclaimed. "I wonder I didn't see it years ago. The reason Duncan resembled Lady Macbeth's father as he slept is that *it actually was her father!*" "Good God!" breathed my companion, softly. "Lady Macbeth's father killed the King," I said, "and, hearing someone coming, thrust the body under the bed and crawled into the bed himself." "But," said the lady, "you can't have a murderer who only appears in the story once. You can't have that." "I know that," I said, and I turned to Act II, Scene 4. "It says here, 'Enter Ross with an old Man.' Now, that old man is never

identified and it is my contention he was old Mr. Macbeth, whose ambition it was to make his daughter Queen. There you have your motive." "But even then," cried the American lady, "he's still a minor character!" "Not," I said, gleefully, "when you realize that he was also *one of the weird sisters in disguise!*" "You mean one of the three witches?" "Precisely," I said. "Listen to this speech of the old man's. 'On Tuesday last, a falcon towering in her pride of place, was by a mousing owl hawk'd at and kill'd.' Who does that sound like?" "It sounds like the way the three witches talk," said my companion, reluctantly. "Precisely!" I said again. "Well," said the American woman, "maybe you're right, but—" "I'm sure I am," I said. "And do you know what I'm going to do now?" "No," she said. "What?" "Buy a copy of 'Hamlet,' " I said, "and solve *that*!" My companion's eye brightened. "Then," she said, "you don't think Hamlet did it?" "I am," I said, "absolutely positive he didn't." "But who," she demanded, "do you suspect?" I looked at her cryptically. "Everybody," I said, and disappeard into a small grove of trees as silently as I had come.

Hi-yo Silver, Away!
Martha Kendall

Kendall's subject is Tonto, the Lone Ranger's faithful Indian companion. Almost everybody has heard of him, but nobody seems to know to what Indian tribe he belongs. In paragraph 2 Kendall states her thesis, first in the form of a question— "Who was that Indian?"—and then in the form of an answer— "Tonto's identity is as enigmatic as the Ranger's." The only clue to Tonto's tribal origin is the phrase *kemo sabe*, and, Kendall claims, "no one actually knows what it means."

The rest of the essay defends the thesis that Tonto's identity cannot be pinned down. Kendall moves from the theory that the key phrase *kemo sabe* is Spanish (paragraphs 3-4) to the theory that it is Indian (paragraphs 5-23). This second theory takes a number of different shapes. Was Tonto a Western

Source. "Hi-yo Silver, Away!" by Martha Kendall. Copyright 1977 Smithsonian Institution, from *Smithsonian* magazine, September 1977. Reprinted by permission of *Smithsonian* magazine.

Apache, a Potawatomi, a Tewa, a Yavapai, a Cree, a Paiute, an Osage, or a Tunica? Kendall tells us the story of her efforts to find out. Her essay thus demonstrates that **narrative** (see p. 7) can be an effective way of organizing evidence.

1   As a child, I was a Lone Ranger *aficionada*. Weekday afternoons at 4:30 the "daring and resourceful masked rider of the Plains" and his faithful Indian companion rode into my life on the family's small-screen television set. As they rode away half an hour later, some minor character from that day's episode inevitably turned to a more knowledgeable other and asked, "Who *was* that masked man?" We in the audience, of course, already knew.

2   But who was that *Indian*? Twenty years had passed and I had earned a PhD in anthropology, with a specialty in American Indian languages, before I realized that Tonto's identity is as enigmatic as the Ranger's. His tribal origin is unknown. He comes from nowhere. He has no Indian friends; he has a horse named Scout. The only clue to his past is a single phrase from an unidentified language: *kemo sabe*, and no one actually knows what it means.

3   Most of my contemporaries seem to think it means "white man" or "friend," but they hazard such guesses on the basis of narrative context more than anything else. A few people suggest that it might be a corruption of Spanish *quien lo sabe?*, "who knows?," or better yet, *el que lo sabe*, "he who knows," "the one who knows." Those who offer this hypothesis bolster it by arguing that *tonto* itself is a perfectly good Spanish word meaning "stupid" or "crazy," and by noting that the Lone Ranger stories are set in just those states where one might expect Indians and lawmen to have some minimal knowledge of Spanish. While this theory is plausible linguistically, it creates a curious impression of the relationship between our two heroes: one habitually calls the other "he who knows" and is addressed as "stupid" in return. If we accept a Spanish etymology for *kemo sabe*, then the Lone Ranger becomes a racist and Tonto a redskinned Stepin Fetchit.

4   It is more logical to assume that *kemo sabe* is an American Indian term; but to claim this is to broaden the field of possibilities, not to narrow it. When white men reached the New World, there were 220-odd mutually unintelligible languages native to America north of the Rio Grande alone—quite a linguistic haystack in which to search for etymological needles. Still, the puzzle intrigued me, so I set out to discover what I could of the mysterious greeting.

5   I reread 10 of the 12 Lone Ranger dime novels that appeared in the 1930s and '40s, looking for clues to Tonto's tribal group. As far as I

could tell, he is never specifically identified with any particular Indian nation, though he seems able to converse in several dialects. From his name and from the setting of the Lone Ranger tales, I first assumed he was a Western Apache, probably a Tonto Apache, but this notion evaporated in the face of counterevidence contained in *The Lone Ranger and the Renegade Savage* (1946). In this adventure the Lone Ranger and Tonto are charged with pacifying the famous Chiricahua Apache chief Geronimo. I was chagrined to learn in the course of reading this story that Tonto could neither converse with nor understand Geronimo, demonstrating conclusively that he could never have been a Western Apache. Western Apaches speak a variant of Apache recognizably distinct from that of the Chiricahuas; nevertheless, the two dialects are similar enough linguistically to be mutually intelligible.

6   Frustrated with this line of pursuit, I tried writing letters to Clayton Moore and Jay Silverheels, who played the Lone Ranger and Tonto respectively in the television serial. I never expected replies from either of them, reasoning that they were heartily sick of being queried about the term *kemo sabe*. My expectations were entirely accurate.

7   I had more success with the Popular Culture Center at Bowling Green University in Ohio. They responded that *kemo sabe* is discussed in Jim Harmon's book *The Great Radio Heroes* (Doubleday, 1967), where it is translated "faithful friend" or "trusty scout." I eagerly read Harmon's chapter on the Lone Ranger and Tonto, only to find that the Indian's nationality is as much a mystery to Harmon as to myself. All he says of Tonto's background, really, is that his dialect is "unique."

8   In the meantime, I located an article entitled "Hi-Yo, Silver," by J. Bryan III, in the *Saturday Evening Post* for October 14, 1939. It contained the startling information that Tonto is supposed to be, theoretically at least, a Potawatomi. I wondered what an Indian from the Great Lakes Region would be doing in the American Southwest and how he would have gotten to know the deserts so well if he had grown up in Michigan with his tribe, but in fiction anything is possible.

9   I learned from Bryan's piece that Tonto's creator, Francis Striker, hailed from Buffalo, New York, and had never been west of that city until he was brought to Detroit to write the famous *Lone Ranger* serial for radio station WXYZ in 1932. He had written several successful radio shows before that, one of which featured a "semi-savage" named Gobo. Apparently, Gobo was metamorphosed into Tonto because the Lone Ranger needed a companion. The poor lawman had appeared alone in nine radio episodes, talking only to himself or to his horse—a practice that necessarily limited opportunities for dramatic scripting. ("They're all around us, boy!" "Whinney.") As to the mystery of *kemo sabe*, Bryan noted that Striker's letters to children always began, "Ta-i ke-mo sah-bee" ("Greetings, trusty scout"). In other words,

Striker made it up. "Ta-i ke-mo sah-bee" is as similar to Potawatomi as "hiya, pal" is to Chinese.

10   Just to tuck in the loose ends, I asked Ives Goddard of the Smithsonian Institution if *kemo sabe* could possibly be from Potawatomi or from a language related to it, since he specializes in that language group. (We were standing around at a conference on American Indian languages in San Francisco.) He said he had heard that theory too, but no, the phrase definitely was not Algonquian in origin. I was about to tell him all about Gobo, when he added "It's Tewa."

11   I couldn't believe my ears. After months of letter-writing and novel-reading, after hours of watching *Lone Ranger* reruns and phoning local television stations to query them about Tonto, I found someone else who not only cared about *kemo sabe*, but also could identify the language it is from. As it turned out, Dr. Goddard and I were not alone. Four or five other serious scholars were interested in the problem, even if only half-seriously. Two provided plausible American Indian sources for the phrase.

12   Goddard had discovered that in J. P. Harrington's "The Ethnogeography of the Tewa Indians," which appeared in 1916 in the *29th Annual Report of the Bureau of American Ethnology*, a Smithsonian Institution publication, a list of Tewa words for other tribes and peoples includes these items:

> "APACHE. *Sabe* of obscure etymology. This is applied to every kind of Apache or Athapascan, including the Navaho. See Chiricahua Apache, Coyotero Apache, Jicarilla Apache, Llanero Apache" . . . . (p. 573).

> "FRIEND. *Kema* 'friend'." (p. 574).

Just above the entry for FRIEND is one reading:

> "COYOTERO APACHE. *Kojoteru, Kojoterusabe* (*Kojoteru* Span. Coyotero; *Sabe* 'Apache')."

It seems incredible, but the words *kema* and *sabe* actually do appear in juxtaposed entries in Harrington's work.

13   Striker, then, may have wanted some authentic American Indian words for Tonto to speak and consequently searched for a book containing native American words short and simple enough for a children's program. Assuming that Striker had wanted Tonto to be a Southwestern Indian, since the masked man was a Texas Ranger, he might have been attracted to a book on the Tewa, who live along the Rio Grande in New Mexico (with one small ethnic outpost among the Hopi in Arizona). While Harrington's monograph on Tewa ethnogeography is a bit arcane for a radio script writer, it is not completely implausible that Striker might have come across it. In the early part of this century there was a veritable glut of these Smithsonian volumes in used-book

shops, since they were distributed free to various politicians who clearly had no use for them. If we assume that Striker or his research assistant found *kema* and *sabe*, scribbled them down hurriedly, and redefined *sabe* somewhat, we have a reasonable explanation of the change in spelling (*kema* becomes *kemo*) as well as the slippage in meaning ("Apache" becomes "Faithful"), and we have a bona fide American origin for Tonto's famous phrase.

14 When I told Alan Shaterian of the University of California at Berkeley about the Tewa hypothesis, he supplied one of his own. His is from Yavapai, an American Indian language spoken in Arizona, and one that I have actually worked on myself. The "Yavapai theory" goes something like this:

15 Striker, knowing nothing about Southwestern Indians, wants to lend an air of authenticity to his characterization of the Lone Ranger and his Indian companion. Rather than hunt around musty old book shops, he goes to Arizona to do some research and lands on an Apache reservation. This particular reservation is the home of the Tontos, so Striker incorrectly assumes that every Indian here is a Tonto. Actually, the Tonto Apache have been associated with the Northern Yavapai for as long as anyone can remember, and have intermarried with them fairly steadily since the turn of the century when they were interned together at San Carlos, Arizona.

16 Now, argues Shaterian, suppose Striker approaches a Yavapai, incorrectly assuming he is a Tonto, and asks the Indian the word for "one who is white" or shows the Indian a picture of the Lone Ranger in his white shirt and trousers and asks him to make up a name for this person in his language.

17 To the first question (how do you say "the one who is white?") a typical Yavapai would respond *kinmasaba*. Faced with the instruction to think up a term of address for someone who habitually dresses in white clothes, a good Yavapai response might be *kinmasabeh*. The difference in ending is that *-a* marks certain kinds of nouns while *-eh* is a vocative marker, used when one addresses another person directly. It might be translated "thou" or "you." *Nmasab* is the color term for white. When used alone it refers to white clothes, cloths or rags, but it never refers to the skin tone of Caucasians. The prefix *ki-* literally means *the one who*, so that the whole construction *ki-nmasab-a* means precisely "the one who is white," while the construction *kinmasab-eh* means, a little less precisely, "thou, white clothing" or, more irreverently, "hey, you, white rags." In casual speech, the Yavapais pronounce *kinmasabeh* in such a way that anyone but a trained linguist probably would hear *kimasabeh*.

18 If Shaterian and Goddard can play this game, so can I. Some casual flipping through American Indian dictionaries produced these possibilities.

CREE: "kemoo'tisew," *He is secret, concealed.*

SOUTHERN PAIUTE: "Qima," *stranger,* plus "sautsi," *to peep* (perhaps a reference to the Lone Ranger's peeping through a mask).

OSAGE: "ke-mo-ge zhu dse," *red-breasted turtle* (admittedly, not very likely).

TUNICA: "koma," *to comb one's* hair, plus either (1) "sara," *to beg or implore*, or (2) "sari," *to hate or detest* (so the Lone Ranger either loved to comb his hair or he hated it; he was fastidious or slovenly).

NAVAJO: (1) "k'ineedlishii," *stink beetle* (perhaps this is what Tonto really thought of him), (2) "k'ineeshbizhii," *dumpling* (he was overweight?), or (3) "kin yaah sizini," *whore* (he was a Midnight Cowboy?).

19   At this point, I decided that I prefer mystery to certainty.
20   Does it matter, ultimately, what *kemo sabe* means? At one time, I passionately thought so. But, then, after all, Tonto and his masked friend are mythic characters, and as such, they do not have to be fixed in historical reality. They exist and continue to exist in the timeless Wild West of the mind. Hi-yo, Silver!

Masculine/Feminine
Prudence Mackintosh

Mackintosh presents her thesis in two places. At the end of paragraph 2, she offers it as a *hypothesis* to be tested: if children are raised properly, they will grow up "free of sex-role stereotypes." In paragraph 14, she says no—sons and daughters *won't* turn out alike. No matter how hard anyone tries, certain natural sex differences, corresponding to some of our stereotypes, will remain.

Most of the evidence consists of examples drawn from the author's personal experience. *The organization of the essay reflects the* **inductive process** *(see p. 92), which moves from a question to be answered, to the evidence, to a conclusion.* You will notice that after arriving at her conclusion (paragraph 14), Mackintosh provides further evidence to reinforce it.

Source. "Masculine/Feminine" by Prudence Mackintosh. Copyright © 1977 by Prudence Mackintosh. First appeared in *Texas Monthly*. Reprinted by permission of the Julian Bach Literary Agency, Inc.

Does one person's experience prove anything? How does Mackintosh try to *generalize* her experience so that her conclusion will seem valid to other people?

1 I had every intention to raise liberated, nonviolent sons whose aggressive tendencies would be mollified by a sensitivity and compassion that psychologists claim were denied their father's generation.

2 I did not buy guns or war toys (although Grandmother did). My boys even had a secondhand baby doll until the garage sale last summer. I did buy Marlo Thomas' *Free to Be You and Me* record, a collection of nonsexist songs, stories, and poems, and I told them time and time again that it was okay to cry and be scared sometimes. I overruled their father and insisted that first grade was much too early for organized competitive soccer leagues. They know that moms *and dads* do dishes and diapers. And although they use it primarily for the convenient bathroom between the alley and the sandpile, my boys know that the storeroom is now mother's office. In such an environment, surely they would grow up free of sex-role stereotypes. At the very least wouldn't they pick up their own socks?

3 My friends with daughters were even more zealous. They named their daughters strong, cool unisex names like Blakeney, Brett, Brook, Lindsay, and Blair, names that lent themselves to corporate letterheads, not Tupperware party invitations. These moms looked on Barbie with disdain and bought trucks and science kits. They shunned frilly dresses for overalls. They subscribed to Feminist Press and read stories called "My Mother the Mail Carrier" instead of "Sleeping Beauty." At the swimming pool one afternoon, I watched a particularly fervent young mother, ironically clad in a string bikini, encourage her daughter. "You're so strong, Blake! Kick hard, so you'll be the strongest kid in this pool." When my boys splashed water in Blakey's eyes and she ran whimpering to her mother, this mom exhorted, "You go back in that pool and shake your fist like this and say, 'You do that again and I'll bust your lights out.' " A new generation of little girls, assertive and ambitious, taking a backseat to no one?

4 It's a little early to assess the results of our efforts, but when my seven-year-old son, Jack, comes home singing—to the tune of *"Frère Jacques"*—"Farrah Fawcett, Farrah Fawcett, I love you" and five minutes later asks Drew, his five-year-old brother, if he'd like his nose to be a blood fountain, either we're backsliding or there's more to this sex-role learning than the home environment can handle.

5 I'm hearing similar laments from mothers of daughters. "She used to tell everyone that she was going to grow up to be a lawyer just like Daddy," said one, "but she's hedging on that ambition ever since she

learned that no one wears a blue fairy tutu in the courtroom.'' Another mother with two sons, a daughter, and a very successful career notes that, with no special encouragement, only her daughter keeps her room neat and loves to set the table and ceremoniously seat her parents. At a Little League game during the summer, fearful that this same young daughter might be absorbing the stereotype "boys play while girls watch," her parents readily assured her that she too could participate when she was eight years old. "Oh," she exclaimed with obvious delight, "I didn't know they had cheerleaders."

6   How does it happen? I have my own theories, but decided to do a little reading to see if any of the "experts" agreed with me. I was also curious to find out what remedies they recommended. The books I read propose that sex roles are culturally induced. In simplistic terms, rid the schools, their friends, and the television of sexism, and your daughters will dump their dolls and head straight for the boardroom while your sons contemplate nursing careers. *Undoing Sex Stereotypes* by Marcia Guttentag and Helen Bray is an interesting study of efforts to overcome sexism in the classroom. After reading it, I visited my son's very traditional school and found it guilty of unabashedly perpetrating the myths that feminists abhor. Remember separate water fountains? And how, even if the line was shorter, no boy would be caught dead drinking from the girls' fountain and vice versa? That still happens. "You wouldn't want me to get cooties, would you, Mom?" my son says, defending the practice. What did I expect in a school where the principal still addresses his faculty, who range in age from 23 to 75, as "girls"?

7   Nevertheless, having been a schoolteacher myself, I am skeptical of neatly programmed nonsexist curriculum packets like Guttentag and Bray's. But if you can wade through the jargon ("people of the opposite sex hereafter referred to as POTOS"), some of the observations and exercises are certainly thought-provoking and revealing. In one exercise fifth-grade students were asked to list adjectives appropriate to describe women. The struggle some of the children had in shifting their attitudes about traditional male roles is illustrated in this paragraph written by a fifth-grade girl who was asked to write a story about a man using the adjectives she had listed to describe women:

> Once there was a boy who all his life was very *gentle*. He never hit anyone or started a fight and when some of his friends were not feeling well, he was *loving* and *kind* to them. When he got older he never changed. People started not liking him because he was *weak, petite*, and he wasn't like any of the other men—not strong or tough. Most of his life he sat alone thinking about why no one liked him. Then one day he went out and tried to act like the other men. He joined a baseball team, but he was no good, he always

got out. Then he decided to join the hockey team. He couldn't play good. He kept on breaking all the rules. So he quit the team and joined the soccer team. These men were *understanding* to him. He was really good at soccer, and was the best on the team. That year they won the championship and the rest of his life he was happy.[1]

8   After reading this paragraph it occurred to me that this little girl's self-esteem and subsequent role in life would be enhanced by a teacher who spent less time on "nonsexist intervention projects" and more time on writing skills. But that, of course, is not what the study was meant to reveal.

9   The junior high curriculum suggested by *Undoing Sex Stereotypes* has some laudable consciousness-raising goals. For example, in teaching units called "Women's Roles in American History" and "The Socialization of Women and the Image of Women in the Media" teenagers are encouraged to critically examine television commercials, soap operas, and comic books. But am I a traitor to the cause if I object when the authors in another unit use *Romeo and Juliet* as a study of the status of women? Something is rotten in Verona when we have to consider Juliet's career possibilities and her problems with self-actualization. The conclusions of this project were lost on me; I quit reading when the author began to talk about ninth-graders who were "cognitively at a formal-operational level." I don't even know what my "external sociopsychological situation" is. However, I think I did understand some of the conclusions reached by the kids:

"Girls are smart."

"If a woman ran a forklift where my father works, there would be a walkout."

"Men cannot be pom-pom girls."

10   Eminently more readable, considering that both authors are educators of educators, is *How to Raise Independent and Professionally Successful Daughters*, by Drs. Rita and Kenneth Dunn. The underlying and, I think, questionable assumption in this book is that little boys have been reared correctly all along. Without direct parental intervention, according to the Dunns, daughters tend to absorb and reflect society's values. The Dunns paint a dark picture indeed for the parents who fail to channel their daughters toward professional success. The woman who remains at home with children while her husband is involved in the "real world" with an "absorbing and demanding day-to-day commitment that brings him into contact with new ideas, jobs, and people (attractive self-actualized females)" is sure to experience lowered IQ, according to the Dunns. They go on to predict

[1] From *Undoing Sex Stereotypes* by Marcia Guttentag and Helen Bray © 1976 McGraw-Hill, Inc. Used with permission of McGraw-Hill Book Co.

the husband's inevitable affair and the subsequent divorce, which leaves the wife emotionally depressed and probably financially dependent on her parents.

11   Now I'm all for women developing competency and self-reliance, but the Dunns' glorification of the professional is excessive. Anyone who has worked longer than a year knows that eventually any job loses most of its glamour. And the world is no less "real" at home. For that matter, mothers at home may be more "real" than bankers or lawyers. How is a corporate tax problem more real than my counseling with the maid whose boyfriend shot her in the leg? How can reading a balance sheet compare with comforting a five-year-old who holds his limp cat and wants to know why we have to lose the things we love? And on the contrary, it is my husband, the professional, who complains of lowered IQ. Though we wooed to Faulkner, my former ace English major turned trial lawyer now has time for only an occasional *Falconer* or Peter Benchley thriller. Certainly there is value in raising daughters to be financially self-supporting, but there is not much wisdom in teaching a daughter that she must achieve professional success or her marriage probably won't last.

12   In a chapter called "What to Do from Birth to Two," the authors instruct parents to introduce dolls only if they represent adult figures or groups of figures. "Try not to give her her own 'baby.' A baby doll is acceptable only for dramatizing the familiar episodes she has actually experienced, like a visit to the doctor." If some unthinking person should give your daughter a baby doll, and she likes it, the Dunns recommend that you permit her to keep it without exhibiting any negative feelings, "but do not lapse into cuddling it or encouraging her to do so. Treat it as any other object and direct attention to other more beneficial toys." I wonder if the Dunns read an article by Anne Roiphe called "Can You Have Everything and Still Want Babies?" which appeared in *Vogue* a couple of years ago. Ms. Roiphe was deploring the extremes to which our liberation has brought us. "It is nice to have beautiful feet, it may be desirable to have small feet, but it is painful and abusive to bind feet. It is also a good thing for women to have independence, freedom and choice, movement, and opportunity; but I'm not so sure that the current push against mothering will not be another kind of binding of the soul. . . . As women we have thought so little of ourselves that when the troops came to liberate us we rushed into the streets leaving our most valuable attributes behind as if they belonged to the enemy."

13   The Dunns' book is thorough, taking parents step-by-step through the elementary years and on to high school. Had I been raising daughters, however, I think I would have flunked out in the chapter "What to Do from Age Two to Five." In discussing development of vocabulary, the Doctors Dunn prohibit the use of nonsensical words for

bodily functions. I'm sorry, Doctors, but I've experimented with this precise terminology and discovered that the child who yells "I have to defecate, Mom" across four grocery aisles is likely to be left in the store. A family without a few poo-poo jokes is no family at all.

14 These educators don't help me much in my efforts to liberate my sons. And although I think little girls are getting a better deal with better athletic training and broader options, I believe we're kidding ourselves if we think we can raise our sons and daughters alike. Certain inborn traits seem to be immune to parental and cultural tampering. How can I explain why a little girl baby sits on a quilt in the park thoughtfully examining a blade of grass, while my baby William uproots grass by handfuls and eats it? Why does a mother of very bright and active daughters confide that until she went camping with another family of boys, she feared that my sons had a hyperactivity problem? I'm sure there are plenty of rowdy, noisy little girls, but I'm not just talking about rowdiness and noise. I'm talking about some sort of primal physicalness that causes the walls of my house to pulsate on rainy days. I'm talking about something inexplicable that makes my sons fall into a mad, scrambling, pull-your-ears-off-kick-your-teeth-in heap just before bedtime, when they're not even mad at each other. I mean something that causes them to climb the doorjamb with honey and peanut butter on their hands while giving me a synopsis of *Star Wars* that contains only five intelligible words: "And then this guy, he 'pssshhhhhhh.' And then this thing went 'vrongggggg.' But this little guy said, 'Nong-neeee-nonh-neee.' " When Jack and Drew are not kicking a soccer ball or each other, they are kicking the chair legs, the cat, the baby's silver rattle, and, inadvertently, Baby William himself, whom they have affectionately dubbed "Tough Eddy." Staying put in a chair for the duration of a one-course meal is torturous for these boys. They compensate by never quite putting both feet under the table. They sit with one leg doubled under them while the other leg extends to one side. The upper half of the body appears committed to the task at hand—eating—but the lower extremities are poised to lunge should a more compelling distraction present itself. From this position, I have observed, one brother can trip a haughty dessert-eating sibling who is flaunting the fact he ate all his "sweaty little peas." Although we have civilized them to the point that they dutifully mumble, "May I be excused, please?" their abrupt departure from the table invariably overturns at least one chair or whatever milk remains. This sort of constant motion just doesn't lend itself to lessons in thoughtfulness and gentleness.

15 Despite my encouragement, my sons refuse to invite little girls to play anymore. Occasionally friends leave their small daughters with us while they run errands. I am always curious to see what these females will find of interest in my sons' roomful of Tonka trucks and

soccer balls. One morning the boys suggested that the girls join them in playing Emergency with the big red fire trucks and ambulance. The girls were delighted and immediately designated the ambulance as theirs. The point of Emergency, as I have seen it played countless times with a gang of little boys, is to make as much noise with the siren as possible and to crash the trucks into each other or into the leg of a living-room chair before you reach your destination.

16   The girls had other ideas. I realized why they had selected the ambulance. It contained three dolls: a driver, a nurse, and sick man on the stretcher. My boys have used that ambulance many times, but the dolls were always secondary to the death-defying race with the fire trucks; they were usually just thrown in the back of the van as an afterthought. The girls took the dolls out, stripped and re-dressed them tenderly, and made sure that they were seated in their appropriate places for the first rescue. Once the fire truck had been lifted off the man's leg, the girls required a box of Band-Aids and spent the next half hour making a bed for the patient and reassuring him that he was going to be all right. These little girls and my sons had seen the same NBC *Emergency* series, but the girls had apparently picked up on the show's nurturing aspects, while Jack and Drew were interested only in the equipment, the fast driving, and the sirens. . . .

17   Of course, I want my sons to grow up knowing that what's inside a woman's head is more important than her appearance, but I'm sure they're getting mixed signals when I delay our departure for the swimming pool to put on lipstick. I also wonder what they make of their father, whose favorite aphorism is "beautiful women rule the world." I suppose what we want for these sons and the women they may marry someday is a sensitivity that enables them to be both flexible and at ease with their respective roles, so that marriage contracts are unnecessary. When my sons bring me the heads of two purple irises from the neighbor's yard and ask, "Are you really the most beautiful mama in the whole world like Daddy says, and did everyone want to marry you?" do you blame me if I keep on waffling?

Part Three
Evaluation: Introductory Essay

Evaluative writing intends to persuade us that *X*—whatever the subject may be—is good or bad, right or wrong, adequate or inadequate. When you say, "that was a great game" or "chicken in pineapple sauce tastes lousy" or "cheap boots aren't really a good buy," you are making an evaluation. When someone else puts a grade on a report you have written or says, "sorry, you're not quite the right person for this job" or pays you $250 for one night's performance on the trombone, you are receiving an evaluation. We are concerned here with evaluations in the form of words on paper.

Kinds of Evaluations

One obligation of written evaluations is to clarify the meaning of such terms as *great* and *lousy* and *good*. Three basic approaches are possible.

(1) The approach can be **utilitarian**: *X* is good, or not good, with reference to a job to be done. In this case, *good* and all other terms of approval mean *useful*. Or (2) the approach can be **ethical**: *X* is good, or not good, with reference to ethical and moral and religious beliefs. In this case, *good* and all other terms of approval mean *inherently right*.

This distinction is important because the same thing can be good in one sense but not in the other. The *Consumer Reports* evaluation of fast foods (p. 175) shows that—on *utilitarian* grounds—one group of fast-food meals provides adequate protein and other nutrients. But someone looking at the rise of fast-food chains in terms of the traditional values of family life and the home—*ethical* grounds—might find fast-food meals far from "good."

There are more difficult instances. Abortion has been defended as "good" on practical, *utilitarian* grounds; it has also been condemned as "bad" on *moral* grounds. When you write an evaluation, you must make clear whether the utilitarian or the ethical approach is more important.

(3) Another approach, the **aesthetic**, applies to evaluations of things that we see as attractive or unattractive—a sunset, a state capitol building, a piece of music, a novel, and so forth. Here the emphasis is on the degree of pleasure that *X* brings us. A good film is one that you enjoy seeing. A good meal (at home or at McDonald's) is—from this viewpoint—one that tastes good. Aesthetic evaluations are often debatable because they are so personal.

The Process of Evaluation

Defining the Subject. Whichever approach you take, the logical process underlying evaluation is the same. **You must first decide exactly what you are evaluating, define it if necessary, and**

limit it to manageable proportions. You would not undertake to evaluate "the automobile" in a short essay, for example. But you might try evaluating *the standard-size cars manufactured by American companies in 1977 and 1978.* The **first step** in the process, then, is **definition.**

Stating Criteria. The next step will be the establishment of *criteria*—**the standards against which** *X* **is to be judged good or bad (or somewhere in between).** The meaning of such terms as *good* must now be made more precise. Let us assume that your approach to the subject of standard-size American cars manufactured in 1977 and 1978 will be utilitarian: are those cars good with reference to the job to be done? The inquiry is still inexact.

Choosing and Ranking the Criteria. There are many possible meanings of "good with reference to the job to be done." In evaluating the cars, that very general phrase suggests at least five different criteria.

1 The cars are inexpensive to operate and maintain.
2 The cars are reliable (they do not have an excessive rate of mechanical failure).
3 The cars provide the passenger and luggage space needed by the average American family.
4 The cars are safe.
5 The cars are attractive to look at and comfortable to ride in.

In order for your evaluation to be responsible, you must know—and your reader must know—exactly what criteria you are applying.

If you decide to apply more than one criterion (to judge the cars, perhaps, in terms of expense, reliability, and safety) you will need to *rank the criteria*—that is, to determine the order of priority among them. Is expense the most important factor, or is reliability, or is

safety? Or are you interested in a concept of total performance, in which a high rating in one area could compensate for a low rating in another?

Making the Criteria Fair. It is pointless to apply a criterion that is unfair to whatever you are evaluating—a criterion intended for a different category of things, or a criterion that unfairly emphasizes one part of the picture. It would be pointless to fault a standard-size passenger automobile for not being as speedy as a racing car. Similarly, to dismiss a film as "bad" because one bit part was inconsistently played, or to praise a dinner as "marvelous" because the olives were perfectly ripe, is unfair because a disproportionate emphasis is placed on one aspect of *X*.

Making the Criteria Precise. Let us assume that you have decided to evaluate cars in terms of comfort alone. That general criterion, which is certainly fair, now needs to be made more precise. What *exactly* does it mean to ask whether the cars are "comfortable"? You may decide to specify that a comfortable car is one that allows its driver's seat to be adjusted to fit people from 5′0″ to 6′2″ (and so forth).

Sometimes, as Claiborne shows in trying to evaluate Wasps (p. 200), it is extremely difficult to establish precise criteria. Sometimes the effort to do so occupies more of the finished piece of writing than does any other part of the evaluative process. Highet spends a large part of his evaluation of the Gettysburg Address (p. 183) establishing his concept of what constitutes a good oratorical performance.

Sometimes it is simply impossible to establish criteria precisely. Gutcheon praises soap operas for trying to educate us about ourselves and about alternative ways of life (p. 213). She does not attempt to specify exactly what proportion of its time on the air a given soap opera should spend on educational matters before deserving the evaluation "good, because educational." It would be silly for her to say that a good soap opera spends 28.2 percent of its time, or 86.1 percent of its time, being educational.

The principle to remember: **make your criteria as precise as you reasonably can.** Somewhere between the extremes of criteria so vague or so overprecise as to be useless lies the right degree of precision for each piece of evaluative writing. The nature of your subject, the space and time you have to spend, the experience and degree of interest of your audience, and your own common sense will help you decide.

Justifying the Criteria. If your criteria are clear, fair, and precise, most of your readers will accept them. But occasionally a criterion will need to be defended. If you want to evaluate a novel, for instance, and your criterion is that it should help you understand yourself, a reader could legitimately ask "Why?" Why should a novel bring pleasure only according to that standard? Couldn't it deserve to be judged "good" if it helped you understand *other* people rather than yourself? Or if it provided an exciting escape from reality altogether?

Whether the criteria will need to be justified depends, as so much else in writing does, on the audience for which you are writing. If you are evaluating your high school education and condemning it for not having taught you a marketable skill, do you need to justify that criterion? Probably not, if your audience consists of teachers and students at a vocational-technical school; they are already committed to career education. Probably yes, if your audience consists of teachers and students in a college-preparatory track; they are likely to see high school as a step toward college, not directly toward a job. The more unusual your

criterion seems to your audience, the more likely it becomes that you should take the time to explain why you feel it is the right one. If you want to evaluate spaghetti in terms of its tensile strength, you'd *certainly* better take the time to explain why.

Collecting Information. In order to see how well *X* measures up to your criteria—once the criteria have been chosen, ranked if there will be more than one, checked for fairness and precision, and justified if necessary—you will have to assemble information about *X*. Otherwise your judgment would be unsubstantiated. Collect the information that corresponds to your chosen criteria. If you are evaluating Levi and Wrangler jeans in terms of how long they last and what they cost (a "cost-effectiveness" analysis), you would not include information on where they are manufactured or what colors are available.

Sometimes the process of collecting the right information is made easier by the preparation of an outline, a chart, or a data sheet like the one at the end of the *Consumer Reports* article on "fast foods" (p. 180).

Making the Judgment. In logical terms (pp. 89–95), the process of making the judgment is a *deductive argument*. We can use the model of the syllogism.

1 A low-cost car is a car that (a) averages at least 20 miles per gallon of gas, (b) needs no more than $10 per month for maintenance and repairs, and (c) has an initial purchase price of no more than $3800 (new, with standard equipment only, not including the interest expense for time payments). [*Major premise.*]
2 My 1977 model Chevrolet (a) gets about 22 miles per gallon and (b) costs me about $9 per month for maintenance and repairs. Its initial purchase price (c) was $3720.46. [*Minor premise.*]

3 The 1977 model Chevrolet is, judging from the evidence available to me, a low-cost car to purchase and to own. [*Conclusion*.]

The major premise, in an evaluative syllogism, is the criterion. If you are using more than one criterion, the major premise may be rather long.

> It is wrong to permit someone to die when the means to prolong life are available—unless the patient is suffering extreme pain, is elderly (65 years old or older), has physical and mental deterioration for which no reversal can be expected, is not known to hold any religious principles requiring the preservation of life to the utmost, and would require medical resources that are needed by somebody more likely to recover. If all those conditions exist, it is *not* wrong to permit the patient to die. If any one of those conditions is missing, it *is* wrong to permit the patient to die.

Similarly, if you have a lot of information about *X* to present, the minor premise too may take several paragraphs—or pages—to present; and you may want to discuss your conclusion at some length. The overall pattern, however, remains the same.

To summarize: the complete (or "full-form") process of evaluation we have been describing contains four elements.

1 Definition of the thing (*X*) to be evaluated.
2 Selection of criteria that are fair and adequately precise, and ranking and justifying of the criteria if necessary.
3 Collection of information about *X* so that it can be compared to the ideal established by the criteria.
4 Comparison of *X* to the criteria and statement of the judgment.

You can see all four elements most clearly in test reports of consumer goods or other evaluations of material items and objects. (See the *Consumer Reports* evaluation of fast foods, p. 175.)

Abbreviated Evaluations. At times, only part of the full logical process of evaluation appears in the written report. What results is called an abbreviated (or "short-form") evaluation. If *X* is something familiar to most of us, no definitions may be necessary. The criteria may be implied—*suggested* by the wording or by the inclusion and omission of certain subjects—rather than explicitly stated and ranked. If a writer discusses only the vitamin A content of different brands of frozen carrots, we can see that the standard of value is simply the amount of vitamin A (not the cost or the taste or the appearance of the carrots). Sometimes even the judgment may be left for the readers to state in their own words.

An abbreviated evaluation is not necessarily an irresponsible one. Whatever can be taken for granted does not need to be spelled out. But how much is it proper to omit?

The test of whether an abbreviated evaluation is responsible is whether the reader can answer the following questions on the basis of material either stated or implied.

1 What exactly is the subject (*X*)?
2 What criteria are being applied?
3 What information about *X* corresponds to those criteria?
4 What is the overall judgment?

Hungiville's essay "Groovin' in Academe" (p. 170) is an abbreviated evaluation, but a responsible one. You may not necessarily agree with it, but you can see what criteria are being used and what the evidence is. The judgment is not made explicit—the essay ends on a question "Is anybody saluting?"—but we can infer it ourselves from the information we have been given. Hungiville, at least, is not saluting at all.

A Special Technique of Evaluation: Satire

Satire is a technique of disapproval: it is a way of writing about *X* so that *X* looks ridiculous or offensive. It involves intentional distortion. The writer chooses only the few characteristics of *X* that will make it look silly or ugly, not the whole picture. Or rather than describing the real *X* at all, the writer instead creates an exaggerated version of it, a *parody*. An example in this book is Baker's "Redesigning Chickens" (p. 208).

Satirical evaluations are not always fair. In fact, they do not try to be fair. They try to emphasize particular characteristics of *X* that seem, to their writers, so disqualifying that *X* does not deserve a standard evaluation. A cartoonist who draws a picture of a politician as all belly is suggesting that this person's greed overwhelms all other characteristics. A *Mad* magazine-type feature portraying news commentators as speaking *only* in meaningless unconnected phrases ("Hello, here we are

Source. By permission of Chicago Tribune-New York News Syndicate.

This political cartoon uses certain characteristics of the *satiric evaluation*. Is it an effective comment? How could you decide whether it is a legitimate (fair) comment?

at . . . now we switch you to . . . on our left we have a . . . tune in again tomorrow!'') is suggesting that the fragmentary nature of TV news presentations is so dominant a characteristic that it blots out all else.

Satirical evaluations are protests against aspects of our world that we may take for granted. The satirist asks, in effect, ''Don't you see how greedy this politician is?'' or ''Don't you see how meaningless the TV news programs are?'' The purpose of satirical evaluations is to make sure that we *do* see. They are useful not as replacements for standard evaluations, but as a means of waking people up when it is wrong—or dangerous—for them to be sleeping. Satirical evaluations are also fun to read and to write.

The Value of Evaluation

In full or abbreviated form, using a utilitarian or ethical or aesthetic approach, written in a straightforward or a satirical style, evaluations respond to the question, ''Is *X* good or bad?'' Many of our most important questions are of this type. Is it wrong to kill people? Is America a good country? Do I have a good relationship with the person I love most? Answering questions such as these often requires an evaluative process extending through a lifetime.

Some questions of evaluation need more urgent answers. Would it be better to live at home, in the dorm, or in an apartment (''better'' for what)? Would courses in acccounting or courses in Russian technical translation be better (more useful) choices for next term? Does the person you are going to marry have the qualities of a good parent? Is a particular friend still compatible after 10 years?

All of us want to make the value judgments that will improve our own lives. All of us want to back a winning horse. To choose a winner—to know which option is best—means to evaluate evidence accurately and to have clear, reasonable standards of measurement.

Summary

1 The process of *formal evaluation* has four elements. You need to (1) *define X*, the thing to be evaluated, or other terms that may be unclear; (2) *select criteria* that are fair and precise—and rank and justify the criteria if necessary; (3) *collect information*, so that the characteristics of *X* can be compared to the standards set by the criteria; and (4) *draw a judgment*. This process resembles a deductive argument, since you are applying general principles of value to specific objects or instances.

2 An *abbreviated evaluation* is appropriate when your reader already understands the limits of your subject, the criteria being applied, or the way that your information leads toward a judgment.

3 A *satirical evaluation*, a special form of abbreviated evaluation, records disapproval or amusement. It works by overemphasizing certain details to make *X* look wrong or silly.

Evaluation, Series One
Readings with Commentary

The Common Stock of the Coca-Cola Company

This selection comes from a booklet evaluating common stocks. (A share of stock represents part ownership of a business.) The booklet is written for people who might want to buy stock as an investment. The company pays stockholders an annual dividend on each share, and the shares can often be sold later at a profit. *The criterion for evaluating stock is the ability of the shares to make money for their owners.*

After a two-sentence introduction to supply general information about the Coca-Cola Company, the writer discusses its recent growth in sales, earnings per share, and dividends. He then distinguishes between income from sales of soft drinks and income from sales of the company's other products. The last paragraph offers a prediction of continued financial strength and the judgment that shares of Coca-Cola's common stock are "attractive" for people who want to see their money grow. *Attractive* clearly means, in this context, appealing not to the eye or the ear or the taste—but to the pocketbook.

1 More than 110-million times a day, someone, somewhere in the world, drinks a Coke—one of the most successful consumer products ever

Source. "The Common Stock of the Coca-Cola Company." Copyrighted 1969 Merrill Lynch, Pierce, Fenner & Smith, Inc. Reprinted by permission from Merrill Lynch, Pierce, Fenner & Smith, Inc. The report does not constitute a recommendation and is accurate only for its own date.

introduced. That success has made the Coca-Cola Company the dominant firm in the soft-drink industry, where it commands about 44% of the domestic market for bottled soft drinks and more than 85% of the market for trademarked fountain drinks. During the five years through 1968, Coca-Cola's sales grew at a compound annual rate of 13%, and earnings per share advanced at a 15% compound rate. The company has paid dividends each year since 1893 and has increased the dividend rate in each of the last seven years. The current annual dividend is $1.32 a share.

2   The company expects its sales of soft drinks in the United States to increase at an annual rate of 9-to-10% during the next three-to-five years, and it expects sales for the foreign division to grow even more rapidly, at a rate approaching 15%. Sales of soft drinks last year accounted for 75% of Coca-Cola's total revenues of $1.2 billion, to which domestic and foreign operations contributed equal amounts.

3   In addition to selling carbonated beverages, Coca-Cola is the world's largest processor of citrus concentrates and drinks and the largest producer of instant coffee and tea sold under private labels. We estimate that 1969 earnings, excluding unremitted foreign profits of about 11¢ a share, will be $2.15-to-2.20 a share compared with $1.93 a share in 1968.

4   In our opinion, Coca-Cola's sales and earnings will continue to expand in coming years. We base that expectation on the company's strong consumer franchise and on projections of increases in population, in standards of living, and in per-capita consumption of soft drinks throughout the world. Although Coca-Cola's outstanding record has not been overlooked by investors, we believe that the investment-grade shares remain attractive for growth.

Commentary

This very short evaluation includes all parts of the full-form evaluation pattern except an explicit statement of the criteria. The important characteristics of X are defined in the first paragraph (Coca-Cola is "the dominant firm in the soft-drink industry," and so forth). The information most relevant to potential purchasers of the shares—information about the company's earnings (which govern its ability to pay dividends) and information about the dividends themselves—is provided in the next two paragraphs. The writer also includes predictions about the financial future to assure readers that if they buy Coca-Cola shares

today, their investments will not be endangered tomorrow. The judgment is compressed into one word of approval: "attractive." And a reason is given to suggest why the approval is no stronger than that: other investors have already bought Coca-Cola stock (the company's "outstanding record has not been overlooked"), so its price may be fairly high.

This very efficient report functions quite satisfactorily without an explicit statement of criteria for two reasons. One is that, since it was written for a booklet issued by a stock-brokers' firm, it was unlikely to reach people who were not interested in making money (the criterion for evaluating stock). The other is that its own language indicates the standard of value being used. The many financial terms *(sales, market, compound annual rate, earnings per share,* and so forth) give adequate evidence of this evaluation's orientation.

Outline

  I Introduction: general information about *X*—paragraph 1

 II Minor premise: information about *X* to correspond with criteria—paragraphs 2-3

III Conclusion: judgment that *X* is "attractive"—paragraph 4

Suggestions for Writing

1 Write a short evaluation using a criterion that is obvious and can therefore remain unstated. For example, using good taste as your criterion, evaluate something you ate for lunch yesterday. You might begin with a one- or two-sentence definition (what you ate). Supply the important information. ("It had a weird taste, as if somebody had taken cold farina and poured latex wall paint on it, hiding a few crumpled international postage stamps here and there for variety. I was aware of a distantly Italian spiciness in one lump, a Chinese crispness in another.") State your judgment at the end, compressing it into one word if possible.

2 Begin with the first sentence of the Coca-Cola evaluation: "More than 110-million times a day, someone, somewhere in the world, drinks a Coke—one of the most successful consumer products ever introduced." Write an evaluation for a different audience, perhaps the members of your class. Use a different criterion (flavor, nutritional value, pleasure), provide the appropriate information, and state your judgment at the end.

The American Cause
John Dos Passos

In this selection, novelist Dos Passos responds to an extremely ambitious writing assignment—a request that he state, in about 300 words, what is good about the United States of America. Dos Passos tries to distinguish between *one class of "good*

Source. "The American Cause" by John Dos Passos. From *The Theme Is Freedom* by John Dos Passos. Copyright by Elizabeth H. Dos Passos and reprinted with her permission.

things," material or superficial benefits, and a *second class of "good things,"* moral qualities such as faith in human dignity and goodness.

Notice that Dos Passos does not have space to present the evidence behind his evaluative statements, to define his terms fully, or to explain and defend his criteria. How successful is his **abbreviated evaluation** (see p. 162)? Does his opinion about the United States match yours?

1   Not long ago I received a letter from some German students asking me to explain to them in three hundred words why they should admire the United States. "Young people in Germany," they wrote, "as in other places in the world, are disillusioned, weary of pronouncements on the slogan level. They are not satisfied with negations, they have been told over and over again what to hate and what to fight. . . . They want to know what to be and what to do."

2   This is what I didn't tell them: I didn't tell them that they should admire the United States for the victories of our armed forces, or because we had first developed the atomic bomb or the hydrogen bomb, or because we had shinier automobiles or more washing machines and deep freezes and televisions, or ran up more passenger miles of airplane travel a year than any other people in the world. I didn't tell them to admire us for getting more productive work done with less backbreaking labor than any other people in the world, or for our high wages or our social security system. I didn't tell them to admire us because our popular leaders had the sweetest smiles before the television cameras, or because we lived on a magnificent continent that offered an unbelievable variety of climates, mountains, plains, rivers, estuaries, seashores. Some of these are very good things, but they are not things that would help them "to know what to be and what to do."

3   This is what I told them: I told them they should admire the United States not for what we were, but for what we might become. Selfgoverning democracy was not an established creed, but a program for growth. I reminded them that industrial society was a new thing in the world, and that although we Americans had gone further than any people in spreading out its material benefits, we were just beginning, amid crimes, illusions, mistakes and false starts, to get to work on how to spread out what people needed much more: the sense of belonging, the faith in human dignity, the confidence of each man in the greatness of his own soul, without which life is a meaningless servitude. I told them to admire our failures because they might con-

tain the seeds of great victories to come, not of the victories that come through massacring men, women and children, but of the victories that come through overcoming the evil inherent in mankind through urgent and warmhearted use of our best brains. I told them to admire us for our foolish trust in other peoples, for our failure to create an empire when empire building was easy. I told them to admire us for our still unstratified society, where every man has the chance, if he has the will and the wit, to invent his own thoughts and to make his own way. I told them to admire us for the hope we still have that there is enough goodness in man to use the omnipotence science has given him to ennoble his life on earth, instead of degrading it. Selfgovernment, through dangers and distortions and failures, is the American cause. Faith in selfgovernment, when all is said and done, is faith in the eventual goodness of man.

Commentary

What makes an evaluation convincing? Sometimes you need to present the full range of evidence, discuss your criteria, even answer objections. However, if you are writing to people who happen to share many of your assumptions about values, they won't be so demanding. And if you happen to be the recognized authority on a certain subject, people are likely to listen to your opinion even if you don't have room to support it fully or if they didn't at first share your assumptions. Dos Passos writes here as a celebrity whose opinions have been requested by a group of people in another country.

Why does Dos Passos include the second paragraph, which lists things some people admire about America—although he doesn't? In part, he answers this question himself in the last sentence of the paragraph, where he ex-

plains that he is interested in what people should be and what they should do. Therefore America's material and other utilitarian qualities are not as important to him as its human opportunities are. He is following the principle that the good characteristics of something can become more evident once the irrelevant or negative characteristics are eliminated. This "elimination of the negative" tactic helps to remove obvious objections and clears the way for agreement about what is left. It also helps convince your audience you are not blind to the problems: you don't like just *everything*.

Dos Passos wrote some 25 years ago to an audience of German students. Which of his claims might have to be modified now? Which do you accept on the basis of your own experience, which on faith?

Outline

I Introduction: description of the situation (paragraph 1)

II Negative detail: characteristics Dos Passos does *not* tell the audience to

admire about America (paragraph 2)

III Positive detail: characteristics Dos Passos *does* tell the audience to admire about America (paragraph 3)

Suggestions for Writing

1 Following Dos Passos' negative-to-positive pattern, write a brief evaluation of some subject on which you are an authority: some aspect of your school or church (or synagogue) or sports team, for example.

2 Following Dos Passos' negative-to-positive pattern if it seems helpful, update his evaluation of America. Since you are not a recognized authority on the subject, you will probably have to provide evidence, such as personal experience, to help make your evaluation convincing.

3 Evaluate Dos Passos' article. Show why it is convincing or unconvincing on the basis of a clear statement about your own standards of value for America.

Groovin' in Academe
Maurice Hungiville

Hungiville is evaluating an advertising campaign—the one recently launched by American colleges.

If you chose your college because it was in your neighborhood or because people you knew had gone there, then you may not have been influenced by the public relations campaigns that many colleges adopted in the 1970s. But you were probably aware of college sales pressure in your high school counselors' offices or in newspaper or TV appeals.

This essay records one person's amusement and indignation at the excesses of college publicity. The implication is that if the colleges actually deliver what they are promising, true education has come to a halt. Either way, the advertising campaign is a bad thing: if the colleges don't deliver, that's fraud; if they do, that's a poor substitute for an education.

1 American colleges did not lack for students in the lush 1960s. A plentiful supply of war babies had come of age, determined to avoid their own war in Vietnam. Given the choice between carrying a book on campus or an M-16 rifle in a far-off jungle, most young men decided to go to college and make grades, not war.

Source. "Groovin' in Academe" by Maurice Hungiville. From *The National Observer*, August 10, 1974. Reprinted with permission of *The National Observer*, © Dow Jones & Company, Inc. 1974. All Rights Reserved. By permission also of the author.

2   Colleges in the 1970s, however, are frequently confronted with steadily shrinking enrollments, sparsely populated classrooms, and half-filled but fully mortgaged dormitories. Many colleges, as a result, have been compelled to sell themselves with all the slogans that we normally associate with odorless underarms or slip-proof dentures. The better (i.e., larger and more generously endowed) colleges may be relatively immune to this kind of hard-sell sales promotion; there is not—yet—any advertising that asks, "Wouldn't you rather have a Harvard?" But the smaller schools, which are only No. 2 or 2,000, must indeed try harder. Their advertisements constitute a curious composite portrait of the college as a commodity and the student as a customer.

Individuality Comes First

3   What follows, then, is an unvarnished, unscientific, unqualified, admittedly impressionistic survey of some prevailing themes in academic advertising. Most of this material is probably presented in fuller more dignified detail in the college catalogs, but it is available in all its gaudy commercial simplicity only in the booklets and brochures that are sent to students.

4   Throughout these brochures certain expressions appear often enough to suggest a significance beyond their banality. Among them the word "individual" thrusts itself forward with all the mechanical predictability of a neon sign. Students at every college are assured that they are "individuals," "unique persons," or "somebodies." The smaller colleges often use these words as incantations to call up terrifying, Kafkaesque visions of impersonality at larger colleges and universities, where a student is merely a "number on a computer card" or an anonymous "face in the crowd."

5   The psychedelic poster put out by Suomi College in Hancock, Michigan, is fairly typical in its emphasis on the individual. Featuring a busty girl wearing an "I'm somebody" T-shirt, the poster promises that Suomi College is "a people place," a "place where you can be the center of a successful educational experience." Additional information about Suomi College—and an affirmation of self—can be had by signing a postcard titled, "Yes, I'm Somebody Too."

"A Piece of the Action"

6   The concern for the personal and the individual that prevails throughout these academic advertisements is invariably combined with assurances that a dazzling array of impersonal technology is also available. Widener College in Chester, Pennsylvania, quite typically features both personalized "mini-courses" along with "full-equipped, multi-

media classrooms" and a learning center that provides "access to instant replays of lectures, dial access to film, video tape and recorded information in controlled acoustics and air-conditioned rooms."

7   In addition to the latest in learning technology, higher education—at least the 1974 model—features student power above all else. What was wrung so slowly from college administrators in the 1960s is now a standard built-in feature of most colleges. Entering freshmen at Macalester College in Minnesota are invited to "voice their opinions at regular monthly meetings of the faculty," while students at Rockford College in Illinois are offered "a piece of the action." At Tarkio College in Missouri, students are urged to "vote with management" on the board of directors. Hood College in Maryland is even more specific in its invitation to "learn governance by governing, by sitting on policy-making college committees, by administering $30,000 in student-activity fees, by helping the college evaluate itself and what it is doing."

8   Throughout these brochures there is a general acceptance of the notion that the student is the best judge of his educational needs. The curriculum, as a result, is often described as a plastic, polymorphously perverse substance that is easily shaped to accommodate itself to shifting student interests. Students at Hood College—and nearly everywhere else—are promised that "we not only listen when you express what you want from life, but we shape our curriculum to your individual needs." At Union College in Schenectady, New York, students are assured that they may "initiate independent courses, interdepartmental and interdisciplinary offerings."

9   If these student-initiated courses prove too constricting, it is also possible for the Union student to undertake "innovative academic options outside the usual class structure" or to pursue "many academically accredited programs away from campus." Elsewhere, students are invited to "create your own major," "design your own curriculum," and "build your own image." The emphasis everywhere is on "free-choice curriculum," or as Carroll College in Wisconsin so succinctly puts it, "courses that are desired rather than required."

Ambush at Podium Gap

10   Some concrete effects of such a "free-choice curriculum" are evident in particular courses. At Western Michigan University the general-education requirements are offered under the tantalizing title of "Getting It Together" The "Getting It Together," or GIT, program includes such courses as "In Pursuit of Awareness," "Beyond Survival," "The Many Faces of Nature," and "Mystic and Creative Mythology." At other colleges students are enticed with new or "recycled" courses

on "Death," "Silence," "Futurism," and "Me-ology," the study of the self.

1　One might expect that the promotion of Cedar Rapids, Iowa, as "a swinging place" would be the campus copy writer's greatest challenge, but many of the brochures seem to have little difficulty in depicting desolate Midwestern prairies as desirable, muggerless, smog-free Edens. Many colleges also have exotic branches in such places as London, Paris, Vienna, and Alexandria, Egypt. Students who tire of Evansville, Indiana, for example, can shuttle over to the University of Evansville's overseas campus in Grantham, England. Here they can pursue their studies at the Harlaxton Study Centre, "a stone mansion in Gothic style standing in 55 acres of garden and park lands."

2　It is the faculty, far more than the locality, that seems to pose the greatest promotional problems. Like the undeniable tar in the filter cigaret or the taste of the most unpleasant mouthwash, the faculty is the part of the product that seems to arouse the greatest consumer resistance. Most schools face this problem by featuring only a few photographs of professors smiling benignly at undergraduates or occasionally lecturing with manic passion. Several schools boast of the number of Ph.D.s on their staff, and one or two event boast about their lack of them.

3　Many colleges are, however, reluctant to suggest that their professors might be excessively learned or interested in anything but teaching. Coe College, for example, announces that all its professors are "hung up on teaching undergraduates" and that Coe occasionally prefers an M.A. "who can communicate to a Ph.D. who can't bridge the podium gap." Professors at Coe, when they are not bridging the podium gap, are poised to engage in "spontaneous and personal dialog with students."

4　Seton College in Yonkers, New York, seems to be most reassuring about faculty. In a full-page ad in *The New York Times*, Seton features several group photographs of students and faculty idling about in joyful intimacy and challenges the reader to guess, "Which one is the professor?" The professor inevitably turns out to be the most garishly dressed, the most fashionably hirsute, and even the most youthful of the group.

5　The promises of power, individuality, and freedom from organized knowledge that dominate the selling of the academy suggest that the radical slogans of the 1960s have been easily assimilated by the advertising of the 1970s. These advertisements may not, of course, be a reliable guide to what is actually happening on campus, but they do reflect student expectations as perceived—and promoted—by the college account executives and the marketing-research specialists. If nothing else, this is what's being run up the flagpole. Is anybody saluting?

173

Commentary

Superficially, Hungiville seems simply to describe the methods colleges use to attract students in the face of shrinking enrollments. (An outline of the essay shows this neutral quality and nothing more, because outlines indicate *what* is being discussed rather than *how*.) At no point does he say, "These methods are good" or "These methods are bad." Yet we know that he rejects the entire advertising procedure. His essay is an indictment, a negative evaluation, of colleges' attempts to sell themselves to students.

How does he succeed in conveying his judgment without openly stating it? **Largely by the use of connotative language,** language that implies evaluation (see Hayakawa, p. 84). Often he exaggerates the inflated claims of the colleges in words that make them sound absurd. For example, "the word 'individual' thrusts itself forward with all the mechanical predictability of a neon sign" (paragraph 4). The comparison to a neon sign highlights the commercialism of the enterprise, while "mechanical predictability" makes the pretense of individuality seem ridiculous. The description of the curriculum as "a plastic, polymorphously perverse substance" (paragraph 8) makes it resemble Silly Putty or modeling clay and so achieves the same purpose of conveying Hungiville's opinion that this is kids' stuff at best. When he gives the "tantalizing title" of general requirements at one school (paragraph 10) or refers to the "muggerless, smog-free Edens" (paragraph 11) of the Midwest, we recognize that these characteristics are nonsensical. Only silly people would find "GIT" or a course in "Me-ology" tantalizing, and the small towns of Iowa qualify as "Edens" no more than small towns in other states do.

These techniques of style are designed to produce a resounding "No!" in answer to Hungiville's rhetorical question at the end. Rather than stating his evaluation, he is trying to produce it in us.

Outline

I Colleges' quests for students in the 1970s—paragraphs 1–2

II Promotional devices—paragraphs 3–14
  A Guaranteed individualism—paragraphs 3–5
  B Participation in governance—paragraphs 6–7
  C Self-selected curricula—paragraphs 8–10
  D Attractive campuses—paragraph 11
  E Attractive faculty—paragraphs 12–14

III Summary—paragraph 15

Suggestions for Writing

1 Evaluate the publicity statements that your college uses for recruiting new students. Get a packet of the materials mailed to prospective students (probably from the Admissions Office) and examine the "sales pitch" used. Do you approve of it?

2 Imitate Hungiville's technique of letting the style do the job. Write an evaluation of any commercial product (cigarettes, cosmetics, plastic Christmas trees, etc.) without openly stating your opinion. Let your choice of words make it clear that you approve or disapprove.

How Nutritious Are Fast-Food Meals?
Consumer Reports

Probably everyone in America has eaten a fast-food meal. Few of us ask, "Exactly how much does my hamburger weigh?" or "Exactly how much carbohydrate does it contain, and how much protein?" Most of us are satisfied with "I love thick shakes" or "*X*'s hamburgers are better than *Y*'s."

The *Consumer Reports* writers, however, are interested in *evaluating* fast-food meals on the criterion of their *nutritional content*. This general criterion breaks down into several components: calories, protein, carbohydrate, fat, and other nutrients—each with a specified amount for adequacy. While your response to a Big Mac or a Whopper might be "it's good," this careful and informative evaluation tells you whether it's good *for* you. (Notice the different meanings of *good*.)

As evaluative writing, this piece stops short of recommendation. The *Consumer Reports* writers are not recommending that we eat in fast-food restaurants. They are not persuading us to spend our money at McDonald's or Arby's rather than at the supermarket. They are simply making clear the value (in nutritional terms) of what McDonald's and Arby's and six other fast-food chains are offering—or were in May 1975.

1 By 1980, if the present trend continues, Americans will eat half their meals outside the home. Doubtless we will eat many of those meals at McDonald's, Kentucky Fried Chicken, Hardee's, or at one or more of the many other fast-food chains that even now serve up some $10-billion worth of meals a year.

2 Reasons for the growing popularity of fast-food chains appear obvious enough. For one thing, the food is generally cheap as restaurant food goes. The most frequently ordered meal at McDonald's—a "Big Mac" hamburger sandwich, french fries, and a chocolate shake—costs only $1.75. That's a bargain when you consider the saved time and effort of the persons who would otherwise cook and clean up at home. The food is filling. And, judging by the fact that customers return to

Source. "How Nutritious Are Fast-Food Meals?". Copyright 1975 by Consumers Union of United States, Inc., Mount Vernon, N. Y. 10550. Reprinted by permission from *Consumer Reports*, May, 1975.

the successful chains time and again, many Americans like the way it tastes.

3   But as fast food assumes an ever more significant role in the diet, it's appropriate to inquire about the nutritional value of such assembly-line eating. That's what CU concentrated on in this project.

4   We bought and tested meals typical of those served up at eight of the biggest chains in the country: Burger Chef, McDonald's, and Burger King, which specialize in variations on the hamburger theme; Pizza Hut; Kentucky Fried Chicken; Hardee's, which builds its meals around a pseudosteak sandwich or hamburger; Arby's, which serves roast beef sandwiches; and Arthur Treacher's Fish & Chips, which specializes in breaded fried fish.

5   We will go into detail on our tests and results later. But first, some highlights:

The meat in McDonald's "Big Mac" hamburger sandwich weighs about 25 per cent less than the meat in Burger Chef's "Super Shef" and Burger King's "Whopper." Yet the McDonald's meal provided ample protein (as much as Burger King's, for example).

Pizza Hut is the protein champion by far (its "Supreme" 10-inch pizza contains plenty of cheese and other protein-rich foods). But none of the other seven meals tested was inadequate in protein.

Nearly all the meals were too heavy on calories. Several of them provided almost one-half the daily ration of calories needed by the typical adult male. Thus, it's likely that a man who ate at one of these chains regularly, and also ate two other substantial meals a day, would put on weight, especially if he sat behind a desk most of the time between meals. (A deskbound woman would put on more weight because she needs fewer calories.)

A lot of those excess calories come in a form almost useless from a nutritional point of view—sugar and other sweeteners that provide a quick shot of energy but no nutrients. Many of these "empty calories" are to be found in the beverage—either a "thick shake" (not to be confused with a *milk* shake, about which more later) or a cola drink.

All the meals were deficient in at least a few nutrients usually considered essential in a well-rounded diet. A small nutrient deficiency is not a matter of great concern. But when a meal falls short in 10 essential nutrients, as Arthur Treacher's did, "Fish & Chips" lovers had best start thinking carefully about what they eat the rest of the day.

Some Nutritional Rules of Thumb

6   The table on page 180 shows the total weight of each meal and the weight of the individual constituents. More significant are the columns

showing the total calories and the amounts of protein, carbohydrate, and fat. Those columns summarize the nutritional pluses and minuses of each meal. Here's a simple guide to interpreting the nutritional information in the table:

Calories

As a guideline for the amount of calories one should consume each day, the National Academy of Sciences-National Research Council (NAS-NRC) has established a Recommended Daily Dietary Allowance (RDA) for both sexes and for various age groups and body weights. For the typical adult man between the ages of 23 and 50, the calorie RDA is 2700; for children from 7 to 10, the calorie RDA is 2400. (The "typical adult man," it should be noted, is 5 feet 9 inches tall and weighs 154 pounds. Bigger men need somewhat more calories; smaller men, somewhat less. Given equal size and weight, women need slightly fewer calories than men.) The calories, which are measurements of energy, come from three principal components of food—protein, carbohydrate, and fat.

Protein

Known as the body's builder and repairer, protein consists of a complex variety of amino acids. Meat, poultry, and fish are rich protein sources. So are milk and most milk products. (But not butter; that's largely fat.) Legumes—dried beans, peas, lentils, and the like—also have lots of protein, as do eggs and peanut butter. The NAS-NRC has established a guideline RDA for protein. For the typical adult man it would be 56 grams; for the typical 7-to-10-year-old child, male or female, 36 grams.

Carbohydrate

Carbohydrates are often associated with the empty calories of refined sugar. But carbohydrates also come from the starches in potatoes and cereal grains and the sugars natural to many other foods that contain a variety of essential nutrients—vitamins and minerals. A good daily diet should include some bread and other grain products, as well as vegetables and fruit. If it does, it will include a certain amount of carbohydrate. But table sugar and other sweeteners are carbohydrate sources that contain only empty calories. There is no specific requirement for carbohydrates in the diet, nor has there been a guideline set for the amount of carbohydrate humans need daily, although the NAS-NRC Food and Nutrition Board has recommended 100 grams as a minimum. Nutritionists generally agree that the amount needed is low, but all our fast-food meals exceed 100 grams of carbohydrates—and

177

thus, as only one of three daily meals, could contribute to a daily diet likely to be overly rich in carbohydrates. Your best guideline is to make sure your family's carbohydrates come mainly from fruit, vegetables, bread, and cereals, rather than from sugar or sweetened food.

Why We Didn't Feed Rats This Time

When CU reported on the nutritional value of breakfast cereals in the February issue, we noted that comparisons could best be made through studies of how rats fared on the cereals. Yet in this report on fast-food meals we compare the nutritional value of the ingredients without having fed the food to rats. How come?

Packaged cereal is a highly processed food. One can't assume that corn will behave like corn in the body once a manufacturer tortures it into *Quisp* or *Sugar Pops*. The food served by fast-food chains, on the other hand, is relatively "natural." We can measure the nutrients through recognized microbiological methods and predict their behavior in the body with accuracy.

Protein is a good example. We know the quality and biological availability of protein from ground beef, chicken, cheese, fish, and other foods. Therefore, a laboratory measurement of the amount of such natural foods present in a meal tells us enough of what we need to know about the adequacy of the protein content. But we don't know what the quality of protein in breakfast cereals is after the cereal-derived starches, flours, and grains have been processed. Some of these proteins may complement each other—and thus improve overall protein quality—and some may not. One good way to determine the quality of such artificial products is to feed them to growing animals and see how the animals make out.

Iodine: A Potential Problem

During our analyses of the meals served at fast-food chains, CU found one nutrient, iodine, present in surprisingly large quantity. On average, the fast-food meals tested for the accompanying report contained more than 30 times the Recommended Daily Allowance for iodine established by the National Academy of Sciences-National Research Council. Small amounts of iodine are necessary in the diet, mainly to prevent goiter. But no one has established how much is too much.

Can a continued high intake of iodine do harm? A recent review made by the Federation of American Societies for Experimental Biology for the Food and Drug Administration concluded that "adverse reactions to iodine in food are not a significant clinical or public health hazard." Yet little is known about a diet that contains as much iodine as we found in fast-food meals, nor did the review mentioned consider regular consumption of such high levels of iodine. It is known that too much iodine could affect the proper functioning of the thyroid gland. Thus, the review made for the FDA concluded that the amounts of iodine in the American diet should be evaluated periodically. We hope the FDA heeds the suggestion.

Where does all that iodine come from? Some of it may come from the iodized salt used in the preparation of the fast-food meals, but not all of it—or the meals would be inedible. There are two other likely sources: the rolls, bread, and breading made by bakeries that probably use high levels of iodates in their processes; or from residues of iodine compounds that may have been used to clean and sterilize food-processing equipment.

Fat

This third source of energy is the one that's usually right before your eyes—on the meat, in the frying pan, in the bottle of oil, or as butter or margarine. It's the most concentrated source of energy, because one gram of fat is converted into nine calories, not the four calories that a gram of protein or carbohydrate produces. Thus, a little fat goes a long way, and a little more goes too far. You do need some fat; it's the only source of linoleic acid (an essential nutrient), and it's a carrier for vitamins A, D, E, and K. There are no guidelines for how much fat one should eat daily. Suffice it to say that most Americans get ample fat, usually far more than they need. Since fat converts into so many calories per gram, it's a good food component to cut down on if your daily diet includes more calories than it should.

Other Nutrients

The body needs many vitamins and minerals as well as protein, and a well-balanced diet, one that contains a variety of foods, will include them all. Recommended Daily Dietary Allowances have not been established for every known essential nutrient. But our consultant did analyze the fast-food meals for a host of nutrients for which RDA's do exist. These include: folacin (folic acid), niacin, thiamine, riboflavin, pyridoxine, vitamins B_{12} and C, total vitamin A (both retinol and carotene), phosphorus, calcium, magnesium, iron, zinc, and iodine. Our consultant also analyzed the meals for biotin, pantothenic acid, and copper- nutrients for which the Food and Drug Administration has established labeling guidelines—and for total minerals, fiber, and moisture. We judged a meal deficient in a nutrient if it failed to provide one-third the daily allowance guideline.

The Beverage Problem

7   The nutritional booby trap common to all the fast-food meals we tested is the beverage. Both the shakes and the cola drinks contributed significantly to the general overabundance of calories and to the excessive amount of carbohydrate found in our analyses.

8   All the shakes are called "thick" shakes—perhaps because they are indeed thick, perhaps because the words "thick" and "milk" have a rough resemblance. They are rarely milk shakes. Milk shakes contain whole milk and ice cream; the sweet, heavy froths served at these fast-food chains usually do not. Judging by the fact that the shakes did contribute to the protein content of the meals, however, they no doubt do contain an appreciable amount of nutritious fat-free milk solids in addition to an appreciable amount of sweetener and chemical thickener. Our shakes averaged about 334 calories, most of them empty calories. (Note, by the way, that the table gives the weight of

beverage in avoirdupois ounces, not the volume in fluid ounces. That's because the shakes are so thick and puffed with air that we couldn't measure their volume accurately.)

9   The cola drinks are, of course, familiar beverages that contain nothing of nutritional value. Our colas averaged 111 calories, all devoid of other nutrients. Cola drinks contain the drug caffeine (as they must by law to be labeled "cola"). The cola drinks we analyzed averaged about 30 milligrams (mg) of caffeine; a brewed cup of coffee contains about 100 mg of caffeine, on average.

10   Given the American appetite for shakes and cola drinks, and given the enormous advertising of cola drinks, one can hardly expect fast-food chains to refrain from offering them. Unfortunately, the ones we visited offered little other choice. Everyone would be better off, in our opinion, drinking water instead of the shakes and cola drinks served at these establishments. If you can't wheedle a glass of water off the assembly line, unsugared tea or black coffee is the next best bet for an adult (neither offers any nutritional value, but neither do they add appreciably to the calorie count), and milk, juice, or a low-calorie soda, where available, would be better for children.

11   People on low-sodium diets face a problem at most fast-food chains. The specialty item is almost always presalted, and the potatoes are usually presalted. The Pizza Hut meal had the highest sodium content of all—four grams. That translates into about 1½ teaspoons of table salt—a full day's supply for a person on the mildest of sodium-restricted diets. The six meat meals each contained nearly one teaspoonful of salt, still a lot for someone on a diet. We found only negligible amounts of sodium in the Arthur Treacher's meal.

THE EIGHT FAST-FOOD MEALS

The three hamburger meals are listed first, in order of amount of protein provided. The other meals follow in protein order. Descriptions of the meals with comments are on the facing page.

	Price	Total weight (oz.)	Meat weight (oz.)	Bread weight (oz.)	Potatoes weight (oz.)	Trimmings weight [A] (oz.)	Beverage weight (oz.)	Total calories	Protein (grams)	Carbohydrates (grams)	Fat (grams)
BURGER CHEF	$1.75	26.9	3.0	4.0	4.1	2.7	12.7	1300	47	181	41
McDONALD'S	1.75	18.7	2.3	2.9	3.5	1.5	8.6	1100	40	143	41
BURGER KING	1.70	20.6	3.2	4.0	2.6	2.2	8.5	1200	40	147	47
PIZZA HUT	2.74	32.2	19.0[B]	—	—	—	13.2	1200	72	152	35
KENTUCKY FRIED CHICKEN	2.08	22.7	7.9[C]	0.8	2.0	—	12.1	1300	65	141	57
HARDEE'S	1.89	21.1	3.2	2.2	4.9	0.3	10.4	1100	41	143	41
ARBY'S	1.95	22.9	2.7	2.8	2.9	2.3	12.2	1200	37	166	40
ARTHUR TREACHER'S	1.84	24.5	2.6	2.6[D]	4.7	—	14.7	900	22	101	42

[A] *Trimmings include sauces, tomato slice, cheese, pickle, onion, lettuce, or cole slaw provided with the meal.*
[B] *Weight of total pizza.*
[C] *Including breading, but without bones.*
[D] *Weight of breading on fish.*

Fast-Food Chains, One Bite at a Time

Here, in summary, is the evaluation of the nutritional quality of each meal we measured.

Our Burger Chef meal consisted of a "Super Shef" hamburger, french fries, and a chocolate shake. It would load children with half their total daily need for calories and come close to supplying half the calorie needs of an adult, too. The greatest nutritional drawback of the Burger Chef meal was its high carbohydrate content—higher in weight than that of any of the other meals. Most of those carbohydrates were empty calories of sweetness in the shake. (The same criticism can be made of the other shakes we tested; see facing page.) The meal was low in biotin, folacin, and pantothenic acid for adult and child; vitamin A for adult.

We ordered a "Big Mac" hamburger, french fries, and a chocolate shake. The McDonald's meal provided less meat than the other burger meals and less total food. So perhaps the familiar advertising theme, "You deserve a break today at McDonald's," refers to the dietary break of slightly fewer calories than you get at the other hamburger chains. The protein content was more than adequate. The meal was low in biotin, pantothenic acid, and total vitamin A for both age groups.

We bought the "Whopper" hamburger, french fries, and a chocolate shake. That meal contained more meat and less potatoes than the other two burger meals—and more fat, which probably came from the meat. As with the Burger Chef meal, calories came to half of a child's daily needs and nearly half of an adult's. The meal was low in biotin, folacin, pantothenic acid, and copper.

Here we bought a 10-inch "Supreme" pizza —a pie appliquéd with tomato sauce, cheese, ground sausage, mushrooms, pepperoni, onions, and green pepper—and a cola drink. It provided the most protein of any of the meals, far exceeding a whole day's RDA for any age. Yet the total calories weren't unusually high, and the fat content was the lowest of all. This was clearly the best food buy, considering that the pizza alone would provide a single meal's worth of protein for two persons. But it's by no means perfect. Surprisingly, considering its constituents, this meal was the only one that failed to have one-third the RDA for vitamin C for both adult and child. (The high baking heat probably destroyed the vitamin C.) The meal was also low in biotin and pantothenic acid for both age groups, and it contained more sodium than anyone on a sodium-restricted diet should have at one meal (see facing page).

Kentucky Fried Chicken

Colonel Sanders' meal contained three pieces of fried chicken, french fries, a roll, and a chocolate shake. That added up to half the daily calorie need of the adult and to more than half of the child's needs. (But it's probably unlikely that many 7-year-olds could chew their way through all that food.) This meal contained considerably more meat than the hamburger meals and, as a direct consequence, a lot more protein—more than a whole day's RDA for adult and child. An excess of protein does no harm other than the harm done by the excess of calories likely to follow too much of any food component. (Note: we weighed the meat without the bone but with the breading—we just couldn't successfully separate the breading from the chicken. However, we believe the weight of the breading was not so high as to affect the general outlines of our findings.) With all that meat came more fat than in any of the other meals tested: The Colonel's frying process results in a greasy bird in hand; not only do your fingers need lickin', they need washin'. All in all, the Kentucky Fried Chicken meal represents a lot of food for the money, perhaps even a surfeit of food. The meal was low in biotin, folacin, and vitamin A for adult and child.

Hardee's

This meal consisted of a flaked and formed steak, a bun, french fries, and a chocolate shake. Calories, protein, carbohydrates, and fat were fairly comparable to that of the burger meals. And the steak was comparable to a hamburger (a "flaked and formed steak" is just shredded meat tenderized and formed into the shape of a steak). The meal was low in biotin, pantothenic acid, and total vitamin A for both age groups.

Arby's

Arby's serves up sliced beef on a bun, two potato patties, and cole slaw (the roast beef plate). We also bought a chocolate shake. Arby's main contribution to fast-food technology appears to be its mastery of the art of paper-thin slicing. We counted an average of 28 slices of beef per sandwich, each slice *nine-thousandths* of an inch thick. But all those slices weighed only 2.7 ounces. That's an adequate portion of meat, but not a generous one. Thus the meal contained less protein than any of the other meat meals, although enough for one of three daily meals. Arby's meal also contained the second highest measure of carbohydrates, and, again, a lot of that was empty calories from the shake. It also fell short in biotin, folacin, pantothenic acid, total vitamin A, and copper for both age groups.

Arthur Treacher's

This meal contained two pieces of breaded fried fish, french fries, and a cola drink. That added up to the fewest total calories and the least amount of protein. We don't mourn the low calorie count, and there was still enough protein to provide one-third the daily needs of man and child. But this meal contained too little biotin, pantothenic acid, niacin, thiamine, total vitamin A, calcium, magnesium, iron, copper, and zinc for both adult and child.

181

12 **Those Missing Nutrients**

The six nutrients most commonly in short supply in fast-food meals are: biotin, folacin, pantothenic acid, total vitamin A, iron, and copper. These nutrients, which perform a variety of functions in growth and life-support, are derived from many food sources, some of which would usually be part of almost any standard diet that includes a variety of foods. If you eat at a fast-food chain regularly, it would be wise to make sure that your other meals include such nutritious foods as beans, dark green leafy vegetables, yellow vegetables, and a variety of fresh fruits. That should overcome the nutritional deficiencies of fast-food meals.

Commentary

The *Consumer Reports* article illustrates the full formal evaluation process (see p. 162). After an introduction that reminds us of the popularity of fast-food restaurants, the writers **limit their topic** to a manageable size and state their general **criterion** (paragraphs 1–4). A quick glance at the major **conclusions** is provided next, for the convenience of readers who are too busy to read through the entire evaluation (paragraph 5). The writers then return to the **criteria**, dividing "nutritional quality" into several categories and carefully explaining each one (paragraph 6). Two problem areas are discussed (paragraphs 7–12). Then the detailed individual evaluations are provided in two ways: first, a table gives the **exact data** for each fast-food meal; second, a brief summary points out the meaning of the data in the table.

You will notice that the sequence of presentation is not the same as the sequence suggested above (p. 162) for the evaluation process itself. Can you see why the *Consumer Reports* writers arranged their material as they did?

The criterion of nutritional quality is utilitarian: the *Consumer Reports* writers want to help you get the most food value for your money. However, that functional intention does not bind them to a dull style. Notice the stylistic jokes in the summaries: a new meaning for "you deserve a break today," and the phrase "not only do your fingers need lickin', they need washin'" used about Kentucky Fried Chicken.

The *Consumer Reports* writers have designed their evaluation for the audience of that magazine. What kinds of people read *Consumer Reports*? What other points of view might you have about fast-food meals? Perhaps nutrition is not all that you expect from a good meal.

Outline

I Introduction: the popularity of fast foods; criterion and scope of this study (paragraphs 1–4)

II General conclusions (paragraph 5)

III Details of criteria (paragraph 6)

IV Two problem areas (paragraphs 7–12)

A Nutrition in beverages (paragraphs 7–11)

B Nutrient shortages (paragraph 12)

V Data and meal-by-meal evaluations (charts)

Suggestions for Writing

1 Adopt the *Consumer Reports* point of view of a person seeking the most utilitarian value for the money, and evaluate some product designed for consumer use. You may deal with only one example of the type (not, as here, with eight), and you may not have access to all the kinds of information used here. But your personal experience evaluation will correspond to the way that most of us decide whether a product we buy once will appear on our shopping list again.

2 Evaluate some item (perhaps fast-food meals) from a perspective other than that of the consumer seeking the most performance for his or her money. What do people look for—aside from utilitarian adequacy at a reasonable price—when they buy houses, cars, clothing? For example, if one value of dinner is the chance for quiet conversation and relaxation from the day's hustle and bustle, how well do fast-food meals meet that criterion? If one value of a house is that it should "feel like home" according to your personal definition of *home*, how good would a high-rise apartment or a trailer or an isolated house in the country be?

The Gettysburg Address
Gilbert Highet

What qualities make us remember the great speeches of American history? Lincoln's collected writings fill several volumes, but only a few short pieces are remembered as great writing. Most contemporary political rhetoric will not deserve to be remembered at all.

Part of the importance of a speech derives from its subject and occasion. Nobody would expect a routine tax message to be of widespread and permanent interest. But among the many speeches devoted to important subjects and significant occasions, those with literary excellence are the ones most likely to survive.

Highet's analysis of Lincoln's Gettysburg Address judges it as "a work of art," specifically as a successful illustration of certain techniques of classical oratory. Do you agree that the style of political addresses is as important as their substance?

Source. "The Gettysburg Address" by Gilbert Highet. From *A Clerk of Oxenford: Essays on Literature and Life* by Gilbert Highet. Copyright © 1954 by Gilbert Highet. Reprinted by permission of Curtis Brown, Ltd.

Fourscore and seven years ago our fathers brought forth on this continent, a new nation, conceived in Liberty, and dedicated to the proposition that all men are created equal.

Now we are engaged in a great civil war, testing whether that nation or any nation so conceived and so dedicated, can long endure. We are met on a great battle-field of that war. We have come to dedicate a portion of that field, as a final resting place for those who here gave their lives that that nation might live. It is altogether fitting and proper that we should do this.

But, in a larger sense, we can not dedicate—we can not consecrate—we can not hallow—this ground. The brave men, living and dead, who sturggled here, have consecrated it, far above our poor power to add or detract. The world will little note, nor long remember, what we say here, but it can never forget what they did here. It is for us the living, rather, to be dedicated here to the unfinished work which they who fought here have thus far so nobly advanced. It is rather for us to be here dedicated to the great task remaining before us—that from these honored dead we take increased devotion to that cause for which they gave the last full measure of devotion—that we here highly resolve that these dead shall not have died in vain—that this nation, under God, shall have a new birth of freedom—and that government of the people, by the people, for the people, shall not perish from the earth.

1 *Fourscore and seven years ago . . .*

2 These five words stand at the entrance to the best-known monument of American prose, one of the finest utterances in the entire language and surely one of the greatest speeches in all history. Greatness is like granite: it is molded in fire, and it lasts for many centuries.

3 Fourscore and seven years ago . . . . It is strange to think that President Lincoln was looking back to the 4th of July 1776, and that he and his speech are now further removed from us than he himself was from George Washington and the Declaration of Independence. Fourscore and seven years before the Gettysburg Address, a small group of patriots signed the Declaration. Fourscore and seven years after the Gettysburg Address, it was the year 1950,[1] and that date is already receding rapidly into our troubled, adventurous, and valiant past.

4 Inadequately prepared and at first scarcely realized in its full importance, the dedication of the graveyard at Gettysburg was one of the supreme moments of American history. The battle itself had been a turning point of the war. On the 4th of July 1863, General Meade repelled Lee's invasion of Pennsylvania. Although he did not follow up his victory, he had broken one of the most formidable aggressive enterprises of the Confederate armies. Losses were heavy on both sides. Thousands of dead were left on the field, and thousands of

---

[1] In November 1950 the Chinese had just entered the war in Korea.

wounded died in the hot days following the battle. At first, their burial was more or less haphazard; but thoughtful men gradually came to feel that an adequate burying place and memorial were required. These were established by an interstate commission that autumn, and the finest speaker in the North was invited to dedicate them. This was the scholar and statesman Edward Everett of Harvard. He made a good speech—which is still extant: not at all academic, it is full of close strategic analysis and deep historical understanding.

5   Lincoln was not invited to speak, at first. Although people knew him as an effective debater, they were not sure whether he was capable of making a serious speech on such a solemn occasion. But one of the impressive things about Lincoln's career is that he constantly strove to *grow*. He was anxious to appear on that occasion and to say something worthy of it. (Also, it has been suggested, he was anxious to remove the impression that he did not know how to behave properly—an impression which had been strengthened by a shocking story about his clowning on the battlefield of Antietam the previous year.) Therefore when he was invited he took considerable care with his speech. He drafted rather more than half of it in the White House before leaving, finished it in the hotel at Gettysburg the night before the ceremony (not in the train, as sometimes reported), and wrote out a fair copy next morning.

6   There are many accounts of the day itself, 19 November 1863. There are many descriptions of Lincoln, all showing the same curious blend of grandeur and awkwardness, or lack of dignity, or—it would be best to call it humility. In the procession he rode horseback: a tall lean man in a high plug hat, straddling a short horse, with his feet too near the ground. He arrived before the chief speaker, and had to wait patiently for half an hour or more. His own speech came right at the end of a long and exhausting ceremony, lasted less than three minutes, and made little impression on the audience. In part this was because they were tired, in part because (as eyewitnesses said) he ended almost before they knew he had begun, and in part because he did not speak the Address, but read it, very slowly, in a thin high voice, with a marked Kentucky accent, pronouncing "to" as "toe" and dropping his final R's.

7   Some people of course were alert enough to be impressed. Everett congratulated him at once. But most of the newspapers paid little attention to the speech, and some sneered at it. The *Patriot and Union* of Harrisburg wrote, "We pass over the silly remarks of the President; for the credit of the nation we are willing . . . that they shall no more be repeated or thought of"; and the London *Times* said, "The ceremony was rendered ludicrous by some of the sallies of that poor President Lincoln," calling his remarks "dull and commonplace." The first commendation of the Address came in a single sentence of the

Chicago *Tribune*, and the first discriminating and detailed praise of it appeared in the Springfield *Republican*, the Providence *Journal*, and the Philadelphia *Bulletin*. However, three weeks after the ceremony and then again the following spring, the editor of *Harper's Weekly* published a sincere and thorough eulogy of the Address, and soon it was attaining recognition as a masterpiece.

8   At the time, Lincoln could not care much about the reception of his words. He was exhausted and ill. In the train back to Washington, he lay down with a wet towel on his head. He had caught smallpox. At that moment he was incubating it, and he was stricken down soon after he reentered the White House. Fortunately it was a mild attack, and it evoked one of his best jokes: he told his visitors, "At last I have something I can give to everybody."

9   He had more than that to give to everybody. He was a unique person, far greater than most people realize until they read his life with care. The wisdom of his policy, the sources of his statesmanship—these were things too complex to be discussed in a brief essay. But we can say something about the Gettysburg Address as a work of art.

10   A work of art. Yes: for Lincoln was a literary artist, trained both by others and by himself. The textbooks he used as a boy were full of difficult exercises and skillful devices in formal rhetoric, stressing the qualities he practiced in his own speaking: antithesis, parallelism, and verbal harmony. Then he read and reread many admirable models of thought and expression: the King James Bible, the essays of Bacon, the best plays of Shakespeare. His favorites were *Hamlet, Lear, Macbeth, Richard III*, and *Henry VIII,* which he had read dozens of times. He loved reading aloud, too, and spent hours reading poetry to his friends. (He told his partner Herndon that he preferred getting the sense of any document by reading it aloud.) Therefore his serious speeches are important parts of the long and noble classical tradition of oratory which begins in Greece, runs through Rome to the modern world, and is still capable (if we do not neglect it) of producing masterpieces.

11   The first proof of this is that the Gettysburg Address is full of quotations—or rather of adaptations—which give it strength. It is partly religious, partly (in the highest sense) political: therefore it is interwoven with memories of the Bible and memories of American history. The first and the last words are Biblical cadences. Normally Lincoln did not say "fourscore" when he meant eighty; but on this solemn occasion he recalled the important dates in the Bible—such as

the age of Abram when his first son was born to him, and he was "fourscore and six years old."[2] Similarly he did not say there was a chance that democracy might die out: he recalled the somber phrasing of the Book of Job—where Bildad speaks of the destruction of one who shall vanish without a trace, and says that "his branch shall be cut off; his remembrance shall perish from the earth."[3] Then again, the famous description of our State as "government of the people, by the people, for the people" was adumbrated by Daniel Webster in 1830 (he spoke of "the people's government, made for the people, made by the people, and answerable to the people") and then elaborated in 1854 by the abolitionist Theodore Parker (as "government of all the people, by all the people, for all the people"). There is good reason to think that Lincoln took the important phrase "under God" (which he interpolated at the last moment) from Weems, the biographer of Washington; and we know that it had been used at least once by Washington himself.

2   Analyzing the Address further, we find that it is based on a highly imaginative theme, or group of themes. The subject is—how can we put it so as not to disfigure it?—the subject is the kinship of life and death, that mysterious linkage which we see sometimes as the physical succession of birth and death in our world, sometimes as the contrast, which is perhaps a unity, between death and immortality. The first sentence is concerned with birth:

> Our *fathers brought forth* a *new* nation, *conceived* in liberty.

The final phrase but one expresses the hope that

> this nation, under God, shall have a *new birth* of freedom.

And the last phrase of all speaks of continuing life as the triumph over death. Again and again throughout the speech, this mystical contrast and kinship reappear: "those who *gave their lives* that that nation might *live*," "the brave men *living* and *dead*," and so in the central assertion that the dead have already consecrated their own burial place, while "it is for us, the *living*, rather to be dedicated . . . to the great task remaining." The Gettysburg Address is a prose poem; it belongs to the same world as the great elegies, and the adagios of Beethoven.

13   Its structure, however, is that of a skillfully contrived speech. The oratorical pattern is perfectly clear. Lincoln describes the occasion, dedicates the ground, and then draws a larger conclusion by calling on his hearers to dedicate themselves to the preservation of the Union.

[2] Gen. 16.16; cf. Exod. 7.7.
[3] Job 18.16–17; cf. Jer. 10.11, Micah 7.2.

But within that, we can trace his constant use of at least two important rhetorical devices.

14   The first of these is *antithesis:* opposition, contrast. The speech is full of it. Listen:

> The world will little *note*
> nor long *remember*   what *we say* here   .
> but   it can never *forget*   what *they did* here.

And so in nearly every sentence: "brave men, *living* and *dead*"; "to *add* or *detract*." There is the antithesis of the Founding Fathers and the men of Lincoln's own time:

> Our *fathers brought forth* a new nation . . .
> now *we* are testing whether that nation . . . can *long endure*.

And there is the more terrible antithesis of those who have already died and those who still live to do their duty. Now, antithesis is the figure of contrast and conflict. Lincoln was speaking in the midst of a great civil war.

15   The other important pattern is different. It is technically called *tricolon*—the division of an idea into three harmonious parts, usually of increasing power. The most famous phrase of the Address is a tricolon:

> government of the people
> by the people
> and   for the people.

The most solemn sentence is a tricolon:

> we cannot dedicate
> we cannot consecrate
> we cannot hallow this ground.

And above all, the last sentence (which has sometimes been criticized as too complex) is essentially two parallel phrases, with a tricolon growing out of the second and then producing another tricolon: a trunk, three branches, and a cluster of flowers. Lincoln says that it is for his hearers to be dedicated to the great task remaining before them. Then he goes on,

> that from these honored dead

—apparently he means "in such a way that from these honored dead"—

> we take increased devotion to that cause.

Next, he restates this more briefly:

> that we here highly resolve . . .

And now the actual resolution follows, in three parts of growing intensity:

> that these dead shall not have died in vain
> that this nation, under God, shall have a new birth of freedom

and that (one more tricolon)

> government of the people
>   by the people
>   and   for the people
> shall not perish from the earth.

Now, the tricolon is the figure which, through division, emphasizes basic harmony and unity. Lincoln used antithesis because he was speaking to a people at war. He used the tricolon because he was hoping, planning, praying for peace.

6   No one thinks that when he was drafting the Gettysburg Address, Lincoln deliberately looked up these quotations and consciously chose these particular patterns of thought. No, he chose the theme. From its development and from the emotional tone of the entire occasion, all the rest followed, or grew—by that marvelous process of choice and rejection which is essential to artistic creation. It does not spoil such a work of art to analyze it as closely as we have done; it is altogether fitting and proper that we should do this: for it helps us to penetrate more deeply into the rich meaning of the Gettysburg Address, and it allows us the very rare privilege of watching the workings of a great man's mind.

W. E. Barton, *Lincoln at Gettysburg* (Bobbs-Merrill, 1930).
R. P. Basler, "Abraham Lincoln's Rhetoric," *American Literature* 11 (1939-40), 167-82.
L. E. Robinson, *Abraham Lincoln as a Man of Letters* (Chicago, 1918).

Commentary

Highet spends his first eight paragraphs identifying his subject and establishing historical background. Although a great deal of information is skillfully compressed into these paragraphs, they are a rather long introduction if his purpose is to demonstrate that the Gettysburg Address is "one of the greatest speeches in all history" (paragraph 2). Is this introductory section justified? What purposes does it serve?

Paragraphs 9–15 examine Lincoln's art: the content and the stylistic devices of the Address. To Highet, who believes in the value of tradition, it is high praise to say that Lincoln's speech belongs in "the long and noble classical tradition of oratory." **He divides this general principle of literary excellence into several specific qualities:** echoes of earlier writings (paragraph 11); a theme of permanent importance (paragraph 12); a clear oratorical pattern (paragraph 13); the devices of antithesis and tricolon (paragraphs 14 and 15). Highet believes that the tricolon is such a valuable device that he uses it himself at the end of paragraph 15 (in describing how Lincoln used it).

Some rhetoricians have claimed that we should not teach people how to write or speak movingly unless we also teach them a sense of responsibility. Otherwise they might use the power of words for evil purposes. Eloquence can be a dangerous weapon, they point out, and we should not put dangerous weapons in the hands of everybody. If you agree with this position, you may evaluate Highet's article as incomplete because it does not try to demonstrate the excellence of Lincoln's ideas.

Should our criteria for evaluating political rhetoric be utilitarian (= does a speech work?) or moral (= does it propose good ideas?) or aesthetic (= does it give us pleasure to hear it?)—or all three?

Outline

I Introduction: the power and permanence of the Address—paragraph 2

II Historical background—paragraphs 4–8
   A Occasion of the Address—paragraphs 4–6
   B Its impact—paragraph 7

III The ''art'' of the Address—paragraphs 9–15
   A Lincoln's training and sources—paragraphs 10–11
   B Themes—paragraph 12
   C Devices of style—paragraphs 13–15

IV Summary of the value of the Address and assertion that analyzing it increases its meaning—paragraph 16

Suggestions for Writing

1 Evaluate an *X* of your own choosing, using Highet's pattern: (1) give background information so that we are familiar with the situation; (2) state your focus—as when Highet says he will comment on Lincoln's speech ''as a work of art''; (3) bring criteria and evidence together.

2 Lincoln once said that a nation must hear ''mystic chords of memory stretching from every battlefield and patriot grave to every living heart and hearthstone.'' Many Americans apparently no longer hear those chords.

   What would the Gettysburg Address mean to a person who does not recognize its sources or accept its patriotic themes? Evaluate Lincoln's speech using not criteria drawn from classical rhetoric but whatever contemporary criteria you think are appropriate.

3 The Roman writer Cicero, himself a master of political rhetoric, thought that the ideal speech should involve three kinds of persuasion: (1) *logical persuasion*, which gives facts and builds a reasonable argument on them; (2) *emotional persuasion*, which uses language to affect the audience's emotions; and (3) *ethical persuasion*, which brings out the speaker's sincerity and other good human qualities in order to earn the audience's trust.

   Evaluate Lincoln's speech using those criteria. Does it use all three kinds of persuasion? How well?

Evaluation, Series Two
Readings without Commentary

The Squirrel Memo
The Wall Street Journal

The subject of this short evaluation is bureaucratic red tape, specifically the endless and senseless forms that government agencies ask people to fill out. An HEW (Department of Health, Education, and Welfare) application form is made to seem ridiculous when someone answers it in terms of squirrels.

The *Wall Street Journal* writer uses the evaluative technique known as "damning with faint praise." He finds something to approve of, but it is so minor a characteristic, and his praise is so lukewarm, that the overall evaluation is clearly negative. Thus the last paragraph finds that it is "nice" (a trivial term) to see a sense of humor in a government agency with "an occupational devotion to red tape." We are meant to remain annoyed with HEW for its red tape. The sense of humor belongs mostly to the university staff member who had the bright idea of sending those nuts a few squirrels.

1 Many releases and handouts that cross newspaper desks each day could be offered as prime exhibits for hiking the postal rates on unsolicited mail. But occasionally there's gold in them thar hills, and we offer as evidence a recent item from the news bureau of Washington and Lee University in Lexington, Virginia.

2 It seems that one Frank Parsons, assistant to the university presi-

Source. "The Squirrel Memo." From *The Wall Street Journal*, October 24, 1974. Reprinted with permission of *The Wall Street Journal*, © Dow Jones & Company, Inc. 1974. All Rights Reserved.

dent, was struggling with a lengthy application for federal funds to be used in building the university's proposed new library. Among other things, HEW wanted to know how the proposed project "may affect energy sources by introducing or deleting electro-magnetic wave sources which may alter man-made or natural structures or the physiology, behavior patterns, and/or activities of 10% of a human, animal or plant population." The questions go on and on, but you get the idea.

3   Assistant Parsons plugged away, dutifully answering as best he could. And then he came to the section on animal populations, where he was asked to list the extent to which the proposed library would "create or precipitate an identifiable long-term change in the diversity of species within its natural habitat."

4   "There are some 10 to 20 squirrels living, or appearing to live, in the site proposed for the new library," he wrote. "Some trees that now provide either homes or exercise areas for the squirrels will be removed, but there appear to be ample other trees to serve either or both of these purposes. No major food source for the squirrels will be affected. It is likely that the squirrels will find no difficulty in adjusting to this intrusion. . . . They have had no apparent difficulty in adjusting to relocations brought on by nonfederally supported projects."

5   To the question of whether the proposal will "create or precipitate an identifiable change in the behavior patterns of an animal population," he assured HEW the squirrels and such would have to make some adjustments but "it will be difficult to tell if they're unhappy about having to find new trees to live in and sport about."

6   Eventually the application was shipped off to Washington, and lo and behold before long HEW official Richard R. Holden actually wrote the president of the school. He said: "Perhaps bureaucracy will tremble, but I salute Washington and Lee University. . . . The mountain of paperwork which confronts me daily somehow seemed much smaller the day I read about the squirrels in Lexington. May they and your great university coexist in harmony for many, many years." As copies of the correspondence zipped throughout federal agencies, with all the speed of a confidential memo destined for Jack Anderson, bureaucrats from all over telephoned their congratulations to the "squirrel memo man."

7   We're still not sure exactly what lesson is to be drawn from all this. Our initial reaction was surprise that anyone actually reads these exhaustive applications, and even now we're undecided whether that's cause for comfort or dismay. Yet while we never doubted that HEW possessed a sense of humor—indeed, we've gotten some of our biggest laughs from proposals emanating from the vicinity of 330 Independence Avenue, S.W.—it's nice to know that an occupational devotion

to red tape has not completely eroded the agency's ability to laugh at itself.

Stereotypes in American History
Vine Deloria, Jr.

This selection is an attack on the "sweetness and light" treatment of American history. Deloria protests two ways of seeing the history of America's minority groups. One way singles out isolated blacks or Indians or Mexicans and exaggerates their part in major historical events. The other depicts each minority group (as a whole) as offering some material contribution to our national welfare. These are bad interpretations, Deloria says, because they do not tell the truth about the painful clashes of our national past. Deloria's criterion, then, is truth—an accurate presentation of the facts. To him, a good version of American history would offer a "balanced story" (paragraph 1), not a pretty but "unrealistic account" (paragraph 7).

Do you agree that the value of history is its truth? Or is it also important for the members of an ethnically diverse culture to learn a version of history that makes them feel more at home?

1 If the weak points of each minority group's history are to be covered over by a sweetness-and-light interpretation based on what we would like to think happened rather than what did happen, we doom ourselves to decades of further racial strife. Most of the study programs today emphasize the goodness that is inherent in the different minority communities, instead of trying to present a balanced story. There are basically two schools of interpretation running through all of these efforts as the demand for black, red, and brown pride dominates the programs.

Source. "Stereotypes in American History" by Vine Deloria, Jr. Reprinted with permission of Macmillan Publishing Co., Inc. from *We Talk, You Listen* by Vine Deloria, Jr. Copyright © 1970 by Vine Deloria, Jr.

2   One theory derives from the "All-American Platoon"[1] concept of a decade ago. Under this theory members of the respective racial minority groups had an important role in the great events of American history. Crispus Attucks, a black, almost single-handedly started the Revolutionary War, while Eli Parker, the Seneca Indian general, won the Civil War and would have concluded it sooner had not there been so many stupid whites abroad in those days. This is the "cameo" theory of history. It takes a basic "manifest destiny" white interpretation of history and lovingly plugs a few feathers, woolly heads, and sombreros into the famous events of American history. No one tries to explain what an Indian is who was helping the whites destroy his own people, since we are now all Americans and have these great events in common.

3   The absurdity of the cameo school of ethnic pride is self-apparent. Little Mexican children are taught that there were some good Mexicans at the Alamo. They can therefore be happy that Mexicans have been involved in the significant events of Texas history. Little is said about the Mexicans on the other side at the Alamo. The result is a denial of a substantial Mexican heritage by creating the feeling that "we all did it together." If this trend continues I would not be surprised to discover that Columbus had a Cherokee on board when he set sail from Spain in search of the Indies.

4   The cameo school smothers any differences that existed historically by presenting a history in which all groups have participated through representatives. Regardless of Crispus Attuck's valiant behavior during the Revolution, it is doubtful that he envisioned another century of slavery for blacks as a cause worth defending.

5   The other basic school of interpretation is a projection backward of the material blessings of the white middle class. It seeks to identify where all the material wealth originated and finds that each minority group *contributed* something. It can therefore be called the contribution school. Under this conception we should all love Indians because they contributed corn, squash, potatoes, tobacco, coffee, rubber, and other agricultural products. In like manner, blacks and Mexicans are credited with Carver's work on the peanut, blood transfusion, and tacos and tamales.

6   The ludicrous implication of the contribution school visualizes the minority groups clamoring to enter American society, lined up with an abundance of foods and fancies, presenting them to whites in a never-ending stream of generosity. If the different minority groups were given an overriding 2 percent royalty on their contributions, the

[1] The "All American Platoon" was a "one each": one black, one Mexican, one Indian, one farm boy from Iowa, one Southerner who hated blacks, one boy from Brooklyn, one Polish boy from the urban slums of the Midwest, one Jewish intellectual, and one college boy. Every possible stereotype was included.

same way whites have managed to give themselves royalties for their inventions, this school would have a more realistic impact on minority groups.

The danger with both of these types of ethnic studies theories is that they present an unrealistic account of the role of minority groups in American history. Certainty there is more to the story of the American Indian than providing cocoa and popcorn for Columbus' landing party. When the clashes of history are smoothed over in favor of a mushy togetherness feeling, then people begin to wonder what has happened in the recent past that has created the conditions of today.

Technology — Hope or Hobgoblin?
Henry B. du Pont

When the late Henry B. du Pont wrote the following evaluation of technology, he was vice-president of one of America's large manufacturing corporations. The selection below was originally part of a speech that du Pont gave to the Association of Land-Grant Colleges and Universities.

Du Pont defends technology on two grounds. First, it has vastly increased the material well-being of the average American worker. Second, it has vastly decreased the difference between the worker's living standard and that of the boss. Technology thus promotes social equality.

More than 25 years have passed since 1952, when du Pont wrote this evaluation. Have the criteria by which you would evaluate technology changed? Has the evidence changed? Do you agree that technology is still "everybody's rich uncle" (paragraph 9)? Are there disadvantages to having a rich uncle?

1 There have been times in the past when fears were expressed that widespread unemployment would result from technological advances.

Source. "Technology—Hope or Hobgoblin?" by Henry B. du Pont. From an address before the Association of Land-Grant Colleges and Universities, November 11, 1952. Reprinted by permission of E. I. du Pont de Nemours & Co., Inc.

195

But today few are deluded by the myth that technology will make displaced persons of our industrial population. If the buggy whip and the livery stable have become extinct, they cannot be mourned by a society that employs 12,000,000 people to make and service the automobile. Today, after the most intensive technological program in history, we have the largest employment force in history.

2 Yet occasionally there have been those who actually called for a moratorium on research and invention. You will recall that such outcries were popular during the Thirties. But let us suppose that all research and development had somehow been halted arbitrarily at some given point in history. Without tractors and machinery and chemical fertilizers, our farms could not have supported our growing population and soon we would have stagnated into a nation of paupers and peasants like India or China, always at the edge of famine. With our food problem solved, people were able to turn their attention to other activities. It is estimated that fully half of the American working population now earns its living producing things unknown in 1902. And even since 1930 we have seen huge gains in employment opportunities—to indicate the fields that new technology has opened we need only to mention such things as air-conditioning, television, synthetic fibers, home freezers, and frozen foods.

3 It is quite true that technology creates problems. No one denies that. And obviously it creates change, like nothing else. It is the greatest revolutionary in history, for it has had a more profound effect upon social custom and social reform than any legislation or any code of law. Let me cite just one example:

4 A hundred years ago, the average American workman had a few simple hand tools, and for power he was limited to his own muscles, plus the help of domestic animals and water wheels. He worked from the time he was through with his elementary schooling until he died. Assuming that he survived for the Biblical three-score-years-and-ten, he probably spent a total of 56 years on the job, 72 hours a week, 52 weeks a year. Add this up, it comes to something like 180,500 hours of his life.

5 The average workman today, with modern machinery and equipment, probably works from the age of 19 to the age of 65, or 46 years. He works only 40 hours a week, and has at least two weeks' vacation. When you total this, you find he works over his productive life less than 90,000 hours—or about half of the time put in by the 1852 worker, and he performs his duties in greater ease, safety and comfort.

6 The reason, of course, is advancing technology. It has been estimated that every horsepower of mechanical or electrical or chemical energy put at his disposal multiplied his own efforts 22 times. He doesn't work shorter hours because some benevolent law permits it.

He works less hours only because with modern machinery he can outproduce his grandfather many times over.

There has also been a remarkable readjustment of the American workman's living pattern. Fifty years ago, the difference in living standards between the wage-roll man and the manager or owner of a plant was very great. They lived in different neighborhoods, wore different kinds of clothes, and had a widely different degree of comforts and diversions.

This picture has changed completely. There may be a difference in income between the workman and his boss, but the difference in their living patterns is small. Each drives to work in a comfortable, dependable automobile—the difference between them is only one of degree. One may drive a Chevrolet, one a Buick—both can and do travel well. Either may spend his vacation in Florida or in traveling through the Rockies. Their homes may differ in size; they differ little in comforts for the family—both have automatic heating units and modern equipment of all kinds in the laundry, the kitchen, and the bathroom. Their own clothing and that of their wives suffer little by comparison. Both see the same TV programs on the same kind of set, attend the same concerts, art galleries, and theaters. This is the only country in the world where this situation exists.

Technology is everybody's rich uncle. But the benefactions of this generous relative will continue only so long as he is alive and healthy; when he dies he takes it with him.

The Bird and the Machine
Loren Eiseley

Eiseley uses **narration** and **comparison** and **contrast** to suggest two concepts of value: the value of "the machine," which is able to get a certain task done efficiently, and the value of living things, which are capable of joy and sorrow. To him, the emotional values of living things are more important. To per-

Source. "The Bird and the Machine" by Loren Eiseley. Copyright © 1955 by Loren Eiseley. Reprinted from *The Immense Journey*, by Loren Eiseley, by permission of Random House, Inc.

suade us to share his viewpoint, he relies on a story about himself. The narrative he chooses embodies both value systems. First it depicts Eiseley as "getting the job done," collecting wild birds because he has been told to do so. Then it depicts him as coming to understand that "to be alive" (paragraph 1) involves higher values.

Eiseley does not really define his terms or explain his criteria. He relies on *suggestive language* to help us see his attitude and on *narration* to make us share it.

1   In the morning, with the change that comes on suddenly in that high country, the mist that had hovered below us in the valley was gone. The sky was a deep blue, and one could see for miles over the high outcroppings of stone. I was up early and brought the box in which the little hawk was imprisoned out onto the grass where I was building a cage. A wind as cool as a mountain spring ran over the grass and stirred my hair. It was a fine day to be alive. I looked up and all around and at the hole in the cabin roof out of which the other little hawk had fled. There was no sign of her anywhere that I could see.

2   "Probably in the next county by now," I thought cynically, but before beginning work I decided I'd have a look at my last night's capture.

3   Secretively, I looked again all around the camp and up and down and opened the box. I got him right out in my hand with his wings folded properly and I was careful not to startle him. He lay limp in my grasp and I could feel his heart pound under the feathers but he only looked beyond me and up.

4   I saw him look that last look away beyond me into a sky so full of light that I could not follow his gaze. The little breeze flowed over me again, and nearby a mountain aspen shook all its tiny leaves. I suppose I must have had an idea then of what I was going to do, but I never let it come up into consciousness. I just reached over and laid the hawk on the grass.

5   He lay there a long minute without hope, unmoving, his eyes still fixed on that blue vault above him. It must have been that he was already so far away in heart that he never felt the release from my hand. He never even stood. He just lay with his breast against the grass.

6   In the next second after that long minute he was gone. Like a flicker of light, he had vanished with my eyes full on him, but without actually seeing even a premonitory wing beat. He was gone straight into that towering emptiness of light and crystal that my eyes could scarcely bear to penetrate. For another long moment there was silence. I could

not see him. The light was too intense. Then from far up somewhere a cry came ringing down.

I was young then and had seen little of the world, but when I heard that cry my heart turned over. It was not the cry of the hawk I had captured; for, by shifting my position against the sun, I was now seeing further up. Straight out of the sun's eye, where she must have been soaring restlessly above us for untold hours,[1] hurtled his mate. And from far up, ringing from peak to peak of the summits over us, came a cry of such unutterable and ecstatic joy that it sounds down across the years and tingles among the cups on my quiet breakfast table.

I saw them both now. He was rising fast to meet her. They met in a great soaring gyre that turned to a whirling circle and a dance of wings. Once more, just once, their two voices, joined in a harsh wild medley of question and response, struck and echoed against the pinnacles of the valley. Then they were gone forever somewhere into those upper regions beyond the eyes of men.

I am older now, and sleep less, and have seen most of what there is to see and am not very much impressed any more, I suppose, by anything. "What Next in the Attributes of Machines?" my morning headline runs. "It Might Be the Power to Reproduce Themselves."

I lay the paper down and across my mind a phrase floats insinuatingly: "It does not seem that there is anything in the construction, constituents, or behavior of the human being which it is essentially impossible for science to duplicate and synthesize. On the other hand . . ."

All over the city the cogs in the hard, bright mechanisms have begun to turn. Figures move through computers, names are spelled out, a thoughtful machine selects the fingerprints of a wanted criminal from an array of thousands. In the laboratory an electronic mouse runs swiftly through a maze toward the cheese it can neither taste nor enjoy. On the second run it does better than a living mouse.

"On the other hand . . ." Ah, my mind takes up, on the other hand the machine does not bleed, ache, hang for hours in the empty sky in a torment of hope to learn the fate of another machine, nor does it cry out with joy nor dance in the air with the fierce passion of a bird. Far off, over a distance greater than space, that remote cry from the heart of heaven makes a faint buzzing among my breakfast dishes and passes on and away.

---

[1] When Eiseley had captured the male hawk the night before, the female hawk had escaped (see paragraphs 1-2).

A Wasp Stings Back
Robert Claiborne

This is an evaluation of a cultural group, the WASPs (White Anglo-Saxon Protestants). This group has become a new collective antihero, condemned by other segments of American society and often by itself. Claiborne, however, says that WASPs deserve our approval for at least one contribution to American culture: the concept of limited government. Beyond that, he claims, they are no worse than other ethnic or religious groups. He points out that the Catholics, who are among the critics of the WASPs, "ripped off" his ancestor's farm and that the persecution of minorities exists also in Third World countries, despite their criticism of WASP persecution of minorities.

Do you think that Claiborne's defense of WASP values is adequate? What seem to be his criteria for judging people?

1   Over the past few years, American pop culture has acquired a new folk antihero: the Wasp. One slick magazine tells us that the White Anglo-Saxon Protestants rule New York City, while other media gurus credit (or discredit) them with ruling the country—and, by inference, ruining it. A Polish-American declares in a leading newspaper that Wasps have "no sense of honor." *Newsweek* patronizingly describes Chautauqua as a citadel of "Wasp values," while other folklorists characterize these values more explicitly as a compulsive commitment to the work ethic, emotional uptightness and sexual inhibition. The Wasps, in fact, are rapidly becoming the one minority that every other ethnic group—blacks, Italians, chicanos, Jews, Poles and all the rest—feels absolutely free to dump on. I have not yet had a friend greet me with "Did you hear the one about the two Wasps who . . .?"—but any day now!

2   I come of a long line of Wasps; if you disregard my French great-great-grandmother and a couple of putatively Irish ancestors of the same vintage, a rather pure line. My mother has long been one of the Colonial Dames, an organization some of whose members consider the Daughters of the American Revolution rather parvenu. My umpty-umpth Wasp great-grandfather, William Claiborne, founded the first European settlement in what is now Maryland (his farm and trading

Source. "A Wasp Stings Back" by Robert Claiborne. From *Newsweek*, September 30, 1974. Copyright 1974 by Newsweek, Inc. All rights reserved. Reprinted by permission.

post were later ripped off by the Catholic Lord Baltimore, Maryland politics being much the same then as now).

The Stereotype

As a Wasp, the mildest thing I can say about the stereotype emerging from the current wave of anti-Wasp chic is that I don't recognize myself. As regards emotional uptightness and sexual inhibition, modesty forbids comment—though I dare say various friends and lovers of mine could testify on these points if they cared to. I will admit to enjoying work—because I am lucky enough to be able to work at what I enjoy—but not, I think, to the point of compulsiveness. And so far as ruling America, or even New York, is concerned, I can say flatly that (a) it's a damn lie because (b) if I *did* rule them, both would be in better shape than they are. Indeed I and all my Wasp relatives, taken in a lump, have far less clout with the powers that run this country than any one of the Buckleys or Kennedys (Irish Catholic), the Sulzbergers or Guggenheims (Jewish), or the late A. P. Giannini (Italian) of the Bank of America.

Admittedly, both corporate and (to a lesser extent) political America are dominated by Wasps—just as (let us say) the garment industry is dominated by Jews, and organized crime by Italians. But to conclude from this that The Wasps are the American elite is as silly as to say that The Jews are cloak-and-suiters or The Italians are gangsters. Wasps, like other ethnics, come in all varieties, including criminals—political, corporate and otherwise.

The Values

More seriously, I would like to say a word for the maligned "Wasp values," one of them in particular. As a matter of historical fact, it was we Wasps—by which I mean here the English-speaking peoples—who invented the idea of *limited governments:* that there are some things that no king, President or other official is allowed to do. It began more than seven centuries ago, with Magna Carta, and continued (to cite only the high spots) through the wrangles between Parliament and the Stuart kings, the Puritan Revolution of 1640, the English Bill of Rights of 1688, the American Revolution and our own Bill of Rights and Constitution.

The Wasp principle of limited government emerged through protracted struggle with the much older principle of unlimited government. This latter was never more cogently expressed than at the trial of Charles I, when the hapless monarch informed his judges that, as an anointed king, he was not accountable to any court in the land. A not dissimilar position was taken more recently by another Wasp head of state—and with no more success; executive privilege went over no better in 1974 than divine right did in 1649. The notion that a king, a President, or any other official can do as he damn well pleases has never played in Peoria—or Liverpool or Glasgow, Melbourne or Toronto. For more than 300 years, no Wasp nation has endured an absolute monarchy, dictatorship or any other form of unlimited government—which is something no Frenchman, Italian, German, Pole, Russian or Hispanic can say.

7   It is perfectly true, of course, that we Wasps have on occasion imposed unlimited governments on other (usually darker) peoples. We have, that is, acted in much the same way as have most other nations that possessed the requisite power and opportunity—including many Third World nations whose leaders delight in lecturing us on political morality (for recent information on this point, consult the files on Biafra, Bangladesh and Brazil, Indian tribes of). Yet even here, Wasp values have played an honorable part. When you start with the idea that Englishmen are entitled to self-government, you end by conceding the same right to Africans and Indians. If you begin by declaring that all (white) men are created equal, you must sooner or later face up to the fact that blacks are also men—and conform your conduct, however reluctantly, to your values.

The Faith

8   Keeping the Wasp faith hasn't always been easy. We Wasps, like other people, don't always live up to our own principles, and those of us who don't, if occupying positions of power, can pose formidable problems to the rest of us. Time after time, in the name of anti-Communism, peace with honor or some other slippery shibboleth, we have been conned or bullied into tolerating government interference with our liberties and privacy in all sorts of covert—and sometimes overt—ways; time after time we have had to relearn the lesson that eternal vigilance is the price of liberty.

9   It was a Wasp who uttered that last thought. And it was a congress of Wasps who, about the same time, denounced the executive privileges of George III and committed to the cause of liberty their lives, their fortunes and—*pace* my Polish-American compatriot—their sacred honor.

The Sociology of the Blender
New Times

This short evaluation attacks the American concept of progress, which leads to technological overkill, "the stunning, wasteful act of drowning a good idea with 'improvements.' " The evidence offered is a history of one American kitchen gadget, the blender. As we watch the blender evolve from the sensible and simple machine of the 1940s into the supercomplicated ego pleaser of our day, we come to share the writer's negative evaluation of the manufacturers who indulge in such overkill— and the consumers who buy it.

Nikita Khrushchev, in one of his lighter moods, once threatened: Russia "will bury you in the dust of our progress." If Nikita had been 10 points brighter, he might have tried: "Russia will bury you in the dust of your *own* progress." We're not talking here about that old bogyman nuclear holocaust, but just plain capitalist overkill: the stunning, wasteful act of drowning a good idea with "improvements." Consider, if you will, the history of that great American institution the blender.

The Beginning (See Figure A)
Before 1922, there was the eggbeater and there was elbow grease. After 1922 there was Stephen Poplawski. A tinkerer from the city of Racine, Wisconsin, Poplawski one day sent away to Washington for a patent on a machine with "an agitating element mounted in the bottom of a cup. . . ." Happily for Americana, Racine also turned out to be home for the Horlick Company, maker of the malted milk; soon Poplawski's machines were mixing Horlick's malteds in Racine's soda fountains. At first, this happened under Poplawski's own name; in 1946, John Oster bought Stephen out, and the Osterizer began beating up the culture.

Source. "The Sociology of the Blender." From *New Times*, April 29, 1977. Reprinted by permission of *New Times*.

3   Into the thick of this plunged Fred Waring, the bandleader. Waring took the blender so seriously that he liked to list himself in *Who's Who* as *the* inventor of the blender, and even patented a new spelling, "blendor." Waring and Oster thought of the blender as the new wheel; it shouldn't be wasted on malteds and bar drinks; it should be used on *everything*.

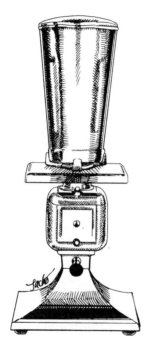

FIGURE A

FIGURE B

1940s (See Figure B)

4   During the war years, however, blenders remained as sensible as toys can remain—they looked like solid beasts of burden with heavy metal bases, thick glass containers and simple on-off toggle switches. If you wanted to "blend," you turned the machine on for a short time; if you wanted to "liquefy," you turned it on for a long time. That was it. An exquisite American invention, built, like the first Fords, to last nearly a lifetime.

Source. All drawings by Shelly Sacks. Used by permission.

1950s (See Figure C)

During the Eisenhower years, the creeping cosmetics began. Waring switched to a two-speed model, offered with this promise: "With a Waring, you'll beat, chop, grate, liquefy, blend and whip at the flick of a switch . . . to perfection." Meanwhile the enthusiastic Oster demonstrators were promising things they couldn't deliver, like suggesting that, by liquefying cucumbers in an Osterizer, one could obtain a longer life. U. S. Guv didn't buy that, even with Abe Fortas defending the company.

FIGURE C

FIGURE D

1960–66 (See Figure D)

By the sixties, blenders were big business. It was no longer a time for practical machines, but sexy ones, and so began the War of the Buttons. In 1964, Oster introduced an eight-speed, push-button model; in 1966, a ten-speed; Sunbeam and a gang of imitators clattered onto the field. As Oster admits today, the speed phenomenon was "about 90 percent sizzle and 10 percent steak," but the race was on.

1966—70 (See Figure E)

7 In one quantum blast, most blender manufacturers doubled their speeds by adding just one more button—a dual-control circuitry switch. Sunbeam's 8 speeds became 16; Waring's 7 became 14, and so on. Waring unqualifiedly crowed: "You'll never need anything more . . . than the new Super Robot Blendor."

FIGURE E

FIGURE F

1970s (See Figure F)

8 Not even Waring could take that last one seriously; by 1970 it had trotted out another refinement: a button to "flash blend" whatever substance you happened to be ogling. Quicker than you could make carrot juice, every blender on the market had a variant. For Osterizer it was a "Pulse-matic" button; for Hamilton-Beach it was "Insta-Blend"; for Sunbeam, "Burst of Power," for "quick, extra power when you need it." And then there were the timers. Apparently, even with transparent containers, customers couldn't be trusted to see when their bananas had liquefied. So blender manufacturers had broken through with a way to keep *time* for them. You could never be too precise about your daquiris. . . .

9 All this time, the War of the Buttons was still on. "It was crazy," remembers Harry Goenner of Proctor Silex, a company that has since opted out of the blender biz. "The more buttons, the better they sold. We got as high as 16, and the things still couldn't do much more than whip cream. At most, there was a 100 rpm difference between one

speed and another—virtually indistinguishable." Another exec recalls: "When we came out with our 16-speed blender, eight of us sat up two nights straight, trying to get words with five letters, each one sounding a bit higher than the other. It was like trying to fit 14 words between 'dull' and 'bright.' "

Finally, the words ran out. When Sunbeam came out with 20 speeds, they had to repeat some. Thus you could "crumb" at 1 and 5, "chop" at 2 and 7, "mince" at 12 and 17, "grind" at 11 and 15. . . .

FIGURE G

1980s and Beyond (See Figure G)

The future? Many companies have withdrawn from the battle while others, as Ford has done, have trimmed back on the trimmings. But last time we checked, Ronson had broken the tape at 24 speeds—not to mention a bunch of bristling attachments, including a knife sharpener and coffee bean grinder. And then there was "infinite speed control," an innovation from Rival, the "electronic" blender. This model featured a "bouncing light" and presumably limitless stops along the way. All this, according to Rival, was achieved with a tiny electronic "brain," that took the "guesswork" out of blending. "Translated into woman's talk," Rival explained, "this means you can dial the exact speed for every blending need. . . . Why, it's almost human."

Well, as they say, *plus ça change, plus c'est la même chose.*[1]

[1] "The more it changes, the more it remains the same."

Redesigning Chickens
Russell Baker

Many people are concerned about the dangers of genetic engineering—the use of technology to redesign living beings.
Baker, however, finds the engineering image of creation silly.
He describes the new featherless chicken in a way that makes
this "improvement" seem a dubious gain. He then provides a
comic **process analysis**, describing the way an engineer might
go about designing "the basic human being," complete with an
add-on gadget to compensate for a major design flaw. Notice
the extent to which Baker's style relies on unexpected *combi-
nations of words* ("Kentucky fried feathers") and *connotative
language* (the new chicken is said to be "naked," not merely
featherless).

If Baker finds efforts at biological design open to mockery,
against what standard is he measuring them? To what extent
can we take this **satiric evaluation** (see p. 163) seriously?

1   God having rested on the seventh day, man gazed upon His creation
and decided it needed improvement. For one thing, all the chickens
had been built with feathers on the outside. The human race lived with
this error in chicken design for a long time. There were, after all, so
many other improvements that had to be made. Recently, however,
genetic engineers at the Universities of Connecticut and Maryland
have finally rebuilt the chicken right. Which is to say, without any
feathers at all.

2   This new improved chicken is nakeder than a jaybird. By breeding
her without feathers, scientists believed, they could raise her economic
efficiency. It seems that ordinary chickens spend a quarter of their
protein intake on developing plumage, and since there is no demand
at all for Kentucky fried feathers this is a waste of investment.

3   There are still bugs in the new design, of course. Chickens that have
to go through life naked are prone to stomach ulcers, chills and nervous
seizures. Some spend so much energy scurrying around to keep warm
that they eat more than feathered chickens. Others, according to Dr.
Ralph Somes of the University of Connecticut, "get so miserable that
they stop eating and simply waste away."

4   Nevertheless, there are signs that the unfeathered chicken is the

fowl of the future. Early models weigh 6 percent more than the original feathered model and, because they develop less fat to shrink during cooking, leave 16 percent more meat in the pan.

I have spent some time trying to imagine what it must feel like to be a chicken doomed to go through life without any feathers on and believe I can understand why many of them develop bad nerves and stomach ulcers, but my ability to sympathize with chickens is slight. I am far more interested in the human implications of such genetic redesigning.

If we can say without blasphemy that God botched the chicken design, and blithely rebuild His work to get rid of the wasteful feathers, may we not also concede that His basic human design also contains absurdities which might better be engineered out of future models?

Do teeth, for example, make any sense at all? Imagine for a moment that you are designing the basic human being and that an assistant comes to you and says, "I think I've licked the eating problem." And then he dumps on your desk several dozen small white objects of varying sizes, and you say, "What's this junk?" and he says, "Teeth."

And you say, "Is this a gag?" And he says, "Listen, all you do is, you put half of these teeth into the upper jaw and half of them into the lower jaw, and then when the jaws move open and shut the teeth will bite and grind against each other until the food is ready for the stomach."

And you say, "What keeps them from falling out?" And he says, "Twice a day and after every meal, the human being will scrub them with a hand brush and soap, and twice a year he will have them all X-rayed and scraped and drilled and tightened up while writhing in agony in a chair."

I don't know what you say then. I think you fire him, or at least take him off the human-being project, possibly by demoting him to chicken design. Why this wasn't done in the beginning I don't know, except that it was a crash project—all done in one day—and a lot of incompetents probably weren't weeded out.

Like the chicken's feathers, human teeth were an error of commission, and it seems very likely that they led to the most singular error of omission in the human structure. I refer to the absence of an eye in the back of the head. Surely this necessary appurtenance must have been planned for in the original blueprint, since at that time there was no way of foreseeing the invention of the rearview mirror.

What happened? My guess is there was one of those confusions in the shop such as account for so much botched auto repair. Once it was decided to go ahead with the teeth, there would have been a terrible job trying to get all the teeth placed correctly in the two jaws. This would have ended with the head lying backside down on a workbench and a great deal of laboring and grunting over the impossible task of getting the wisdom teeth properly occluded, eliminating over-bite between the incisors, and so forth. At the finish of this job, with the head lying faceup, even an assiduous designer might easily have failed to notice that nobody had remembered to install the eye in the back of the head.

13 Whether geneticists can amend this oversight is doubtful, but the mistake in the eating mechanism is easily changed. Breeding toothless humans should be as easy as breeding featherless chickens. And once we are rid of teeth, it will be a simple business to equip every person with an electric food chewer, which when placed on tables will chew food to a scientifically calculated consistency perfect for swallowing and transmit measured portions to the diner's mouth.

14 Will there be philosophical objections to this refinement on divine work? Very likely, for man in his present state is sometimes said to have been made in the image of God. As Mark Twain noted, however, the only authority we have for this information is man, that redesigner of chickens.

Thinking Like a Mountain
Aldo Leopold

Leopold first introduces his subject as "a deep chesty bawl . . . an outburst of wild defiant sorrow" (paragraph 1). He then expands to a larger subject: the relationships of wolves to men on the one hand, and to the natural life of mountains on the other. As the howl suggests the whole meaning of the wolf, so the wolf suggests the whole meaning of our human way of thinking. We think too much in terms of safety, Leopold believes, while "too much safety seems to yield only danger in the long run" (paragraph 10).

In this expanding structure that moves from (1) the howl to (2) the wolf to (3) our human response to the wolf and finally to (4) the difference between human modes of thought and the

Source. "Thinking Like a Mountain" by Aldo Leopold. From *A Sand County Almanac* with other essays on conservation from "Round River" by Aldo Leopold. Copyright © 1949, 1953, 1966; renewed 1977 by Oxford University Press, Inc. Reprinted by permission.

way a mountain thinks, Leopold comes close to **symbolism, the use of one object or image to stand for a whole category or idea.** Of what is the wolf a symbol?

Leopold's evaluative conclusion is: it's better to be wild than tame. Is that conclusion clear enough? Exactly what does it mean to "think like a mountain"? According to what value system (utilitarian, ethical, aesthetic) does Leopold claim it is good to think this way?

A deep chesty bawl echoes from rimrock to rimrock, rolls down the mountain, and fades into the far blackness of the night. It is an outburst of wild defiant sorrow, and of contempt for all the adversities of the world.

Every living thing (and perhaps many a dead thing as well) pays heed to that call. To the deer it is a reminder of the way of all flesh, to the pine a forecast of midnight scuffles and blood on the snow, to the coyote a promise of gleanings to come, to the cowman a threat of red ink at the bank, to the hunter a challenge of fang against bullet. Yet behind these obvious and immediate hopes and fears there lies a deeper meaning, known only to the mountain itself. Only the mountain has lived long enough to listen objectively to the howl of a wolf.

Those unable to decipher the hidden meaning know nevertheless that it is there, for it is felt in all wolf country, and distinguishes that country from all other land. It tingles in the spine of all who hear wolves by night, or who scan their tracks by day. Even without the sight or sound of wolf, it is implicit in a hundred small events: the midnight whinny of a pack horse, the rattle of rolling rocks, the bounds of a fleeing deer, the way shadows lie under the spruces. Only the ineducable tyro can fail to sense the presence or absence of wolves, or the fact that mountains have a secret opinion about them.

My own conviction on this score dates from the day I saw a wolf die. We were eating lunch on a high rimrock, at the foot of which a turbulent river elbowed its way. We saw what we thought was a doe fording the torrent, her breast awash in white water. When she climbed the bank toward us and shook out her tail, we realized our error: it was a wolf. A half-dozen others, evidently grown pups, sprang from the willows and all joined in a welcoming mêlée of wagging tails and playful maulings. What was literally a pile of wolves writhed and tumbled in the center of an open flat at the foot of our rimrock.

In those days we had never heard of passing up a chance to kill a wolf. In a second we were pumping lead into the pack, but with more excitement than accuracy: to aim a steep downhill shot is always confusing. When our rifles were empty, the old wolf was down, and a pup was dragging a leg into impassable slide-rocks.

6   We reached the old wolf in time to watch a fierce green fire dying in her eyes. I realized then, and have known ever since, that there was something new to me in those eyes—something known only to her and to the mountain. I was young then, and full of trigger-itch; I thought that because fewer wolves meant more deer, no wolves would mean hunters' paradise. But after seeing the green fire die, I sensed that neither the wolf nor the mountain agreed with such a view.

7   Since then I have lived to see state after state extirpate its wolves. I have watched the face of many a wolfless mountain, and seen the southfacing slopes wrinkle with a maze of new deer trails. I have seen every edible bush and seedling browsed, first to anemic desuetude, and then to death. I have seen every edible tree defoliated to the height of a saddle-horn. Such a mountain looks as if someone had given God a new pruning shears, and forbidden Him all other exercise. In the end the starved bones of the hoped-for deer herd, dead of its own too-much, bleach with the bones of the dead sage, or moulder under the high-lined junipers.

8   I now suspect that just as a deer herd lives in mortal fear of its wolves, so does a mountain live in mortal fear of its deer. And perhaps with better cause, for while a buck pulled down by wolves can be replaced in two or three years, a range pulled down by too many deer may fail of replacement in as many decades.

9   So also with cows. The cowman who cleans his range of wolves does not realize that he is taking over the wolf's job of trimming the herd to fit the range. He has not learned to think like a mountain. Hence we have dustbowls, and rivers washing the future into the sea.

We all strive for safety, prosperity, comfort, long life, and dullness.

10   The deer strives with his supple legs, the cowman with trap and poison, the statesman with pen, the most of us with machines, votes, and dollars, but it all comes to the same thing: peace in our time. A measure of success in this is all well enough, and perhaps is a requisite to objective thinking, but too much safety seems to yield only danger in the long run. Perhaps this is behind Thoreau's dictum: In wildness is the salvation of the world. Perhaps this is the hidden meaning in the howl of the wolf, long known among mountains, but seldom perceived among men.

There Isn't Anything Wishy-Washy About Soaps
Beth Gutcheon

Gutcheon defends a much-attacked form of popular culture, the TV soap opera. Her favorable evaluation of the "soaps" is based on two qualities she finds in recent productions: (1) the attempt to educate audiences about contemporary problems, and (2) the attempt to make people question their own way of life. The evidence that the "soaps" are fulfilling these goals consists of plot summaries of a number of recent programs and information drawn from interviews. Gutcheon avoids making an exaggerated claim for the virtues of her subject. As she summarizes (paragraph 17), "I'm not suggesting that soaps are great art; just that they are often good television, and that there are legitimate uses (as well as abuses) of television."

Do you agree that "good television" means television programs with an educational or social purpose and that the "soaps" have such purposes?

In case you haven't tuned in since the days of "Mary Noble, Backstage Wife" (or Mary, Noble Backstage Wife), soap operas have come a long way. The organ music, the convoluted and bathetic plots persist—but with a twist. Soap writers are increasingly using the serial form—as Charles Dickens once did—to educate audiences or lead them to question their insular attitudes in ways that little else in their lives may do.

Consider the way some soaps have come to handle members of the groups my upstairs neighbor refers to as "those people." CBS's "Search for Tomorrow," for example, introduced a black orderly, developed him as all jive and sass, and established a polarity between him and a wealthy respectable bigot out to get him fired. But after the writers have set us up for weeks the orderly is revealed to be a talented Vietnam-trained paramedic who saves the bigot's life while all the doctors are at lunch. Similarly, NBC's "Somerset" gave us a hippie wanderer with long hair and no history; after arousing our suspicion and dislike, he turned out to be a shell-shocked war hero with amnesia and a chestful of medals. CBS's "As the World Turns" uses its access to some 8 million viewers daily to investigate prejudice against white lawyers with beards and bad manners: hirsute attorney Grant Colman offended almost everybody when he came to town, and glamorous oft-married widow Lisa Miller Hughes Shea didn't like him one little bit. But the better she knows him. . . .

3   Some soaps use this familiar "hero-disguised" device more creatively. For instance, "Search for Tomorrow" evolved a long romantic plot line featuring a mysterious character who was deaf and unable to speak (played by Linda Bove, who is also deaf). When the suds settled, viewers had learned a good deal of sign language; they were also exposed in considerable depth to the ways in which families, schools, communities, and society at large discriminate against the handicapped. The heroine's elegant wealthy parents, preoccupied with their own pain, had sent her to special schools that tried to teach her to "talk" rather than those that would encourage her family and community to learn her language. Her parents responded with such shock and embarrassment to the awkward lowing sounds she made that she ran away. It was not until they found her months later, betrothed to a fine young doctor and chattering gaily with her hands to her new neighbors, that they began to see that she could be accepted as she was by a "normal" community.

4   "Search for Tomorrow," still doing business with the same old characters at the same old stand for 23 years, has somehow become the most forthrightly feminist soap on the air. In the past year, husband and wife writers Ralph Ellis and Eugenie Hunt have developed a woman lawyer who chooses not to have children because she prefers her career (and her husband encourages her). At the office, she does research and legwork while her husband, whose credentials are the same as hers, is given important briefs and litigation to handle. She quits (again applauded by her husband). A black woman, denied a bank loan because she is a woman (*not* because she is black), is successfully defended by the woman lawyer—the bank unsuccessfully defended by her ex-boss, Doug Martin, who has for umpteen years been one of the sympathetic stalwarts of the show. Then Doug Martin's nice little wife Eunice takes up part-time free-lance writing (she works at home, doesn't neglect the baby, and still has dinner ready at six every night). Nice old Doug erupts into a fever of *macho* pigginess that ends with mayhem, murder, adultery, and divorce; all clearly established as caused by, not justifying, his irrational behavior. Incidentally, "Search" has the largest proportion of male viewers—16 percent, or nearly one million—of any on the air.

5   When I asked Agnes Nixon, queen of the soap writers, how she—and others—got off the nonstop, pro-marriage, baby-boom go-round

popular for so long, she took the novel view that the best way to entertain people is to make them think. She holds what may be a unique record in the industry for entertaining people. Nixon created "Search for Tomorrow," the longest continuously running program of any kind on television. With the legendary late Irna Phillips she co-created "As the World Turns," which, after 18 years, still has one of the highest ratings.

Nixon likes to beef up the suds with high-protein filler. Soap operas are considered audio entertainment; it is assumed that the viewer is looking at the enzyme presoak most of the time and not at the screen. So whatever the actors are doing, it's up to the writer to keep the dialogue continuous, which explains all that homey chitchat about meat loaf and slipcovers. Agnes Nixon, however, drops in one-liners about pollution or zero population growth. As long as the ratings are up and the sponsors happy, she can even elevate a public service conversation to a subplot. On "One Life To Live" (ABC), she had young Cathy Craig, ace reporter, bend everyone's ear about a story she was writing on the VD epidemic. The article was then offered free to the viewers, and 10,000 of them requested copies.

Earlier, when Cathy Craig was found to be "experimenting with drugs," Nixon arranged with drug therapist Dr. Judianne Densen-Gerber to have "Cathy" participate in a group therapy program at New York's Odyssey House. Taped segments of the real thing were integrated into the soap. ABC and Odyssey House were swamped with calls from people who don't watch documentaries, or read the New York *Times*, and perhaps could not have been reached any other way.

Nixon respects her audience to a certain extent; enough, for example, not to offer to them a staged drug-rehabilitation therapy group when she could get them the real thing. But by far the more telling motive for her innovations has been respect for her own power. Nixon's position is unique because after many years of reviving slumped ratings for CBS and NBC, she moved to ABC on her own terms: she owns the soaps she writes. She created "One Life To Live," but recently sold it to the network to give herself time to act as consultant for their made-for-women afternoon movies, called "Afternoon Playbreaks." She still owns and head-writes "All My Children."

On "All My Children," Nixon's popular bitch goddess Erica Martin had television's first legal abortion. The network went nuts ("You're teaching our daughters and wives how to get abortions we don't want them to have"), but network rage doesn't bother Nixon much. She's the one soap writer who cannot be fired (the rest are replaced about yearly). And viewer rage bothers her not at all: "An angry viewer is a hooked viewer." Robert Cenedella, another long-running soap writer, tells of the viewer who wrote him: "If Rachel ["Another World," NBC] isn't punished by next week, I am going to stop watching." She wrote him the same letter, twice a month, for four years.

10   The question of content in soaps depends on ratings first, with morals, taste, audience response, and responsibility running a distant second. Content is proposed by head writers, then approved, abridged, or vetoed by the network or sponsors, or both. (Even Nixon must submit to this sort of review, but as a soap owner, she has the last word.) Murders, marriages, organized crime, diseases, and psychoses are soap staples, as they are on prime time. Race and class issues are rarely met head-on—a fairly suspicious circumstance since demographics indicate that a sizable proportion of the audience is blue collar or black, or both. Except for a janitor on "General Hospital" and a waitress on "One Life To Live" (both ABC) and a woman who works in a factory on "The Young and the Restless" (CBS), the social scale ranges from absurdly prosperous nurses, doctors, lawyers, and executives right on up to the congenitally wealthy. Only "One Life To Live" has ever evolved a major plot line focusing on (rather than pointedly ignoring) race. With actress Ellen Holly, Agnes Nixon created a black woman who passed for white because as a light-skinned black she had been rejected by both white and black communities. The point was to examine the motivations and consequences of denying race and heritage: the woman, established as white, fell in love with a black man. Throughout the romance only the writers knew she was going to turn out to be black, and the moment the couple first kissed, every TV set below the Mason-Dixon line went blank.

11   Genuine social issues are high-risk material—not at all what the networks had in mind when they brought soaps to TV back in the fifties. In those days, Irna Phillips (creator of "The Guiding Light," "Young Doctor Malone," "Love Is a Many Splendored Thing," and "As the World Turns") ruled the roost.

12   Phillips had a dream, or more precisely a magic formula: a folksy American vision of a vast community of nice, wholesome middle-class people, all of whom care deeply and without malice about the most trivial details of each other's lives. Everyone works who wants to, but the need to earn money never features as motive for anything—a dream you can see functioning to this day on "As the World Turns" without the slightest reference to contemporary, or any, reality. I am sorry to report that, with a 33 percent audience share, it is one of the most popular soaps on the air and has been since 1961. I personally find it salacious, depressing, and rather offensive. After all, if you expunge all consciousness of war, racism, sexism, inflation, unemployment, poverty, or politics, you are pretty much left with pregnancy, crime, and illness. The children have heart conditions, the

women are all pregnant, mostly by men other than their husbands, and the death rate is simply terrific—which is probably a good thing, since no one has heard of contraception or abortion yet, and the place is a one-town population explosion.

3   Nevertheless, I sometimes watch it. I started in the last months of my pregnancy, and I still tune in, even though the writers have so little regard for my sense of probability that they allowed one character (who was a loathsome, wet, sentimental specimen) to kill herself, on the morning after her wedding, by falling *up* the stairs. (I think it likely that I watch because of incidents like that. Months later, when I entered a lonely, diaper-ridden period of my life, I needed a good laugh.)

4   On the other hand, I turn off the sound before I answer the phone, lest anyone know I'm watching. Now why is that? My husband watches the World Series and has to wade through such lard as a pregame interview on the subject of what Yogi Berra had for breakfast (answer—a western omelet), and he doesn't feel personally threatened. It doesn't affect anyone's opinion of his general intelligence. Why should I feel responsible for the occasional flotsam on soap operas? It hasn't rotted my brain. If anything, it has sharpened my sense of satire. Yet the fact that you're watching soaps isn't the sort of thing you want to get around.

5   I think that people are contemptuous not of the serial form, nor of the content, but of the audience. Women. Women who stay home. Women who "don't work." Housewives. One CBS daytime executive, for example, volunteered the information that he had defended a fine, sensitive plot line for "The Young and the Restless," involving a young woman who is raped. He added, however, that he killed writer William Bell's suggestion of a plot in which the same character, although highly qualified, is denied a job simply because she is a woman. He told me that his audience doesn't know from jobs; they stay home, they're not interested. Viewers are hooked on all those women doctors and lawyers because of their personal struggles, not their professional ones.

6   If he asked me—and he didn't—I would have said that people don't get addicted to soap operas or anything else because they are smug and satisfied. Certainly for the time in my own life when I was most wired on soaps, when, all kidding aside, I really *needed* to tune in tomorrow, the reason was precisely that I was dying to work. I had chosen to take a year out of my life to spend with my infant son, yes, but in terms of daily reality, I had One Life To Live and I appeared to be spending it peeling carrots. If I had allowed myself to focus on carrots completely, I'd have been a candidate for a straitjacket. Why shouldn't I listen to soap operas? At the same time in my life, I

developed a temporary passion for mystery novels, which no one thought at all funny, though most of them were not as well written as the soaps.

17   I'm not suggesting that soaps are great art; just that they are often good television, and that there are legitimate uses (as well as abuses) of television. Soaps, regardless of their plots, consistently deal with aspects of women's physical and emotional health that one certainly finds nowhere else on television. On "Love Is a Many Splendored Thing" (CBS), a young mother faced advanced cervical cancer because she neglected to have a Pap test. On "The Guiding Light" (CBS), Janet Norris's (woman) doctor tells her firmly that her self-effacing absorption with her home and baby is not noble but neurotic, that it indicates an unwillingness to face something basically painful in her life situation. (Janet has also had trouble "responding" to her husband since the birth of her daughter. Apparently that's not uncommon, but I wouldn't have known it if they hadn't told me.) On "The Edge of Night" (CBS), a menopausal woman is suffering "empty nest syndrome." On "The Secret Storm" (CBS), shortly before its cancellation last February, the neighborhood shrink gently explained to Laurie Reddin that her growing obsession with fantasy was also a symptom of something in her life that she was afraid to face (her husband, the ex-priest, is angry and drinks).

18   I like soaps because they are about women and because they occasionally have ideas in them; further, I prefer the serial form to the episodic because I am interested in the details of life as well as the climaxes. "All My Children" may be sentimental, but currently it's unfolding a plot about the causes and consequences of child abuse. As a daughter and a mother I'm interested in the ways parents damage children—so when it's my turn to wash the dishes I'll probably do them at one o'clock while I listen—maybe I'll find out why I sometimes feel like slugging my son. Maybe I'll find out why my mother slugged me. (No, Dr. Welby, it has nothing to do with being adopted or illegitimate—it has to do with my looking exactly like her.) And NBC recently introduced a new soap called "How To Survive a Marriage." Hampered as it sometimes is by pseudo-hip dialogue, it is at least founded squarely on the proposition, may Irna Phillips rest in peace, that marriage can be damaging.

19   Soaps may be melodramatic and predictable, but they are never as devoid of intellectual content as "Cannon" or "Mannix" or the Daddy-figure prime-time doctor/lawyer things. Soaps are better than those and watching them hasn't made me any more ridiculous than I was before. Soaps are a phenomenon touching the lives of an estimated 30 million women daily—no laughing matter. I'm tired of seeing soaps treated as a joke—partly because the writers and actors honestly deserve better, and partly because the joke is really aimed at me.

After the Paint Wears Off: the 1955 Chevrolet Six 2-Door
Ted West

West's title, together with the fact that his article appeared in *Road & Track*, suggests that he will evaluate 1955 Chevies. As we quickly learn, however, his real purpose is to entertain us with an account of his personal experience with one '55 Chevy. This evaluation is almost a satiric version (see p. 163) of the typical automobile test report. The standard ingredients are there—complete with cost accounting—but West's approach is so flip and personal that his evaluation of X is not likely to be taken seriously.

What kind of reader (audience) does West assume? What peculiarities of style do you notice? Are they justified?

1   You could hear it in there, subtle as an Italian wedding, the old engine just kind of taking a little rest every sixth stroke. But I needed a car for school and $125 for a 1955 Chevy Six 2-door was about right. And besides, what's so bad about five cylinders? I mean, hell, that was two more than my old Porsche had.

2   As I was pulling out of the back lot I caught the salesman crossing himself and had the oddest feeling he was being absolutely literal when he said, "Take it around the block." The road test (data not available) didn't prove much except that the car was capable of going forward, stopping and, with tactful use of the clutch, backing up. The column shift proved a little weak-kneed and you couldn't get it into first or reverse without scraping your knuckles on the back of the steering wheel, but since I hadn't planned on having to downshift into first too often—I mean, how many three mile an hour corners *are* there?—that didn't seem too crucial.

3   There was one hang-up, though. A deep depression had been worn away in the driver's seat so that you sank in about six inches and couldn't comfortably rest an elbow on the window sill. Now this elbow on the window sill, as you know, is standard equipment on all American cars. And besides, the way the seat had been gouged out in the center it felt like you were sitting on a toilet seat. The salesman

Source. "After the Paint Wears Off: the 1955 Chevrolet Six 2-Door" by Ted West. From *Road & Track*. Reprinted by permission of the author.

219

gallantly offered me a piece of foam rubber to plug the gap and that settled that.

4   In all other respects, though, the car suited my every requirement. It was dirt cheap.

5   It was now time to take a long hard look at the car and see what damage had been done to my image. You remember about a year ago there was an article on a Jag 3.8 and the owner summed the car up by saying it was "conspicuously inconspicuous, the very essence of snob appeal." Well, if that's snob appeal, then my car had just the reverse. It was so inconspicuously inconspicuous that just sitting in it for two minutes qualified you for a Missing Persons Report.

6   In deference to the car's dignity I won't even try to guess how many previous owners there had been. Somewhere along the line, though, someone had given it a nice inconspicuous light tan paint job. Now this was a real work of art. You could find places here and there where the artist, refusing to be limited by convention, came as close as one inch from the chrome. At other points the chrome was fully protected with a rich coat of enamel, giving the car's basic design a wonderfully varied sense of line. The outer appearance was otherwise undistinguished except for a fender-long gash at the right rear. The gash had suffered neither the violence of the body man's hammer, nor the indignity of Bond-O, since well before this inspired paint job. A somewhat rumpled chrome strip had been neatly attached to the fender with sheet metal screws so it would not fly off at speed—a tribute to the artist's respect for auto safety. The final nuance of the car's style— which was Early Mexican Taxicab—was its headliner. A friend suggested that it might have been used for gunnery practice. A rather nice patriotic touch, I thought. Otherwise the car had that generally forlorn aspect that any car takes on after 12 years of being driven like a Hungarian violin.

7   Mechanically, with the exception of the engine (a minor point), the car was in remarkable condition. Though you had to double-clutch for all downshifts, and before upshifting it was advisable to count to five so everything in there had time to slow down, still the transmission had a refreshing tendency not to pop out of gear. On occasion this tendency was so pronounced that I would have to get out into the brisk evening air with a flashlight, crawl underneath, and pull the shifting arm out of first manually, but you can't have everything. The brakes were fine, arousing suspicions that the former owner had let some mechanic tamper with them. The U-joint whine in high was cured by a little oil, which reassured me that the former owner hadn't let mechanics tamper with nature *too* often. The steering was very tight, though it didn't bind, and sure enough, I found an alarmingly new steering box hiding under cakes of oil and road grime. The front suspension looked a little flatfooted—mildly suggesting the rear cam-

ber of a VW with 12 buffaloes in the back seat—but it seemed to point in a generally straight line, so it took me four months and a recap and a half to find out that the right wheel was severely toed-in. The speedometer didn't go below 30 and I didn't go above 30, so it served a largely decorative function on the dashboard, which was reminiscent of one of those rounded-off 1950 plastic radios. Everything else, though—oil and generator lights, gas and temperature gauges, high beams and even the dashlight—worked like champs. Even if I *did* get going "that fast" I could steer and I could stop, so the car seemed quite safe.

Now saying that such-and-such components work fine is one thing, but actually driving the 1955 Chevy is truly an amazing experience. It's like some design engineer sat down in front of a tape-recorder that was saying, "Smooth ride, smooth ride," over and over again, drank 14 beers to kind of get the feel of it, and started drawing. The car feels like it's got marshmallows for springs. The ride is so smooth that, on a dark enough night, you could drive over an 80-ft cliff and think all you had was a flat. Nothing, I mean *nothing*, gets through. And then you'll be driving along on a freeway and you get your tires caught in one of those seams between lanes and the car will heel over 45 degrees and you'll tug on the wheel until the cords in your neck stand out and finally the car will move an inch off the seam. And then you get this wonderful rocking effect for a few hundred yards. The first time it happened I thought I was going to be sea sick. But all these characteristics total "smooth ride." Nothing jerky, mind you. Nauseating maybe. But *smooth*.

Maintenance

Are you kidding? After 12 years and 180,000 miles? Have a heart. I mean I get nervous just guessing at the mechanical indignities this car has suffered in its lifetime. The bandana I found tied around the carburetor to hold on the air cleaner implies atrocities better left to the infinite mercy of the dim past.

Did I mention something about blue smoke? Well, the day I bought the car the salesman said all it needed to stop the smoke was a little clean oil. The next day I put five quarts of Shell Premium 30W detergent in the car and then the long slow descent began. After 50 miles, I had to add another quart of Shell and, sure this would cure everything but the dents, put in a can of STP. That lasted another two days. This time I *really* bombed it with three more cans of STP (I now recommend peanut butter). Two days later I slipped down to second quality 40W non-detergent. Finally a month later I discovered those $1.25 gallon cans of 40W they sell at supermarkets and chain drug stores. You will notice in the list of costs that I have not included oil consumption.

221

The reason is that in all those frustrated Friday nights hanging around the Thrifty Drug Store oil counter I no doubt forgot to write down a few gallons. In the interests of accuracy, I have not tried to guess how many I missed.

11   Apparently, though, the engine was quite ready to plug along like that year after year, just as long as I kept the oil level up. Now this situation had distinct rewards. For instance, everytime I drove the

---

1955 Chevrolet Six 210

Repairs & Replacement Costs from miles 173,584 to 180,867

Replacement engine (including extra generator)	$ 60.00
Engine installation (includes hoist, throw-out bearing, 5 pilot bushings)	20.00
Radio (includes $12 charge for 5-minute installation)	27.00
Seat covers ("Universal" fit—unfortunately my car is not a Universal)	7.00
One tire (includes $1.50 mounting charge)	4.25
Two tires (mounted them myself; one gouged, other's tread separated one month later)	10.00
One tire (tread separated after two months)	9.00
One tire (excellent buy)	2.00
Master cylinder rebuild	8.05
Transmission linkage bushings	0.25
Hub caps (Midnight Auto Supply)	0.00
Spare keys (two for the price of one)	0.50
Left rear grease seal & safety check required by insurance company	22.00
8 remanufactured spark plugs (lasted 2 weeks before fouling)	1.25
Total	$171.30

Maintenance

Alignment & balance (includes toe-in adjustment, ignored shot bushings)	$10.00
Full tune-up (includes 6 real spark plugs, distributor points, deluxe screw job)	24.00
Full chassis lube (shot bushings still squeaked)	4.50
Brake adjustment	2.00
Total	$40.50

```
                        Overall costs

Delivered price ........................................ $125.00
License and taxes ......................................   26.00
Insurance ..............................................   94.67
Gasoline and other liquids (includes STP, radiator stop-leak,
   top oil; does not include engine oil) ................  124.00
Repairs & replacements .................................  171.30
Maintenance ............................................   40.50
                                                         _____
   Total costs ......................................... $581.47
Value of car at end of period ..........................  125.00
                                                         _____
   Cost of driving 7283 miles .......................... $456.47
Overall cost per mile ..................................    6.3¢
Note: Actual overall cost per mile is fractionally higher due to cost of oil
which has been omitted in the absence of satisfactory records. The differ-
ence would be less than 0.1¢ higher, however.
```

hundred miles from Santa Barbara to Los Angeles, I was obliged to stop and check the percolator at least once every 40 miles. As a result, I am on a first-name basis with several cows along the Santa Paula road and know better than to pet one particularly friendly looking German Shepherd.

Anyone who is krautish-minded enough to have supported a dying Porsche for three years, though, cannot be satisfied with a car which burns two quarts of oil every hundred miles. It's zo . . . zo imprezeiss! At first I was too busy with school and settled for getting to know Suzy down at the Thrifty Drugs oil counter, but finally I graduated and had time to stew over the engine. But then I was intermittently down to four cylinders—neck-and-neck with the Porsche—and something had to be done.

I went to a local auto wrecker—same breed as the used car salesman except he didn't wash his hands as often—and told him my problem. "Just happened to get one in yesterday. Hard to find, Chivvy Sixes." Sure, sure. We started it up and it sounded real good, so I gave him 60 bucks and he dropped the thing off on a friend's front lawn. Now I'm not being facetious, believe me, but I *doan know nothin'* about mechanics. I mean, I understand some theory and I can change plugs and add oil but that's about it. Well, I decided, if you're ever going to learn, a Chivvy Six is the place to start. And besides, my friend *just happened* to know all about engine swapping. Unknown to me, though, he had an accident the night before and was in the hospital, so I was

223

on my own. Three 12-hour days later—you think I'm kidding, don't you—I got the new engine kind of jammed in there and a few bolts tightened down and the thing actually started! I drove around the block at a stately five miles per hour grinning like an assassin and waving at people I've never seen before. Everything was delirious until I started cleaning up and found two nasty big bolts in the bottom of the tool box. They looked alarmingly familiar.

14   We put the car up on the lift and looked everywhere, but everything seemed bolted up fine. Days later, fortified against the sticky feeling in my socks by a couple beers, I tried a downshift and the engine stayed in the car—and, as a matter of fact, has ever since.

15   With the exception of the engine—a minor point, as I said—maintenance has been relatively light. There have been the *major* improvements, of course—a radio, new seat covers, the set of hubcaps which mysteriously appeared on the car one night at no cost to the owner (it helps to know members of the industry)—but, generally, the costs have been minimal.

Conclusion

16   Would I buy another Chevy Six? What the hell do I need *another* one for? This thing's going to run the rest of my life, anyway. And besides, with all that inconspicuousness, even after it quits running I'll keep it around just to sit down in when I want to get away from it all.

Star Wars:
Two Reviews

In 1977, almost everyone saw the film *Star Wars*. Such words as Artoo Deetoo (or R2D2), Chewbacca the Wookie, and Ben Obi-Wan Kenobi joined our language. Some moviegoers liked the film for its symbolism, for its use of cowboy and hot-rod themes, or for its exciting plot. These two reviews show two professional film reviewers applying their own criteria.

Judith Crist is interested in the *emotional effect* of the film.

Its blend of nostalgia, fantasy, good-versus-evil adventures, familiar charactertypes, and sheer "magic" leaves us feeling, as she puts it, "satisfied." She refers to this criterion at once (in her title and in paragraph 1, in the phrase "The era of the 'feel good' movie . . ."). As she gives us information about the film, she tries to capture the ingredients that produce "that satisfied Saturday-afternoon-at-the-movies smile" (paragraph 5).

Michael Rogers, on the other hand, is interested in the *technology behind the film's special effects*. To him, this is the valuable feature of *Star Wars*. To help us appreciate its "elegant technological features," he calls attention to forthcoming films that will imitate *Star Wars* and compares it to earlier films that it surpasses. These comparisons help us understand the film's technological originality. However, Rogers is writing mostly for people who are not experts on film technology. How does he try to hold our interest?

Crist's criterion of value seems to be that a film should make us feel good. Rogers' seems to be that it should be technologically skillful. What other criteria might there be? What do you look for in films?

"Feel Good" Film
Judith Crist

1 The era of the "feel good" movie, launched by *Cousin, Cousine* and *Rocky*, is upon us—with *Star Wars* to offer lavish, glittering, and nostalgic confirmation thereof.

2 It is fitting that *Star Wars* is the creation of George Lucas, whose last film, in 1973, was that utterly charming re-creation of an adolescent yesterday, *American Graffiti*. This time the thirty-two-year-old writer-director has re-created the fantasies of a childhood soaked in adventure fictions, ranging from the respectability of Camelot and Oz to the trashery of comic strips and Saturday-afternoon serials. The last have provided the format for his chivalric science-fiction tale: he is

Source. "Feel Good' Film" by Judith Crist. From *Saturday Review*, July 9, 1977. Reprinted by permission of the author.

giving us that very special Saturday when the printed prologue (appropriately moving off screen into the vast beyond) bring us up to date on the rebellion against the evil Galactic Empire and plunks us down into the final series of misadventures that will precede the breathtaking triumph of good over evil and the comforting assurance that the good will flourish happily ever after. Do children of all ages ask for anything more?

3   Lucas made an intriguing science-fiction 15-minute short as a student at the University of Southern California, won a National Student Film Festival prize with it in 1968, and was given a Warner Bros. contract to expand it to feature length. The result, 1971's *THX 1138*, was a clinical fantasy set in the twenty-fifth century but bearing all the philosophical earmarks of *1984* and the technological sci-fi clichés of 1960s television. But for *Star Wars*, set "a long time ago" in a "galaxy far, far away," his imagination is unbridled, his vision unbound. We are whisked from deserts to teeming cities to the super spaces of a super space station, all inhabited by a vast variety of men and beasts and machines and mutations thereof; we travel through galaxies and touch down at various and new worlds—with infinity and a new experience ever in the offing, so suffused in inventiveness and refreshing conception are the film's creators.

4   The plot is simply a series of chases, captures, and escapes as the good guys set out to rescue the princess—yes, it is Princess Leia Organa (Carrie Fisher), the sweet-faced, lush-figured, feisty leader of the rebellion, who has fallen into the hands of the vile, führer-like Grand Moff Tarkin (Peter Cushing) and his black knight, Lord Darth Vader (David Prowse behind the armor, given voice by James Earl Jones), aboard their super-Pentagonish space station, *Death Star*. As familiar-but-gussied-up as the villains are the good guys: Luke Skywalker (Mark Hamill), a blond, blue-eyed farm boy and crack pilot recruited by Ben "Obi-Wan" Kenobi (Alec Guinness), a hermit, last of the Jedi Knights, who believed in "the force" (as in "may the force be with you"), a belief that constituted "the old religion"; Han Solo (Harrison Ford), a hotshot pilot and mercenary who proves himself true-blue; Chewbacca, Solo's first mate, a gigantic, monkeylike creature who purrs and growls and bears a striking resemblance to the Cowardly Lion; and two Mutt-and-Jeff-like robots, See Threepio (C3PO), a gold-plated Tin Man programmed for diplomatic missions and therefore British-accented and prissy, and Artoo-Dee-too (R2D2), a round little machine stuffed with data and given to chirps and burbles.

5   There are memorable moments along the way and a simply whizbang dazzle of battling spaceships for a climax, with the happy ending all it should be. The joy of it all is that everyone is playing it straight, no bogging down in messages or monoliths on the one hand, no camp-

ing it up on the other. It is simply a triumph of creativity and technology by masters thereof, people who very obviously delight in doing
what only the medium of film can do in the creation of magic. They
are all listed at the end of the film and well deserve the applause you'll
find yourself giving them—before you exit with that satisfied Saturday-
afternoon-at-the-movies smile that feels so good.

Special Effects—the
Real Stars
Michael Rogers

1 *Star Wars* marks the opening salvo of what could become a pitched
battle of special effects—as well as a watershed in the nature of special
effects itself. It has effortlessly outstripped the classic *2001* in terms
of opticals, miniatures, and miscellaneous amazement—even a brief
comparison of the show-stopping ''Blue Danube'' sequence in *2001*

Source. ''Special Effects—the Real Stars'' by Michael Rogers. Appeared as ''Grand
Illusions'' by Michael Rogers, Rolling Stone Issue # 246, August 25, 1977. © 1977 by
Straight Arrow Publishers Inc. All Rights Reserved. Reprinted by permission.

and the final dogfight in *Star Wars* underscores just how far the technology has evolved. *2001* was itself a landmark: the first giant step past the era when stars were clearly painted on a background and the sparks from a rocket's exhaust inevitably fell toward the bottom of the frame. Yet, while *2001* was a stunning achievement for 1968, it involved, in all, only 35 special-effects shots—all virtual set pieces—as compared to 365 for *Star Wars*. And *Star Wars* actually cost half a million dollars less to produce.

2   Appropriately, 30-year-old John Dykstra, the special photographic effects supervisor for *Star Wars*, received much of his basic training work with Doug Trumbull—the special-effects wizard responsible for *2001*. And, in fact, the next big special-effects film, to be released late this year, will also be a project of Trumbull's. It is Steven Spielberg's $18 million *Close Encounters of the Third Kind,* a film about man's first face-to-face encounter with extraterrestrials that will almost certainly offer some legendary special effects of its own.

3   Past that, the $20-million production of *Superman*, due next summer, includes footage on the planet Krypton and is predicted to be no special-effects slackard itself. During Christmas of 1978, Walt Disney Productions is scheduled to present a $10-million epic called *Space Station One*, which reportedly involves a mile-long space station in imminent danger of falling into a black hole.

4   Special effects is the area of filmmaking that incorporates the widest range of science and technology—from optics and the chemistry of film emulsions to mechanical engineering, physics and electronics. And so it is also the area most affected by scientific progress—and *Star Wars* is a perfect example.

5   The film is, of course, filled with remarkable effects achieved through the clever use of existing technology. An example that comes to mind immediately is the use of videotape images, printed onto film, to yield the holographic look on both Artoo Detoo's projected image of Princess Leia and the monster figures used as pieces in the chess game aboard Han Solo's ship.

6   But *Star Wars'* real contribution to special-effects technoloogy was something altogether new: a fundamentally different way of shooting the kind of deep-space action characterized by both the *2001* "Blue Danube" sequence and the *Star Wars* dogfights. Each of *Star Wars'* special-effects shots required the use of from two to 12 individual elements—ranging from spacecraft models to animated laser beams—separately photographed and then added together, one atop the next, to create finally the total scene. In all, 3,838 individual elements were required for those 365 scenes. Sandwiching together planets, stars and stationary spacecraft is tricky enough, but by no means particularly new. In the case of moving spacecraft, however—especially two or

more spacecraft moving relative to one another—the problem becomes far more complex.

The rebel X-wing fighter one sees swooping and soaring in *Star Wars* was actually standing perfectly still, attached solidly to a plastic pylon during the shooting. It was the *camera* that moved, in such a fashion as to create the illusion of spacecraft motion. If one wanted *two* moving spacecraft—to add, say, an Empire fighter dogging the X-wing's trail—it was necessary to film the Empire fighter separately, moving the camera differently, and then put the two films together to make a single coordinated scene (not to mention adding stars, planets, animated laser fire, etc.).

There was yet another challenge, however: suppose you also wanted the camera's point of view to change during the course of the shot. In traditional filmmaking, pans and tilts and dolly shots are used regularly. But in a situation like the deepspace battle scenes—where the camera was *already* moving to lend the appearance of motion to the stationary spacecraft miniatures—adding yet another component of camera movement is complex indeed. And when there were two or more moving spacecraft in the scene to begin with, that meant that while the camera moved separately to simulate motion during each individual spacecraft shot, it also had to retain, intact and exact, frame by frame, the components of what was to appear as its *own* motion— so that when the composite scene was assembled, the shifting points of view matched identically.

This was the most difficult problem solved by the *Star Wars* group. And, almost predictably, the immediate mind behind those complex camera moves was a computer. Properly programmed and feeding instructions to a set of electric motors, the computer led the camera through an intricate series of maneuvers—and remembered frame by frame just what it had done and then repeated it, with any necessary variations thrown in. The result was that in *Star Wars*, for the first time, director George Lucas could not only place the camera where he wanted it in space—but could actually move it around, just like a director in real time.

The opening scene of *Star Wars* was an exuberant announcement of filmmaking's new capabilities. Once the printed prologue runs off against the stars, the camera—apparently suspended in midspace— leisurely tilts down from the black sky to survey the curling edge of the planet Tatooine, as if it had been there all along. Moments later, a rebel space cruiser roars up from the bottom of the frame, closely pursued by an Empire warship, lasers firing. And then both vessels plummet, scale diminishing rapidly, toward the surface of the planet.

While running no more than a minute or so, this is a scene guaranteed to make special-effects people fall off their chairs. And the rest of the audience—the people who don't know a multi-element matched-move matte shot from an explosion enhancement—can't help but love it too. But for a different reason: suddenly they are part of the story, sucked out of their seats and right into that galaxy far, far away. And sooner or later they may even stop noticing the elegant technologic details of the special-effects work altogether.

Part Four
Recommendation: Introductory Essay

Speak roughly to your little boy,
And beat him when he sneezes
He only does it to annoy
Because he knows it teases.
(*Alice's Adventures in Wonderland*)

This curious bit of advice, given to a wondering Alice by a thoroughly insane Duchess, is not one that we are expected to follow. There are many times, however, when one person wants to tell another what to do, what to say, what to think, or where to get off—in other words, to make a recommendation—and to have it taken seriously.

You have already examined ways to *define a subject*, to *substantiate a thesis* made about it, to *evaluate* it as good or bad. You may now be ready to **persuade** people to do something about it. This final step is not always necessary. If your purpose is to describe a merry-go-round or to evaluate this year's World Series, there is no need to do anything further. But if your purpose is to help handicapped people or to convince students that buying term papers is a bad idea, then your writing task will not be complete until you persuasively advocate a course of action or the adoption of a new attitude. Many of our most urgent questions ask, "What should we do?" The essays that answer such questions are called **recommendations**.

Jefferson in the Declaration of Independence (p. 255) and Lincoln in the Gettysburg Address intended to stimulate action. Their recommendations have great visibility for historical reasons. But the methods of these writers may well be used by the ordinary citizen who writes a letter to a local newspaper in support of a zoning ordinance or by the student who writes a proposal to undertake a special project. Even a letter home asking for money is an exercise in persuasion: you are recommending a course of action that you hope your family will accept.

Recommendations are often particularly satisfying to write. Sometimes, having completed a piece of writing of another kind, you may suspect that your readers will think, "Okay, but so what?" In a recommendation, you have the opportunity to make the "so what" perfectly clear: you want people to behave or believe in a certain way, and you tell them so.

The most primitive form of recommendation, in fact, does no more than flatly state what ought to be done. This primitive form is the command: "Stop" or "Stop or I'll shoot!" When the word *Stop* appears on a red-and-white road sign, it is a recommendation with the authority of the law behind it. When "Stop or I'll shoot!" is shouted by a person taking aim with a revolver, it is a recommendation with the authority of force behind it. Other commands, like the "eat here" signs along the highway, function as invitations rather than orders. Still others, like the advice to "Insert Tab A into Slot B," function as instructions. All commands, however, are recommendations with an implicit "or else": stop or you'll be sorry, eat here or you'll miss a good meal, insert Tab A into Slot B or the gadget won't work. **In a formal recommendation essay, as we see below, the "or else"—the reason why something ought to be done, the type of loss we will suffer if we don't do it—is fully spelled out.**

A more complex form of recommendation than the simple command is the advertisement. Americans spend billions of dollars a year following the advice of advertisements. The term *Madison Avenue* has become a household word because of the remarkable influence exerted by the advertising agencies on that New York City street—and they sell not only bleaching compounds and breakfast cereals, but also politicians and philosophies.

Ads usually rely on emotional associations rather than on logical argument. They may use no words at all. Sometimes a photograph of a gorgeous landscape through which two beautiful young people walk, carrying a bottle of Brand *X* Scotch or proffering each other a

"*I have not yet begun to fight...*"

Can you remember the vivid mental images conjured up so many years ago by your history teacher as she described the dire straits of the **Bonhomme Richard** — flagship of the flimsy revolutionary fleet? She was dis-masted, dead in the water, holed below the water line, sinking from below and burning from above. Yet her master John Paul Jones, when asked to surrender, defiantly spoke those stirring words: "I have not yet begun to fight."

And it is important to remember also that he went on to win. Not only the battle, but to win the war.

As I think of that story, I see a great lesson in it for all of us — and particularly for businessmen.

Today, American business is very much like the Bonhomme Richard. American business is still the great and powerful flagship of our fleet of state, but she is very definitely under attack. Huge tax levies have taken the wind out of her sails; regulations on top of regulations have turned once-safe harbors into dangerous minefields. Environmentalists have stalled, if not stopped, conversion to alternate sources of power. The crew, once a proud and motivated group sharing common dreams and goals, has today turned into a listless, aimless, too often incompetent conglomeration that would strike if they could find the energy.

Yet the captain of the ship, the captains of industry, still tread that quarterdeck. Their defiance, their determination, their actions say louder than words: 'I HAVE NOT YET BEGUN TO FIGHT!'.

It is because of these men that the Hagoth Corporation was founded.

Source. Reprinted with permission from Hagoth Corporation.

Notice the use of *analogy* (see p. 24) in this ad (the product being sold is a $1500 lie detector). Why does the Hagoth Company want you to see American business as if it were like John Paul Jones's ship? Is the analogy an appropriate one?

Brand *Y* cigarette, seems to be all that is needed. A five-word slogan appealing to hunger, sex drives, or snobbery may suffice to sell candy or engine oil. Gasoline additives are inseparable from sexy women; virile and successful men use underarm deodorant. However untrue such associations may be, they seem to work—at least on people who don't think.

Essays of recommendation are based on the assumption that people can and do think.

The Formal Recommendation

Formal recommendations, sometimes called **proposals**, often follow a pattern composed of four elements.

(1) **Establishing the Need to Do Something.** Whether the issue is "I need a new car" or "something must be done to increase our energy supply," recommendations assume that there is a problem (*X*) requiring a solution. But most people would rather ignore problems—especially somebody else's—and therefore **the first obligation of a formal recommendation is to explain exactly what the problem is and why it requires attention *now*.** As a writer, if you want to move your audience off dead center, you will have to show that a failure to move will cause harm to someone (or everyone).

A charitable organization recently ran a fund-raising campaign using the slogan "Give to Birth Defects!" A wealthy and usually generous old man, approached for his contribution, snapped, "Why should I? Birth defects are doing well enough without my help." The people who planned the campaign failed twice. They failed to define the problem and were thus thought to be claiming that birth defects needed support. And they failed to prove that the problem was serious enough to

make that skeptical old man reach for his checkbook. The example is an extreme one, but the reaction of the old man is not. Most people, when told to do something, are going to ask (or think), "Why should I?" and it is risky to fail to answer that question.

The Declaration of Independence is the most famous recommendation written in America and one of the most effective. It won widespread endorsement for a radical change. It begins with a discussion of the problem: "When . . . it becomes necessary . . . to dissolve the political bands. . . ." The audience's immediate response was probably to ask *why* it was necessary, and the Declaration answers this question by providing an extensive list of reasons: the king's "long train of abuses" over a lengthy historical period.

(2) **Considering the Alternatives.** If the first section of a formal recommendation has done its job, the reader should now agree: "Yes, we'd better do something about *X*. Things can't go on this way any longer." **The next step is to define the types of "something" that we might do—in other words, to set forth the alternative solutions.** If there is a shortage of electricity in Dutchess County, New York, the alternatives might be to build a dam on the Hudson River, or to construct an atomic power plant or a plant powered by coal or solar energy, or to cut power consumption and learn to live within our electrical means. Unless you consider all reasonable alternatives, the reader will suspect you of being ill informed or of having an ulterior motive in concealing some of the solutions and expressing others.

The writers of the Declaration of Independence wanted people to know not only what grievances existed, but also what solutions less drastic than revolution had already been tried. "In every stage of these oppressions we have petitioned for redress," they wrote.

233

They explained that they had sought satisfaction by peaceful means so that readers should not think they were militarists who agitated for war at the drop of a hat (or hike of a tax).

(3) **Choosing the Best Solution. The next step is to determine which of the possible solutions would be the best one.** At this point an evaluation is to be made, and it will be necessary to choose—and probably state—the criteria. If the only criterion in solving a power shortage is money, then the cheapest source of energy will be best. But perhaps the cheapest solution to the energy shortage would destroy the beauty of a river and the habitats of wildlife. Choosing what is best becomes harder when multiple—and conflicting—criteria must be met. Often the best solution is a compromise: a power-generating source not as cheap as some, but not as damaging to the environment as others.

Sometimes all that must be done to determine the best solution is to point out that the others have already failed. The most famous passage in the Declaration is the one beginning, "We hold these truths to be self-evident." This section, which states the "unalienable rights" of all people, served as the standard by which the writers evaluated governments. It was clear, from the list of the British government's "abuses," that the colonial system had failed to provide the kind of government the colonists wanted. And it was clear, from the statement that petitions and other traditional means of adjusting differences had been useless, that the colonial system had been given every chance.

(4) **Demonstrating Feasibility. Once the best solution has been chosen, it is still necessary to show that it is** *feasible*—**in other words, that no insurmountable obstacle stands in its way.** This can usually be established by showing that money is available for your project, that a majority of the people affected by it approve, or that any legal or moral objections can be overcome.

You can tell exactly what sort of feasibility demonstration your recommendation needs by asking, "What will it take to get this done?" and then checking to see that the necessary ingredients are within reach. If you are uncertain, be honest about your uncertainty. "If we can find a large enough room in any building near the center of campus," you may have to write, "we can have an African Studies Center, since everything else we need is available."

Sometimes you may discover, as you try to demonstrate feasibility, that the best solution—the one that comes nearest to meeting the criteria—is simply not feasible and must be discarded in favor of a next-best solution.

As for American independence, the Declaration itself demonstrates the feasibility of making such a recommendation. The feasibility of a successful revolution, however, was a different matter. The signers knew that while it was easy enough to declare a war, it wasn't going to be easy to win one. Instead of itemizing their resources, which might have given too much information to the enemy, they simply pledged everything they had to offer: "our lives, our fortunes, and our sacred honor." If other colonists did the same, the war could be won. History shows that their assessment of the Revolution's feasibility was correct.

A formal recommendation, then, defines the problem and establishes the need to do something about it, considers the alternative solutions, chooses the best solution, and demonstrates that the chosen solution is feasible. Concelman, in "Brotherhood Means Paying the Bills" (p. 268), follows this pattern. The ingredients need not always be presented in this order—although the order is a logical one for both writer and reader to follow.

You will notice that this model for making

recommendations involves the other kinds of writing you have studied. It involves **definition**—both the problem and the solutions have to be defined, **substantiation**—a number of theses may have to be substantiated (e.g., the thesis that the problem needs attention, or the thesis that the solution is feasible), and **evaluation**—competing solutions have to be evaluated on the basis of criteria in order to single out the best one.

What is new here is the open call to action, the movement from "this is best" to "let's get it done, and now." Sometimes the call to action is not so urgent—tomorrow or next year will do. And sometimes the call is not for *action*, but for a change in our *thoughts* or *attitudes*. But the overall intention is the same. **The writer wants to urge change in the readers, to move them toward a new goal.**

The Abbreviated Recommendation

Some recommendations, like some evaluations, omit part of the full logical model given above. Someone writing to recommend a particular form of cancer research does not need to spend time demonstrating that cancer is a problem we should care about; we are already familiar with its importance. Someone writing to recommend that we turn the lights off when we don't need them on does not need to explain why this course of action is better than the alternative.

In addition, the writer often cannot complete all parts of the model because some information is not available, or because no single course of action can be endorsed, or because the intention is only to arouse concern about the problem and leave the specific decision up to us. Weinberg's "Disability Isn't Beautiful" (p. 246) discusses the need for action but stops short of a specific "Do *this*" recommendation.

The Negative Recommendation

A special form of abbreviated recommendation is the negative recommendation, which says, "*Don't* do this" or "*Stop* doing this." Its purpose is to persuade us that a certain course of action, or way of thinking, does *not* deserve our endorsement. It usually does not tell us what to do or think instead. Clubb's short article "And God Created Person" (p. 243) recommends that we *not* try to solve problems of sex discrimination by replacing the word *man* with *person*.

A negative recommendation can back up its thesis, "*Don't* do this," by attacking any part of the *standard recommendation* model. If your thesis is "Let's *not* have separate men's and women's sex-education classes," you can show that *there is no problem* (step 1) with the current mixed classes; or that separating the classes by sex would be irrelevant to whatever problem exists—*not a reasonable alternative* to consider (step 2); or that this is *not the best alternative* (step 3); or that *it isn't feasible* (step 4) because federal laws prohibit sex discrimination and reject "separate but equal" schooling.

The negative recommendation is often a useful and even necessary step in solving complex problems. We need to guard against wasting our energies on pseudo-solutions—solutions that look as if they will work but really won't. The negative recommendation acts like a warning flag to protect us from such pitfalls. But unless a negative recommendation can provoke us to think toward a new positive solution, it runs the risk of accomplishing next to nothing.

The Mock Recommendation

Sometimes a writer will begin by recommending a course of action that seems extreme, even a little absurd. The more we read, the more absurd the proposal seems, until we reject it altogether. *This is exactly the effect the writer wants.* The real purpose in saying, "Let's do this" while making the proposal sound wrong or ridiculous is to say, "Let's *not* do this—it's wrong (or ridiculous)." The mock or satiric recommendation is thus one type of negative recommendation. Huff's "How to Lie with Statistics" (p. 291) is a good example; Swift's "Modest Proposal" (p. 299) is another.

Mock recommendations are fun, but risky. If readers fail to sense the satiric purpose and take the mock advice for *real* advice, they may act on the mock advice, which is just the opposite of what the writer intends. Or they may reject the writer as silly or stupid. If you write a mock recommendation, then, be sure that something in your essay—an utterly fantastic setting, a wildly improbable detail of the proposal—will let the audience know that this one isn't for real.

Recommendations and the Writer's Involvement

Once there was a student who wrote one failing paper after another. Nothing she put down on paper was ever any good, and both she and her English teacher knew it. Toward the end of her first year in college, someone broke into her dormitory room and stole her radio and typewriter. Furious, she wrote a letter to the editor of the campus newspaper, explaining how hard she had worked to earn the money to buy those things and how unfair she though it was for people to steal. She also wrote a letter to the Dean in charge of dormitories, pointing out that the locks on the rooms in her dorm were almost useless. Students who forgot their keys could open their doors with someone else's key or even with a hairpin, a piece of hanger wire, or a thin screwdriver. This situation practically invited theft. It put the dormitory's residents, who

paid as much for their room contracts as students in newer and better-protected buildings, at a disadvantage. She called for the entire set of locks in the dormitory to be replaced at once.

The remarkable thing about these two letters was that they were outstanding examples of good writing. There were no errors in grammar or punctuation or spelling. The prose flowed when it should have flowed, was crisp when it should have been crisp. It was full of the right information, in the right place, at the right time—in other words, full of dramatic power. Despite a series of failing compositions, this student knew how to write—*when she felt she had something important to say and someone to say it to.*

Knowing how to write recommendations will help you say something important to somebody. When your proposal matters to you, you have every incentive to get the facts right as you define the problem and substantiate the thesis that we must do something about it. You have every incentive to consider the alternative solutions, evaluate them honestly to identify the best one, and demonstrate that the solution you recommend is feasible.

Language is power. At least some of the time, the pen is mightier than the sword. And language is the civilized way to bring about change, to remake the world so that it conforms a little more to the image of the world we want.

That last word, *want*, points out a critical element of good writing: writing is most likely to be good when the writer *wants* it to be, when the degree of involvement in the subject is high, when the feeling behind the sentences is genuine. When you write a recommendation—or any other types of essay—say what you *want* to, in such a way that your readers will be persuaded to accept your goals as theirs also. Writing is a way of bringing people together.

236

Summary

1 The process of *formal recommendation* has four steps: (1) define the problem and establish the need to do something about it; (2) consider alternative solutions; (3) choose the best solution; and (4) demonstrate the feasibility of this solution.

2 Many recommendations are *abbreviated*—they omit some part of the formal recommendation because it is obvious or for some other reason unsuitable to include.

3 Special forms of recommendation are (1) the *negative recommendation*, which says, "*Don't* do that" and attacks any weakness in the four-step logic of formal recommendation, and (2) the *mock recommendation*, which uses exaggeration to urge an action or conclusion opposite from the apparent thesis.

4 Recommendations—and other forms of writing—are likely to be good when the writer's sense of involvement is strong.

Recommendation, Series One

Readings with Commentary

The Intellectual Taxicab Company
Peter Carlson

Carlson, a college student majoring in journalism, is about to have a personal confrontation with a widespread problem: getting a job. He and other educated people are finding that there is a very small market for the intellectual skills they have learned and enjoy practicing. The alternatives for the liberal-arts graduate seem to be to go to graduate school or drive a taxicab.

Carlson proposes a "simple answer" to this problem. Why not combine the intellectual training of young people with their ability to drive cars? As drivers for "The Intellectual Taxicab Company," college students could "bring adult education to the streets" by providing, simultaneously, a ride and a quick summary of the latest news in psychology, economics, or English literature.

1   My friend Danny hung his Boston University diploma below the hack license in his cab.

2   After seventeen years of education in the finest schools in America, Danny, at 22, couldn't fix his stopped sink, repair a burnt connection in his fuse box, replace a pane of glass in his kitchen, or locate the carburetor in his car.

3   Danny is an educated man. He is a master of writing research papers, taking tests, talking and filling out forms. He can rattle off his social-security number as easily as he can his name because it was also his student identification number. He can analyze Freud from a Marxian viewpoint and he can analyze Marx from a Freudian viewpoint.

4   In short, Danny is an unskilled worker and he has a sociology degree to prove it. He is of very little use to American industry.

5   This is nothing new. Colleges have been turning out unskilled workers for decades. Until five years ago, most of these unskilled workers took their degrees in sociology, philosophy, political science or history and marched right into the American middle class. Some filled executive positions in business and government but many, if not most, went into education, which is the only thing they knew anything about. Once there, they taught another generation the skills necessary to take tests and write papers.

6   But that cycle broke down. Teachers are overabundant these days, college applications are down, plumbers are making $12 an hour and liberal-arts graduates are faced with a choice—graduate school or the taxicab.

7   Danny chose the taxicab because driving was about the only marketable skill he possessed. Danny refers to his job as "Real World 101." He has been shot at, punched, sideswiped and propositioned. But he has also acquired some practical skills—he can get his tickets fixed; he knows how to cheat the company out of a few extra dollars a week; he found his carburetor and he can fix it.

8   Soon, I will be in the same position. I'll graduate from Boston University with a B.S. in journalism. Whatever skills that degree symbolizes are not currently in demand. I suppose I could go to graduate school, but, Christ, I've been doing the same thing for seventeen years and I'm getting a little tired of it. Besides, there are a lot of grad-school graduates who are driving cabs, too.

9   And that brings me to the Intellectual Taxicab Company.

10   Danny and I were discussing the hack business recently and we came up with the idea. It is the simple answer to a simple question: why should all that college education go to waste reading road signs when masses of people are looking for knowledge and riding in cabs?

11   What America needs is a system to bring together all the knowledgeable cabbies and the undereducated rest of the country. The system we propose is the Intellectual Taxicab Company.

12   The Intellectual Taxicab Company would consist of a dispatcher and a fleet of cabs driven by recent college graduates. When you need a ride, you call the company and say something like: "I'd like to go from Wall Street over to East 83rd and I'd like to discuss the world monetary situation."

3   "All right, sir, we'll have an NYU economics graduate over in five minutes."

4   Or: "Hello, I'm in Central Square and I'd like to go to Brookline and discuss whether or not there is a God."

5   "You're in luck, madame, we have a Harvard philosophy graduate who minored in Comparative Religions right in the neighborhood."

6   The educational possibilities of this plan are staggering. English and Drama graduates could take the after-theater run, explaining the literary ramifications of the shows. Political Science graduates could hack around Capitol Hill or City Hall. Regular bus runs could be set up to conduct seminars on popular topics.

7   The Intellectual Taxicab Company would bring adult education to the streets. It would also give all those alienated college graduates a feeling that they didn't waste four years and all that tuition money. And it would elevate the snotty cabdriver to an art form: cabbies would quote Voltaire while they rant about how bad the mayor is.

8   Surely there must be some foundation money or unimpounded Federal funds available to begin such a noble experiment in education. If there is, Danny and I are ready to start immediately. In fact, Danny is licking his lips in anticipation. "Just think how much my tips will go up," he said.

Commentary

Carlson begins with the story of his friend Danny to capture our interest. Danny, we find, represents a whole generation of young people with a problem (paragraphs 1 to 7). The writer belongs to this group too. (Why do you think he decided to describe Danny in the first paragraphs rather than himself?) Nearly half of this short article is spent acquainting us with the problem.

In paragraphs 9 and 10 we are introduced to Carlson's "simple answer to a simple question," the Intellectual Taxicab Company. Then we are told exactly how this multipurpose operation would work so that we can accept it as feasible. At the end of the article, Carlson summarizes the benefits of his proposal, suggests that somebody offer him an initial stake to get the business under way, and conveys his desire to get something done *now* by remarking that he and his friend are "ready to start immediately."

This short recommendation moves from a definition of the problem, to a brief mention of two alternatives (graduate school and ordinary taxi-driving), **to a presentation of the alternative the writer prefers, to a demonstration of its feasibility, to an evaluation of its usefulness, and finally to a summarizing call for action.** It corresponds almost exactly to the model for recommendations discussed in the introduction to this section.

But how is this proposal intended? Carlson's exaggerated language leads us to suspect that he is at least half in jest. We get suspicious when he calls the employment problem "simple" (paragraph 10). We get more suspicious when he introduces his solution with the grand phrase "What America needs is a system . . ." (paragraph 11). We have seen so many systems come and go that we doubt whether America needs one more. Similarly, when Carlson calls the educational possibili-

241

ties of his idea "staggering" (paragraph 16), he is not credible.

What, on the whole, do you think his recommendation is? Does he really want to start an Intellectual Taxicab Company? Perhaps he is proposing "Let's do *something*. If you think my idea is silly, think of a better one."

Outline

I The problem—paragraphs 1–6

II The alternatives

  A Alternatives rejected: standard taxi-driving, graduate school—paragraphs 7–8

  B Alternative recommended: Intellectual Taxicab Company—para-graphs 9–16

    1 This alternative is *preferable*—paragraph 11

    2 This alternative is *feasible*—paragraphs 12–16

III Summary: benefits of proposal, call to action—paragraphs 17–18

Suggestions for Writing

1 Write a recommendation suggesting a "simple answer to a simple question." You may be fully serious or only partly so. For example, given the problem of the high cost of sugar, propose that we simply do without sugar; given the problem of highway deaths—some 60,000 a year—propose that we simply close all the highways; given the problem of racial discrimination, propose that we all wear paper bags over our heads and mittens on our hands so that nobody can see our skin.

2 Carlson says (paragraph 4) that Danny, educated in sociology, is "of very little use to American industry." But maybe Carlson is wrong. Write a letter of recommendation for Danny or someone else like him: a person educated not in a production-oriented skill but in a liberal-arts subject (history, philosophy, social science, literature, etc.) that has trained him to think clearly, to express himself well, and to see the human side of problems. Recommend this person for a job in some part of "American industry." For example, recommend him for a job as an encyclopedia salesman, a loan officer in a bank, a department-store purchaser of furniture, a caseworker in a government welfare office, an on-the-job counselor for "unemployables" being employed in an auto factory.

And God Created Person
Merrel D. Clubb, Jr.

"In the beginning was the word," as the Bible says, recognizing the immense power of language. Clubb's essay (actually a letter to an editor) is a vehement **negative recommendation** about words. His thesis is that we should not replace the word *man* by the word "person." This might seem harmless enough—except that his recommendation occurs in the context of a national controversy about the liberation of women and the way that language influences our perceptions of one another.

Clubb defends *man* as the preferable alternative by appealing to the history of words and by citing term after term, phrase after phrase, in which the *-person* suffix sounds awkward or silly. He seems to be suggesting that our new sensitivity to the sexist connotations of ordinary words is silly. Do you agree, or do you think that he is behaving too much like a *maleperson?*

To the Editor:

The women's liberation movement has, of course, given birth to many worthwhile improvements, but it has also spawned at least one linguistic monstrosity. One can, with some ease, accept the new form *Ms* as filling an empty slot in our language; but is *chairperson*, or even *chairwoman* really necessary? *Chairperson* is fast infiltrating our newspapers and magazines, but when it begins to appear in the publications of our most august Modern Language Association of America, it is time for those concerned with the "purity" of our language to cry forth. If we go the route of *chairperson* we may just as well start talking about *clergyperson, churchperson, countryperson, journeyperson, kinsperson, longshoreperson, foreperson, postperson, brakeperson, milkperson, Redperson, Peking person, inner person,* and *freshperson; personhour, personhunt, personservant, personslaughter, personhole, personmade, personkind, personhood, personly,* and *personliness; person of the world, person in the street, person of God, person of straw, person of war,* and *person o'war bird.* We may even talk about *personing the ship* and *personing the production lines.* And finally, *Persons' Room.* Now surely, we would

Source. "And God Created Person" by Merrell D. Clubb, Jr. Reprinted by permission.

want to be able to tell what is behind the door labeled "Persons' Room," wouldn't we? So, we will have to start talking about *Persons' Room* in contrast to *Wopersons' Room*. This will lead to *flagperson* and *flagwoperson, policeperson* and *policewoperson, salesperson* and *saleswoperson, personish* and *wopersonish, person of the house* and *woperson of the house,* and—*chairperson* and *chairwoperson.* Most surely, wopersons—or fepersons—would wish to distinguish *woperson power* from *person power, woperson suffrage* from *person suffrage,* and most of all, *wopersons' lib* from *persons' lib!*

2   The insistence on such forms as *chairperson, cochairperson,* and *chairpersonship* only goes to show how uninformed avid wopersons and their campfollowers can be. What does the form *man* mean in its various contexts? The modern *man* comes from Old English *man* (in various spellings, as early as 971 A.D.). The meaning of Old English *man* along with its cognates in all the Germanic languages was twofold: (1) "an adult male human being" and (2) "a human being of either sex." Moreover, the more common meaning of *man* in Old English was the latter—"human being or person" without reference to age or sex—and the distinctive sex terms were *wer,* "man, adult male" and *wif,* "woman, adult female." The forerunner of modern *woman,* Old English *wifman,* meant literally "female human being" or "female person." The dual meaning of *man* has continued in English down to the present day, although the meaning "human being" has become somewhat more constricted in that it occurs now only in general or indefinite applications. In many words such as *swordsman, penman, policeman, chairman,* etc., the unstressed form *man* is no longer even a word, but, in effect, a derivational suffix with meanings of, roughly, "one who is skilled in the use of something" (a sword, a pen) or "one who is connected with some act" (policing, chairing). In short, why bring in a relative Johnny-come-lately *person* (originally from Old French) to replace a perfectly good English form *man?* Do we really want to talk about Shakespeare's *Two Gentlepersons of Verona,* Pope's *An Essay on Person,* Shaw's *Person and Superperson,* O'Neill's *The Iceperson Cometh?* Must we open Milton's *Paradise Lost* and read: "Of Person's First Disobedience, and the Fruit/Of that Forbidden tree . . ."?

Merrel D. Clubb, Jr.
University of Montana

Commentary

A recommendation logically involves all the forms of writing previously examined in this text: *definition, substantiation, and evaluation.* They can be presented within a very short space, as Clubb's two-paragraph recommendation shows—with room to spare for a good amount of specific data supporting the writer's proposal. This letter to an editor shows how effective such a "high compression" technique can be.

The first sentence supplies background, functioning as a **definition** of the situation; the second sentence provides a **thesis** in the form of a question: Is the word *chairperson* necessary? The third sentence presents the author's **recommendation** to "cry forth" against this "monstrosity," and those words themselves indicate his **evaluation**: negative. The remainder of the first paragraph shows that if you consistently substitute *person* for *man*, you create absurdities. (This tactic is called **reductio ad absurdum**, *reducing something to absurdity*.) Paragraph 12 argues that *man* hasn't historically meant *male* in any case, and therefore it doesn't need to be replaced to be fair to women (*wopersons*). The final sentence provides a slightly different kind of argument: to require *person* would destroy some of the poetry of our language.

Outline

I Introduction: women's lib has created a context—paragraph 1 (first sentences)

II Statement of recommendation: let's not adopt *chairperson*—paragraph 1

III Defense of the chosen alternative: *-person* formations are silly—paragraph 1

IV Defense of the chosen alternative: *man* doesn't mean "male" anyway—paragraph 2

V Defense of the chosen alternative: we have some fine poetry using *man*—paragraph 2

Suggestions for Writing

1 Not long ago, leaders of the Black Liberation Movement endorsed calling one another *man* as a symbol of defiance against whites who referred condescendingly to adult blacks as *boys*. You may still hear people sprinkle their conversation with the word *man* as a way of asserting their status. Like cool, man! Write an essay recommending that this functional use of *man* be encouraged and paralleled by a similar use of *woman*: Like cool, woman! Or write an essay recommending the opposite.

2 Write an essay recommending the retention or expulsion of another controversial word. For example, should the indefinite pronoun *he* be replaced by the phrase *he or she*, or perhaps by a new indefinite pronoun altogether, such as *'e*? (This last was the proposal of a two-year-old child who was unsure which adults were male and which were female anyway, and hit upon *'e* as a way of never being definitely wrong about the pronoun.) Other sexless pronouns that have been proposed are *hesh* (he/she), *hirs* (his/hers), and *herm* (him/her).

3 Clubb attacks *chairperson* and similar words on linguistic grounds: they sound awkward or foolish as words. Defend or attack the use of *chairperson* on other grounds, for example, its social, psychological, or political implications.

4 Language is not the only element of our culture open to criticism for the attitudes it implies. Write an essay recommending, or recommending against, a change in the conventions of dress (for instance, some restaurants require that a man wear a jacket and tie; many local ordinances require that a woman—but not a man—wear upper-body clothing) or sports

245

(most sports are sex-segregated). Should there be a Persons' Football Team?

5 The following prose-poem reflects an attitude toward language different from Clubb's.

Myth

Long afterward, Oedipus, old and blinded, walked the roads. He smelled a familiar smell. It was the Sphinx. Oedipus said, "I want to ask one question. Why didn't I recognize my mother?" "You gave the wrong answer," said the Sphinx. "But that was what made everything possible," said Oedipus. "No," she said. "When I asked, What walks on four legs in the morning, two at noon, and three in the evening, you answered, Man. You didn't say anything about woman." "When you say Man," said Oedipus, "you include women too. Everyone knows that." She said, "That's what you think."[1]

Because Oedipus assumed that women were simply included in the category Man, he was made to suffer—and his mother and other people of both sexes suffered too.

If you share Rukeyser's viewpoint, write a recommendation in contrast to Clubb's. What should we do to give separate recognition to women? Similarly, should we give separate recognition to children and other groups? If so, how?

[1] "Myth" by Murial Rukeyser; Reprinted by permission of Monica McCall, International Creative Management. Copyright © 1973 Muriel Rukeyser. From *Breaking Open* by Muriel Rukeyser, published 1973 by Random House, Inc., New York, p. 388.)

Disability Isn't Beautiful
Nancy Weinberg

This selection demonstrates how recommendation relies upon *definition, substantiation,* and *evaluation.* Weinberg's recommendation is that handicapped people be given the same rights and opportunities as other minority groups. To persuade us to support this position, she must *explain what a minority group is* (definition), *demonstrate that handicapped people indeed qualify as a minority group* (substantiation), and *make us feel that the current treatment of the handicapped is wrong* (evaluation).

Source. "Disability Isn't Beautiful" by Nancy Weinberg. From *The New York Times*, January 8, 1977. Op-ed. © 1977 by The New York Times Company. Reprinted by permission.

1   The law barring Federal agencies and holders of Federal contracts from discriminating against the physically handicapped has not been actively enforced during its three years of existence. And though the handicapped are legally entitled to the same protection as other minority groups, they continue to be a target of discrimination while the Government acts as if they were different from other minorities.

2   Three characteristics define a minority. The first is easy identification. Recognition of a physically disabled person is usually simple on the basis of appearance alone. However, the physically disabled may attempt "to pass" by concealing their handicap. Deaf people, for example, will sometimes avoid using manual communication, especially in public. This refusal to use manual communication is similar to hair-straightening, skin-bleaching and other examples of minority members' attempts to deny their identity.

3   Another feature of a minority group is the negative prejudgment made about the behavior and abilities of its members. When able-bodied individuals are surveyed and asked to describe a disabled person or another able-bodied person, their descriptions of the former are more negative than those of the latter. Blind persons, deaf persons and individuals confined to wheelchairs are all viewed as less intelligent, less happy, less popular, less likeable, and less self-confident than the able-bodied.

4   The final feature of a minority group is the threat, real or imagined, that it poses to the comfort of the majority. The physically handicapped threaten the social comfort of the able-bodied. Research indicates that the able-bodied feel more uncomfortable and show greater physiological stress when interacting with a disabled person than with an able-bodied person. In addition, possibly to avoid further tension, people interacting with the disabled tailor their opinions so they are in closer agreement with the disabled and terminate their interactions with the disabled sooner than with others.

5   As well as meeting the three defining characteristics of a minority group, the physically handicapped experience disadvantages that other minorities do not face.

6   People in racial and ethnic minorities grow up with other members of those minorities. They learn from others in their group how to deal with the majority culture.

7   In contrast, a child born with a handicap is generally brought up around the nonhandicapped. The child has little opportunity to learn coping skills from others with similar handicaps. He or she is soon socialized to have the same values about the importance of physical perfection as the rest of society. (When able-bodied children and disabled children are asked to arrange pictures of children with and without handicaps from "most liked" to "least liked," both groups order the pictures in the same manner, with the able-bodied child

247

always being liked best.) The sense of pride in a certain identity that can be fostered when people of the same religious or ethnic group come together is absent. There is no natural grouping to support a "disability is beautiful" movement.

8 Finally, even when people with disabilities are given opportunities, they are often unable to take advantage of them because of physical barriers: steps and curbs, inaccessible elevators, narrow corridors, revolving doors, a lack of accessible public transportation and a lack of accessible housing. According to a Government report, 20 million people with handicaps are "built out of normal living by unnecessary barriers."

9 The physically handicapped have the liabilities of a minority group. Shouldn't they be given the rights of a minority group? The answer is affirmative. It is time the action was also.

Commentary

This essay was written in 1977. By now, nearly everyone has seen sidewalk curbs with ramps for wheelchairs, or special restroom facilities for the handicapped. Weinberg's call for affirmative action, which she shows is logically necessary, has been answered—to some extent. *Notice that Weinberg does not consider whether her proposal is completely feasible:* whether it is economically feasible to break down *all* the physical barriers that restrict handicapped people. At what point might someone recommend that we concentrate our efforts on the needs of other groups

of people instead?

Weinberg decides to exclude the *mentally* handicapped. What recommendations might one make for them?

Many writers, having chosen this subject, would include brief narratives about specific people whose opportunities in life were unfairly restricted by physical barriers. Weinberg, however, does not include such case histories; **she chooses to let the logic of the situation do the job.** Do you think that her recommendation would be more effective if she had used specific instances?

Outline

I Introduction: the physically handicapped have been excluded from affirmative action—paragraph 1
II Liabilities that qualify the physically handicapped as a minority group—paragraphs 2–8

A Problems shared with other minorities—paragraphs 2–4
B Problems added to those of other minorities—paragraphs 5–8
III Call for affirmative action—paragraph 9

Suggestions for Writing

1 Recommend some action that the majority might take to reduce discrimination

against the physically handicapped. Choose an instance with which you are

248

familiar—for example, recommend that the light switches in an office building in which you have worked be lowered so that people in wheelchairs can reach them.

2 Describe some action that has helped reduce discrimination against some minority group and recommend that it be extended to the handicapped. For example,

negative images of racial or ethnic minority groups have been countered by public relations campaigns. How could positive images of the handicapped be reflected in your local newspapers or other media? Could you persuade an advertiser to show Grandpa with a hearing aid—rather than granddaughter with her teddy-bear—enjoying Yummo's bread?

Classified Ads that Click
Champ Clark

This selection makes a recommendation about writing. Clark is writing an ad (in a manner of speaking) on behalf of good ad writing. His essay must itself illustrate the *X* he is recommending. Has he complied with all of the applicable rules that he cites, and has he avoided the bad practices? Which recommendations about ad writing also apply to writing in general?

```
WATCHMAKER WANTED
with references who can furnish tools.
State age, experience, and salary re-
quired.
                 T 39, Daily News
```

It was short, simple and straight-forward. It stated the conditions without flimflam. It cntnd nt 1 sngl dmnd abbvn. It cost only 80¢ for one day's insertion—but it did the job. It was placed under Help Wanted in the classified advertising section of the Chicago Daily News on April 1, 1887 by a man named Richard Sears. It was answered by artisan Alvah Roebuck.

2   Classified ads rarely make such mercantile history. Yet they are a large and significant factor in the American marketplace; estimates are that in 1974, more than 300 million classified ads, adding up (including repeats) to well over 3 billion lines, appeared in U.S. daily newspapers at a cost of about $2.1 billion. (These computations do not take into account magazines, weekly papers or other places where want ads are carried.)

3   Unfortunately, millions of these classified ads failed to bring advertiser and customer together. The list of possible reasons why is almost endless. An advertiser may put a price on an item that is simply out of sight, for example. Or there may be a complete dearth of demand for, say, pet capuchin monkeys no matter how "clean & friendly" the little beasts may be. But it is safe to say that the most likely reason for an ad's falling flat is bad writing: either the style is confusing or the content is inadequate—or both.

4   I am (or was) a long-time member of that pitiable minority that writes unrequited want ads. In my younger days, my main concern was with unloading much-used autos that came into my possession from time to time, usually by way of classified ads. I was addicted to describing these vehicles as either "nifty" or "spiffy" or sometimes both; upon more mature reflection, I can now understand why the best I ever managed to do was sell, without advertising aid, a 1951 Nash to a neighbor's kids for $1. In later and slightly more affluent years, my interest occasionally turned to selling houses ("By Owner— No Brokers"), and my favorite words were "lovely" and "extraordinary"; I often wondered why the ad taker at the other end of the telephone seemed suddenly afflicted by a bad cold.

5   Lately, after talking extensively to want-ad takers, users and industry groups, I've found out why. Each major category of classified ads—Houses for Sale, General Merchandise, Help Wanted, and Autos—has its particular requirements, but certain general principles apply to the writing of all want ads. Here are some to keep in mind:

6   • Remember that a classified ad does not sell. It merely sets up a situation for selling (or hiring, or whatever). In almost every instance, a face-to-face meeting between advertiser and prospective customer is necessary before a transaction can be completed. Therefore, in writing a want ad, don't lie or even embellish too much. Anyone you trick or mislead into taking the trouble to see your product has a moral right to punch you in the nose. Make yourself as easy as possible to reach; if a prospective buyer can't find you quickly, he'll take his business elsewhere. At the very least, list your phone number and the times you will be available to take calls. Except in special cases—as, for example, when job résumés are desired—box numbers are bad news.

7   • Give facts. Each classified category has certain facts that are con-

sidered essential to almost every ad. Others are optional and should be selected according to the specific features of the item you are selling. In general, the more complete the facts, the better the response to the ad. There is another side to this coin: flossy descriptive phrases—nonfacts—can irritate readers (for a sample of what not to do, see the box in suggestion 1 below). One or two, especially when used as a headline for an ad, may be okay. But don't overdo it.

• Write in English. Short, complete sentences are best. Avoid telegraphese and unfamiliar words. (A glebe house is a rural parsonage, but if you want to sell your house in the country, don't advertise it as a glebe house.) Above all, as a cardinal rule of want-ad writing, abbreviations are anathema. The reason may be illustrated by a sample from a recent issue of a New York daily. Would you be interested in buying this house in the Flatbush section of Brooklyn?

> FLTB—dbl lvl u & d L-shpd ktch gly dec.
> Nice ngbh. Gldn opp. AC-DC. Owner.
> $62,500

• Use common sense about want-ad costs. If you hope to sell a used ten-speed bicycle, it is silly to spend anything above the bare minimum to juice up an ad. On the other hand, if your $50,000 house is at stake, it may well be wise to pay enough to offer additional facts, a heading and some eyestopping white space. Classified-ad costs are almost impossible for the layman to figure for himself. Basically, they are computed per line of agate print, with about five words to the line; larger print and white space count as more lines. Rates generally go according to the circulation of the paper. Discounts are offered for consecutive-day ads and other things. I suggest that you write your ad in two ways: first, the way you would really like to see it; second, with an eye to saving space. Then call the classified-ad department of your chosen paper, read both versions and get costs on each. Use your own judgment as to whether the extra lineage is worth it. It probably is—at least on major items.

In addition to these general rules, consider some categorical specifics:

House for Sale

Facts are especially important in house-for-sale ads, and there is, happily, a recognizable order of factual importance. Surveys indicate that by far the most essential fact is location. In writing an ad, be specific about the area, district, neighborhood, street and even the number. Next comes price—and any attractive financial terms you're able to offer. Some experts argue this point, insisting that it is not really necessary to cite price; all I can say is that the price had better be there if you expect me to do so much as lift a telephone. Next on the list comes the number of bedrooms (bathrooms, equally important to me, rank surprisingly far down in the surveys).

12   Those three facts—location, price and number of bedrooms—are vital. The omission of any will make a dramatic difference, for the worse, in the response to an ad. But the Big Three are closely followed by other factors: condition of the house; convenience to schools, shopping centers, churches, commuter trains (but watch this one— you don't want to brag about your house being *too* close to the tracks); number of rooms of all types (a specific listing of rooms is even better); type and quality of architecture and construction, and the age of the house. In these days of high fuel costs, the type of heating takes on added significance—and fireplaces become more than a grace note. Any or all of these optional facts should be used—if they make a positive point—along with any other feature that might enhance the value of a house. But take warning: gimmicks don't sell. I have yet to hear of anyone buying a house because it had, say, electronically controlled garage doors.

Merchandise

13   The use of a brand name helps (unless, of course, it's a bad brand). With or without a brand name, a stove is a stove—so don't oversell. Always describe the condition of what you are selling (unless it is in horrible condition, in which case it probably won't sell anyway). Always say when and where an item may be inspected—as it is certain to be. But the main thing to remember is that the merchandise classifieds are a vehicle for comparison shopping. Listing the price is essential.

Help Wanted

14   In this category, we are restricting ourselves to the sort of help an individual might need—domestic help, mothers' helpers, companions for elderly persons, a doctor's receptionist-secretary, etc. It is most important to give a full and accurate description of what the job entails. Be careful about wording: light housekeeping, for example, means light housekeeping—not waxing floors and washing windows. State whether or not experience is necessary. Ask for references—and check on them.

15   Fringe benefits such as pensions and health insurance plans are of course rare in this kind of job. But pleasant surroundings may be an enticement; if you can offer them, describe them. Wages are generally negotiable, but it's useful to indicate roughly what you're willing to pay.

Autos

Auto ads are probably the easiest of all classifieds to write well—and they're the most poorly written. Abbreviations are a special curse. Ridiculous phrases like "Must see to appreciate" are rampant. Extras are endlessly listed, although the classified-ad professionals agree that most prospective used-car buyers don't care about minor extras like wheel covers or fog lights if the price of the basic auto is right. To write a perfectly passable used-car ad all one needs to do is list the year, make and body type of the car, the kind of transmission—and the price. If the mileage is low, it is all right to mention it; the condition of the car is also okay to include. Add one or two more features of which you are especially proud and you are in business.

To test this theory, I went to Arthur Einstein Jr., senior vice president and copy director of the New York advertising agency of Lord, Geller, Federico, Inc. For years Einstein wrote flowing prose for the national advertising of automobile companies, including Ford and Renault; he is also an auto hobbyist and a frequent contributor to Automobile Quarterly. I asked him how he, as an expert on a loftier plane, would write an auto classified ad; I confess that I expected something souped up. But as it happened, he had written one for himself only three months before:

1968 VW CONVERTIBLE
Automatic stick. Air conditioned. Four new tires. New battery. Very clean car with only 22,500 miles. Asking $1295.

Art Einstein sold his car almost immediately at his asking price. That is my kind of want ad. It is short, simple and straightforward. It states the facts without flimflam. It cntns nt 1 sngl dmn abbvn. It cost only $4.70 for one insertion in the East Hampton (N.Y.) Star—but it did the job. Mr. Sears, meet Mr. Roebuck.

Commentary

This recommendation is a set of instructions, a "how-to." It uses most of the parts of the formal recommendation (see pp. 233–235). Clark begins by explaining his subject—using *definition by example*—and by citing figures to show us that ads are numerous and hence important. They represent over $2 billion worth of business each year, or did in 1974. Clark then tells us what the problem is: millions of ads don't work, including ads that Clark used to write himself. Note that he brings in personal experience to help us relate "millions of ads" to our individual situations.

Clark spends most of the rest of his time explaining the *alternative* to badly written ads. His criterion of value is utilitarian: a good ad is one that sells. First he states four general rules for ad writing (paragraphs 6–9), and then uses *division and classification* to present the large category "classified ads" in smaller and more useful units—house ads, merchandise ads, help-wanted ads, car ads. An example at

253

the end of the article parallels the example at the beginning, giving the article a balanced structure that ends where it began: with a good ad. These examples show that writing good ads is *feasible*.

How persuasive is Clark's recommendation? What hard evidence does he supply to

convince you that if you tell the truth, give facts, and write short, complete sentences, your want ad will bring results? Many ads use an alternative approach, called the *hard sell*. To what kinds of ads do you respond favorably?

Outline

I The subject (classified ads) and the problem (classified ads that don't sell)—paragraphs 1–4
II General rules for writing good ads—paragraphs 5–9

III Applications to specific kinds of ads—paragraphs 10–16
IV Concluding example—paragraphs 17–18

Suggestions for Writing

1 Clark provides an example of a bad want-ad (printed in the box below).

Just give the news, please

Make Your Nest Egg
HATCH
This Comfortable Nest

A top-hat-and-tails neighborhood where dollars live a merry life. Tudor so truly English you drop your aitches at the front door. 4 bedrooms: Master—insomnia is just a dim memory in this dim sleeping room; one with a romantic Romeo and Juliet balcony for teen-age daughter. 2 baths: Helen of Troy had nothing like these perfect appointments. Breakfast room to give morning eggs farm fresh appeal. Kitchen where your Queen of Hearts will love to make tarts. Dining room a beautiful shell to hold years of delectable meals. Living room a completely charming shell to enclose all the joy of a real home. Den designed for a heap of living. Attic a delight for families who just can't help collecting things. Basement a secret, safe meeting place for young underground members. Hot water heat makes late parties end on a warm note. Grounds just like a gaily embroidered green pocket handkerchief. Best offer.

Believe it or not, these descriptive phrases are taken verbatim from a 22-page, 1,200-item, attic-to-basement suggestion list that the New York Times provides its ad sellers. Nobody seriously recommends using large doses of this sort of language; indeed, even in small doses it may put off as many buyers as it attracts.

Following his directions, rewrite the ad.
2 Collect several good and bad want ads from your local newspaper. Test them on your friends or classmates and then write an analysis (evaluation) of why the best ad is good, the worst one bad.
3 Clark warns against telling lies in want ads. Should his warning be extended to all advertisers? Write a recommendation against the practice of using deceptive words or images in merchandise or political advertising, citing examples that you have collected.
4 Write a "how-to" on a subject of your own choosing. Follow Clark's process if you like: identify the problem, give general principles, use division and classification to divide the subject into smaller units to which more specific rules apply, and conclude with an example that parallels one you used in the introduction.

You might want to prepare the text and illustrations for a "how-to" pamphlet.

The Declaration of Independence
Thomas Jefferson and Others

A "declaration" or "manifesto" is not simply an announcement that somebody is going to do something. It is also a call to action—a recommendation, even an impassioned plea—to other people to contribute their energies and if necessary their lives. The writers of a declaration must therefore not only explain their program (*definition*), but also demonstrate that a problem exists (*substantiation*), convince us that what they want to do is right (*evaluation*), and ask us to support them (*recommendation*).

Jefferson and the other delegates of the Continental Congress accomplish all of these functions in the Declaration of Independence. They appeal to our subjective beliefs by stating the philosophical principles they live by and are willing, if need be, to die by. But they also invite an objective assessment by rehearsing "the facts" as proof of the reasonableness of their action.

In CONGRESS, July 4, 1776
The Unanimous Declaration of the Thirteen United
States of America,

When in the Course of human events, it becomes necessary for one people to dissolve the political bands which have connected them with another, and to assume, among the powers of the earth, the separate and equal station to which the Laws of Nature and of Nature's God entitle them, a decent respect to the opinions of mankind requires that they should declare the causes which impel them to the separation.

We hold these truths to be self-evident: that all men are created equal; that they are endowed by their Creator with certain unalienable Rights; that among these are Life, Liberty, and the pursuit of Happiness. That to secure these rights, Governments are instituted among Men, deriving their just powers from the consent of the governed. That whenever any Form of Government becomes destructive of these ends, it is the Right of the People to alter or to abolish it, and to institute a new Government, laying its foundation on such principles,

255

and organizing its powers in such form, as to them shall seem most likely to effect their Safety and Happiness. Prudence, indeed, will dictate that Governments long established should not be changed for light and transient causes; and accordingly all experience hath shewn, that mankind are more disposed to suffer, while evils are sufferable, than to right themselves by abolishing the forms to which they are accustomed. But when a long train of abuses and usurpations, pursuing invariably the same Object, evinces a design to reduce them under absolute Despotism, it is their right, it is their duty, to throw off such Government, and to provide new Guards for their future security. Such has been the patient sufferance of these Colonies; and such is now the necessity which constrains them to alter their former Systems of Government. The history of the present King of Great Britain is a history of repeated injuries and usurpations, all having in direct object the establishment of an absolute Tyranny over these States. To prove this, let Facts be submitted to a candid world:

3   He has refused his Assent to Laws, the most wholesome and necessary for the public good.

4   He has forbidden his Govenors to pass Laws of immediate and pressing importance, unless suspended in their operation till his Assent should be obtained; and when so suspended, he has utterly neglected to attend to them.

5   He has refused to pass other Laws for the accommodation of large districts of people, unless those people would relinquish the right of Representation in the Legislature, a right inestimable to them and formidable to tyrants only.

6   He has called together legislative bodies at places unusual, uncomfortable, and distant from the depository of their public Records, for the sole purpose of fatiguing them into compliance with his measures.

7   He has dissolved Representative Houses repeatedly, for opposing with manly firmness his invasions of the rights of the people.

8   He has refused for a long time, after such dissolutions, to cause others to be elected; whereby the Legislative powers, incapable of Annihilation, have returned to the People at large for their exercise; the State remaining in the mean time exposed to all the dangers of invasion from without, and convulsions within.

9   He has endeavoured to prevent the population of these States; for that purpose obstructing the Laws for Naturalization of Foreigners; refusing to pass others to encourage their migrations hither, and raising the conditions of new Appropriations of Lands.

10   He has obstructed the Administration of Justice, by refusing his Assent to Laws for establishing Judiciary powers.

11   He has made Judges dependent on his Will alone for the tenure of their offices, and the amount and payment of their salaries.

He has erected a multitude of New Offices, and sent hither swarms of Officers to harass our people, and eat out their substance.

He has kept among us, in times of peace, Standing Armies, without the Consent of our legislatures.

He has affected to render the Military independent of and superior to the Civil power.

He has combined with others to subject us to a jurisdiction foreign to our constitution, and unacknowledged by our laws; giving his Assent to their Acts of pretended Legislation:

For quartering large bodies of armed troops among us;

For protecting them, by a mock Trial, from punishment for any Murders which they should commit on the Inhabitants of these States;

For cutting off our Trade with all parts of the world;

For imposing Taxes on us without our Consent;

For depriving us in many cases of the benefits of Trial by Jury;

For transporting us beyond Seas to be tried for pretended offenses;

For abolishing the free System of English Laws in a neighbouring Province, establishing therein an Arbitrary government, and enlarging its Boundaries so as to render it at once an example and fit instrument for introducing the same absolute rule into these Colonies;

For taking away our Charters, abolishing our most valuable Laws and altering fundamentally the Forms of our Governments;

For suspending our own Legislatures, and declaring themselves invested with power to legislate for us in all cases whatsoever.

He has abdicated Government here by declaring us out of his Protection and waging War against us.

He has plundered our seas, ravaged our Coasts, burnt our towns, and destroyed the lives of our people.

He is at this time transporting large Armies of foreign Mercenaries to compleat the works of death, desolation, and tyranny, already begun with circumstances of Cruelty & perfidy scarcely paralleled in the most barbarous ages, and totally unworthy the Head of a civilized nation.

He has constrained our fellow Citizens taken Captive on the high Seas to bear Arms against their Country, to become the executioners of their friends and Brethren, or to fall themselves by their Hands.

He has excited domestic insurrections amongst us, and has endeavoured to bring on the inhabitants of our frontiers the merciless Indian Savages, whose known rule of warfare is an undistinguished destruction of all ages, sexes, and conditions.

21   In every stage of these Oppressions, We have Petitioned for Redress in the most humble terms. Our repeated Petitions have been answered only by repeated injury. A Prince, whose character is thus marked by every act which may define a Tyrant, is unfit to be the ruler of a free people.

22   Nor have We been wanting in attentions to our British brethren. We have warned them from time to time of attempts by their legislature to extend an unwarrantable jurisdiction over us. We have reminded them of the circumstances of our emigration and settlement here. We have appealed to their native justice and magnanimity, and we have conjured them by the ties of our common kindred to disavow these usurpations, which would inevitably interrupt our connections and correspondence. They too have been deaf to the voice of justice and of consanguinity. We must, therefore, acquiesce in the necessity, which denounces our Separation, and hold them, as we hold the rest of mankind, Enemies in War, in Peace Friends.

23   WE THEREFORE the Representatives of the UNITED STATES OF AMERICA, in General Congress Assembled, appealing to the Supreme Judge of the world for the rectitude of our intentions, do, in the Name, and by Authority of the good People of these Colonies, solemnly publish and declare, That these United Colonies are and of Right ought to be FREE AND INDEPENDENT STATES; that they are Absolved from all Allegiance to the British Crown, and that all political connection between them and the State of Great Britain is and ought to be totally dissolved; and that as FREE AND INDEPENDENT STATES, they have full Power to levy War, conclude Peace, contract Alliances, establish Commerce, and to do all other Acts and Things which INDEPENDENT states may of right do. AND for the support of this Declaration, with a firm reliance on the protection of divine Providence, we mutually pledge to each other our Lives, our Fortunes, and our sacred Honor.

Commentary

The Declaration begins by announcing what its signers intend to do. It then proceeds to explain the beliefs they hold—standards that serve as the basis for judging King George's government. It is only because the signers believe that governments exist to secure the inherent rights of "life, liberty, and the pursuit of happiness" that they can condemn the British rule. (If you believe, for instance, that governments exist to secure their own prosperity, you might find that the British rule was admirably trying to perform its job.) The ex-

planation of concepts of government (paragraph 2) is appropriate here, therefore, because it functions as the statement of criteria for an evaluation. The writers of the Declaration are not simply sounding off.

Similarly, the rehearsal of the colonists' grievances against the king (paragraphs 3 to 29) is appropriate because it provides evidence. The largest part of the Declaration consists of this list of grievances. The decision on the part of Jefferson and his comrades to devote so much of their document to presenting "the facts" shows the very high value they put on the rational abilities of the human mind. (Their era is sometimes called the Age of Reason and they themselves Rationalists.) Without this section, the Declaration would sound merely like the angry protest of an unreasoning loser or the tantrum of a child. The colonists do not want to be mistaken for children.

After the presentation of evidence, the Declaration asserts that the preferable alternative to war—peaceful redress of grievances—has been tried and found ineffective. This claim justifies (note the transitional "therefore,"

paragraph 32) the conclusion that the colonists now have no alternative except independence.

There is very little discussion of feasibility here. To present details about the resources available for war might have divulged too much information to the enemy. To demonstrate the feasibility of the endeavor, the writers simply assert that they will rely upon God and upon their own willingness to sacrifice everything for this cause. The eloquent last phrases are a summons to everyone else who shares their beliefs and has suffered from the same injustices to do the same.

Outline

I Introduction: statement of the problem—paragraph 1

II Demonstration that something must be done: that British rule has repeatedly violated the basic principles of true government—paragraphs 2-29

   A Principles of government—paragraph 2

   B British violations of those principles—paragraphs 3-29

III Consideration of the alternatives: peaceful negotiation has failed—paragraphs 30-31

IV Choice of the remaining best (only) alternative, brief demonstration of feasibility, and call to action—paragraph 32

SUGGESTIONS FOR WRITING

1 Following the pattern of the Declaration of Independence, write a manifesto of your own. Show that a problem exists because someone or something does not conform to your criteria and that other alternatives have been tried but have not worked. Conclude with an invitation to others to join you. Use some of the language of the Declaration if that seems appropriate.

2 Recommend a specific change in the governance structure of your dormitory group, student government, family, etc. Who should have authority? How should decisions be reached?

Recommendation, Series Two

Readings without Commentary

A Message to America's Car Buyers

R. C. Gerstenberg

This selection, like Champ Clark's "Classified Ads that Click" (p. 249), demonstrates the very close relationship between advertisements and recommendations. It appeared as an ad in a newspaper read by middle-class people. To attract this audience, the copywriter decided to rely on arguments rather than emotional associations or a pretty picture. The ad that resulted includes most of the elements of a formal recommendation. It identifies the problem ("inflation-weakened America"), considers alternatives ("common-sense conservation" versus "empty austerity"), uses an example (a chilly house) to persuade us that conservation is better than austerity, and concludes by recommending that we enact a policy of conservation by buying new cars: buying cars will benefit the economy. The only thing missing is the demonstration of feasibility, and even this is hinted at: if you "see your dealer," the ad implies, you'll be able to make a deal.

Like many ads, this one uses repetition to drive its car home. Having said "no growth makes no sense," the ad says it again ("not for America") and a third time ("not for anyone")—and, in case the message might have been missed by a really dim-witted reader, it concludes with a blunt "Right now is the time to buy a new car." Our impulse is directed toward General Motors showrooms specifically by the advice under the com-

Source. "A Message to America's Car Buyers" by R. C. Gerstenberg. Reprinted by courtesy of *Barron's National Business and Financial Weekly.* Copyright © 1974.

pany's name: "See your Chevrolet, Pontiac, Oldsmobile, Buick or Cadillac dealer today."

What makes you respond favorably (or not) to this recommendation?

A message to America's car buyers...

Inflation-weakened America needs common-sense conservation, not empty austerity. Conservation is insulating the attic and saving fuel; austerity is shivering in your living room.

In a similar way, when new cars replace old, the nation's primary means of transportation gains efficiency. Our new 1975 cars conserve gasoline, even as they emit less pollution, provide more safety features, and cost less to operate and maintain than earlier models.

The purchasing of new cars is the common-sense conservation we need. It keeps the wheel of progress rolling. It means growth and investment. This means more jobs for our people, more revenue for our government, more value for our customers, and more dividends for our stockholders.

No growth makes no sense; not for America, not for anyone.

Right now is the time to buy a new car.

R.C. Gerstenberg

R.C. Gerstenberg
Chairman
General Motors Corporation

General Motors

See your Chevrolet, Pontiac, Oldsmobile, Buick or Cadillac dealer today.

A Two-Hundred-Year Conversation
Lewis Thomas

Many people are interested in whether there is intelligent life elsewhere in the universe. If there is, what will it mean to us? If we do make contact with extraterrestrial beings, what should we say to them? It might well take 200 years for us to get a reply to our opening remark. This delay makes it hard to choose the information we should send about ourselves and the questions we should ask in return.

You may find Thomas's recommendations rather odd. Consider how well he defends. How would *you* write the script for the first intercosmic conversation?

1   Let us assume that there is, indeed, sentient life in one or another part of remote space, and that we will be successful in getting in touch with it. What on earth are we going to talk about? If, as seems likely, it is a hundred or more light years away, there are going to be some very long pauses. The barest amenities on which we rely for opening conversations—"Hello, are you there?" from us, followed by "Yes, hello," from them—will take two hundred years at least. By the time we have our party we may have forgotten what we had in mind.

2   We could begin by gambling on the rightness of our technology and just send out news of ourselves, like a mimeographed Christmas letter, but we would have to choose our items carefully, with durability of meaning in mind. Whatever information we provide must still make sense to us two centuries later, and must still seem important, or the conversation will be an embarrassment to all concerned. In two hundred years it is, as we have found, easy to lose the thread.

3   Perhaps the safest thing to do at the outset, if technology permits, is to send music. This language may be the best we have for explaining what we are like to others in space, with least ambiguity. I would vote for Bach, all of Bach, streamed out into space, over and over again. We would be bragging, of course, but it is surely excusable for us to put the best possible face on at the beginning of such an acquaintance. We can tell the harder truths later. And, to do ourselves justice, music

Source. "A Two-Hundred-Year Conversation" by Lewis Thomas. From *The Lives of a Cell: Notes of a Biology Watcher* by Lewis Thomas. Copyright © 1972 by the Massachusetts Medical Society. Reprinted by permission of The Viking Press.

would give a fairer picture of what we are really like than some of the other things we might be sending, like *Time*, say, or a history of the U.N., or Presidential speeches. We could send out our science, of course, but just think of the wincing at this end when the polite comments arrive two hundred years from now. Whatever we offer as today's items of liveliest interest are bound to be out of date and irrelevant, maybe even ridiculous. I think we should stick to music.

4   Perhaps, if the technology can be adapted to it, we should also send some paintings. Nothing would better describe what this place is like, to an outsider, than the Cézanne demonstrations that an apple is really part fruit, part earth.

5   What kinds of questions should we ask? The choices will be hard, and everyone will want his special question first. What are your smallest particles? Did you think yourselves unique? Do you have colds? Have you anything quicker than light? Do you always tell the truth? Do you cry? There is no end to the list.

6   Perhaps we should wait a while, until we are sure we know what we want to know, before we get down to detailed questions. After all, the main question will be the opener: "Hello, are you there?" If the reply should turn out to be "Yes, hello," we might want to stop there and think about that, for quite a long time.

Words
William K. Zinsser

Zinsser offers a negative recommendation: don't write "journalese." To convince us to follow this advice, he first *defines journalese* (paragraphs 2–3), using both *lexical definition* and *illustrations*. He *substantiates* his claim that journalese is tiresome by giving us a sample as evidence (paragraph 4). Then he *evaluates* that sample, pointing out just what makes it bad according to his criteria of badness in writing—laziness and lack of originality (paragraph 6).

The positive side of this recommendation is reserved for the end. Now that journalese has been cleared out of the way, Zinsser suggests a better attitude towards words (paragraph 7).

Source. "Words" by William K. Zinsser. From *On Writing Well* by William K. Zinsser. Copyright © 1976 by William K. Zinsser. Reprinted by permission of William K. Zinsser.

1   There is a kind of writing that might be called journalese, and it is the death of freshness in anybody's style. It is the common currency of newspapers and of magazines like *Time*—a mixture of cheap words, made-up words, and clichés which have become so pervasive that a writer can hardly help using them automatically. You must fight these phrases off or you will sound like every hack who sits down at a typewriter. In fact, you will never make your mark as a writer unless you develop a respect for words and a curiosity about their shades of meaning that is almost obsessive. The English language is rich in strong and supple words. Take the time to root around and find the ones you want.

2   What is "journalese"? It is a quilt of instant words patched together out of other parts of speech. Adjectives are used as nouns ("greats," "notables"). Nouns are used as adjectives ("top officials," "health reasons") or extended into adjectives ("insightful"). Nouns are used as verbs ("to host"), or they are chopped off to form verbs ("enthuse," "emote"), or they are padded to form verbs ("beef up," "put teeth into").

3   This is a world where eminent people are "famed" and their associates are "staffers," where the future is always "upcoming" and someone is forever "firing off" a note. Nobody in *Time* has merely sent a note or a memo or a telegram in years. Famed Diplomat Henry Kissinger, who hosts foreign notables to beef up the morale of top State Department staffers, sits down and fires off a lot of notes. Notes that are fired off are always fired in anger and from a sitting position.

4   Here, for example, is a *Time* article of several years ago that is hard to match for sheer fatigue:

> Last February, Plainclothes Patrolman Frank Serpico and two other New York City policemen knocked at the door of a suspected Brooklyn heroin pusher. When the door opened a crack, Serpico shouldered his way in only to be met by a .22-cal. pistol slug crashing into his face. Somehow he survived, although there are still buzzing fragments in his head, causing dizziness and permanent deafness in his left ear. Almost as painful is the suspicion that he may well have been set up for the shooting by other policemen. For Serpico, 35, has been waging a lonely, four-year war against the routine and endemic corruption that he and others claim is rife in the New York City police department. His efforts are now sending shock waves through the ranks of New York's finest. . . . Though the impact of the commission's upcoming report has yet to be felt, Serpico has little hope that anything will really change. . . .

5   The upcoming report has yet to be felt because it is still upcoming, and as for the "permanent deafness," it is still a little early to tell. And what makes those buzzing fragments buzz? I would have thought that by now only the head would be buzzing.

265

6   But apart from these lazinesses of logic, what makes the story so infinitely tired is the failure of the writer to reach for anything but the nearest cliché. "Shouldered his way," "only to be met," "crashing into his face," "waging a lonely war," "corruption that is rife," "sending shock waves"—these dreary phrases constitute journalese at its worst and writing at its most banal. We know just what to expect. No surprise awaits us in the form of a bizarre word, an oblique look. We are in the hands of a hack and we know it right away.

7   Don't let yourself get in this position. The only way to fight it is to care deeply about words. If you find yourself writing that someone recently "enjoyed" a spell of illness or that a business has been "enjoying" a slump, stop and think how much they really enjoyed it. Notice the decisions that other writers make in their choice of words and be finicky about the ones that you select from the vast supply. The race in writing is not to the swift but to the original.

Brotherhood Means Paying the Bills
Jim Concelman

This proposal concerns a problem all too familiar in fraternities, sororities, communes, and other social groups: some members fail to pay their way. Concelman begins by presenting the problem. He uses *specific information* (a $3854 deficit) to substantiate his claim that a major difficulty exists and *causal analysis* to explain how it came about. He then states the *criteria* by which any recommendation will have to be judged, lists the *alternatives,* and chooses and defends the *solution* that seems best.

Notice the ways in which Concelman appeals to his intended audience—his fraternity brothers, on whom acceptance of the proposal depends. His appeal begins in the letter accompanying the proposal. The letter prepares the brothers for some kind of bad news about the fraternity's finances, but postpones the details.

Source. "Brotherhood Means Paying the Bills" by Jim Concelman. Source: A student paper. Reprinted by permission of the author.

(Concelman's approach persuaded his fraternity brothers to accept the "get tough" proposal, as the postscript shows.)

Penn State Chapter

Delta Chi Fraternity

The Pennsylvania State University
424 E. Fairmount Avenue   State College, Pennsylvania 16801

July 5, 1978

Dear Brothers:

"Neither a borrower nor a lender be. . . ." Certainly these words suggest the sticky situations that dealing with money can lead to. Still, financial problems must be addressed. We hope we have done so equitably – – but that is for you to decide.

The bill—collection proposal that follows is the work of the Finances Committee, consisting of the Alumni Board of Trustees and of brothers Thumma, Clark, Gallagher, Kelmar, and myself. We considered many solutions, most of which are represented in the report. However, our biggest problem was defining the problem: what <u>exactly</u> has gone wrong with the house's finances? Once this became clear, the proper solution seemed to us to be almost self—evident.

Although we feel that our proposal thoroughly solves the problem of bill collection, we encourage your questions and comments because the new regulations, if accepted, will work only if all the brothers understand them.

This proposal will be brought before the chapter at our meeting on July 10, 1978, for our discussion and vote.

Fraternally,

James Concelman

Jim Concelman
For the Finances Committee

The Problem

Delta Chi is no different from any other consumer: we must promptly pay our bills for goods delivered and services rendered. We receive no special consideration because we are a fraternity.

We may soon have trouble meeting our bills because some brothers are reluctant to pay their house dues and other debts. With $3854 in dues and debts outstanding, special funds—such as the House Improvement Fund or the House Emergency Account—may have to be diverted to the general account for normal operating expenses. This reallocation would not only involve needless paperwork for the Alumni Board of Trustees (ABOT), but would also set an unwanted precedent and would solve the problem only temporarily. What we need is reliable and prompt collection of the money that the brothers owe to the house. However, such bill collection is hampered by several factors:

3   • Friends find it difficult to collect money from friends. The treasurer, a brother, too easily succumbs to impassioned appeals for more time or to other excuses. Also, since the job of treasurer is rather thankless—$60 a term is small compensation for the many hours of work required—the treasurer may be reluctant to continually chase after delinquent house bills.

4   • Brothers are not required to sign a lease or contract. Therefore, no legal means of collection applies. The agreement is only an understanding: "If you want to live here, you must help meet the expenses." Expulsion is the house's only recourse, and that action doesn't pay the accumulated debts. And expulsion may not be possible because, by our rules, it requires the vote of two-thirds of the brothers, who may not want to expel a close friend no matter what the financial circumstances are.

5   In the past, brothers owing large amounts over long periods have been asked to appear before ABOT to explain their delinquency. The idea is a stern show of concern: "Let's put him on the spot." Although moderately successful in extreme cases, this vague procedure promotes a lackadaisical attitude towards paying promptly. This attitude means that the treasurer and ABOT must chase after house bills that, with a small effort by the brother who owes the money, could have been paid on time.

6   What is needed, then, are regulations in the bylaws that will facilitate prompt payment and punish brothers for lateness or nonpayment. However, we should have some provision for delayed payment since some brothers rely on loans or jobs, or face other circumstances preventing full payment at the beginning of each term. Whatever we do should be effective and consistent with our goals as a brotherhood and should make minimal claims on our time.

The Options

7   We see the following possible courses of action.

8   1 Do nothing. In the end, most of the money is paid, proving that the

system usually works as it stands. Regulations might only increase the pressure on brothers already pressed for money.

9   2 Keep the same procedure, but add to it a requirement that offenders appear before a house meeting of the brotherhood. In other words, increase the peer pressure through a confrontation with the chapter.

0   3 Institute late-payment fees. Specify a date by which all bills must be paid (e.g., 10 to 14 days after the first day of classes). After that date an additional amount would be added to the bill.

1   4 Institute loss of privileges for debtors. Any brother owing more than a certain amount would lose seniority in making room choices, etc., as long as the debt is outstanding.

2   5 Institute mandatory expulsion. If a debt is not paid within a specified period, expulsion would be automatic, bypassing the two-thirds vote needed in cases of expulsion for other reasons.

3   6 Require all brothers to sign a lease or other contract. The threat of legal prosecution would encourage payment, and, if needed, prosecution would guarantee eventual collection of the money.

Recommendations

4   We feel that suggestions 1 and 2 will not solve the problem because they do not establish concrete guidelines. Suggestions 5 and 6 are too harsh; they are not consistent with our ideals of brotherhood. We recommend that suggestions 3 and 4 be incorporated into the bylaws in the following language:

5   A All house bills must be paid to the treasurer within ten business days after the first day of classes each term. After the tenth day, a late-payment fee of $10 shall be added to all unpaid house bills.

6   B Any brother who, because of special problems, needs an extension or an installment plan must appear before ABOT prior to the tenth-day deadline to avoid the late-payment fee.

7   C Any brother who owes the house $100 or more (any kind of debt) loses all privileges of seniority until the debt is paid, at which point all privileges will be restored.

8   This proposal offers two advantages. Regulations A and C are absolute: no person or board need make a decision; the late-payment fee or loss of privileges is automatic. The brothers know in advance that these penalties are indisputable because they appear in the bylaws. As for the loss of privileges, we feel that this penalty is consistent with our ideals. A brother who owes the house money does not deserve a better room (room choice is the greatest advantage of seniority) than a brother who pays all his bills when they are due.

9   In summary, this proposal recommends a clear and simple procedure to handle the collection of delinquent house dues and other debts. It

is designed to replace a haphazard and unreliable system that has proven inadequate—to the tune of $3854 this year. We recommend that it be given permanence and authority by incorporation into the bylaws. We encourage all brothers to read the proposed new bylaws thoroughly and to think them over. Feel free to raise any doubts at the July 10 house meeting, since our proposal will be useful only if it is completely understood and accepted.

[*Postscript*—The above proposal was accepted by the fraternity, and written into the bylaws, with the following amendments: the late-payment fee was raised to $30, the deadline was extended to 14 days after the first day of classes, and the loss-of-privileges debt figure was dropped to $50.]

The God That Failed
Richard Wright

During the 1930s, Richard Wright was an enthusiastic supporter of the Communist Party. Black, poor, and living in a Chicago slum, he believed that communism could provide a solution to racial problems as well as to other varieties of human injustice. The selection below reports part of his gradual disillusionment with the Party. The time is 1936; the scene, a Party parade for May Day. Wright's essay moves from a *narrative* showing that one course of action does not work—at least for him—to an *analysis* in which he formulates a new *alternative*: no longer able to endorse the Party, he resolves to speak as a person "really alone now" (paragraph 34).

We are not explicitly asked or told to do anything, but the concept Wright recommends is clear. We should work for progress not by joining mass protest movements but by trying, as individuals, to understand how to live a genuinely "human" life (paragraph 33).

Source. "The God That Failed" by Richard Wright. From pp. 159–162 by Richard Wright from *The God That Failed* edited by Richard Crossman. Copyright 1944 by Richard Wright. Reprinted by permission of Harper & Row, Publishers, Inc.

As May Day of 1936 approached, it was voted by the union member-ship that we should march in the public procession. On the morning of May Day I received printed instructions as to the time and place where our union contingent would assemble to join the parade. At noon, I hurried to the spot and found that the parade was already in progress. In vain I searched for the banners of my union local. Where were they? I went up and down the streets, asking for the location of my local.

"Oh, that local's gone fifteen minutes ago," a Negro told me. "If you're going to march, you'd better fall in somewhere."

I thanked him and walked through the milling crowds. Suddenly I heard my name called. I turned. To my left was the Communist Party's South Side section, lined up and ready to march.

"Come here!" an old Party friend called to me.

I walked over to him.

"Aren't you marching today?" he asked me.

"I missed my union local," I told him.

"What the hell," he said. "March with us."

"I don't know," I said, remembering my last visit to the headquar-ters of the Party, and my status as an "enemy."

"This is May Day," he said. "Get into the ranks."

"You know the trouble I've had," I said.

"That's nothing," he said. "Everybody's marching today."

"I don't think I'd better," I said, shaking my head.

"Are you scared?" he asked. "This is *May Day*."

He caught my right arm and pulled me into line beside him. I stood talking to him, asking about his work, about common friends.

"Get out of our ranks!" a voice barked.

I turned. A white Communist, a leader of the district of the Com-munist Party, Cy Perry, a slender, close-cropped fellow, stood glaring at me.

"I—It's May Day and I want to march," I said.

"Get out!" he shouted.

"I was invited here," I said.

I turned to the Negro Communist who had invited me into the ranks. I did not want public violence. I looked at my friend. He turned his eyes away. He was afraid. I did not know what to do.

"You asked me to march here," I said to him.

He did not answer.

"Tell him that you did invite me," I said, pulling his sleeve.

"I'm asking you for the last time to get out of our ranks!" Cy Perry shouted.

I did not move. I had intended to, but I was beset by so many impulses that I could not act. Another white Communist came to assist

Perry. Perry caught hold of my collar and pulled at me. I resisted. They held me fast. I struggled to free myself.

27   "Turn me loose!" I said.

28   Hands lifted me bodily from the sidewalk; I felt myself being pitched headlong through the air. I saved myself from landing on my head by clutching a curbstone with my hands. Slowly I rose and stood. Perry and his assistant were glaring at me. The rows of white and black Communists were looking at me with cold eyes of nonrecognition. I could not quite believe what had happened, even though my hands were smarting and bleeding. I had suffered a public, physical assault by two white Communists with black Communists looking on. I could not move from the spot. I was empty of any idea about what to do. But I did not feel belligerent. I had outgrown my childhood.

29   Suddenly, the vast ranks of the Communist Party began to move. Scarlet banners with the hammer and sickle emblem of world revolution were lifted, and they fluttered in the May breeze. Drums beat. Voices were chanting. The tramp of many feet shook the earth. A long line of set-faced men and women, white and black, flowed past me.

30   I followed the procession to the Loop and went into Grant Park Plaza and sat upon a bench. I was not thinking; I could not think. But an objectivity of vision was being born within me. A surging sweep of many odds and ends came together and formed an attitude, a perspective. "They're blind," I said to myself. "Their enemies have blinded them with too much oppression." I lit a cigarette and I heard a song floating over the sunlit air:

Arise, you pris'ners of starvation!

31   I remembered the stories I had written, the stories in which I had assigned a role of honor and glory to the Communist Party, and I was glad that they were down in black and white, were finished. For I knew in my heart that ī should never be able to write that way again, should never be able to feel with that simple sharpness about life, should never again express such passionate hope, should never again make so total a commitment of faith.

A better world's in birth. . . .

32   The procession still passed. Banners still floated. Voices of hope still chanted.

33   I headed toward home alone, really alone now, telling myself that in all the sprawling immensity of our mighty continent the least-known factor of living was the human heart, the least-sought goal of being was a way to live a human life. Perhaps, I thought, out of my tortured feelings I could fling a spark into this darkness. I would try, not because I wanted to, but because I felt that I had to if I were to live at all.

I would hurl words into this darkness and wait for an echo; and if an echo sounded, no matter how faintly, I would send other words to tell, to march, to fight, to create a sense of the hunger for life that gnaws in us all, to keep alive in our hearts a sense of the inexpressibly human.

Hey Kid, Wanna Buy a Used Term Paper?
Phyllis Zagano

Zagano shows how easy (and legal) it is for students to "beat the system" by plagiarizing. Yet she believes that such cheating is wrong. If the purpose of education is to foster learning, buying your way through is fraud, and honest people are its victims. (You would not want to pay for advice from an architect or lawyer or medical doctor with a "bought" degree.)

Zagano argues mainly in terms of law. Her conclusion *recommends federal legislation as the only feasible remedy* for term-paper fraud. But will a person who sees nothing immoral about buying term papers stop doing so if term-paper companies become illegal? Could Zagano strengthen her case by additional recommendations directed at (1) individual morality, or (2) the practices of educational institutions that seem to some people almost to invite cheating?

The term-paper companies that gained considerable notoriety in the early 1970's are neither gone nor forgotten. Ready-made term papers, once hawked from dingy storefronts near college campuses, are now offered for sale through the mails. Affluent students can purchase by mail papers that are written to their specifications.

During the past few months, I've completed the same procedure any enterprising student with a Master Charge card can go through if he's unwilling to write an assigned paper. All it takes is a few weeks and between \$14 and \$35 to get any assignment, no matter how specialized, written by someone else.

3   Just days after I wrote to Research Assistance, Inc., in Los Angeles, I held in my hands Volume 6 of the "Nation's Most Extensive Library of Research Material"—184 closely typed pages of merchandise with a table of contents running from Advertising to Women Studies (*sic*). I had over 6,000 titles from which to choose. I chose two: No. 1439, "The Treatment of Death by Emily Dickinson" ("Contends that the poet's attitude toward death influenced her use of words in unconventional ways. Quotes from poems and critics. f.n. Bib. 5pp.") and No. 3473, "American Literature from Colonial Times to the 1860's" ("Reviews several books to illustrate their contrasting of Civilized (Old World) and Wilderness life (New World) 5pp."). Each retailed for \$13.75. The unimpressive results seemed to be photocopies of papers previously submitted elsewhere. One had handwritten corrections and comments on it. But, undaunted, I continued with my plan.

4   Professors Miriam Baker and Peter Shaw, of the Stony Brook English Department, had both agreed in advance to read "my" papers. Well, I got the papers back the other day, and it seems that the classic rip-off can be a rip-off itself. Shaw gave me a C-minus. Baker failed me. Baker, an assistant professor of English and a Dickinson scholar, wrote that "the writer failed utterly to make any genuine statement about the poet as an artist and instead falls back on commonplace and genuinely erroneous biographical ideas." An undergraduate who doesn't know anything about Emily Dickinson doesn't have to pay \$13.75 for erroneous biographical ideas. He can make them up on his own.

5   All was not lost. I still had the C-minus from Shaw, an associate professor of English and the author, most recently, of *The Character of John Adams*. The paper managed a C-minus only because it was marked as a freshman paper.

6   In essence, what I did was pay a company \$28.20 ("Include 70¢ extra for postage and handling") to help me pass two courses. While I really managed to pass only one, there are thousands of students across the country who regularly make use of these services and regularly pass courses using bought papers.

7   You really *can* get through school on a credit card. And it's not illegal.

8   Both New York and California have laws that regulate the sale of term papers—but just the sale. I purchased my papers from a Los Angeles firm that is prohibited by California law from selling papers that will be presented for academic credit in the State of California. I'm in New York, and there is nothing outlawing my action. I am bound only by my own college's regulations (if I am caught). New York has a similar law, which classes the sale of term papers as a

Class B misdemeanor. But a law firm specializing in criminal law has advised me that it would be difficult, if not impossible, to prove that Research Assistance, Inc., is doing business in New York.

The country's first legislation outlawing the sale of term papers came in North Carolina in 1969. Since then, several other states besides New York and California—among them, Illinois, Massachusetts, Connecticut, Pennsylvania, and Maryland—have acted to try and prohibit an activity that seems tantamount to fraud.

The state legislatures are still at it. In Washington State, the Subcommittee on Postsecondary Education of the House of Representatives' Higher Education Committee has drafted a law it hopes will end the state's problem with plagiarism. The law has passed the House, and is awaiting action in the Senate. Washington is the home of several typical term-paper mills, as well as of Research Unlimited, a more specialized firm.

Research Unlimited set up offices there in 1972, shortly after term-paper laws were enacted in its home state, Illinois. Its brochure offers a complete line of individually written academic assignments, including doctoral dissertations: "In the case of larger and more complex projects, such as theses and dissertations, we offer a complete service, beginning with the proposal and ending with the abstract. In addition to preparing all of the written texts, we compile and assemble the bibliographic material required and perform any statistical analysis that may be involved." I found out about Research Unlimited through an ad in *The New York Times Book Review*. The Washington law is similar to those in other states; it will prevent such companies only from doing business within the state. It won't prevent their moving to another state, or advertising and doing business by mail in states where laws have yet to be enacted.

While the Washington State law is constitutionally defensible, the nationwide pastiche of laws has not been effective in dealing with term-paper companies. Probably the only thing that can put an end to them is a national law.

It's fraud. It's fraud and conspiracy to commit fraud through interstate commerce. Injunctions have come out of the courts against term-paper companies based on common-law fraud principles. And there is nothing constitutional about fraud.

Those who say it is up to the university to protect itself against plagiarism are begging the question. The recommended remedies—specialized assignments, more in-class writing, more examinations—forget that it is the nature of the true scholar to find a topic and deal with it in writing. The university is interested in fostering scholarship, and it is hampered by the fact that honest students are competing against professionally written material that has been tailor-made and is therefore untraceable.

15   Congress should be willing to protect the reputation of an educational system it pours so many millions of dollars into. After all, while I've completed a process that is seemingly illegal, it turns out that, in the State of New York at least, I can't even get myself arrested for it.

Marriage Today
Vance Packard

This section of Packard's book *The Sexual Wilderness* considers the problem of what to do about marriage—how to modify the traditional institution of marriage to make it fit the needs of people now. Packard first *explains* what is wrong with traditional marriage and what makes it valuable nevertheless (paragraphs 1–7). He then uses *division and classification* to present eight *alternatives* to traditional marriage (paragraphs 8–19). He briefly *evaluates* these alternatives, using as *criteria* the good characteristics of traditional marriage (paragraphs 20–21). Most of the eight alternative proposals, he finds, should be rejected.

Does Packard give us adequate guidance for arriving at a positive recommendation? If you agree that "The institution of marriage is obviously in need of modifications," what changes would you propose? What has Packard gained (or lost) by excluding morality from his discussion?

1   Most of the rules regulating marriages and their dissolution were made in eras when the bride and groom could look forward to fewer than half the number of years together that the couples marrying in the next few years can anticipate. For that reason alone, entering into wedlock calls for a new high level of prudence. There is now obviously a greater chance the partners will outgrow each other, lose interest, or become restless. In the past quarter century, instead of greater pru-

dence, however, we have seen a considerable increase in imprudent embarkations upon marriage.

Wives in the future surely will spend an increasing proportion of their married life as equal partners of the husband free of the "motherhood-service role," and so will have more options for the outlet of their surplus energy. They can no longer view marriage as a haven where they will be looked after by a husband in return for traditional services rendered.

Instead, more than ever before, women will have not only the opportunity but the expectation to push out for themselves and function as autonomous individuals who happen to have marriage partners. Marriages will apparently continue to be brittle for some time. Families in the immediate future will be expected to be highly mobile, and ever smaller in size.

While, as noted, the traditional economic functions of marriage have shrunk, there are two particularly compelling reasons looming why people will be marrying in the coming decade despite the relatively free availability of unmarried sexual partners:

1 The warm, all-embracing companionship that in marriage can endure through the confusion, mobility, and rapid social change of our times.
2 The opportunity to obtain immortality and personal growth for married individuals who perpetuate themselves through reproduction as they help mold personalities of their children and proudly induct them into the larger community.

This opportunity is so profoundly desired by most adult humans who are capable of reproduction that childlessness by choice would seem to be almost as difficult to popularize on any large scale as singleness by choice. Both would probably require intensive, prolonged social conditioning.

The institution of marriage is obviously in need of modifications to fit the modern needs. Author Jerome Weidman made an important point in his book *Your Daughter Iris* when he wrote of today's marriages: "Human beings do not obtain permanent possession of each other when they marry. All they obtain is the right to work at the job of holding on to each other." In pressing for modification of marriage as an institution we should seek above all to assure that the two functions of marriage just stated be fulfilled.

A variety of predictions and proposals are being heard today as to how the male-female liaison will or should evolve in the next few decades to meet the changing conditions of modern life. Here, for example, are eight possible patterns of marriage or near-marriage that are being discussed:

10   1 *Serial mating.* Sometimes it is called serial monogamy, sometimes serial polygamy, sometimes consecutive polygamy. But the basic idea is pretty much the same for all. It would assume a turnover of partners over the 50-odd years that a man and a woman can expect to live after they first consider marriage. Swedish sociologist Joachim Israel suggested that four or five marriages might be about par for a lifetime. The mood behind such proposals was summed up by a New York model when she said, "Why lie to yourself? We know we're not going to love one man all our lives." Among others, a psychologist-social worker in California, Virginia Star, has advocated the adoption of renewable marriage contracts. She suggests the contract lapse unless renewed every five years.

11   2 *Unstructured cohabitation.* These are the prolonged affairs without any assumption of permanence or responsibility. Such so-called unstructured liaisons—long popular in the lower classes—have been springing up in many of the larger universities in the off-campus housing. A psychiatrist at the University of California in Berkeley has suggested these liaisons may be the shape of the future. He said, "Stable, open non-marital relationships are pushing the border of what society is going to face in 10 years."[1]

12   A man's magazine in the mid-1960s presented some unconventional views of a woman who had been involved in a national controversy. During the presentation, she was asked, "How many lovers have you had, if you don't mind our asking?"

13   She responded, "You've got a helluva nerve, but I really don't mind. I've had five, if you count my marriage as an affair . . . five affairs, all of them really wing-dings."

14   3 *Mutual polygamy.* At a conference of marriage specialists in 1966 one expert from a Midwestern university speculated, "If we are moving into a new pattern where we are not claiming that marriage can do all the things that have been assumed, we may be moving into a kind of situation where there will be more than one partner. A compartmentalizing." Each partner in any particular marriage might have several mates, each chosen for a special purpose—for example, economic, recreational, procreational. A more informal variant of this would be "flexible monogamy," which in the view of Phyllis and Eberhard Kronhausen would frankly allow "for variety, friendships, and even sexual experiences with other individuals, if these are desired."[2]

15   4 *Single-parent marriages by intent.* These, on the Swedish model,

---

[1] "Unstructed Relations," *Newsweek*, July 4, 1966.

[2] Phyllis and Eberhard Kronhausen, *The Sexually Responsive Woman* (New York: Grove Press, 1964), p. 236.

would be the females—and occasional males—who yearn for parenthood without the burdens of wedlock.

5 *Specialists in parenthood.* Anthropologist Margaret Mead, in looking a few decades ahead, suggests the time may come when pressures to keep the birth rate low will produce a social style "in which parenthood would be limited to a smaller number of families whose principal function would be child-rearing; the rest of the population would be free to function—for the first time in history—as individuals."[3]

6 *Communal living.* In such a situation, several adult females and several adult males might live together in the same large dwelling and consider themselves an enlarged communal family, much as the hippies and other unconventional family groups have already been doing for some time.

7 *Legalized polygamy for senior citizens.* This is a form of polygamy that enables a man to have several wives at the same time. It has been advanced as a way to ease the demographic problem created by the fact that after the age of 60 there are increasingly more females than males in the population. One such proposal was advanced in the magazine *Geriatrics* by Dr. Victor Kassel, of Salt Lake City (the Mormon capital). The idea was taken seriously enough to be debated and unofficially turned down by the National Council of the Aging. A widow in South Carolina gave one feminine viewpoint when she said, "I am lonesome—but not that lonesome!"

8 *A variety of liaison patterns functioning in society simultaneously.* David Mace suggests we are moving toward a 3-layer cake type of society as far as male-female liaisons are concerned. He speculated that there may be a coexistence of several patterns. One pattern, as he sees it, will be that a proportion of the people will settle for sex freedom. They will not marry, but will drift into liaisons of long and short terms. There will be no attempt to punish or suppress such persons. He suggested that the second layer of this cake would involve somewhat more structuring, with a number of people choosing to go in and out of marriage and probably having several marriages in a lifetime, as in the common Hollywood pattern. Probably in this second layer there will be an attitude of freedom regarding extramarital sex while the couples are married. He suggested that in the third layer of the cake will be those who accept the concept of exclusive monogamy, preceded in at least some cases by premarital chastity.

Moral standards aside, one complication of most of the eight pos-

[3] Margaret Mead, "The Life Cycle and Its Variants: The Division of Roles," *Daedalus*, Summer, 1967.

sible patterns cited above is that they do not allow sufficiently for the intense desire that most women have for a secure arrangement—or at least women have had this intense desire until very recent times. They have had greater difficulty accepting fluid arrangements, especially after they pass the age of 30, than males.

21   An even bigger complication is that while most of these arrangements might seem attractive in terms of providing the companionship so important to male-female partnerships today, they do not come to terms with the second crucial ingredient of modern marriages: a partnership where there is a sound environment for reaching for immortality through the rearing of children. Thus most should be rejected from serious consideration as socially unfeasible—at least for people interested in having children, and we suspect that those who don't will remain a small minority.

The Special Joys of Super-Slow Reading
Sydney Piddington

There is a story about a young man who completed a "speed-reading" course and boasted that he had just read Tolstoy's *War and Peace* in 47 minutes flat. "What's it about?" someone asked. "Russians," he replied.

Piddington recommends reading not for speed but for "delight." He offers no statistics and no testimonials, only an account of how slow reading functioned as therapy for him in times of trouble: during the frustration of a day when everything went wrong on the job and during the fearful boredom of three and a half years as a prisoner of war.

1   Even for the pressure-cooker world of advertising, it had been a frustrating, tension-building day. I took home a briefcase full of troubles. A major contract was in danger of being lost at the last minute,

two executives of a company with whom we hoped to clinch a deal were being elusive, and a strike threatened the opening of a business that held my money and my future.

2   As I sat down on that hot and humid evening, there seemed to be no solutions to the problems thrashing around in my brain. So I picked up a book, settled into a comfortable chair and applied my own special therapy—super-slow reading.

3   I spent three hours on two short chapters of *Personal History* by Vincent Sheean—savoring each paragraph, lingering over a sentence, a phrase, or even a single word, building a detailed mental picture of the scene. No longer was I in Sydney, Australia, on a sticky heatwave night. Relishing every word, I joined foreign correspondent Sheean on a mission to China and another to Russia. I lost myself in the author's world, *living* his book. And when finally I put it down, my mind was totally refreshed.

4   Next morning, four words from the book—"take the long view"— were still in my mind. At my desk, I had a long-view look at my problems. I concluded that the strike would end sooner or later, so I made positive plans about what to do then. The two executives would see me eventually; if not, I would find other customers. That left me free to concentrate on the main thing, saving the contract. Once more, super-slow reading had given me not only pleasure but perspective, and helped me in my everyday affairs.

5   I discovered its worth years ago, in the infamous Changi prisoner-of-war camp in Singapore. I was 19, an artillery sergeant, when the city fell to the Japanese on February 15, 1942. Waiting with other Australian POWs to be marched off, I tried to decide what I should take in the single pack permitted. The only limit was what a weary man could carry the 17 miles to Changi. Our officer thoughtfully suggested, "Each man should find room for a book."

6   So I stuffed into my pack a copy of Lin Yutang's *The Importance of Living*—a title of almost macabre appropriateness—and began a reading habit that was to keep me sane for the next three and a half years. Previously, if I had been really interested in a book, I would race from page to page, eager to know what came next. Now, I decided, I had to become a miser with words and stretch every sentence like a poor man spending his last dollar.

7   During the first few days at Changi, I took Lin Yutang out of my pack three or four times, just gazing at the cover, the binding and the illustrated inside cover. Finally, as the sun went down one evening, I walked out into the prison yard, sat down on a pile of wood and, under the glare of prison lights, slowly opened the book to the title page and frontispiece. I spent three sessions on the preface, then two whole evenings on the contents pages—three and a half pages of chapter headings with fascinating subtitles—before I even reached

page one. Night after night I sat there with my treasure. Fellow prisoners argued, played cards and walked about all around me. I was oblivious. I disappeared so completely into my book that sometimes my closest friends thought I had gone bonkers.

8   I had started with the practical object of making my book last. But by the end of the second week, still only on page ten, I began to realize how much I was getting from super-slow reading itself. Sometimes just a particular phrase caught my attention, sometimes a sentence. I would read it slowly, analyze it, read it again—perhaps changing down into an even lower gear—and then sit for 20 minutes thinking about it before moving on. I was like a pianist studying a piece of music, phrase by phrase, rehearsing it, trying to discover and recreate exactly what the composer was trying to convey.

9   It is difficult to do justice to the intensity of the relationship. When Lin Yutang wrote of preparations for a tea party, I could see the charcoal fire, hear the tinkle of tiny teacups, almost taste the delicate flavor of the tea. I read myself in so thoroughly that it became not a mass of words but a living experience.

10   It took me something like two months to read Lin Yutang's book. By then, his philosophy on tea-making had become my philosophy on reading: You can do it fast, but it's a whole lot better done slowly. I held to the method, even after we had persuaded the Japanese to give us several hundred books from the famous Raffles library in Singapore.

11   The realization dawned on me that, although my body was captive, my mind was free to roam the world. From Changi, I sailed with William Albert Robinson, through his book *Deep Water and Shoal*. In my crowded cell at night, lying on a concrete floor, I felt myself dropping off to sleep in a warm cabin, the boat pitching under me. Next day, I'd be on deck again, in a storm, and after two or three graphic paragraphs I'd be gripping the helm myself, with the roar of the wind in my ears, my hair thick with salt. I wouldn't let go of the helm until we sailed into the calmer waters of a new chapter. If I had read with my old momentum, it would have been like viewing Sydney Harbor from a speedboat, instead of experiencing it from the deck of my own yacht.

12   My voyage took me just short of eight weeks. Had I raced through the book at my former speed, I could never have experienced the blessed release of Robinson's reality becoming so vividly mine.

13   Sitting on a woodpile in the prison yard or crouched on my haunches in any unoccupied corner, I slow-read biographies, philosophy, encyclopedias, even the *Concise Oxford Dictionary*. One favorite was W. Somerset Maugham's *The Summing Up*. I was no longer on a rough prison woodpile, wasting away from hunger; I was in an elegant drawing room on the French Riviera, a decanter of old port at hand,

282

listening to a great writer talking just to me about his journey through life, passing on the wisdom he had gained.

4 An average speed reader might dispose of *The Summing Up* in 50 minutes. But he wouldn't be living that book with the writer, as I did during the nine weeks I took to read its 379 pages. (A slow reader himself, Maugham wrote scathingly of those who "read with their eyes and not with their sensibility. It is a mechanical exercise like the Tibetans' turning of a prayer wheel.") I handled *The Summing Up* so much that it fell to pieces in the tropical heat. Then I carefully rebound it with dried banana leaves and rubber gum. I still have it, the most treasured volume in my bookcase.

5 I developed the habit in Changi of copying passages that especially appealed to me. One of these, from Aldous Huxley's *Ends and Means,* told how training is needed before one can fully savor anything—even alcohol and tobacco:

> First whiskies seem revolting, first pipes turn even the strongest of boyish stomachs. . . . First Shakespeare sonnets seem meaningless; first Bach fugues a bore, first differential equations sheer torture. But in due course, contact with an obscurely beautiful poem, an elaborate piece of counterpoint, or of mathematical reasoning, causes us to feel direct intuitions of beauty and significance.

6 I defy anyone to pick anything really significant out of a book like that by speed reading. It would be like playing a Beethoven record at the wrong speed!

7 Once, something I copied proved useful in camp. Our own commander had ordered us to give any spare clothing to our officers so they could appear immaculately dressed before the Japanese. The order incensed everybody. I pinned over my bunk some words from T. E. Lawrence's *Seven Pillars of Wisdom:*

> Among the Arabs there were no distinctions, traditional or natural, except the unconscious power given a famous sheik by virtue of his accomplishment, and they taught me that no man could be their leader except that he ate the ranks' food, wore their clothes, lived level with them, and yet appeared better in himself.

8 That night hundreds of slips of paper bearing these words were pinned up all over Changi, a possible nasty conflict averted.

9 Beyond giving me the will to survive in Changi, slow reading helps me today. Of course, super-slow reading is not for the man clearing out his briefcase or dealing with the Niagara of paper flowing across his desk. I can skim an inter-office memo as fast as the next person.

But when faced with a real problem, to clear my mind of everyday clutter I will sit down quietly at home and slowly read myself into another world.

20   As Lin Yutang wrote:

> There are two kinds of reading, reading out of business necessity, and reading as a luxury. The second kind partakes of the nature of a secret delight. It is like a walk in the woods, instead of a trip to the market. One brings home, not packages of canned tomatoes, but a brightened face and lungs filled with good clear air.

21   That is what super-slow reading is all about. Try it. As I read somewhere, a man is poor only when he doesn't know where his next book is coming from. And if he can get out of a book everything the author put into it, he is rich indeed.

When Freedom is Difficult to Live With
James J. Kilpatrick

Kilpatrick discusses one of the recurrent questions of our time: what to do when freedom seems to be getting out of hand. He focuses on the obscenity conviction of Larry Flynt, publisher of the pornographic magazine *Hustler*. **Kilpatrack** *first consider one way* of dealing with Flynt and his kind: send them to prison for publishing smut. *This recommendation must be rejected,* Kilpatrick finds, for several reasons. Legally, there is no firm definition of obscenity. Charges are not being brought against other smut peddlers. The Constitution is not being applied in the same way everywhere. Furthermore, it is dangerous to permit local juries to restrain the national press.

What alternative solution is available to people who, like Kilpatrick, believe in the "old-fashioned morality" and are offended by pornography? The public display of pornography could be controlled. **Kilpatrick** *offers another recommendation:* "Don't buy the stuff." If it doesn't sell, like any other unprofitable product it will disappear from the marketplace.

Source. "When Freedom is Difficult to Live With" by James L. Kilpatrick. From *Nation's Business,* April 1977. Reprinted with permission from *Nation's Business.*

How persuasive is this advice? What if enough people continue to buy enough pornography to keep it profitable?

1　No obscenity case in a long time—certainly not since the Ginzburg and Mishkin cases more than a decade ago—has raised more troublesome questions than the case of Larry Flynt, publisher of *Hustler* magazine. Flynt was convicted in Cincinnati in January under Ohio law; he was sentenced to serve from seven to 25 years in the Ohio penitentiary.

2　The pornography business is a big business, but it is not the kind of enterprise ordinarily discussed in *Nation's Business*. Flynt is a pornographer. He sells licentiousness as other men sell shoes or steel or coffee beans. His stock in trade is lewdness. He has been enormously successful. Flynt launched his magazine in July of 1974. Its circulation now approaches three million a month. Flynt's corporation, based in Columbus, Ohio, employs 250 persons and earns him between $10 million and $12 million a year. His associated enterprise, Leasure Time Products, brings in additional profits from the sale of "love kits," novelty jewelry, and the like.

3　It is the magazine that concerns us. The magazine, if one may judge from the March issue, is tasteless, crude, vulgar, patently offensive. The editorial content, such as it is, is pitched at the literary level of an army latrine. Except for a couple of articles, one on the grisly "sport" of dog-fighting and another a self-serving piece on First Amendment law, the contents deal almost entirely with carnality. The cartoons amount to little more than witless and unfunny graffiti. The photographs of female models emphasize the genitalia in explicit detail. This is *Hustler*. It is as crummy a publication as one can find on a newsstand anywhere—sleazy, morbid, dirty, contemptible.

4　But the question is: Should Larry Flynt be sent to prison for publishing it? Reluctantly, glumly, I have to say no. This is a position I take with no enthusiasm whatever. When this smut peddler invokes the First Amendment as a shield for his sordid publication, I want to retch. If it were not for other considerations, I could see this rogue in prison and never shed a tear.

5　The other considerations come first. One such consideration is the rule of law. Another is the nature of a free society. Here we deal with fundamental principles; and these principles are far too precious to be compromised for anything so cheap, and so relatively harmless, as *Hustler* magazine.

6　Let me touch on the rule of law. This was not a civil proceeding, brought with the intention of confiscating copies of the magazine or enjoining their sale or display. This was a criminal proceeding. Once that line is crossed, from the civil to the criminal, all the familiar requirements of due process come into play. The accused is entitled to all the protections arising both from the Constitution and from the inheritance of centuries of common law. He must be proved guilty beyond a reasonable doubt. Guilty of what? Guilty of the crime with which he is charged. What was this crime? It was charged that Flynt, in association with others, had published and distributed in the state of Ohio an obscene publication. And what is an "obscene" publication?

7   There the chain of questions breaks down. In every other field of the criminal law, the elements of the crime are precisely defined. We know what is meant by murder, rape, assault, burglary, embezzlement, counterfeiting, and auto theft. In these areas there is nothing vague. If Flynt had been indicted for robbing a cab driver, his trial would have proceeded routinely from the fact to the inquiry: The crime of robbery had been committed. Did Flynt commit it?

8   Only in the field of obscenity is everything turned upside down. Here there was no question of Flynt's conduct. He published *Hustler*. But was this a crime? The jury said it was. In reaching this verdict, the jury relied on the nebulous criteria established by the Supreme Court in a series of decisions dating back to the Roth-Alberts cases of 1957. But these criteria, in terms of criminal law, are as gauzy as mist, as insubstantial as sand. They boil down to subjective determinations of what is "serious" or what is "prurient." In the end, obscenity falls into a class with beauty and ugliness, which lie in the eye of the beholder. This is the rule of law with no rules. I am troubled that any person should be deprived of his liberty thereby.

9   Another aspect troubles me. One of the great principles of American jurisprudence—a principle engraved in stone on the front of the Supreme Court itself—is equal justice under law. This is the unattainable ideal; it is one of the aims our system of government strives for. In the case at hand, my thought is that Flynt is the subject not of equal justice, but of capricious and selective justice. The newsstands of Cincinnati, Cleveland, Columbus, and every other Ohio city are crowded with magazines in the same class with *Hustler*. The dirty jokes in the March *Playboy* are indistinguishable from the dirty jokes in the March *Penthouse*. The lip-licking sexual "advice" is served up in identical fashion. A dozen "men's magazines" depict the female sex organs as explicitly as *Hustler* depicts them. And beyond these magazines are the filthy little peep-show houses that abound in truly hard-core pornography. If Flynt is criminally guilty, what of hundreds of others who peddle smut in Ohio? It is not as if the evidence were hard to come by. The evidence everywhere confronts the sensual eye.

10   Much more troublesome is the constitutional question arising from

the First Amendment. This says that Congress shall make "no law" abridging freedom of the press. Over the past 50 years the prohibition imposed upon Congress under the First Amendment has been extended to the states under the Fourteenth. I confess my own mystification at this judicial legerdemain, but put that argument aside. For all practical purposes Ohio is subject to the same First Amendment that applies everywhere else.

1   Now virtually no one—not even Mr. Justice Douglas and the late Hugo Black—would construe "no law" to read "positively and absolutely no law whatever." Freedom of speech and of the press are subject to all sorts of constitutional limitations. But no matter how the First Amendment is construed, in terms of its application to libel, advertising matter, postal regulations, newspaper mergers, or whatever, the same constitutional constructions apply universally. Except as to obscenity.

2   This inexplicable inconsistency lies at the heart of the case of Larry Flynt. The First Amendment deals not only with free speech and free press, but also with establishments of religion and the free exercise thereof. When the Supreme Court rules against prayers in the public schools of New York, the court effectively rules against prayers in public schools anywhere. When the court deals with the rights of Amish parents in Wisconsin, it lays down principles that apply in every other state also. The Sullivan doctrine as to libel began with *The New York Times* in Alabama, but local juries in every jurisdiction are bound by its teachings. We have one Constitution. It sets forth "the supreme law of the land; and the judges in every State shall be bound thereby, any thing in the constitution or laws of any State to the contrary notwithstanding."

3   It is difficult for me to understand, as a nonlawyer, how the First Amendment can have one meaning in Cincinnati and another meaning in New York. The Supreme Court got itself into this fix in the Roth-Alberts cases by leaving obscenity to be determined by the average person "applying contemporary community standards," but the meaning of "community" was not specifically narrowed until the Miller case in June of 1973. Is a community a town, a city, a county, a metropolitan area? Is it a federal judicial district? The concept of constitutional construction by community appears nowhere else. We do not have community standards for auto theft or bank robbery. How is it that obscenity got to be different?

4   So much for questions of law. The Flynt case raises other questions that go to the nature of a free society, and these questions are as intractable and puzzling as the others. Freedom has this in common with Christianity and with other faiths also: It is fearfully difficult to

live up to. Consistently to practice the teachings of Christ is a demanding assignment. As D. Keith Mano has observed, being a good Christian is like keeping in shape: You have to work at it. It is the same thing with practicing one's faith in a free society. Not many of us are up to it. Plenty of businessmen, for one example, make Rotary speeches in praise of free enterprise—and then lobby for protection against competition.

15   Why the backsliding? It is because freedom, like competition, can be awfully uncomfortable to live with. This is especially true when we get to free speech and free press. Eight years ago, when student demonstrations were heating up, we had the spectacle of students proclaiming their faith in free speech by throttling army recruiters. On the other hand, we witnessed efforts to stifle the young radicals. And more to the point: Since the days of Anthony Comstock, our putatively free society has had to deal with efforts to censor publications that treat the subject of sex.

16   If we believe in freedom—truly believe in freedom—we ought to undertake such efforts with great care. If our faith in freedom is not strong enough to stomach a *Hustler* magazine, it is perhaps not very strong. It is no big thing, except for Flynt, of course, if Flynt goes to prison. But the law lives on precedents. And once a precedent is established by which local juries may convict the editors of national publications, we may have lost far more than we have gained.

17   I am a newspaperman. I love freedom; I abhor censorship. I am a writer. I live by the language; I despise the pornographer's defilements of speech. Simply as a human being, as a father and grandfather, I am saddened at the debasement of a loving sexual relationship by the cheap carnality of the smut peddlers. Obscenity is a kind of pollution: It stinks, it tastes bad, it fouls the clean air of old-fashioned morality. But precisely as businessmen object to governmental efforts to eliminate every last vestige of industrial pollution because the price is too high for the value received, so we ought to be cautious about eliminating forms of sexual expression that may be merely distasteful.

18   Society is not helpless. A large body of law supports the concept of protecting juveniles. Pornographers can be prevented from public display of their offensive wares. The producers of hard-core films can be reached through laws against prostitution. Through the vigorous, voluntary efforts of schools, churches, and individuals, much more could be done to promote decency and to shame the producers and purchasers of obscene publications. This is the certain remedy: Don't buy the stuff. In a reasonably free marketplace, good products will triumph over bad ones. This is part of our faith in free enterprise, and it ought to work for a free press as well.

How to Lie with Statistics
Darrell Huff

This selection is a *mock recommendation*. The superficial proposal, as suggested by the title, is that we should use statistics
dishonestly. The real proposal, stated in the last paragraph, is
that we should become familiar with the dishonest uses of
statistics in order to avoid being deceived by them. Unless we
learn the con game, we will become its victims.

Do you think that Huff's real purpose—to tell us *"Don't* be
deceived by statistical lies"—is adequately served by this presentation? Or does the tactic of explaining the con game run the
risk that some people will learn it only too well? What other
ways are there to convince readers that statistics can lie and
that they must know how to protect themselves?

1 "The average Yaleman, Class of '24," *Time* magazine reported last
year after reading something in the New York *Sun*, a newspaper
published in those days, "makes $25,111 a year."

2 Well, good for him!

3 But, come to think of it, what does this improbably precise and
salubrius figure mean? Is it, as it appears to be, evidence that if you
send your boy to Yale you won't have to work in your old age and
neither will he? Is this average a mean or is it a median? What kind
of sample is it based on? You could lump one Texas oilman with two
hundred hungry free-lance writers and report *their* average income as
$25,000-odd a year. The arithmetic is impeccable, the figure is con-
vincingly precise, and the amount of meaning there is in it you could
put in your eye.

4 In just such ways is the secret language of statistics, so appealing
in a fact-minded culture, being used to sensationalize, inflate, confuse,
and oversimplify. Statistical terms are necessary in reporting the mass
data of social and economic trends, business conditions, "opinion"
polls, this year's census. But without writers who use the words with
honesty and understanding and readers who know what they mean,
the result can only be semantic nonsense.

5 In popular writing on scientific research, the abused statistic is
almost crowding out the picture of the white-jacketed hero laboring

Source. "How to Lie with Statistics" by Darrell Huff. From *Harper's Magazine*,
August 1950. © 1950 by *Harper's Magazine*. Reprinted by permission of the author.

overtime without time-and-a-half in an ill-lit laboratory. Like the "little dash of powder, little pot of paint," statistics are making many an important fact "look like what she ain't." Here are some of the ways it is done.

The Sample with the Built-In Bias

6 Our Yale men—or Yalemen, as they say in the Time-Life building—belong to this flourishing group. The exaggerated estimate of their income is not based on all members of the class nor on a random or representative sample of them. At least two interesting categories of 1924-model Yale men have been excluded.

7 First there are those whose present addresses are unknown to their classmates. Wouldn't you bet that these lost sheep are earning less than the boys from prominent families and the others who can be handily reached from a Wall Street office?

8 There are those who chucked the questionnaire into the nearest wastebasket. Maybe they didn't answer because they were not making enough money to brag about. Like the fellow who found a note clipped to his first pay check suggesting that he consider the amount of his salary confidential: "Don't worry," he told the boss. "I'm just as ashamed of it as you are."

9 Omitted from our sample then are just the two groups most likely to depress the average. The $25,111 figure is beginning to account for itself. It may indeed be a true figure for those of the Class of '24 whose addresses are known and who are willing to stand up and tell how much they earn. But even that requires a possibly dangerous assumption that the gentlemen are telling the truth.

10 To be dependable to any useful degree at all, a sampling study must use a representative sample (which can lead to trouble too) or a truly random one. If *all* the Class of '24 is included, that's all right. If every tenth name on a complete list is used, that is all right too, and so is drawing an adequate number of names out of a hat. The test is this: Does every name in the group have an equal chance to be in the sample?

11 You'll recall that ignoring this requirement was what produced the *Literary Digest*'s famed fiasco. When names for polling were taken only from telephone books and subscription lists, people who did not have telephones or *Literary Digest* subscriptions had no chance to be in the sample. They possibly did not mind this underprivilege a bit, but their absence was in the end very hard on the magazine that relied on the figures.

12 This leads to a moral: You can prove about anything you want to by letting your sample bias itself. As a consumer of statistical data— a reader, for example, of a news magazine—remember that no statis-

tical conclusion can rise above the quality of the sample it is based upon. In the absence of information about the procedures behind it, you are not warranted in giving any credence at all to the result.

The Truncated, or Gee-Whiz, Graph

If you want to show some statistical information quickly and clearly, draw a picture of it. Graphic presentation is the thing today. If you don't mind misleading the hasty looker, or if you quite clearly *want* to deceive him, you can save some space by chopping the bottom off many kinds of graphs.

Suppose you are showing the upward trend of national income month by month for a year. The total rise, as in one recent year, is 7 per cent. It looks like this:

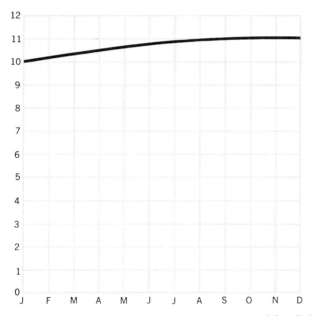

That is clear enough. Anybody can see that the trend is slightly upward. You are showing a 7 per cent increase and that is exactly what it looks like.[1]

But it lacks schmaltz. So you chop off the bottom, this way:

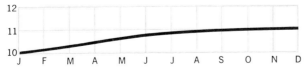

[1] It looks like 10 percent to us. Perhaps what Huff has in mind is a 7 percent annual *rate* of increase, compounded monthly.—Eds., with thanks to Cindy Bernstein of Texas A&M University.

The figures are the same. It is the same graph and nothing has been falsified—except the impression that it gives. Anyone looking at it can just feel prosperity throbbing in the arteries of the country. It is a subtler equivalent of editing "National income rose 7 per cent" into ". . . climbed a whopping 7 per cent."

16   It is vastly more effective, however, because of that illusion of objectivity.

The Souped-Up Graph

17   Sometimes truncating is not enough. The trifling rise in something or other still looks almost as insignificant as it is. You can make that 7 per cent look livelier than 100 per cent ordinarily does. Simply change the proportion between the ordinate and the abscissa. There's no rule against it, and it does give your graph a prettier shape.

18   But it exaggerates, to say the least, something awful:

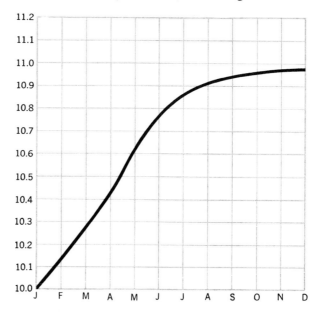

The Well-Chosen Average

19   I live near a country neighborhood for which I can report an average income of $15,000. I could also report it as $3,500.

20   If I should want to sell real estate hereabouts to people having a high snobbery content, the first figure would be handy. The second figure, however, is the one to use in an argument against raising taxes, or the local bus fare.

21   Both are legitimate averages, legally arrived at. Yet it is obvious that at least one of them must be as misleading as an out-and-out lie.

The $15,000-figure is a mean, the arithmetic average of the incomes of all the families in the community. The smaller figure is a median; it might be called the income of the average family in the group. It indicates that half the families have less than $3,500 a year and half have more.

Here is where some of the confusion about averages comes from. Many human characteristics have the grace to fall into what is called the "normal" distribution. If you draw a picture of it, you get a curve that is shaped like a bell. Mean and median fall at about the same point, so it doesn't make very much difference which you use.

But some things refuse to follow this neat curve. Income is one of them. Incomes for most large areas will range from under $1,000 a year to upward of $50,000. Almost everybody will be under $10,000, way over on the left-hand side of that curve.

One of the things that made the income figure for the "average Yaleman" meaningless is that we are not told whether it is a mean or a median. It is not that one type of average is invariably better than the other; it depends upon what you are talking about. But neither gives you any real information—and either may be highly misleading—unless you know which of those two kinds of average it is.

In the country neighborhood I mentioned, almost everyone has less than the average—the mean, that is—of $10,500. These people are all small farmers, except for a trio of millionaire week-enders who bring up the mean enormously.

You can be pretty sure that when an income average is given in the form of a mean nearly everybody has less than that.

The Insignificant Difference or the Elusive Error

Your two children Peter and Linda (we might as well give them modish names while we're about it) take intelligence tests. Peter's IQ, you learn, is 98 and Linda's is 101. Aha! Linda is your brighter child.

Is she? An intelligence test is, or purports to be, a sampling of intellect. An IQ, like other products of sampling, is a figure with a statistical error, which expresses the precision or reliability of the figure. The size of this probable error[2] can be calculated. For their test the makers of the much-used Revised Stanford-Binet have found it to be about 3 per cent. So Peter's indicated IQ of 98 really means only that there is an even chance that it falls between 95 and 101. There is an equal probability that it falls somewhere else—below 95 or above 101. Similarly, Linda's has no better than a fifty-fifty chance of being within the fairly sizeable range of 98 to 104.

---

[2] "Probable error," as a statistical term, identifies the range in which 50 percent of the tested subjects will be. Here, 50 percent of the children will be within 3 points—up or down—of their score.—Eds.

29   You can work out some comparisons from that. One is that there is rather better than one chance in four that Peter, with his lower IQ rating, is really at least three points smarter than Linda. A statistician doesn't like to consider a difference significant unless you can hand him odds a lot longer than that.

30   Ignoring the error in a sampling study leads to all kinds of silly conclusions. There are magazine editors to whom readership surveys are gospel; with a 40 per cent readership reported for one article and a 35 per cent for another, they demand more like the first. I've seen even smaller differences given tremendous weight, because statistics are a mystery and numbers are impressive. The same thing goes for market surveys and so-called public-opinion polls. The rule is that you cannot make a valid comparison between two such figures unless you know the deviations. And unless the difference between the figures is many times greater than the probable error of each, you have only a guess that the one appearing greater really is.

31   Otherwise you are like the man choosing a camp site from a report of mean temperature alone. One place in California with a mean annual temperature of 61 is San Nicolas Island on the south coast, where it always stays in the comfortable range between 47 and 87. Another with a mean of 61 is in the inland desert, where the thermometer hops around from 15 to 104. The deviation from the mean marks the difference, and you can freeze or roast if you ignore it.

The One-Dimensional Picture

32   Suppose you have just two or three figures to compare—say the average weekly wage of carpenters in the United States and another country. The sums might be $60 and $30. An ordinary bar chart makes the difference graphic. That is an honest picture. It looks good for American carpenters, but perhaps it does not have quite the oomph you are after. Can't you make that difference appear overwhelming and at the same time give it what I am afraid is known as eye-appeal? Of course you can. Following tradition, you represent these sums by pictures of money bags. If the $30 bag is one inch high, you draw the $60 bag two inches high. That's in proportion, isn't it? The catch is, of course, that the American's money bag, being twice as tall as that of the $30 man, covers an area on your page four times as great. And since your two-dimensional picture represents an object that would in fact have three dimensions, the money bags actually would differ much more than that. The volumes of any two similar solids vary as the cubes of their heights. If the unfortunate foreigner's bag holds $30 worth of dimes, the American's would hold not $60 but a neat $240.

294

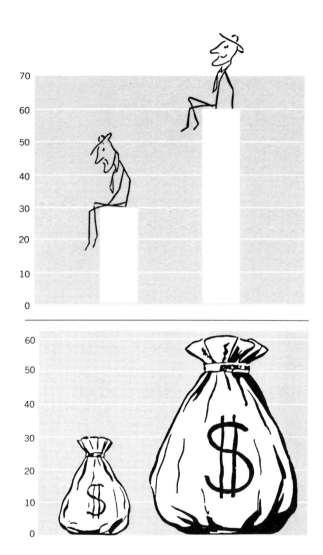

You didn't say that, though, did you? And you can't be blamed, you're only doing it the way practically everybody else does.

The Ever-Impressive Decimal

For a spurious air of precision that will lend all kinds of weight to the most disreputable statistics, consider the decimal.

Ask a hundred citizens how many hours they slept last night. Come out with a total of, say, 781.3. Your data are far from precise to begin with. Most people will miss their guess by fifteen minutes or more and some will recall five sleepless minutes as half a night of tossing insomnia.

295

36   But go ahead, do your arithmetic, announce that people sleep an average of 7.813 hours a night. You will sound as if you knew precisely what you are talking about. If you were foolish enough to say 7.8 (or "almost 8") hours it would sound like what it was—an approximation.

The Semi-Attached Figure

37 If you can't prove what you want to prove, demonstrate something else and pretend that they are the same thing. In the daze that follows the collision of statistics with the human mind, hardly anybody will notice the difference. The semi-attached figure is a durable device guaranteed to stand you in good stead. It always has.

38   If you can't prove that your nostrum cures colds, publish a sworn laboratory report that the stuff killed 31,108 germs in a test tube in eleven seconds. There may be no connection at all between assorted germs in a test tube and the whatever-it-is that produces colds, but people aren't going to reason that sharply, especially while sniffling.

39   Maybe that one is too obvious and people are beginning to catch on. Here is a trickier version.

40   Let us say that in a period when race prejudice is growing it is to your advantage to "prove" otherwise. You will not find it a difficult assignment.

41   Ask that usual cross section of the population if they think Negroes have as good a chance as white people to get jobs. Ask again a few months later. As Princeton's Office of Public Opinion Research has found out, people who are most unsympathetic to Negroes are the ones most likely to answer yes to this question.

42   As prejudice increases in a country, the percentage of affirmative answers you will get to this question will become larger. What looks on the face of it like growing opportunity for Negroes actually is mounting prejudice and nothing else. You have achieved something rather remarkable: the worse things get, the better your survey makes them look.

The Unwarranted Assumption, or Post Hoc Rides Again

43 The interrelation of cause and effect, so often obscure anyway, can be most neatly hidden in statistical data.

44   Somebody once went to a good deal of trouble to find out if cigarette smokers make lower college grades than non-smokers. They did. This naturally pleased many people, and they made much of it.

45   The unwarranted assumptions, of course, was that smoking had produced dull minds. It seemed vaguely reasonable on the face of it, so it was quite widely accepted. But it really proved nothing of the sort, any more than it proved that poor grades drive students to the solace of tobacco. Maybe the relationship worked in one direction,

maybe in the other. And maybe all this is only an indication that the sociable sort of fellow who is likely to take his books less than seriously is also likely to sit around and smoke many cigarettes.

Permitting statistical treatment to befog causal relationships is little better than superstition. It is like the conviction among the people of the Hebrides that body lice produce good health. Observation over the centuries had taught them that people in good health had lice and sick people often did not. *Ergo*, lice made a man healthy. Everybody should have them.

Scantier evidence, treated statistically at the expense of common sense, has made many a medical fortune and many a medical article in magazines, including professional ones. More sophisticated observers finally got things straightened out in the Hebrides. As it turned out, almost everybody in those circles had lice most of the time. But when a man took a fever (quite possibly carried to him by those same lice) and his body became hot, the lice left.

Here you have cause and effect not only reversed, but intermingled.

There you have a primer in some ways to use statistics to deceive. A well-wrapped statistic is better than Hitler's "big lie": it misleads, yet it can't be pinned onto you.

Is this little list altogether too much like a manual for swindlers? Perhaps I can justify it in the manner of the retired burglar whose published reminiscences amounted to a graduate course in how to pick a lock and muffle a footfall: The crooks already know these tricks. Honest men must learn them in self-defense.

A Modest Proposal
Jonathan Swift

When a person unknowingly says something contrary to fact, he is simply wrong, perhaps foolish. When he says something that he *knows* is contrary to fact, he is lying. But when both speaker and audience know that the superficial meaning is not the real one, speaker and audience share a trick, and we call this *irony*. Some taint of its kinship to the lie makes irony more or less harsh, often cruel. Such is the case with Swift's essay, which is one of the most famous instances of irony in the

English language. Written in 1729, it records Swift's indignation against the English government's inhumane treatment of the Irish people.

Some readers have mistaken the serious tone and precise detail as signs that Swift really meant to endorse cannibalism, as the essay superficially proposes. However, you will notice that Swift makes his speaker (the *persona*, the politician who seems to be talking) unpleasant in order to make us suspicious of him.

You may begin to question the *persona* when he refers to "a child just dropped from its dam" (paragraph 4) or to wives as "breeders" (paragraph 6) or to a population "whereof only one fourth part [is] to be males, which is more than we allow" to animals (paragraph 10). The casual way in which Swift's *persona* equates people to sheep or pigs should make you dislike him. By paragraph 12, the trick becomes more obvious when Swift has the speaker compare the landlords' figurative "devouring" of parents by exhorbitant rents to the literal eating of children. This comparison gives us a glimpse of Swift's real target. What the heartless politician accepts, we reject. The politician regards both forms of exploitation of suffering people as reasonable; therefore we regard both as *un*reasonable. Swift himself believes that the rich should *not* be allowed to prey upon the poor.

A Modest Proposal
For Preventing the Children of Poor People in Ireland
from Being a Burden to Their Parents or Country,
and for Making Them Beneficial to the Public

1 It is a melancholy object to those who walk through this great town or travel in the country, when they see the streets, the roads, and cabin doors, crowded with beggars of the female-sex, followed by three, four, or six children, all in rags and importuning every passenger for an alms. These mothers, instead of being able to work for their honest livelihood, are forced to employ all their time in strolling to beg sustenance for their helpless infants, who, as they grow up, either turn thieves for want of work, or leave their dear native country to fight for the Pretender in Spain, or sell themselves to the Barbadoes.[1]

2 I think it is agreed by all parties that this prodigious number of

[1] That is, contract themselves to work in order to pay the cost of transportation to a colony.

children in the arms, or on the backs, or at the heels of their mothers, and frequently of their fathers, is in the present deplorable state of the kingdom a very great additional grievance; and therefore whoever could find out a fair, cheap, and easy method of making these children sound, useful members of the commonwealth would deserve so well of the public as to have his statue set up for a preserver of the nation.

But my intention is very far from being confined to provide only for the children of professed beggars; it is of a much greater extent, and shall take in the whole number of infants at a certain age who are born of parents in effect as little able to support them as those who demand our charity in the streets.

As to my own part, having turned my thoughts for many years upon this important subject, and maturely weighed the several schemes of other projectors, I have always found them grossly mistaken in their computation. It is true, a child just dropped from its dam may be supported by her milk for a solar year, with little other nourishment; at most not above the value of two shillings, which the mother may certainly get, or the value in scraps, by her lawful occupation of begging; and it is exactly at one year old that I propose to provide for them in such a manner as instead of being a charge upon their parents or the parish, or wanting food and raiment for the rest of their lives, they shall on the contrary contribute to the feeding, and partly to the clothing, of many thousands.

There is likewise another great advantage in my scheme, that it will prevent those voluntary abortions, and that horrid practice of women murdering their bastard children, alas, too frequent among us, sacrificing the poor innocent babes, I doubt, more to avoid the expense than the shame, which would move tears and pity in the most savage and inhuman breast.

The number of souls in this kingdom being usually reckoned one million and a half, of these I calculate there may be about two hundred thousand couples whose wives are breeders; from which number I subtract thirty thousand couples who are able to maintain their own children, although I apprehend there cannot be so many under the present distresses of the kingdom; but this being granted, there will remain an hundred and seventy thousand breeders. I again subtract fifty thousand for those women who miscarry, or whose children die by accident or disease within the year. There only remain an hundred and twenty thousand children of poor parents annually born. The question therefore is, how this number shall be reared and provided for, which, as I have already said, under the present situation of affairs, is utterly impossible by all the methods hitherto proposed. For we can neither employ them in handicraft nor agriculture; we neither build houses (I mean in the country) nor cultivate land. They can very seldom pick up a livelihood by stealing till they arrive at six years old, except where they are of towardly parts; although I confess they learn the rudiments much earlier, during which time they can however be looked upon only as probationers, as I have been informed by a principal gentleman in the county of Cavan, who protested to me that he never knew above one or two instances under the age of six, even in a part of the kingdom so renowned for the quickest proficiency in that art.

7   I am assured by our merchants that a boy or a girl before twelve years old is no salable commodity; and even when they come to this age they will not yield above three pounds, or three pounds and half a crown at most on the Exchange; which cannot turn to account either to the parents or the kingdom, the charge of nutriment and rags having been at least four times that value.

8   I shall now therefore humbly propose my own thoughts, which I hope will not be liable to the least objection.

9   I have been assured by a very knowing American of my acquaintance in London, that a young healthy child well nursed is at a year old a most delicious, nourishing, and wholesome food, whether stewed, roasted, baked, or boiled; and I make no doubt that it will equally serve in a fricassee or a ragout.

10   I do therefore humbly offer it to public consideration that of the hundred and twenty thousand children, already computed, twenty thousand may be reserved for breed, whereof only one fourth part to be males, which is more than we allow to sheep, black cattle, or swine; and my reason is that these children are seldom the fruits of marriage, a circumstance not much regarded by our savages, therefore one male will be sufficient to serve four females. That the remaining hundred thousand may at a year old be offered in sale to the persons of quality and fortune through the kingdom, always advising the mother to let them suck plentifully in the last month, so as to render them plump and fat for a good table. A child will make two dishes at an entertainment for friends; and when the family dines alone, the fore or hind quarter will make a reasonable dish, and seasoned with a little pepper or salt will be very good boiled on the fourth day, especially in winter.

11   I have reckoned upon a medium that a child just born will weigh twelve pounds, and in a solar year if tolerably nursed increaseth to twenty-eight pounds.

12   I grant this food will be somewhat dear, and therefore very proper for landlords, who, as they have already devoured most of the parents, seem to have the best title to the children.

13   Infant's flesh will be in season throughout the year, but more plentiful in March, and a little before and after. For we are told by a grave author, an eminent French physician,[2] that fish being a prolific diet,

---

[2] Rabelais.

there are more children born in Roman Catholic countries about nine months after Lent than at any other season; therefore, reckoning a year after Lent, the markets will be more glutted than usual, because the number of popish infants is at least three to one in this kingdom; and therefore it will have one other collateral advantage, by lessening the number of Papists among us.

I have already computed the charge of nursing a beggar's child (in which list I reckon all cottagers, laborers, and four fifths of the farmers) to be about two shillings per annum, rags included; and I believe no gentleman would repine to give ten shillings for the carcass of a good fat child, which, as I have said, will make four dishes of excellent nutritive meat, when he hath only some particular friend or his own family to dine with him. Thus the squire will learn to be a good landlord, and grow popular among the tenants; the mother will have eight shillings net profit, and be fit for work till she produces another child.

Those who are more thrifty (as I must confess the times require) may flat the carcass; the skin of which artificially dressed will make admirable gloves for ladies, and summer boots for fine gentlemen.

As to our city of Dublin, shambles may be appointed for this purpose in the most convenient parts of it, and butchers we may be assured will not be wanting; although I rather recommend buying the children alive, and dressing them hot from the knife as we do roasting pigs.

A very worthy person, a true lover of his country, and whose virtues I highly esteem, was lately pleased in discoursing on this matter to offer a refinement upon my scheme. He said that many gentlemen of this kingdom having of late destroyed their deer, he conceived that the want of venison might be well supplied by the bodies of young lads and maidens, not exceeding fourteen years of age nor under twelve, so great a number of both sexes in every county being now ready to starve for want of work and service; and these to be disposed of by their parents, if alive, or otherwise by their nearest relations. But with due deference to so excellent a friend and so deserving a patriot, I cannot be altogether in his sentiments; for as to the males, my American acquaintance assured me from frequent experience that their flesh was generally tough and lean, like that of our schoolboys, by continual exercise, and their taste disagreeable; and to fatten them would not answer the charge. Then as to the females, it would, I think with humble submission, be a loss to the public, because they soon would become breeders themselves: and besides, it is not improbable that some scrupulous people might be apt to censure such a practice (although indeed very unjustly) as a little bordering upon cruelty; which, I confess, hath always been with me the strongest objection against any project, how well soever intended.

But in order to justify my friend, he confessed that this expedient was put into his head by the famous Psalmanazar, a native of the island Formosa, who came from thence to London above twenty years ago, and in conversation told my friend that in his country when any young person happened to be put to death, the executioner sold the carcass to persons of quality as a prime dainty; and that in his time the body of a plump girl of fifteen, who was crucified for an attempt to poison the emperor, was sold to his Imperial Majesty's prime minister of state, and other great mandarins of the court, in joints from the gibbet, at four hundred crowns. Neither indeed can I deny that if the same use were made of several plump young girls in this town, who without one single groat to their fortunes cannot stir abroad without a chair, and appear at the playhouse and assemblies in foreign fineries which they never will pay for, the kingdom would not be the worse.

19   Some persons of a desponding spirit are in great concern about that vast number of poor people who are aged, diseased, or maimed, and I have been desired to employ my thoughts what course may be taken to ease the nation of so grievous an encumbrance. But I am not in the least pain upon that matter, because it is very well known that they are every day dying and rotting by cold and famine, and filth and vermin, as fast as can be reasonably expected. And as to the younger laborers, they are now in almost as hopeful a condition. They cannot get work, and consequently pine away for want of nourishment to a degree that if at any time they are accidentally hired to common labor, they have not strength to perform it; and thus the country and themselves are happily delivered from the evils to come.

20   I have too long digressed, and therefore shall return to my subject. I think the advantages by the proposal which I have made are obvious and many, as well as of the highest importance.

21   For first, as I have already observed, it would greatly lessen the number of Papists, with whom we are yearly overrun, being the principal breeders of the nation as well as our most dangerous enemies; and who stay at home on purpose to deliver the kingdom to the Pretender, hoping to take their advantage by the absence of so many good Protestants, who have chosen rather to leave their country than to stay at home and pay tithes against their conscience to an Episcopal curate.

22   Secondly, the poorer tenants will have something valuable of their own, which by law may be made liable to distress, and help to pay their landlord's rent, their corn and cattle being already seized and money a thing unknown.

23   Thirdly, whereas the maintenance of an hundred thousand children, from two years old and upwards, cannot be computed at less than ten shillings a piece per annum, the nation's stock will be thereby increased fifty thousand pounds per annum, besides the profit of a new

dish introduced to the tables of all gentlemen of fortune in the kingdom who have any refinement in taste. And the money will circulate among ourselves, the goods being entirely of our own growth and manufacture.

Fourthly, the constant breeders, besides the gain of eight shillings sterling per annum by the sale of their children, will be rid of the charge of maintaining them after the first year.

Fifthly, this food would likewise bring great custom to taverns, where the vintners will certainly be so prudent as to procure the best receipts for dressing it to perfection, and consequently have their houses frequented by all the fine gentlemen, who justly value themselves upon their knowledge in good eating; and a skillful cook, who understands how to oblige his guests, will contrive to make it as expensive as they please.

Sixthly, this would be a great inducement to marriage, which all wise nations have either encouraged by rewards or enforced by laws and penalties. It would increase the care and tenderness of mothers toward their children, when they were sure of a settlement for life to the poor babes, provided in some sort by the public, to their annual profit instead of expense. We should see an honest emulation among the married women, which of them could bring the fattest child to the market. Men would become as fond of their wives during the time of their pregnancy as they are now of their mares in foal, their cows in calf, or sows when they are ready to farrow; nor offer to beat or kick them (as is too frequent a practice) for fear of a miscarriage.

Many other advantages might be enumerated. For instance, the addition of some thousand carcasses in our exportation of barreled beef, the propagation of swine's flesh, and improvement in the art of making good bacon, so much wanted among us by the great destruction of pigs, too frequent at our tables, which are no way comparable in taste or magnificence to a well-grown, fat, yearling child, which roasted whole will make a considerable figure at a lord mayor's feast or any other public entertainment. But this and many others I omit, being studious of brevity.

Supposing that one thousand families in this city would be constant customers for infants' flesh, besides others who might have it at merry meetings, particularly weddings and christenings, I compute that Dublin would take off annually about twenty thousand carcasses, and the rest of the kingdom (where probably they will be sold somewhat cheaper) the remaining eighty thousand.

I can think of no one objection that will possibly be raised against this proposal, unless it should be urged that the number of people will be thereby much lessened in the kingdom. This I freely own, and it was indeed one principal design in offering it to the world. I desire the reader will observe, that I calculate my remedy for this one individual kingdom of Ireland and for no other that ever was, is, or I think ever can be upon earth. Therefore let no man talk to me of other expedients: of taxing our absentees at five shillings a pound: of using neither clothes nor household furniture except what is of our own growth and manufacture: of utterly rejecting the materials and instruments that promote foreign luxury: of curing the expensiveness of pride, vanity, idleness, and gaming in our women: of introducing a vein of parsimony, prudence, and temperance: of learning to love our country, in the want of which we differ even from Laplanders and the inhabitants of Topinamboo[3]: of quitting our animosities and factions, nor acting any longer like the Jews, who were murdering one another at the very moment their city was taken: of being a little cautious not to sell our country and conscience for nothing: of teaching landlords to have at least one degree of mercy toward their tenants: lastly, of putting a spirit of honesty, industry, and skill into our shopkeepers; who, if a resolution could now be taken to buy only our native goods, would immediately unite to cheat and exact upon us in the price, the measure, and the goodness, nor could ever yet be brought to make one fair proposal of just dealing, though often and earnestly invited to it.[4]

30   Therefore I repeat, let no man talk to me of these and the like expedients, till he hath at least some glimpse of hope that there will ever be some hearty and sincere attempt to put them in practice.

31   But as to myself, having been wearied out for many years with offering vain, idle, visionary thoughts, and at length utterly despairing of success, I fortunately fell upon this proposal, which, as it is wholly new, so it hath something solid and real, of no expense and little trouble, full in our own power, and whereby we can incur no danger in disobliging England. For this kind of commodity will not bear exportation, the flesh being of too tender a consistence to admit a long continuance in salt, although perhaps I could name a country which would be glad to eat up our whole nation without it.

32   After all, I am not so violently bent upon my own opinion as to reject any offer proposed by wise men, which shall be found equally innocent, cheap, easy, and effectual. But before something of that kind shall be advanced in contradiction to my scheme, and offering a better, I desire the author or authors will be pleased maturely to consider two points. First, as things now stand, how they will be able to find food and raiment for an hundred thousand useless mouths and backs. And secondly, there being a round million of creatures in human figure throughout this kingdom, whose sole subsistence put into a common stock would leave them in debt two millions of pounds sterling, adding those who are beggars by profession to the bulk of

[3] A district in Brazil.
[4] Swift himself made these proposals in his own earlier works.

farmers, cottagers, and laborers, with their wives and children who are beggars in effect; I desire those politicians who dislike my overture, and may perhaps be so bold to attempt an answer, that they will first ask the parents of these mortals whether they would not at this day think it a great happiness to have been sold for food at a year old in the manner I prescribe, and thereby have avoided such a perpetual scene of misfortunes as they have since gone through by the oppression of landlords, the impossibility of paying rent without money or trade, the want of common sustenance, with neither house nor clothes to cover them from the inclemencies of the weather, and the most inevitable prospect of entailing the like or greater miseries upon their breed forever.

I profess, in the sincerity of my heart, that I have not the least personal interest in endeavoring to promote this necessary work, having no other motive than the public good of my country, by advancing our trade, providing for infants, relieving the poor, and giving some pleasure to the rich. I have no children by which I can propose to get a single penny; the youngest being nine years old, and my wife past childbearing.

Politics and the English Language
George Orwell

Orwell's essay, which has been popular for more than 30 years, urges us to save our language from vagueness and pretentiousness. Orwell begins by asserting the *political importance of language*: if we use words more carefully, we will be able to think more clearly, and by thinking more clearly we may be able to regenerate our society. He then *cites examples* to prove that our language is being abused, *analyzes the ingredients of bad style*, and clarifies its relationship to such qualities of *bad thinking* as insincerity and hypocrisy. He concludes by *recommending six rules* for the improvement of style.

Source. "Politics and the English Language" by George Orwell; From *Shooting an Elephant and Other Essays* by George Orwell, copyright, 1945, 1946, 1949, 1950, by Sonia Brownell Orwell; renewed, 1973, 1974 by Sonia Orwell. Reprinted by permission of Harcourt Brace Jovanovich, Inc.

1   Most people who bother with the matter at all would admit that the English language is in a bad way, but it is generally assumed that we cannot by conscious action do anything about it. Our civilization is decadent and our language—so the argument runs—must inevitably share in the general collapse. It follows that any struggle against the abuse of language is a sentimental archaism, like preferring candles to electric light or hansom cabs to aeroplanes. Underneath this lies the half-conscious belief that language is a natural growth and not an instrument which we shape for our own purposes.

2   Now, it is clear that the decline of a language must ultimately have political and economic causes: it is not due simply to the bad influence of this or that individual writer. But an effect can become a cause, reinforcing the original cause and producing the same effect in an intensified form, and so on indefinitely. A man may take to drink because he feels himself to be a failure, and then fail all the more completely because he drinks. It is rather the same thing that is happening to the English language. It becomes ugly and inaccurate because our thoughts are foolish, but the slovenliness of our language makes it easier for us to have foolish thoughts. The point is that the process is reversible. Modern English, especially written English, is full of bad habits which spread by imitation and which can be avoided if one is willing to take the necessary trouble. If one gets rid of these habits one can think more clearly, and to think clearly is a necessary first step towards political regeneration: so that the fight against bad English is not frivolous and is not the exclusive concern of professional writers. I will come back to this presently, and I hope that by that time the meaning of what I have said here will have become clearer. Meanwhile, here are five specimens of the English language as it is now habitually written.

3   These five passages have not been picked out because they are especially bad—I could have quoted far worse if I had chosen—but because they illustrate various of the mental vices from which we now suffer. They are a little below the average, but are fairly representative samples. I number them so that I can refer back to them when necessary:

(1) I am not, indeed, sure whether it is not true to say that the Milton who once seemed not unlike a seventeenth-century Shelley had not become, out of an experience ever more bitter in each year, more alien [*sic*] to the founder of that Jesuit sect which nothing could induce him to tolerate.

PROFESSOR HAROLD LASKI
(Essay in *Freedom of Expression*).

(2) Above all, we cannot play ducks and drakes with a native battery of

idioms which prescribes such egregious collocations of vocables as the Basic *put up with* for *tolerate* or *put at a loss* for *bewilder*.

PROFESSOR LANCELOT HOGBEN (*Interglossa*).

(3) On the one side we have the free personality: by definition it is not neurotic, for it has neither conflict nor dream. Its desires, such as they are, are transparent, for they are just what institutional approval keeps in the forefront of consciousness; another institutional pattern would alter their number and intensity; there is little in them that is natural, irreducible, or culturally dangerous. But *on the other side,* the social bond itself is nothing but the mutual reflection of these self-secure integrities. Recall the definition of love. Is not this the very picture of a small academic? Where is there a place in this hall of mirrors for either personality or fraternity?

Essay on psychology in *Politics* (New York).

(4) All the "best people" from the gentlemen's clubs, and all the frantic fascist captains, united in common hatred of Socialism and bestial horror of the rising tide of the mass revolutionary movement, have turned to acts of provocation, to foul incendiarism, to medieval legends of poisoned wells, to legalize their own destruction of proletarian organizations, and rouse the agitated petty-bourgeoisie to chauvinistic fervor on behalf of the fight against the revolutionary way out of the crisis.

Communist pamphlet.

(5) If a new spirit *is* to be infused into this old country, there is one thorny and contentious reform which must be tackled, and that is the humanization and galvanization of the B.B.C. Timidity here will bespeak canker and atrophy of the soul. The heart of Britain may be sound and of strong beat, for instance, but the British lion's roar at present is like that of Bottom in Shakespeare's *Midsummer Night's Dream*—as gentle as any sucking dove. A virile new Britain cannot continue indefinitely to be traduced in the eyes or rather ears, of the world by the effete languors of Langham Place, brazenly masquerading as "standard English." When the Voice of Britain is heard at nine o'clock, better far and infinitely less ludicrous to hear aitches honestly dropped than the present priggish, inflated, inhibited, school-ma'amish arch braying of blameless bashful mewing maidens!

Letter in *Tribune*

Each of these passages has faults of its own, but, quite apart from avoidable ugliness, two qualities are common to all of them. The first is staleness of imagery; the other is lack of precision. The writer either has a meaning and cannot express it, or he inadvertently says something else, or he is almost indifferent as to whether his words mean anything or not. This mixture of vagueness and sheer incompetence is the most marked characteristic of modern English prose, and especially of any kind of political writing. As soon as certain topics are raised, the concrete melts into the abstract and no one seems able to think of turns of speech that are not hackneyed: prose consists less and less of *words* chosen for the sake of their meaning, and more and more of *phrases* tacked together like the sections of a prefabricated hen-house. I list below, with notes and examples, various of the tricks by means of which the work of prose-construction is habitually dodged:

Dying Metaphors

5 A newly invented metaphor assists thought by evoking a visual image, while on the other hand a metaphor which is technically "dead" (e.g. *iron resolution*) has in effect reverted to being an ordinary word and can generally be used without loss of vividness. But in between these two classes there is a huge dump of worn-out metaphors which have lost all evocative power and are merely used because they save people the trouble of inventing phrases for themselves. Examples are: *Ring the changes on, take up the cudgels for, toe the line, ride roughshod over, stand shoulder to shoulder with, play into the hands of, no axe to grind, grist to the mill, fishing in troubled waters, on the order of the day, Achilles' heel, swan song, hotbed.* Many of these are used without knowledge of their meaning (what is a "rift," for instance?), and incompatible metaphors are frequently mixed, a sure sign that the writer is not interested in what he is saying. Some metaphors now current have been twisted out of their original meaning without those who use them even being aware of the fact. For example, *toe the line* is sometimes written *tow the line.* Another example is *the hammer and the anvil,* now always used with the implication that the anvil gets the worst of it. In real life it is always the anvil that breaks the hammer, never the other way about: a writer who stopped to think what he was saying would be aware of this, and would avoid perverting the original phrase.

Operators or Verbal False Limbs

6 These save the trouble of picking out appropriate verbs and nouns, and at the same time pad each sentence with extra syllables which give it an appearance of symmetry. Characteristic phrases are *render inoperative, militate against, make contact with, be subjected to, give rise to, give grounds for, have the effect of, play a leading part (role) in, make itself felt, take effect, exhibit a tendency to, serve the purpose of, etc., etc.* The keynote is the elimination of simple verbs. Instead of being a single word, such as *break, stop, spoil, mend, kill,* a verb becomes a *phrase*, made up of a noun or adjective tacked on to some general-purpose verb such as *prove, serve, form, play, render.* In

addition, the passive voice is wherever possible used in preference to the active, and noun constructions are used instead of gerunds (*by examination of* instead of *by examining*). The range of verbs is further cut down by means of the *-ize* and *de-* formations, and the banal statements are given an appearance of profundity by means of the *not un-* formation. Simple conjunctions and prepositions are replaced by such phrases as *with respect to, having regard to, the fact that, by dint of, in view of, in the interests of, on the hypothesis that;* and the ends of sentences are saved from anticlimax by such resounding common-places as *greatly to be desired, cannot be left out of account, a development to be expected in the near future, deserving of serious consideration, brought to a satisfactory conclusion,* and so on and so forth.

Pretentious Diction

Words like *phenomenon, element, individual* (as noun), *objective, categorical, effective, virtual, basic, primary, promote, constitute, exhibit, exploit, utilize, eliminate, liquidate,* are used to dress up simple statements and give an air of scientific impartiality to biased judgments. Adjectives like *epoch-making, epic, historic, unforgettable, triumphant, age-old, inevitable, inexorable, veritable,* are used to dignify the sordid processes of international politics, while writing that aims at glorifying war usually takes on an archaic color, its characteristic words being : *realm, throne, chariot, mailed fist, trident, sword, shield, buckler, banner, jackboat, clarion.* Foreign words and expressions such as *cul de sac, ancien régime, deus ex machina, mutatis mutandis, status quo, gleichschaltung, weltanschauung,* are used to give an air of culture and elegance. Except for the useful abbreviations *i.e., e.g.,* and *etc.,* there is no real need for any of the hundreds of foreign phrases now current in English. Bad writers, and especially scientific, political, and sociological writers, are nearly always haunted by the notion that Latin or Greek words are grander than Saxon ones, and unnecessary words like *expedite, ameliorate, predict, extraneous, deracinated, clandestine, subaqueous* and hundreds of others constantly gain ground from their Anglo-Saxon opposite numbers.[1] The jargon peculiar to Marxist writing (*hyena, hangman, cannibal, petty bourgeois, these gentry, lacquey, flunkey, mad dog, White Guard,* etc.) consists largely of words and phrases translated from Russian, German or French; but the normal way of coining a new word is to

[1] An interesting illustration of this is the way in which the English flower names which were in use till very recently are being ousted by Greek ones, *snapdragon* becoming *antirrhinum, forget-me-not* becoming *myosotis,* etc. It is hard to see any practical reason for this change of fashion: it is probably due to an instinctive turning-away from the more homely word and a vague feeling that the Greek word is scientific.

use a Latin or Greek root with the appropriate affix and, where necessary, the *-ize* formation. It is often easier to make up words of this kind (*deregionalize, impermissible, extramarital, non-fragmentary* and so forth) than to think up the English words that will cover one's meaning. The result, in general, is an increase in slovenliness and vagueness.

Meaningless Words

8 In certain kinds of writing, particularly in art criticism and literary criticism, it is normal to come across long passages which are almost completely lacking in meaning.[2] Words like *romantic, plastic, values, human, dead, sentimental, natural, vitality,* as used in art criticism, are strictly meaningless, in the sense that they not only do not point to any discoverable object, but are hardly ever expected to do so by the reader. When one critic writes, "The outstanding feature of Mr. X's work is its living quality," while another writes, "The immediately striking thing about Mr. X's work is its peculiar deadness," the reader accepts this as a simple difference of opinion. If words like *black* and *white* were involved, instead of the jargon words *dead* and *living,* he would see at once that language was being used in an improper way. Many political words are similarly abused. The word *Fascism* has now no meaning except in so far as it signifies "something not desirable." The words *democracy, socialism, freedom, patriotic, realistic, justice,* have each of them several different meanings which cannot be reconciled with one another. In the case of a word like *democracy,* not only is there no agreed definition, but the attempt to make one is resisted from all sides. It is almost universally felt that when we call a country democratic we are praising it: consequently the defenders of every kind of régime claim that it is a democracy, and fear that they might have to stop using the word if it were tied down to any one meaning. Words of this kind are often used in a consciously dishonest way. That is, the person who uses them has his own private definition, but allows his hearer to think he means something quite different. Statements like *Marshal Pétain was a true patriot, The Soviet Press is the freest in the world, The Catholic Church is opposed to persecution,* are almost always made with intent to deceive. Other words used in variable meanings, in most cases more or less dishonestly, are: *class, totalitarian, science, progressive, reactionary, bourgeois, equality.*

[2] Example: "Comfort's catholicity of perception and image, strangely Whitmanesque in range, almost the exact opposite in aesthetic compulsion, continues to evoke that trembling atmospheric accumulative hinting at a cruel, an inexorably serene timelessness. . . . When Gardiner scores by aiming at simple bull's-eyes with precision. Only they are not so simple, and through this contented sadness runs more than the surface bitter-sweet of resignation." (*Poetry Quarterly.*)

Now that I have made this catalogue of swindles and perversions, let me give another example of the kind of writing that they lead to. This time it must of its nature be an imaginary one. I am going to translate a passage of good English into modern English of the worst sort. Here is a well-known verse from *Ecclesiastes:*

I returned and saw under the sun, that the race is not to the swift, nor the battle to the strong, neither yet bread to the wise, nor yet riches to men of understanding, nor yet favour to men of skill; but time and chance happeneth to them all.

Here it is in modern English:

Objective consideration of contemporary phenomena compels the conclusion that success or failure in competitive activities exhibits no tendency to be commensurate with innate capacity, but that a considerable element of the unpredictable must invariably be taken into account.

This is a parody, but not a very gross one. Exhibit (3), above, for instance, contains several patches of the same kind of English. It will be seen that I have not made a full translation. The beginning and ending of the sentence follow the original meaning fairly closely, but in the middle the concrete illustrations—race, battle, bread—dissolve into the vague phrase "success or failure in competitive activities." This had to be so, because no modern writer of the kind I am discussing—no one capable of using phrases like "objective consideration of contemporary phenomena"—would ever tabulate his thoughts in that precise and detailed way. The whole tendency of modern prose is away from concreteness. Now analyse these two sentences a little more closely. The first contains forty-nine words but only sixty syllables, and all its words are those of everyday life. The second contains thirty-eight words of ninety syllables: eighteen of its words are from Latin roots, and one from Greek. The first sentence contains six vivid images, and only one phrase ("time and chance") that could be called vague. The second contains not a single fresh, arresting phrase, and in spite of its ninety syllables it gives only a shortened version of the meaning contained in the first. Yet without a doubt it is the second kind of sentence that is gaining ground in modern English. I do not want to exaggerate. This kind of writing is not yet universal, and outcrops of simplicity will occur here and there in the worst-written page. Still, if you or I were told to write a few lines on the uncertainty of human fortunes, we should probably come much nearer to my imaginary sentence than to the one from *Ecclesiastes*.

As I have tried to show, modern writing at its worst does not consist in picking out words for the sake of their meaning and inventing images in order to make the meaning clearer. It consists in gumming together long strips of words which have already been set in order by someone else, and making the results presentable by sheer humbug. The attraction of this way of writing is that it is easy. It is easier—even quicker, once you have the habit—to say *In my opinion it is not an unjustifiable assumption that* than to say *I think*. If you use ready-made phrases, you not only don't have to hunt about for words; you also don't have to bother with the rhythms of your sentences, since these phrases are generally so arranged as to be more or less euphonious. When you are composing in a hurry—when you are dictating to a stenographer, for instance, or making a public speech—it is natural to fall into a pretentious, Latinized style. Tags like *a consideration which we should do well to bear in mind* or *a conclusion to which all of us would readily assent* will save many a sentence from coming down with a bump. By using stale metaphors, similes and idioms, you save much mental effort, at the cost of leaving your meaning vague, not only for your reader but for yourself. This is the significance of mixed metaphors. The sole aim of a metaphor is to call up a visual image. When these images clash—as in *The Fascist octopus has sung its swan song, the jackboot is thrown into the melting pot*—it can be taken as certain that the writer is not seeing a mental image of the objects he is naming; in other words he is not really thinking. Look again at the examples I gave at the beginning of this essay. Professor Laski (1) uses five negatives in fifty-three words. One of these is superfluous, making nonsense of the whole passage, and in addition there is the slip *alien* for *akin*, making further nonsense, and several avoidable pieces of clumsiness which increase the general vagueness. Professor Hogben (2) plays ducks and drakes with a battery which is able to write prescriptions, and, while disapproving of the everyday phrase *put up with*, is unwilling to look *egregious* up in the dictionary and see what it means; (3), if one takes an uncharitable attitude towards it, is simply meaningless: probably one could work out its intended meaning by reading the whole of the article in which it occurs. In (4), the writer knows more or less what he wants to say, but an accumulation of stale phrases chokes him like tea leaves blocking a sink. In (5), words and meaning have almost parted company. People who write in this manner usually have a general emotional meaning—they dislike one thing and want to express solidarity with another—but they are not interested in the detail of what they are saying. A scrupulous writer, in every sentence that he writes, will ask himself at least four questions, thus: What am I trying to say? What words will express it? What image or idiom will make it clearer? Is this image fresh enough to have an effect? And he will probably ask himself two more: Could I put it more shortly? Have I said anything that is avoidably ugly? But you are not obliged to go to all this trouble. You can shirk it by simply throwing your mind open and letting the ready-made phrases come crowding in. They will construct your sentences for you—even think your thoughts for you, to a certain extent—and at need they will perform the important service of partially concealing your meaning even from yourself. It is at this point that the special connection between politics and the debasement of language becomes clear.

In our time it is broadly true that political writing is bad writing. Where it is not true, it will generally be found that the writer is some kind of rebel, expressing his private opinions and not a "party line." Orthodoxy, of whatever color, seems to demand a lifeless, imitative style. The political dialects to be found in pamphlets, leading articles, manifestos, White Papers and the speeches of under-secretaries do, of course, vary from party to party, but they are all alike in that one almost never finds in them a fresh, vivid, home-made turn of speech. When one watches some tired hack on the platform mechanically repeating the familiar phrases—*bestial atrocities, iron heel, blood-stained tyranny, free peoples of the world, stand shoulder to shoulder*—one often has a curious feeling that one is not watching a live human being but some kind of dummy: a feeling which suddenly becomes stronger at moments when the light catches the speaker's spectacles and turns them into blank discs which seem to have no eyes behind them. And this is not altogether fanciful. A speaker who uses that kind of phraseology has gone some distance towards turning himself into a machine. The appropriate noises are coming out of his larynx, but his brain is not involved as it would be if he were choosing his words for himself. If the speech he is making is one that he is accustomed to make over and over again, he may be almost unconscious of what he is saying, as one is when one utters the responses in church. And this reduced state of consciousness, if not indispensable, is at any rate favorable to political conformity.

In our time, political speech and writing are largely the defence of the indefensible. Things like the continuance of British rule in India, the Russian purges and deportations, the dropping of the atom bombs on Japan, can indeed be defended, but only by arguments which are too brutal for most people to face, and which do not square with the professed aims of political parties. Thus political language has to consist largely of euphemism, question-begging and sheer cloudy vagueness. Defenceless villages are bombarded from the air, the inhabitants driven out into the countryside, the cattle machine-gunned, the huts set on fire with incendiary bullets: this is called *pacification*. Millions of peasants are robbed of their farms and sent trudging along the roads with no more than they can carry: this is called *transfer of population* or *rectification of frontiers*. People are imprisoned for years without trial, or shot in the back of the neck or sent to die of scurvy in Arctic lumber camps: this is called *elimination of unreliable elements*. Such phraseology is needed if one wants to name things without calling up mental pictures of them. Consider for instance some comfortable English professor defending Russian totalitarianism. He cannot say outright, ''I believe in killing off your opponents when you can get good results by doing so.'' Probably, therefore, he will say something like this:

> While freely conceding that the Soviet régime exhibits certain features which the humanitarian may be inclined to deplore, we must, I think, agree that a certain curtailment of the right to political opposition is an unavoidable concomitant of transitional periods, and that the rigors which the Russian people have been called upon to undergo have been amply justified in the sphere of concrete achievement.

15   The inflated style is itself a kind of euphemism. A mass of Latin words falls upon the facts like soft snow, blurring the outlines and covering up all the details. The great enemy of clear language is insincerity. When there is a gap between one's real and one's declared aims, one turns as it were instinctively to long words and exhausted idioms, like a cuttlefish squirting out ink. In our age there is no such thing as ''keeping out of politics.'' All issues are political issues, and politics itself is a mass of lies, evasions, folly, hatred and schizophrenia. When the general atmosphere is bad, language must suffer. I should expect to find—this is a guess which I have not sufficient knowledge to verify—that the German, Russian and Italian languages have all deteriorated in the last ten or fifteen years, as a result of dictatorship.

16   But if thought corrupts language, language can also corrupt thought. A bad usage can spread by tradition and imitation, even among people who should and do know better. The debased language that I have been discussing is in some ways very convenient. Phrases like *a not unjustifiable assumption, leaves much to be desired, would serve no good purpose, a consideration which we should do well to bear in mind*, are a continuous temptation, a packet of aspirins always at one's elbow. Look back through this essay, and for certain you will find that I have again and again committed the very faults I am protesting against. By this morning's post I have received a pamphlet dealing with conditions in Germany. The author tells me that he ''felt impelled'' to write it. I open it at random, and here is almost the first sentence that I see: ''[The Allies] have an opportunity not only of achieving a radical transformation of Germany's social and political structure in such a way as to avoid a nationalistic reaction in Germany itself, but at the same time of laying the foundations of a co-operative and unified Europe.'' You see, he ''feels impelled'' to write—feels, presumably, that he has something new to say—and yet his words, like cavalry horses answering the bugle, group themselves automatically into the familiar dreary pattern. This invasion of one's mind by ready-made phrases (*lay the foundations, achieve a radical transfor-*

mation) can only be prevented if one is constantly on guard against them, and every such phrase anaesthetizes a portion of one's brain.

I said earlier that the decadence of our language is probably curable. Those who deny this would argue, if they produced an argument at all, that language merely reflects existing social conditions, and that we cannot influence its development by any direct tinkering with words and constructions. So far as the general tone or spirit of a language goes, this may be true, but it is not true in detail. Silly words and expressions have often disappeared, not through any evolutionary process but owing to the conscious action of a minority. Two recent examples were *explore every avenue* and *leave no stone unturned*, which were killed by the jeers of a few journalists. There is a long list of flyblown metaphors which could similarly be got rid of if enough people would interest themselves in the job; and it should also be possible to laugh the *not un-* formation out of existence,[3] to reduce the amount of Latin and Greek in the average sentence, to drive out foreign phrases and strayed scientific words, and, in general, to make pretentiousness unfashionable. But all these are minor points. The defence of the English language implies more than this, and perhaps it is best to start by saying what it does *not* imply.

To begin with it has nothing to do with archaism, with the salvaging of obsolete words and turns of speech, or with the setting up of a "standard English" which must never be departed from. On the contrary, it is especially concerned with the scrapping of every word or idiom which has outworn its usefulness. It has nothing to do with correct grammar and syntax, which are of no importance so long as one makes one's meaning clear, or with the avoidance of Americanisms, or with having what is called a "good prose style." On the other hand, it is not concerned with fake simplicity and the attempt to make written English colloquial. Nor does it even imply in every case preferring the Saxon word to the Latin one, though it does imply using the fewest and shortest words that will cover one's meaning. What is above all needed is to let the meaning choose the word, and not the other way about. In prose, the worst thing one can do with words is to surrender to them. When you think of a concrete object, you think wordlessly, and then, if you want to describe the thing you have been visualizing you probably hunt about till you find the exact words that seem to fit it. When you think of something abstract you are more inclined to use words from the start, and unless you make a conscious effort to prevent it, the existing dialect will come rushing in and do the job for you, at the expense of blurring or even changing your meaning. Probably it is better to put off using words as long as possible and get

---

[3] One can cure oneself of the *not un-* formation by memorizing this sentence: *A not unblack dog was chasing a not unsmall rabbit across a not ungreen field.*

one's meaning as clear as one can through pictures or sensations. Afterwards one can choose—not simply *accept*—the phrases that will best cover the meaning, and then switch round and decide what impression one's words are likely to make on another person. This last effort of the mind cuts out all stale or mixed images, all prefabricated phrases, needless repetitions, and humbug and vagueness generally. But one can often be in doubt about the effect of a word or a phrase, and one needs rules that one can rely on when instinct fails. I think the following rules will cover most cases:

(i) Never use a metaphor, simile or other figure of speech which you are used to seeing in print.
(ii) Never use a long word where a short one will do.
(iii) If it is possible to cut a word out, always cut it out.
(iv) Never use the passive where you can use the active.
(v) Never use a foreign phrase, a scientific word or a jargon word if you can think of an everyday English equivalent.
(vi) Break any of these rules sooner than say anything outright barbarous.

These rules sound elementary, and so they are, but they demand a deep change of attitude in anyone who has grown used to writing in the style now fashionable. One could keep all of them and still write bad English, but one could not write the kind of stuff that I quoted in those five specimens at the beginning of this article.

19   I have not here been considering the literary use of language, but merely language as an instrument for expressing and not for concealing or preventing thought. Stuart Chase and others have come near to claiming that all abstract words are meaningless, and have used this as a pretext for advocating a kind of political quietism. Since you don't know what Fascism is, how can you struggle against Fascism? One need not swallow such absurdities as this, but one ought to recognize that the present political chaos is connected with the decay of language, and that one can probably bring about some improvement by starting at the verbal end. If you simplify your English, you are freed from the worst follies of orthodoxy. You cannot speak any of the necessary dialects, and when you make a stupid remark its stupidity will be obvious, even to yourself. Political language—and with variations this is true of all political parties, from Conservatives to Anarchists—is designed to make lies sound truthful and murder respectable, and to give an appearance of solidity to pure wind. One cannot change this all in a moment, but one can at least change one's own habits, and from time to time one can even, if one jeers loudly enough, send some worn-out and useless phrase—some *jackboot, Achilles' heel, hotbed, melting pot, acid test, veritable inferno* or other lump of verbal refuse—into the dustbin where it belongs.

Author Notes

Baker, Russell (1925–). Born: Loudoun County, Virginia. Educ.: Johns Hopkins, BA 1947; Hamilton College, L.H.D.; Princeton Univ., Union College. Newspaperman, political observer, social critic.

Bates, Daisy. Journalist.

Bibby, T. Geoffrey (1917–). Born: Heversham, England. Educ.: Cambridge, BA 1939, MA 1946. Works in Denmark Historical Museum; mountain climber, science-fiction buff.

Carlson, Peter. Educ.: Boston Univ., BS in journalism 1974.

Claiborne, Robert Watson, Jr. (1919–). Born: Wycombe, Buckinghamshire, England. Educ.: MIT; New York Univ., BA 1942. Factory worker, folksinger, journalist writing on science and society.

Clark, Champ. (1923–). Born: St. Louis, Missouri. Educ.: Univ. of Missouri. Reporter, writer, editor.

Clarke, Gerald.

Clubb, Merrel Dare, Jr. (1921–). Born: New Haven, Connecticut. Educ.: Oklahoma A&M College, BA 1943; Yale, MA 1949; Univ. of Michigan, PhD 1953. Linguist.

Concelman, James (1955–). Born: Pittsburgh, Pennsylvania. Educ.: Penn State Univ., BA 1976. Works for an international bank in Pittsburgh.

Crane, Stephen (1871–1900). Born: Newark, New Jersey. Educ.: Lafayette College, Syracuse Univ. Novelist, war correspondent, free-lance writer.

Crist, Judith (1922–). Born: New York, New York. Educ.: Hunter College, AB 1941; Columbia Univ., MSc 1945. Film and drama critic.

Deloria, Vine, Jr. (1933–). Born: Martin, South Dakota. Educ.: Iowa State Univ., BS 1958; Lutheran School, MTh 1963. Educator, commentator on the American Indians.

Didion, Joan (1934–). Born: Sacramento, California. Educ.: Univ. of California, Berkeley, BA 1956. Editor, columnist, shortstory writer.

Dillard, Annie (1945–). Born: Pittsburgh, Pennsylvania. Educ.: Hollins College, BA 1967, MA 1968. Editor, writer.

Donald, William Spooner (1910). Born: Carlisle, England. Educ.: attended Lime House, Wetheral and Royal Naval College, Dartmouth. Royal Navy, fishing-management posts, journalist, playwright, broadcaster.

Dos Passos, John (1896–1970). Born: Chicago, Illinois. Educ.: Harvard, AB 1916. Writer of poetry, drama, prose.

DuBois, Cora (1903–). Born: New York, New York. Educ.: Barnard College, BA 1927; Columbia Univ., MA 1928; Univ. of California, Berkeley, PhD 1932. Educator, anthropologist.

duPont, Henry B. American industrialist.

Eiseley, Loren (1907-1977). Born: Lincoln, Nebraska. Educ.: Univ. of Nebraska, BA 1933; Univ. of Pennsylvania, AM 1935, PhD 1937. Anthropologist, historian of science, philosopher of science.

Forster, E. M. (1879-1970). Born: England. Educ.: Cambridge Univ. Novelist, short-story writer, scholar, critic.

Fuller, Edmund (1914-). Educator, novelist, critic.

Gerstenberg, Richard Charles (1909-). Born: Little Falls, New York. Educ.: Univ. of Michigan, BA 1931. Automotive executive.

Gutcheon, Beth (1945-). Born: Sewickley, Pennsylvania. Educ.: Radcliffe, BA 1967. Writer on quilting, abortion, popular culture, and the media.

Haley, Alex. Born: Henning, Tennessee. Writer.

Hayakawa, Samuel Ichiye (1906-). Born: Vancouver, British Columbia. Educ.: Univ. of Manitoba, BA 1927; McGill, MA 1928; Univ. of Wisconsin, PhD 1935. Linguist, educator, academic administrator, Congressman.

Highet, Gilbert (1906-). Born: Glasgow, Scotland. Educ.: Glasgow Univ., BA 1929; Oxford Univ., MA 1936. Professor of Classics, translator, critic.

Hollister, George E. (1905-). Born: Erwin, South Dakota. Educ.: George Peabody College, BS 1930, MA 1932; Univ. of Minnesota, PhD 1947. Professor of Education at the Univ. of Wyoming, emphasizing arithmetic for elementary schools.

Huff, Darrell (1913-). Born: Gowrie, Iowa. Educ.: State Univ. of Iowa, BA 1938, MA 1939. Editor (*Better Homes and Gardens*), author of "hundreds of articles in popular magazines."

Hughes, Richard Arthur Warren (1900-). Born: Weybridge, England. Educ.: Oxford, BA 1922. Poet, dramatist, novelist.

Hungiville, Maurice N. (1936-). Born: Bradford, Pennsylvania. Educ.: St. Bonaventure Univ., BA 1959; Western Reserve Univ., MA 1963; Univ. of Tennessee, PhD 1969. Teacher.

Huxley, Julian Sorell (1887-). Born: London, England. Educ.: Oxford, BA 1909. Biologist, philosopher, former Director-General of UNESCO.

Inouye, Daniel K. (1924-). Born: Honolulu, Hawaii. Educ.: Univ. of Hawaii, BA 1950; George Washington Univ., JD 1952. United States Senator.

Jeans, Sir James (1877-1946). Born: London, England. Educ.: Cambridge Univ. Mathematician, physicist, astronomer, writer.

Jefferson, Thomas (1743-1836). Born at "Old Shadwell," Gochland (now Albermarle County), Virginia. Educ.: William and Mary College. Third President of the United States.

Karp, Walter.

Kendall, Martha. Anthropologist; teaches at Vassar College, Poughkeepsie, New York.

Kilpatrick, James L. Newspaperman.

Kramer, Judith Rita (1933-). Born: New York, New York. Educ.: Barnard College, BA 1953; Univ. of Minnesota, MA 1954, PhD 1958. Sociologist.

Lambert, Abigail. Truck driver.

Mackintosh, Prudence.

Orwell, George (Eric Blair) (1903-1950). Born: India. Educ.: Eton. Served the British government in India, fought in the Spanish Civil War. Essayist, novelist, satirist, best known for *Nineteen Eighty-Four* and *Animal Farm*.

Packard, Vance (1914-). Born: Granville Summit, Pennsylvania. Educ.: Penn State Univ., BA 1936; Columbia Univ., MS 1937; Monmouth College, LittD 1975. Author, social critic.

Piddington, Sidney. Born: Australia. Advertising executive.

Rodriguez, Armando M. (1921-). Born: Mexico. Educ.: San Diego State College, BA 1949, MA 1951. Educator, specialist in bilingual education.

Rogers, Michael (1950-). Born: Santa Monica, California. Educ.: Stanford Univ., BA 1972. Journalist, fiction writer.

Stegner, Wallace E. (1909-). Born: Lake Mills,

Iowa. Educ.: Univ. of Utah, BA 1930; State Univ. of Iowa, MA 1932, PhD 1935. College teacher, novelist, commentator on the American West.

Swift, Jonathan (1667-1745). Irish writer, satirist, poet, novelist, best known for *Gulliver's Travels*; also a churchman.

Thomas, Lewis (1913-   ). Born: New York, New York. Educ.: Princeton, BS 1933; Harvard, MD 1937; Yale, MA 1969. Physician, educator, medical administrator.

Thurber, James Grover (1894-1961). Born: Columbus, Ohio. Educ.: Ohio State Univ. Artist, humanist, cartoonist.

Toffler, Alvin (1928-   ). Born: New York, New York. Educ.: New York Univ., AB 1949. Newspaper correspondent, social critic.

Weinberg, Nancy. Educator (University of Illinois School of Social Work).

West, Rebecca (Cicily Fairfield Andrews) (1892-   ). Educ.: Watson's Ladies College, Edinburgh, Scotland. Novelist, critic, journalist.

West, Ted.

Wilford, John Noble (1933-   ). Born: Camden, Tennessee. Educ.: Univ. of Tennessee, BS 1955; Syracuse Univ., MA 1956; Columbia Univ. Journalist, reporter, writer on science and on international affairs.

Woolf, Virginia (1882-1941). Born: London, England. Educ.: at home by father, Sir Leslie Stephen. Novelist, critic.

Woollcott, Alexander (1887-1943). Born: Phalanx, New Jersey. Educ.: Central High School of Phila., BA 1905; Hamilton College, PhD 1913. Drama critic, journalist.

Wright, Richard (1908-1960). Born: Natchez, Missouri. Educ.: attended Seventh Day Adventist School. Novelist.

Zagano, Phyllis. Lecturer in English (State University of New York at Stony Brook).

Zinsser, William K. (1922-   ). Born: New York, New York. Educ.: Princeton Univ., AB 1944. Writer, editor, entertainment critic.

Glossary

Abstract words: words that name a general quality or property of a thing (e.g., the coldness of snow), usually contrasted with *concrete words:* words that name a specific quality or property of a thing (e.g., an individual snowflake has a temperature of 28° F.).

Analogy: resemblance between some features of otherwise unlike things, used in explanations of unfamiliar things by means of familiar things (see p. 22). For example, the remark attributed to Einstein, "God does not play at dice with the world," involves an analogy between God (the unfamiliar) and a gambler (the familiar).

Analysis: process of breaking a whole thing into parts in order to understand its nature or essential features. See *Synthesis*.

Analysis of cause and effect: a technique of definition in which X, the thing to be defined, is explained in terms of what causes it or what its effects are (see p. 9).

Anecdote: a brief narrative, often humorous, of an event involving human interest and often suggesting some lesson.

Antithesis: a sharp contrast of ideas, as in "We must go to war to secure peace."

Argument: 1. a coherent presentation of reasons or facts to establish a point of view; see *deductive arguments* (p. 89) and *inductive arguments* (p. 92). 2. a complete piece of writing that aims at persuading readers of the rightness of its point of view; in this book, "argument" is divided into Substantiation, Evaluation, and Recommendation.

Assertion: a statement declaring that something is the case. "You're late again" is an assertion. "Ouch!" is not. (It's an exclamation.)

Assumption: something taken for granted. "Shut the door" assumes, for instance, that there is a door, and that it is open. "Human beings are basically good" assumes that we know what "good" means.

Attribution: a statement asserting that something or some quality belongs to a person or object.

Audience: the group of potential readers by whom a writer hopes his work will be read and whose characteristics partly determine how he expresses his ideas.

Authority, appeal to: citation of professional opinions—the opinions of people who are acknowledged authorities on a subject—to support an assertion.

Beginning: see *Introduction*.

Bibliography: a list of published writings related to a subject.

Cause and effect: see *Analysis of cause and effect*.

Chronological order: presentation of events or things in normal time sequence, usually contrasted

321

with "chronological displacement," in which time is disrupted by flashbacks or depiction of future events.

Classification: see *Division*.

Cliché: a trite, overused, or stereotyped expression.

Coherence: the inner connectedness of an argument, essay, or paragraph: each part contributes to the unity of the whole.

Colloquial: conversational, as distinct from formal, language.

Comparison and contrast: a technique of definition in which the similarities and differences between things are clarified; often used to identify the unknown by separating it from the known.

Conclusion: 1. the final statement of a logical argument; 2. the ending of an essay, which may summarize, demonstrate the significance of the material, or in some other way bring the piece of writing to its goal and let us know that we have in fact arrived.

Concrete: see *Abstract*.

Connotation and denotation: connotation signifies the emotion associated with a word or expression; denotation signifies the literal meaning of a word or expression. For example, the word "mother" *connotes* all the emotions that we associate with that unique and necessary person; the word *denotes* simply "female parent."

Context: the sentences or paragraphs that surround a word or group of words and given them a particular meaning or connotative value.

Contrast: see *Comparison*.

Criterion (plural, **criteria**): a standard on which judgments or evaluations may be based (see pp. 160–161).

Deduction: the process of deriving conclusions from premises (see p. 89).

Definition: 1. determination of a word's meaning by stating the class of items to which it belongs (genus) and supplying terms (differentia) to distinguish it from the other items in its class; 2. in this book, "definition" includes all compositions in which the writer's primary purpose is to explain the meaning of the subject.

Denotation: see *Connotation*.

Description: 1. verbal depiction of the sensory characteristics of things, or of the intellectual characteristics of ideas; 2. in this book, "description" is presented as a method of defining (see p. 8).

Development: the use of examples, arguments, and so forth, to support a proposition or to make an idea advance ("develop"); see *Paragraph*.

Dialogue: a record of direct speech; conversation.

Dichotomy: a division of something into two parts.

Diction: a writer's choice of words. Good diction means words chosen for their effectiveness and clarity, taking into account the subject, audience, and occasion.

Division and classification: a technique of definition in which a subject is divided into its main parts and the parts are arranged (classified) according to some principle, for example, simple to complex (see p. 8).

Documentation: evidence (usually in the form of footnotes or appendices) furnished to verify facts, support theories, or identify the sources of information.

Drafting: includes everything from doodles and single words or phrases to a preliminary outline or first copy. Here you translate what is in your mind (*prewriting*) to paper—often a messy process because you are trying to organize pieces into a whole.

Emphasis: special significance given to some element(s) of a piece of writing for logical effect or emotional appeal. Means of giving emphasis include position (the beginning and end are usually emphatic positions), repetition, or such stylistic devices as the capitalization of words.

Ending: see *Conclusion*.

Essay: literally an "attempt" or "trial," an attempt

to translate thought into language; a composition that defines, interprets, or advocates.

Evaluation: a composition in which the writer's primary purpose is to justify a judgment about something, often by means of stated criteria. In this book, evaluations are "moral" if the criteria are defined in ethical terms, "utilitarian" if the criteria are defined in practical terms (see p. 159).

Evidence: any fact, opinion, or idea that serves to prove something else. Evidence ranges from the report of a personal experience, to extensive statistical data, to summaries of the viewpoints of authorities.

Exposition: writing that presents, explains, describes, and so forth; called "Definition" in this book.

Fallacy: an erroneous idea or conclusion that may seem plausible but is based on invalid argument or incorrect inference. It is a fallacy, for example, to claim that since B follows A, B is a *result* of A ("She smoked for twenty years and then died of cancer: the smoking must have caused the cancer"). It is possible that B resulted from some other factor (radiation?) altogether.

Fiction: experience, revised and edited.

Functional definition: defining a thing in terms of how it works or what it does, rather than what it is (see p. 24).

Generalization: a principle or concept derived from particular information (see p. 88).

Hypothesis: a tentative proposition asserted in order to discover whether it can be validated by facts or reasons (see p. 88).

Illustration: the use of examples to develop a generalization or clarify an idea (see p. 22).

Implication: an idea suggested, not stated. "Run, here comes Mama!" suggests (but does not state) that the speaker has done something Mama will not like.

Induction: a process of reasoning in which particular observations or other forms of evidence are assembled and then summarized in a conclusion that is more general than the evidence (see p. 92). The movement from the evidence to the conclusion is called the *inductive leap* (see p. 92).

Interpretation: a statement that goes beyond a simple record or report of an experience to explain what the experience means. A report: "A man slapped a child between the shoulder blades." An interpretation: "The man was angry at the child." An alternative interpretation: "The man was trying to dislodge a cherry pit the child had swallowed."

Intrinsic: a trait that naturally belongs to someone or something, as opposed to *extrinsic*, a trait imposed or acquired from outside. A love of warmth is an intrinsic quality of cats; a fondness for automobile travel is an extrinsic quality that some cats acquire.

Introduction: a beginning; not simply *any* beginning but one designed to lead us toward whatever is coming next (etymologically, the word means "a leading into"). You could begin a car journey by driving off in any direction, but a wiser plan is to choose roads that lead where you want to go.

Intuition: a nonrational (or partly rational) way of knowing, usually used to describe a sudden understanding of a problem or an unsupported expectation. "My intuition tells me that the new mailman will bite the dog instead of vice versa." (See p. 95).

Invention: see *Prewriting*.

Irony: statements that say one thing but mean the opposite (see p. 229).

Irrelevant: see *Relevant*.

Jargon: a special vocabulary known only to a small group of people. Jargon may be legitimate in speaking or writing to an audience consisting only of those people; otherwise it is out of place. Example: "interdigitational encounter" for "holding hands."

Judgment: a conclusion drawn about something, usually about the value of something. "*Tom Sawyer* is a marvelous book" is a judgment. (So is "*Tom Sawyer* is *not* a marvelous book.") A judgment is *premature* when it is made before all of the evidence has been considered ("I'm only half through *Tom Sawyer* but I can tell you it's marvelous" is premature; the only judgment justified so far would be "the first half is marvelous").

Justifying the criteria: defending the choice of criteria being used in an evaluation—usually explaining why the criteria are fair (see p. 161). If you are using a criterion of usefulness to evaluate kangaroos, for most American readers you will need to defend that criterion.

Logic: reasoning according to certain accepted patterns, specifically *deduction* and *induction* (see pp. 89–95), in contrast to nonrational ways of knowing such as *intuition* (see p. 95).

Major premise: the first statement of a deductive argument (see p. 89), usually a general statement such as "All men are mortal."

Matters of fact, matters of inference, matters of opinion: a *matter of fact* concerns a simple statement of experience ("I ate six bananas yesterday"), while a *matter of inference* or a *matter of opinion* concerns our responses to experience ("You're a pig"). (See p. 89.)

Metaphor: a figure of speech in which one thing stands for another; an implied likeness. In the phrase "the milk of human kindness," milk stands for all the intangible forms of kindness; the implied likeness is that both milk and kindness nourish.

Minor premise: the second statement of a deductive argument (see p. 89), usually a statement about some particular person or thing, such as "Socrates is a man."

Moral evaluation: see *Evaluation.*

Narration: the retelling of a sequence of events; *narrative* is frequently a synonym for "story." In this book, narration is presented as a way of defining or clarifying something.

Negative detail: the technique of describing something by negatives, providing details of what it is *not*, usually in order to eliminate misconceptions. "A whale is not a fish."

Objective/subjective: *objective* statements involve

a minimal amount of our own personalities ("It's forty degrees out today"), while *subjective* statements involve our personal likes and dislikes ("It's too cold to go swimming"—maybe for us, but not for walruses). On objective and subjective definition, see p. 20.

Outline: a division of a piece of writing into its parts so that its themes and structure become apparent.

Parable: a brief fictional narrative told to make a point about how people should (or should not) behave.

Paradox: an apparent contradiction, as in "a false truth."

Paragraph: a unit of writing that is also a unit of thought or idea; one full step in the development of an idea. Compare the stones of a stone wall: they may differ in size and shape, but each contributes something necessary to the whole structure. Unlike the single sentence, the paragraph *develops* its idea. Typical forms of *paragraph development* include the simple-to-complex pattern (and vice versa), chronological sequence, spatial arrangement (near-to-far, top-to-bottom, etc.), and the "thesis-sentence" pattern in which the paragraph opens with a general summarizing statement followed by the evidence on which that statement depends.

Parallel structure: the repetition of words or grammatical sequences to emphasize the relatedness of ideas, as in "I spent the morning writing my uncle a mad letter, and the afternoon regretting it." The grammatical parallelism of "writing" and "regretting" (both are gerunds) helps link the ideas.

Parody: an exaggerated and mocking imitation, usually one that ridicules something by emphasizing a few peculiarities and ignoring all normal characteristics.

Persona: the character and voice that you adopt when writing nonautobiographically. See Swift's "A Modest Proposal," pp. 297.

Personification: the presentation of a thing or an animal as if it were a person, as in "That collapsible chair lay in wait for me, rejoicing silently in its nasty yellow canvas heart as it watched me approach.''

Persuasion: a form of writing in which the primary purpose is to convince readers that they should share the author's desires or convictions. In this book, three types of persuasion are presented separately: *substantiation*, in which the author tries to make his readers accept his logical conclusions; *evaluation*, in which he tries to make his readers accept his value judgments; *recommendation*, in which he tries to make his readers accept his proposals for change.

Prediction: a statement about the future based on our knowledge of the present and the past.

Prewriting: thinking before you write. Not only what you have to say but how you mean to say it will determine your strategies of presentation. At this stage, "editing" (grammar, punctuation, spelling, etc.) are unimportant.

Recommendation: a composition in which the writer proposes changes in action or attitude to solve some problem (see p. 231).

Refutation: the process of arguing successfully against someone else's theories.

Relevant/irrelevant: a detail or a paragraph or any ingredient in writing is *relevant* if it contributes to the main purpose or idea, *irrelevant* otherwise (no matter how interesting it may be). If your purpose is to define "the mayor-council form of municipal government," the fact that you first learned about this form of government in a course taught by a descendant of the Spanish monarchy, while interesting, is not relevant.

Reports: statements of observation ("The car's gas gauge reads 'empty' and the engine won't start''), in contrast to statements of interpretation ("The car is out of gas").

Rewriting: *not* copying an early draft but revising paragraphs and sentences into finished form. This is the time to "edit," that is, to get your spelling, punctuation, and other choices right (see p. 13).

Rhetorical question: a question to which the answer is obvious, such as God's question to Job: "Is it *you* who commands the morning to dawn?" (Here the answer is so obviously "No" that Job does not need to reply to the question.)

Satire: a witty, ironic, or sarcastic piece of writing that makes use of exaggeration, simplification, or stereotypes to ridicule, scorn, deride, or expose some evil, outworn convention, or eccentricity. It may be applied to both individuals and societies, and its purpose may range from advocating reform to merely affording insight.

Sensory evidence: see *Evidence*.

Simple to complex: see *Paragraph*.

Spatial development: see *Paragraph*.

Specification: an assertion about a specific individual or thing (as opposed to a *generalization*, which is an assertion about a whole category). (See p. 88.)

Stereotype: a conventionalized description of a group of people, animals, and the like usually used thoughtlessly without testing its accuracy.

Style: all qualities of language beyond what is strictly necessary to "do the job." (Both a brand new Rolls Royce and a 1955 Chevrolet will get you to town; the difference is style.) Options which help a writer individualize style—make style reflect personality—include diction, punctuation, organization, even the decision to leave certain things out.

Subjective: see *Objective/subjective*.

Substantiation: a composition in which the writer's primary purpose is to demonstrate the soundness of the reasoning and the *validity* of the conclusion (thesis).

Sufficiency: one of the criteria for evaluating evidence. The evidence is sufficient if it is complete or if it is a representative sample (see p. 92).

Summary: 1. a brief overview of ideas and information more fully developed elsewhere; the final paragraph of an essay is sometimes a summary; 2.

a statement that adds up the evidence and tries to avoid *interpretation*.

Syllogism: a pattern of *deduction*; it usually consists of two premises and a conclusion (see p. 88).

Symbol: an individual, object, or event used to stand for a general or abstract idea. Symbols may be divided into *natural*, in which basic qualities of the symbol suggest its meaning (the sea naturally suggests flux), *conventional*, in which culturally shaped qualities suggest the meaning (to Eskimos, the sea may be a symbol of nourishment), and *personal*, in which individual experience determines the meaning (to you, the sea may suggest the end of a love affair).

Syntax: the arrangement of words into sentences. Each language has its own patterns of syntax, which help determine the meanings of sentences. In English, for example, the standard syntactical pattern *Subject* plus *Verb* plus *Complement* helps us know what the sentence "Wilhelmina bit the dentist" means: Wilhelmina did the biting, and the dentist needs the bandage. A writer can choose among various syntactical patterns in order to individualize his style.

Synthesis: process of combining different things into a coherent whole. See *Analysis*.

Theme: 1. often a synonym for a written composition or essay; 2. the subject of a piece of writing.

Thesaurus: a book listing approximate synonyms for words.

Thesis: 1. the central idea of a composition. *Thesis sentence:* a sentence that summarizes the main idea. 2. the conclusion of a logical argument. A

hypothesis (see p. 88) becomes a "thesis" when its validity has been tested and sustained.

Tone: accent or inflection of a speaker or writer that signifies an attitude toward the subject and the audience, usually conveyed by level of diction (e.g., formal or colloquial) and choice of syntax. Tone is sometimes used as a synonym for style, but more frequently, tone is associated with the writer's emotions ("an angry tone"), while style includes a wider range of qualities.

Transition: words and expressions that connect and show relationships between elements of a composition, such as "therefore" (indicating that what follows is a logical outgrowth of what precedes), or "however" (signalling a turn).

Truth: see *Validity*.

Unity: literally, "oneness"; the quality of having all elements coherent with each other and contributing to a central purpose.

Utilitarian evaluation: see *Evaluation*.

Validity: the quality of being probable beyond a reasonable doubt, the quality of conforming to the evidence. A statement that is valid may nevertheless not be *true;* "truth" implies an absolute rightness, rarely available to us. (In everyday language, however, "truth" is often used for "validity." We say "It's true that he's coming tomorrow" when a strict use of the words would require us to say "It is valid—it conforms to all the evidence we now have—to say that he will come tomorrow.")

Verification: the process of confirming the validity or accuracy of an assertation. Verification often involves the collection of further evidence or the practical testing of a theory.

Thematic Contents

The primary organization of this book is rhetorical—in other words, the selections are arranged by types of writing rather than by subject matter. However, the readings can be chosen so as to form subject matter "clusters," groups of four or five or more selections about the same major theme. The Thematic Contents below present 12 such clusters. You may find them useful for a thematically organized course or for the preparation of longer compositions requiring reference to several published articles on one subject.

1. The American Scene

2. The Consumer

3. Education

329

6. Heroes (And Anti-Heroes)

7. Human Values: The Responsible Man

8. Language, Literature, and Style

9. Our Living Environment

Definition

Substantiation

Evaluation

10. Personal Reports: The Individual Experience

Definition

Substantiation

Evaluation

11. Science

12. Technology and Man